DATE DUE

D1173934

‹ ›

LIBERTY SECURED?
BRITAIN BEFORE AND AFTER 1688

THE MAKING OF MODERN FREEDOM

General Editor: R. W. Davis

LIBERTY SECURED?
BRITAIN BEFORE AND AFTER 1688

< >

Edited by J. R. Jones

STANFORD UNIVERSITY PRESS
STANFORD, CALIFORNIA
1992

Stanford University Press
Stanford, California
© 1992 by the Board of Trustees of the
Leland Stanford Junior University
Printed in the United States of America

CIP data appear at the end of the book

≺ ≻

Series Foreword

T HE STARTLING AND MOVING events that swept from China to
Eastern Europe to Latin America and South Africa at the end of
the 1980s formed one of those great historic occasions when calls
for freedom, rights, and democracy echoed through political upheaval. A clear-eyed look at any of those conjunctions—in 1776 and
1789, in 1848 and 1918, as well as in 1989—reminds us that freedom, liberty, rights, and democracy are words into which many different and conflicting hopes have been read. The language of freedom—or liberty, which is interchangeable with freedom most of the
time—is inherently difficult. It carried vastly different meanings in
the classical world and in medieval Europe from those of modern
understanding, though thinkers in later ages sometimes eagerly
assimilated the older meanings to their own circumstances and
purposes.

A new kind of freedom, which we have here called modern,
gradually disentangles itself from old contexts in Europe, beginning
first in England in the early seventeenth century and then, with
many confusions, denials, reversals, and cross-purposes, elsewhere
in Europe and the world. A large-scale history of this modern, conceptually distinct, idea of freedom is now beyond the ambition of
any one scholar, however learned. This collaborative enterprise, tentative though it must be, is an effort to fill the gap.

We could not take into account all the varied meanings that freedom and liberty have carried in the modern world. We have, for example, ruled out extended attention to what some political philosophers have called "positive freedom," in the sense of self-realiza-
tion of the individual; nor could we, even in a series as large as this,
cope with the enormous implications of the four freedoms invoked
by Franklin D. Roosevelt in 1941. Freedom of speech and freedom of

the press will have their place in the narrative that follows, certainly, but not the boundless calls for freedom from want and freedom from fear.

We use freedom in the traditional and restricted sense of civil and political liberty—freedom of religion, freedom of speech and assembly, freedom of the individual from arbitrary and capricious authority over persons or property, freedom to produce and to exchange goods and services, and the freedom to take part in the political process that shapes people's destiny. In no major part of the world over the past few years have aspirations for those freedoms not been at least powerfully expressed; and in most places where they did not exist, strong measures have been taken—not always successfully—to attain them.

The history we trace was not a steady march toward the present or the fulfillment of some cosmic necessity. Modern freedom had its roots in specific circumstances in early modern Europe, despite the unpromising and even hostile characteristics of the larger society and culture. From these narrow and often selfishly motivated beginnings, modern freedom came to be realized in later times, constrained by old traditions and institutions hard to move, and driven by ambition as well as idealism: everywhere the growth of freedom has been *sui generis*. But to understand these unique developments fully, we must first try to see them against the making of modern freedom as a whole.

The Making of Modern Freedom grows out of a continuing series of conferences and institutes held at the Center for the History of Freedom at Washington University in St. Louis. Professor J. H. Hexter was the founder and, for three years, the resident gadfly of the Center. His contribution is gratefully recalled by all his colleagues.

R.W.D.

Contents

≺ ≻

Acknowledgments

Several foundations have generously supported The Making of Modern Freedom series, and this volume in particular. The National Endowment for the Humanities provided funding for planning meetings. Liberty Fund Inc. sponsored the autumn 1987 conference where the volume was first discussed. The John M. Olin Foundation contributed towards meeting administrative expenses and salaries at the Center for the History of Freedom. Last, but far from least, of our outside supporters is the Lynde and Harry Bradley Foundation. This volume was largely written in the first of our annual Institutes in the spring semester of 1988. The Institutes, which bring the authors together as Fellows of the Institute for the History of Freedom, are fully funded by the Bradley Foundation. We are grateful for all the support we have received, including the strong backing we have always enjoyed from Washington University.

R.W.D.

CONTRIBUTORS

G. C. Gibbs
Birkbeck College, University of London (Emeritus)

Henry Horwitz
University of Iowa

J. R. Jones
University of East Anglia

John Miller
Queen Mary College, University of London

Howard Nenner
Smith College

Gordon J. Schochet
Rutgers University

Lois G. Schwoerer
George Washington University

R. K. Webb
University of Maryland-Baltimore County

Kathleen Wilson
State University of New York at Stony Brook

LIBERTY SECURED?
BRITAIN BEFORE AND AFTER 1688

Introduction

J. R. JONES

HISTORIANS WRITING IN the nineteenth century about the Revolution of 1688–89 presented it as an event of central importance in the history not only of Britain but of the whole civilized world. Thomas Babington Macaulay, in what for long was accepted as the definitive history of the Revolution, saw it as the decisive development that shaped all future progressive changes in Britain. He asserted that although the Bill of Rights, its central document, "made nothing law which had not been law before," it contained "the germ" of every good law (good, that is, by his own liberal standards) passed since 1688, and even of every good law which should be passed "in ages hereafter" to promote the public welfare.[1] Other classic "Whig" historians, writing in the same liberal tradition, expanded Macaulay's interpretation to develop an anglocentric view of modern world history, in which the Revolution appeared to be the necessary first step in Britain's emergence as the dominant world power exporting its constitutional principles and institutions to other countries.[2]

Inevitably, with the end of the British Empire and the questioning of liberal principles such interpretations now seem outdated, and consequently the significance of the revolution appears to become localized and parochial. This has been reflected in the switch of historical attention away from the Revolution of 1688–89 to the study of the English revolution of the 1640s and 1650s on the grounds that developments in this earlier period possess much wider and more fundamental significance. It was then, according to Marxist historians, that the new bourgeois epoch of history began with the first overthrow of the feudal order in a major European country. Although Karl Marx himself, while rejecting Macaulay's liberal principles and conclusions, agreed with him in seeing the Revolution of 1688–89 as marking the historically necessary triumph of the English bourgeoisie, his twentieth-century followers have almost without exception relegated it to the status of a "palace coup," as no more than a postscript to the decisive developments of the earlier one.[3] More generally these latter developments have afforded rich and varied material for historical research and debate, whereas by comparison the Revolution of 1688–89 has been seen to lack its social, economic, and intellectual dimensions, giving the impression of being little more than a matter of high politics, a transfer of power quickly achieved between competing sections of the governing elite.

≺ I ≻

The authors represented in this volume do not claim that the Revolution of 1688–89 in itself constituted an epoch-making event in an unfolding history of progress and freedom. Their chapters are certainly not based on, or geared to, any such teleological assumptions. They see the Revolution as a stage—although an important stage with many and long-term effects—in the processes of change that were affecting virtually all aspects of English life in the last decades of the seventeenth century. To use a term and concept much employed at that time, there was a conjunction or coming together of many trends, changes, and developments in the years before and after 1688. However it would be simplistic to assert that there were direct causal connections between these changes and the Revolution itself. Although there was a general awareness of processes of change in different areas of life, attitudes towards them varied greatly. Major advances in knowledge by use of the new experimental method, what we know as the Scientific Revolution, were over-optimistically expected to produce great material benefits. Judgments were divided on the demographic trend towards urban growth, and on the desirability of industrial and colonial development, and also on the effects of agricultural improvements that banished the specter of famine but also led to over-production and low prices for food and land.

So far as the constitution and the liberties of the nation were concerned the prevailing orthodox attitude was still to see all forms of innovation and change as pernicious. Changes were symptoms of decay and deterioration. Either they were the result of the passage of time itself, as in human life, or they were the result of the actions of evil or ambitious persons—kings, ministers, soldiers, fanatics, or demagogues. Consequently the purpose of the Revolution was not to change the constitution or transform the system of government, but to recover, declare, and protect the rights and liberties that the nation had inherited from the past, but which James II either subverted or threatened.

The explicitly limited objectives of the chief participants in 1688–89 have contributed to the wide acceptance of the thesis that the Revolution was only an episode, an essentially reactionary affair. More generally the attempt to restore and perpetuate the old constitution is placed in the same category of historical futility as the Bourbon regime that collapsed in France in 1830, and the parody embodied in Napoleon III's second empire. Influenced by the world-shaking developments that followed events in France in and after 1789, and in Russia in and after 1917, most historians have regarded revolutions as major motor forces in bringing about and intensifying processes of historical change, whereas restorations like those of 1660 and 1688–89, as well as 1815 and 1851, have been dismissed as attempts to turn back the historical clock.

Indeed systems of historical thought based on linear conceptions of history as progress find it difficult to accommodate the possibility of a successful, enduring restoration. Consequently the concept and practice of restorations as a subject has been neglected. But with the collapse of Marxist-Leninist regimes in East European states in the late 1980s, and the restoration of individual rights, the rule of law, political pluralism, and market economies in most of them, perspectives are altering. These modern examples of attempted restorations throw light on the situations that arise when revolutions die and regimes based on arbitrary power collapse with the same kind of suddenness that marked events in England in 1688. Equally the uncertainties, phases of disillusionment, and unexpected complexities and problems that have followed the collapse of twentieth-century authoritarian regimes illuminate the difficulties involved in the consolidation of the Revolution of 1688–89. No regime since 1640 had achieved political stability, national unity, and a relationship of mutual confidence and common interest between government and governed. It is not surprising, then, that the success of the Revolution settlement was for many years in doubt and that under the pressure of events (and especially the fiscal and economic strains of the long war against France) the unity of 1688 dissolved into factionalism with widespread popular disillusionment.

The actual revolution was only the beginning of a long process, and it was not until its success was assured that the natural rights theories of John Locke became influential. Until then ideology was a dangerously divisive factor. It was not until the next century that radical Whigs expounded a coherent critique of the Revolution settlement itself, as distinct from attacking its corrupt operation by Whig oligarchs. They were chiefly concerned to make Parliament more representative by extending the franchise and reforming the constituencies. These radical Whigs raised the question of whose freedom should be embodied in the law, a question that their predecessors had not succeeded in putting on the political agenda in 1688–89, when the primary concern was overwhelmingly how to protect and preserve the institution of Parliament itself.

≺ II ≻

In 1688–89, as in 1628, 1640, and 1660, the active agent in the repeated attempts at political recovery and renewal was Parliament. J. H. Hexter emphasized the crucial and central position which Parliament came to occupy when he first announced the enterprise, the Making of Modern Freedom, of which this volume is a part. He propounded the thesis that developments during the seventeenth century gradually imprinted on the consciousness of Englishmen the conclusion "that their liberties required the survival of representative institutions, and that the freedom guaranteed by those institutions was their highest political priority."[4]

In the preceding volume of this series the key word "liberties" is shown to have acquired a distinct meaning during the first quarter of the seventeenth century, and one that is implicit in the legislation that followed the Revolution. Liberties were "specific rights and freedoms that followed from being a freeman under the English law."[5] They were more than a mere aggregate of separate franchises and immunities. First this was because every free person formed part of a community, with rights that were unequal but were all secured by law. For most this meant that they could not be deprived of life, liberty, or property except after due process of law, involving a verdict by a jury of their peers. For the significant minority who constituted what is known as the political nation, liberties also entailed a right (or rather obligation) to take a positive and active part in public business. This participation by subjects, together with the obligation set on governors to rule within the boundaries marked out by the law, acted as the guarantees of the rights and liberties of the nation.

In 1628 John Pym, the preeminent parliamentarian of his generation, described government in England as embodying a two-way relation between government and governed: "every part and member" gave strength to the whole in the pursuit of the common good, and in return received from it "strength and protection in their several stations and degrees." This "mutual relation and intercourse . . . concord and interchange of support" preserved the unity of the community, acted as a restraint on government, and ensured that it would operate for the good of the subjects.[6]

On occasions this relationship broke down and governors, both legitimate and usurpers, ruled without regard to the limits set by the laws. In the 1620s and 1630s, as described in the previous volume, the Crown and its servants allegedly manipulated the law and undermined liberties: in 1640–41 the Long Parliament set itself to recompose the constitution and "repair the breaches." In the next twenty years it was the Long Parliament itself which appropriated power, giving credibility to Charles I's warnings about its arbitrary behavior. When facing a sentence of death and execution Charles effectively passed sentence of death on all successive Commonwealth regimes when he rightly predicted that there could be no "hope of settlement . . . so long as power rules without rule or law, changing the whole frame of that government under which this kingdom has flourished."[7] Whatever the Commonwealth's pretensions as a free state, its several regimes whose authority derived from the barrels of the army's guns never gained general acceptance. Similarly James II, relying on prerogative powers and a standing army, freed himself from having to rely on the unforced cooperation of his subjects in governing the kingdom, so contradicting his claim that in granting religious liberty he was establishing a civil interest that united king and subjects.

The most immediately dangerous of James's policies was his attempt to pack a Parliament pre-engaged to legislate according to royal directives. Consequently, in 1688 as in 1660, a "free Parliament" provided the rallying call around which the nation united. The conventions of 1660 and 1689 had the primary duty of reconstructing and recomposing not only the privileges of Parliament but the ancient constitution itself, shattered before 1660, threatened in 1688. This must necessarily be done in accordance with custom and precedent, with the "first institution and ordinance" of government. They were to reestablish old rights, not create new ones. English liberties could be traced back to Saxon times.[8] Parenthetically it can be noted that in the only other major European state in which government depended on representative principles and practice—the Dutch Republic—constitutional theorists went back even further to find the origins of their freedom in the Batavians who resisted Roman conquest and inspired the sixteenth-century revolt against Spanish tyranny. The first chapter in this volume contains a brief comparative examination of English with Dutch liberties, leaving this subject for fuller treatment in a later volume of this series.

Because it was summoned by William explicitly to secure liberties and rights which James had tried to alter, the 1689 convention could not itself contemplate making arbitrary changes in the constitution. As a result although the convention changed the relation between Crown and nation by disposing of the succession by statute, disabling Catholic heirs, and formulating new oaths to be taken by sovereigns and subjects, the rights enjoyed by the latter were not extended. However there was, as Howard Nenner concludes in his chapter, a most significant change in the character (or tenure) of these rights. Before 1688 these were often stated to be rights derived from royal grant or concession; but now they became the inalienable property of subjects or institutions, which they had inherited from previous generations. These rights had been retained, that is not conceded to the sovereign, when government was originally established. It followed that they could not be arbitrarily revoked. It was the duty of the courts of law and of Parliament to ensure universal compliance with the law and, as the Revolution demonstrated, this included the king himself. The resulting new perspectives about rights and liberties went far beyond traditional views on custom and prescription. The concept of a liberty came to mean something that subjects possessed as property, as inviolable right. It followed that any attempt to invade this property deprived the perpetrator of his right. In legal terms the Crown ceased to be regarded as an estate in fee, but became an estate in trust, held for the benefit of subjects.

In other respects the Revolution settlement took the form, as John Miller shows in his chapter, of a set of compromises that were illogical and in the view of the radical Whigs incomplete. The implications of what had been done and, perhaps even more important, what had not been done in 1689 took time to be realized, and developments over the next three decades were to be largely concerned with working them out. But in some areas this complex process was to take over a century to complete, and it is this fact that determines the plan of this volume.

< III >

Two sets of paired chapters deal with areas of life in which the Revolution brought about no formal securing of rights. In 1688–89 neither William's declaration nor the Declaration and Bill of Rights even mentioned freedom of the press. Lois Schwoerer deals with the attitudes of successive governments towards the press in the period up to the lapsing of the Licensing Act in 1695, a change which she shows was due to practical considerations, and in no way due to any change of principles. Graham Gibbs describes what followed this end of pre-publication censorship. Ministers developed new methods to restrain the press and techniques of information management to mold the new force of informed public opinion. The principles of freedom of expression and publication were slow to appear.

The second pair of linked chapters deal with religious liberty, another concept notably absent from the legislation that followed the Revolution. The so-called Toleration Act of 1689 did no more than exempt most, but not all, Dissenters from the penal laws, and Catholics gained nothing. In Chapter 4 Gordon Schochet reconstructs the intellectual context that explains this meager outcome, examining the strong arguments that were deployed against, as well as for, the institution of anything approximating to religious liberty and the concession of full civil rights to Dissenters. Yet even the very modest provisions of the act had important implications in the long term. Dissenting churches took on a permanent and legal character as voluntary entities; in the complementary chapter by Robert Webb the changing patterns of thought about the relations between these churches, the state, and the established church during the century and a half after 1688 are analyzed. As well as explaining why progress from grudging acceptance of religious diversity to the inauguration of religious liberty took so long, Webb discusses the contributions made by Dissenters (and especially by the Unitarians) to the movements pressing for political reform and in the debates which saw the articulation of new concepts about liberty.

These movements and debates form the subject of the last chapter, by Kathleen Wilson, who takes an equally lengthy time-span in her study of a radical tradition which was based on libertarian and populist readings of the principles of the Revolution. Using the centenary celebrations of the Revolution as one of three perspective points, she traces the re-emergence of an active body of radical opinion which derived from the Revolution and from its missed opportunities a strategy for the transformation of the institutions of government. She contrasts this with the complacent and self-congratulatory orthodox interpretation of the Revolution as making any further fundamental changes unnecessary.

The more immediate intellectual and especially legal readjustments which were produced by the major changes that followed the Revolution provide the main subjects of Henry Horwitz's chapter. Two long wars of attrition required major administrative and financial reorganization. The economy and society of Britain began to experience previously unknown processes of change. Consequently the volume of new legislation increased substantially, and the emergence of new forms of wealth required some modifications in legal practice. How far were changes in the ways in which the law was administered consciously intended to benefit the propertied? How far was the law adapted to meet the changing needs of an increasingly commercial society? Did the conduct of juries represent an effective means for popular opinions, interests, and prejudices to influence the administration of justice? These are some of the questions which Horwitz explores through the first seven decades of the eighteenth century.

≺ IV ≻

What, then, did the Revolution of 1688–89 achieve, in terms of the furtherance or development of the kind of freedoms that exist at the end of the twentieth century? In terms of negative freedom, it represented a momentous defeat in one country of the principles and practices that characterized the ancien régime monarchies of contemporary Europe. It ended the threat to rights from arbitrary monarchy, securing the place of Parliament as a representative institution within a "mixed" government, even though the system of representation increasingly worked in favor of an oligarchy.[9] The Revolution safeguarded the principle and practice of participation in governmental processes by independent subjects, albeit drawn from the ranks of the propertied and excluding non-Anglicans for over a century. The liberty established in 1688–89 did not confer on all subjects an equality of rights.

The Revolution established in Britain a representative system of government, but it had little immediate influence on other countries. However, Britain stood at the threshold of changes in every aspect of life such as no other country, economy, or society had ever experienced before. A comprehensive and definitive settlement purporting to embody fixed and immutable principles would soon have become obsolete, whereas a series of pragmatic changes (even though often belated and partial) allowed governmental institutions and mentalities to adapt as the relentless processes of modernization transformed Britain.

The Revolution in Context

J. R. JONES

IN GENERAL TERMS the motives of those who carried through the Revolution of 1688–89 were to recompose the frame of government in accordance with its ancient constitution, reestablishing the liberties of the nation and reinstituting the rule of law. In 1688–89, as in 1660, the overriding aim was to put an end to a period of arbitrary rule and prevent its repetition: James II had attempted to obtain for himself a commanding position which would enable him to rule without regard to any legal restrictions, so that all the rights of institutions and individuals would be held and exercised at "his pleasure," that is only with his consent.

The essential characteristic of the periods of misrule, under the Commonwealth and James II equally, was not corruption or mismanagement but the existence of a conscious design to alter the frame of government. This was the situation in which the philosopher John Locke, who watched developments after 1683 from exile in the Dutch Republic, explicitly justified the right of subjects to "rouse themselves and endeavor to put the rule into such hands which may secure to them the ends for which government was at first erected."[1] For Locke and his contemporaries, the events of 1688–89 constituted a revolution in that they completed a cycle in human affairs. The rule of law had been reestablished in 1660, but Charles II and James had tried to free themselves from its restraints. The latter by suspending the operation of the laws and trying to manipulate the legislature freed his subjects from their obligation to obey his authority. When in 1689 a free Parliament recovered the rights of the nation it completed the historical cycle, and by doing so gave the political nation a new opportunity to achieve what had not been achieved in the years after 1660. Consequently in trying to

understand the actions and objectives of those who were active during the Revolution, and who established and implemented the subsequent legislative settlement, it has to be remembered that for
them its purpose was restorative and conservationist. They did not
aim, like the dominant revolutionaries in France a century later, at
transforming government, the law, society, and changing the status
of all the individuals who composed the nation.

<   I   >

The Restoration of 1660 had centered on the recovery by Charles II
of his right—on which all other legal rights depended. In sequence
of time, however, the restoration of Parliament came earlier, and the
first component of the legal order to be restored was the former political nation. The recovery of its freedom to act, within the limits
set by the law, initiated the process that produced the easy and unconditional restoration of the king, and a similarly composed political nation was to share with William the responsibility for the Revolution and to return the convention of 1689–90 that worked out the
subsequent legislative settlement. The political nation can be defined as comprising all those with some degree of rights to participate in the transaction of public affairs—as peers, parliamentary
candidates and electors, members of grand and petty juries, aldermen and common councillors in boroughs, the Anglican clergy, even
parish officers. These rights took very unequal forms, but the crucial
point was that those who possessed them did not do so at the king's
pleasure, whereas by contrast the JPs who administered the counties
were appointed by the king and could be removed at his will.[2] All
these possessors of active forms of freedom suffered in the course of
James's political campaigning in 1687–88 when he brought sustained pressure to bear on parliamentary electors and potential candidates, on peers, and on the clergy, and when he carried out widespread and repeated purges of corporations.[3]

Only a minority had the right to participate in public affairs. All
adult males possessed certain general freedoms, as distinct from the
positive freedoms to act in a public capacity. Everyone regardless of

status or gender had a right to trial by jury, according to the precise forms of law. Adult males and unmarried adult females possessed the right to hold property. Apart from married women, minors, and apprentices, who were subject to husbands, fathers, and masters who could forcibly detain and chastise them, the law protected all subjects from arbitrary action against their lives and persons as well as their property either by fellow subjects or by royal servants.

While he consciously strained the law in order to strike severely at political offenders whom he could only charge with lesser offenses (in 1689 the Declaration of Rights pronounced against the "illegal and cruel punishments" which he had inflicted for intimidatory purposes),[4] James did not launch any general invasion of basic legal rights. The mass executions and transportations of Monmouth's rebels in 1685, usually accounted an atrocity, were actions undertaken entirely within the draconian limits of the law of treason. Yet in the course of 1687 and 1688 James did set out systematically to alter the character of the political nation that had been restored in 1660—and that thanks to the Revolution was to survive almost intact until 1832. And William's propagandists persuaded most people that his attacks on the political nation represented the preliminary stage in a strategy of reducing everyone and all rights and properties to a state of total dependence on the pleasure of the king. They argued that only by defeating James's policy of trying to create a new political nation could the general freedoms shared by all subjects be made secure—not only against James, but against all future arbitrary acts of governments.

< II >

In the political nation of 1660, peers came first in terms of status. Neither Charles nor James brought improper pressure to bear on the Lords, although rumors spread in 1688 that James intended to create a majority of dependents by the mass creation of new peers. Constitutionally nothing could stop a sovereign doing so, but only once, at the end of 1711, did the Crown make tactical use of this power to create a majority in the Lords.[5] When fundamental changes in the character of the Lords were made it was by statutes: restoration of the bishops (1661), the test excluding Catholic peers (1678), and the admission of elected Scottish peers (1707).[6]

Unlike the Lords, the Commons possessed in its privileges constitutional means of preventing arbitrary and external changes in its composition. By all modern standards the entire representative system was defective, and the Commons frequently abused its privileges to advance personal or party interest. The justification for regarding the House as an authentic if imperfect champion of the principle and practices of representative governmental systems is to be found in the institutional independence which it had achieved in the century before 1660, and which it defended vigorously in the following decades.[7] Exclusive control over the voting of extraordinary taxes gave the Commons not only political leverage to extract concessions and force policy changes but opportunities to champion national and sectional interests. In addresses MPs explicitly justified making general representations on the state of the nation by citing its representative character. Officials resisted, arguing that addresses ought to be limited to statements of specific grievances because general complaints in effect told the people that they were not being well governed, and had helped to provoke rebellion in 1642. MPs replied that James I had welcomed such representations, and if this had continued, with resulting rectification of grievances, demagogues could not have fomented rebellion.[8]

The Commons became final arbiter of issues affecting its own composition during Charles II's reign. It decided disputed elections and this often involved determining the franchise in boroughs. In terms of genuine representation the proceedings at elections were frequently fraudulent or corrupt, and the Commons and its committee of elections often showed themselves scandalously partisan. But this independent exercise of decision ensured the independence of the Commons, and the composition of the urban electorate was not susceptible to royal control. James tried to change this in 1687–88 by his systematic campaign to pack a dependent Parliament by preengaging peers, candidates, and voters; and by filling municipal offices with pledged collaborators. By nominating and removing corporation officers and members at will, James confidently expected to create a dependent electorate in the constituencies that returned most of the Commons. His purges affected several thousand individuals, for whom the Revolution was not a matter of abstract principle or high politics but the way by which they could recover their local standing and influence.[9]

≺ III ≻

The Commons remained constantly alert to protect property rights, although neither Charles nor James revived the prerogative devices used by their father to raise money without parliamentary consent. James's levying of customs and excise duties immediately after his accession, explaining that it was necessary to meet an imminent threat of rebellion, caused disquiet before Parliament retrospectively legalized his action.[10] The only major invasion of property rights during the Restoration period, the 1672 stop of the exchequer, raised new but absolutely fundamental issues. The stop consisted of a unilateral suspension of the repayment of advances which had been made by bankers on the security of tax revenues: interest was promised, but in non-specific terms. Bankers were generally detested as usurers and conspicuous *nouveaux riches* in a period of depression and heavy taxation, but this arbitrary action against them provoked the Commons; MPs reacted strongly against "so high a violation of property."[11] They saw money as a particularly vulnerable form of property, and the consequences of its subversion as critically dangerous: one MP declared that "no point of our liberty is dearer to us than that of our money: with it we lose our liberty." Acting consciously as the "people's trustees" the Commons forced Charles to disclaim any right to suspend laws which concerned the properties, rights, and liberties of subjects, although a bill to prevent all forms of illegal exaction of money from subjects lapsed.[12]

This defense of the bankers by the Commons provides an early example of the emerging alliances between important groupings in Parliament and those in the financial world who can be termed proto-capitalists. It was based on fears that some of the arbitrary practices used by contemporary continental absolute rulers might be introduced into England: imposition of variations in the value of the currency to enhance royal revenues, defraud creditors and exploit the public; mass creations and sales of offices and privileges; partisan inquisitions into governmental financial transactions leading to confiscations of private fortunes; repudiation of debts. On the other hand there was nothing inevitable about an association between emergent capitalism and forms of government based on cooperation with representative institutions. A prudent awareness of the constant danger of arbitrary official action led financiers in France to accept the privileged position of governmental clients. As the later association of the monied interest with the regime of Sir Robert Walpole was to show, the possessors of great wealth tended to follow the men of power, whoever they might be and whatever their governmental methods.[13]

< IV >

Although the restored monarchy acted arbitrarily, infringing the personal liberties of political activists whom it judged were a danger to the regime, the legal rights of ordinary people received substantial and permanent reinforcement. The judgment in *Bushell's Case* gave immunity from fines and imprisonment to jurors who returned perverse verdicts, that is against the directions given them from the judicial bench.[14] In 1679 Parliament passed the Habeas Corpus Amendment Act, which stopped the use of practices designed to evade writs so as to prolong detention without trial.[15] The judges ruled in the case of *Thomas v. Sorrell* (1674) that the king could not use his dispensing powers to set aside the operation of a statute if doing so meant that the action which he thereby authorized would cause damage to a third party.[16]

The king's legal officers responded by developing new techniques to circumvent these safeguards, particularly in cases where royal interests were involved—for example in what can be termed political trials. Sheriffs were expected to pack juries.[17] The Crown relied on judges, whose commissions reverted to formulas permitting arbitrary dismissal, to intimidate juries, set bail and impose fines at unattainably high levels, and inflict "cruel and unusual" punishments on political activists convicted of noncapital offenses. However it was not the cruel but the arbitrary nature of these practices that led to their being declared illegal in the Declaration of Rights.[18] The most widespread interference with personal rights arose from the intermittent but often severe enforcement of the religious laws passed by the Cavalier Parliament between 1661 and 1670. The enforcement obviously was politically motivated, since religious dissent was explicitly linked to political faction and recent patterns of rebellion; there were, however, complex and sophisticated arguments for believing that the restoration of religious unity was both necessary and practicable. Even harsher treatment was intermittently meted out to Catholics. Any historian who tries to trace the development of freedom in the England of the seventeenth century confronts a major contradiction in this area. Almost without exception those who acted consciously in the defense of constitutional liberties and the rule of law also showed themselves to be oppressors of the Catholic minority.[19]

How is this paradox to be explained? Some politicians were entirely cynical in their exploitation of popular prejudices against popery and in particular played on the traditional anticlerical sentiment directed against the Catholic clergy because this could also be used against the high Anglican clergy and their pretensions. But there were two lines of argument that explain the hold that anti-popery retained on all sections of society. First Catholicism was regarded as being indissolubly connected with absolutism, not only because the major European Catholic kingdoms were ruled by absolute monarchies, but also because it was argued that no Catholic sovereign could ever expect to receive the voluntary cooperation of his Protestant subjects. Therefore he would have no option but to free himself from dependence on institutions in which they participated—juries, the militia, and corporate bodies, as well as Parliament. Second, anti-popery provided the only convincing and legally safe way of conducting opposition activities. It legitimated what otherwise would appear to be factious or even rebellious behavior and also provided the demagogically inclined with opportunities for evoking popular support by whipping up passions. Given this context of deeply rooted, xenophobic, and popular prejudice it was inevitable that hostility to James II's religion played an important role in the Revolution, so that the Settlement did not result in the establishment of religious freedom: as Robert Webb explains, this was to remain in the realm of aspiration for over a century. Those who worked in the convention of 1689 to establish constitutional liberties did not think it necessary to complement them with the establishment of freedom of conscience.

≺ V ≻

Gordon Schochet examines the intellectual debate about toleration and religious liberty, which engaged considerable attention among the educated laity as well as the clergy. Most significantly James ignored all theoretical justifications of toleration in his declarations of indulgence; and his apologists similarly avoided intellectual arguments in favor of toleration, preferring to emphasize political and economic advantages that they claimed would accrue to all subjects. In the 1687 declaration James explained his desire to unite all subjects to their ruler "by inclination as well as duty," that is by appealing to their interests, an appropriation of the Whig thesis that religious freedom would promote the wealth of the nation and enable individuals to concentrate on their own crafts, industries, and vocations, and so produce contentment.[20] Some propagandists developed this theme further, arguing that religious indulgence would benefit the economically most useful members of society, those engaged in industry and foreign trade; they explicitly categorized those concerned with agriculture and production for the home market as less deserving of encouragement because they contributed less to national wealth.[21] These were of course the landowners and their tenants, who made up the bulk of the Tory party and with whom James had broken.

James was intent on winning the support of the commercial and industrial sections of society, of the leading elements in the towns, of those who were either dissenters or sympathetic to them, and of all who had been formerly induced to support the Whigs. He had to distance himself from Louis XIV. The latter's Edict of Fontainebleau (October 1685), by which he revoked the toleration granted to the French Protestants by the Edict of Nantes, created great alarm in England. This alarm was sustained by an incoming flood of refugees, which peaked in 1687, the year of James's first declaration.[22] Contemporaries believed that religious persecution and the consequent emigration were precipitating the collapse of the French economy. James emphasized his belief that toleration and prosperity were indissolubly connected, and his propagandists argued that because the revocation was having such damaging economic effects there was no danger of James, with his concern for the expansion of trade, ever imitating Louis's action.[23]

James found in arguments about establishing government on the "civil interest," that is the identity of interest between king and the subjects, a substitute for the divine right principles on which he, like his Stuart predecessors, had relied.[24] Until the eve of William's invasion, James was not concerned by the alienation of many of the Anglican clergy which the declarations of indulgence were causing, because he consciously discarded them as essential props of the monarchy. He gave pragmatic reasons in the declarations for abandoning all attempts to produce religious unity by coercive methods. They had been tried since 1558 but they had failed. In emphasizing these pragmatic arguments James was being disingenuous, but he did give an oblique indication of why he believed that the attempted inculcation of the principles of loyalty and obedience by the Anglican clergy provided no sure basis for monarchical government. After describing the failure of attempts to establish religious unity, he concluded "the difficulty is invincible"; that is, it would never be overcome.[25]

What does this reveal? It explains James's break with the Church of England, which many historians have found to be inexplicable because of the clergy's constant advocacy of unconditional loyalty and their conspicuous services in defending James's right to the succession against the Whig attempts to pass the Bill of Exclusion. One has to return to the central point in James's life, his conversion to Catholicism. By this act he repudiated the claim of the Church of England to be a true church; he would not accept its sacraments, because they were not, and could not be, efficacious. Consistently with this rejection of the Church of England in his own personal quest for salvation, he was bound to reject the Anglican claim that its theological (as well as political) attachment to, and promulgation of, the principles of Divine Right were a sure foundation for the monarchy.[26] Furthermore, and this was the central argument being advanced at this time by Bishop Jacques-Benigne Bossuet, the most formidable Catholic polemicist of the age, the failure of the Church of England to establish religious unity was in itself an unanswerable objection to its being a "true," divinely instituted church.[27]

James's actions in dealing with its clergy were entirely consistent with his belief that the Church of England was not a true church. In his *Directions to Preachers* he showed that he expected some clergy to abandon their asserted principles of loyalty when faced with the prospect of losing their privileges; the *Directions* prohibited the exposition of polemical views because many clergy planted in the minds of their hearers "an evil opinion of their Governors by insinuating fears and jealousies."[28] James used his prerogative powers to create an ecclesiastical commission to supervise and discipline the clergy. Many lawyers regarded it as an illegal court, but they had no way of disputing its legality or preventing the enforcement of its decrees.[29] James's two declarations of indulgence undermined the legal position of the established church. In the 1672 declaration Charles carefully and explicitly gave the church guarantees as an institution.[30] In 1687 and 1688 James refrained from following his example, giving only limited undertakings.[31] James was reducing the established church to a position similar to that of the Dissenters, dependent on concessions granted by the king at his pleasure, which meant that they could be varied at some future date.

James's second major religious initiative raised the issue of England's independence as a state, providing the constitutional justification for the clause in the Bill of Rights (still operative in the late twentieth century) that bars Catholics from the succession. After the declarations, the Catholic church could operate an open organization, and to direct it James permitted the establishment of an embryonic Catholic hierarchy, four vicars apostolic.[32] This move raised fundamental issues about the sovereign powers of the Crown. The vicars apostolic derived their authority from the pope, not the king. By permitting them to operate, James made a concession of power to delegates of a foreign sovereign, surrendering some of the powers vested in the Crown of England by the (unrepealed) statutes of the Henrician Reformation. England could cease to be an *imperium*, a state independent of all supra-national forms of authority; and ultimately the questions raised by the co-existence of royal with papal authority would have to be regulated by a concordat with the Vatican. Having been instituted with James's approval the vicars issued a pastoral letter to the clergy and laity whom they claimed to be in their care. This meant that there were now two rival systems of ecclesiastical government. One had been established by laws—which the king had partially suspended; the other depended on the king's acceptance of an authority external to the kingdom.[33]

However, James tried to pre-empt a possible Protestant reaction at the future succession of a Protestant daughter by including Dissenters in the toleration he established and by conferring civil as well as religious rights on them. More specifically, as a means of dispersing suspicions about his sincerity as the advocate of toleration, James associated himself with a proposal that originated with William Penn, the Quaker founder of Pennsylvania, where religious toleration was a fundamental right.[34] This proposal represented an appropriation of a traditional concept cherished by the Whigs; it envisaged the passage of a new Magna Carta as security for the permanent inviolability of religious toleration. The forthcoming, pre-engaged Parliament would enact this in the form of a statutory declaration of liberty of conscience as an inalienable right. All office holders, peers, and MPs would be obliged to take an oath to respect it and not to attempt its repeal or amendment.

Analysis reveals this magna carta of religion to be a strange hybrid. It incorporated a concept of fundamental and irrevocable rights similar to that which the Levellers had formulated, putting them above statute. One supporting pamphleteer cited the jurist Sir Edward Coke in order to legitimize the notion of a declaration of liberty immune from subsequent statutory alteration or repeal; Coke had said that any statute contrary to a fundamental right of the subject is void and null, and religious liberty should now be seen as such a fundamental right.[35] The proposal that peers and MPs should take an oath to respect toleration, obviously aimed at preventing repeal if and when Mary succeeded, came from a very different source—the Anglican test bills of 1665 and 1675 which would have prevented any attempt by a peer or MP to alter the established government of either church or state.[36] Like those tests, the projected magna carta of religion would have removed religious affairs from the scope of the legislature, but it would not have produced a separation of church and state. In practice religious affairs would have become an area exclusively subject to the prerogative powers of the king.

≺ VI ≻

Many historians have expressed skepticism about James's chances of success in the ambitious campaign on which he embarked in 1687 and with which he persisted until the eve of William's invasion, the packing of a pre-engaged Parliament. His abandonment of the alliance between the Crown and the Tory aristocracy and landowning gentry seems unrealistic. It certainly flew in the face of conventional wisdom. James Harrington's explanation of the causes of the political upheavals of the 1640s and 1650s was widely accepted; political power and influence were directly related to the ownership of land, and the transfer of landed wealth from the Crown and church to the gentry had given the Commons predominant influence.[37] James moved in the opposite direction, abandoning an alliance with the predominantly landowning Tories in order to establish an entirely new connection with the Dissenters and townsmen (and Catholics and opportunistic Whigs) who appear to be an infinitely weaker combination.

James's switch of alliances makes sense when it is realized that there was no necessary connection between landed wealth and parliamentary representation. The pioneer political economist Sir William Petty demonstrated this statistically at the time.[38] In the county seats, where James's electoral agents made comparatively little progress, there were 160,000 freeholders with votes; Petty estimated their wealth as being approximately £160,000,000. But they returned only 91 MPs. James's agents targeted the parliamentary boroughs, which altogether returned 418 MPs; Petty estimated that their electorate numbered fewer than 40,000 and were worth less than £20,000,000 (with a high percentage of this in London). In another calculation he suggested that all county and borough elections were in practice decided by an elite of fewer than 2000 persons— patrons, employers, candidates, and their connections. James's electoral agents set out to eliminate or counter the influence of this elite, substituting for them a small set of royal collaborators, backed by royal influence in the form of direct intervention in borough affairs, and with an expectation that returning officers nominated by the king would work in their favor.

Contemporaries became extremely alarmed that James's electoral campaign would secure the return in October 1688 of sufficient pre-engaged candidates to give James the ability to control Parliament. If he was assured of a Commons composed of MPs whom "he could be assured would comply with his pleasure," he would be able to subvert the integrity and independence of Parliament.[39] By using repeated personal pressure to extract pre-engagements from voters as well as candidates, James was destroying the share in government that every enfranchised commoner possessed as a right. Even more widely, he would if successful infringe the right possessed by all subjects, of being governed only by laws which had been freely passed by men representative of the entire community. Moreover by his intervention in the corporate boroughs James was corrupting an essential part of the body politic. By surrendering charters to the king, and then by accepting royal nomination to municipal office in return for engagements to vote for royal candidates, James's local collaborators were betraying the liberties of the entire nation.[40]

Similarly parliamentary candidates who pre-engaged themselves to follow royal directives would destroy the existing frame of government. One hostile pamphlet described James's aim as "endeavoring of an Alteration of the Government." If he succeeded, it would mean the dissolution of the constitution and its replacement by a sovereign who possessed the power to rule arbitrarily by manipulating a dependent Parliament and enforcing its statutes via a dependent judiciary and magistrature.[41] It was essential for William to intervene before James could assemble such a Parliament. Consequently his declaration denounced James's electoral preparations, and these made it plausible for him to claim that, like Monck in 1660, he was intervening for no other purpose than to ensure a free Parliament.[42]

< VII >

In addition to safeguarding the rights of the church and Parliament, the other principal concern in 1688–89 was to guarantee the rule of

law. For contemporaries this meant ensuring the impartial administration of justice, by judges and juries who were not subject to
direction and control; there was to be no distinction between the
areas of public (or royal) and private concern. As Howard Nenner
demonstrates, the Revolution marked the triumph of a new concept
of liberty. The liberties and rights of the nation were not to be seen
as having originated in royal grants, which would mean that they
could be revoked if the king considered this to be necessary. Instead
rights became property, belonging to the nation, which the people
retained because they had never conceded them to their ruler. The
purpose of the laws was to prevent these rights being infringed by
anyone; anyone meant not merely common criminals but also the
king and his ministers and officials.

James possessed a very different conception of the relationship
between the Crown and the laws. By his use of the suspending and
dispensing powers he acted as if he were not bounded or fenced in
by the laws. He claimed powers to set aside the operation of the
laws, as an inherent and irreducible part of his royal prerogative.
Unlike his predecessors James had to make systematic use of both
the suspending and the dispensing powers because he had committed himself to achieving specific policy objectives by means of
his prerogative powers.

The Bill of Rights declared the suspending power illegal without
any qualification:

the pretended power of suspending of laws or the execution of laws by regal
authority without consent of Parliament is illegal.[43]

However it should be noted that this clause takes away a suspending power only from the monarch personally and does nothing
to entrench the liberties of individuals or corporate bodies. The 1689
Bill of Rights does nothing to secure liberty against encroachment
or even subversion by means of regular legislation. It is entirely
within the British constitution for a king or queen in Parliament, by
means of statutes, to suspend the operation of the laws and established legal rights. This has been frequently done, in what can be
seen objectively as emergency circumstances; but there is no objective criterion of what constitutes an emergency, anymore than there
was in the 1620s and 1630s. As early as 1689 a statute suspended
Habeas Corpus for a stipulated period, to permit the detention of

Jacobite suspects against whom there was insufficient evidence to bring treason charges.[44] In 1941 in *Liversidge v. Anderson* it was ruled that under the provisions of the Defence of the Realm Act the courts had no power to elicit and review a minister's reasons for ordering the internment without trial of a suspected subversive or of a tribunal operating secretly which upheld the decision without stating its reasons.[45] Under the British constitution, statute remains sovereign in an absolute, almost Hobbesian or omnipotent, sense; and unlike an American citizen, who possesses constitutional rights, an individual Briton is still technically a subject, with no constitutional defenses against the power of statutes. No mechanism exists by which a statute can be declared unconstitutional, so that the only defense of specific rights against repressive legislation would lie in the exercise of the long-disused royal veto power.

< VIII >

There was an all-important difference in the background to the two convention parliaments of 1660 and 1689–90. In 1660 everyone knew that once a free Parliament met it would restore the monarchy. But William's 1688 declaration, with its explicit call for a free Parliament, merely made it clear that he would not attempt to impose a settlement. When the convention met in January 1689, peers and MPs were not committed in advance to any particular form of constitutional, political, and religious settlement.[46] Nor did they receive directions as to how to proceed. In his October declaration William went into detail only on how a free Parliament was to be elected—according to the former charters and franchises. In order to widen his appeal William placed all the responsibility for recent breaches of laws, liberties, and religious rights on James's evil councillors, not on the king himself.[47] Obviously William could not denounce James at an early stage, for fear of arousing suspicions that he intended to seize the Crown for himself or for Mary—an argument that James briefly tried to develop.[48] Similarly the declaration was prudently vague about the legislation that would be needed to prevent any repetition of recent invasions of the laws, although these were described fully. From his own experience of English poli-

tics and politicians William knew that the resolution of the crisis
would not be an easy process.[49] General statements about the need
to prevent arbitrary government appeared in the other declarations
which appeared during the Revolution, complementing William's
own declaration but not identical with it. These declarations were
the work of William's provincial adherents, who staged a number of
risings as his army advanced on London.[50] These risings represented
a political development of the greatest significance: a reassertion of
independent influence and self-determination on the part of the
members of the former political nation whom James had displaced.
At Nottingham, Northampton, Derby, and York, in Cheshire and
Worcestershire, groups of peers, gentry, and townsmen assembled in
arms and subscribed to public declarations. In the circumstances attempts were made to draft them in such a way as to attract the widest possible support—Tory as well as Whig. Consequently these declarations contributed to the conservationist character of the Revolution by laying emphasis on regaining and then preserving the
fundamental rights, liberties, properties, and religion of the nation.
A troop of volunteers even took as its slogan the medieval baronial
rallying call: "we do not wish the laws to be changed." The subscribers to most declarations explained with emphasis that they could
not be regarded as rebels because they were defending the laws: only
in one Whig-influenced manifesto was the right (or indeed duty) to
resist tyrants clearly stated.[51]

The radical Whigs failed to seize their opportunities in 1688, either by staging a rising in London or by issuing a general manifesto.
They published pamphlets advocating specific and fundamental political changes, but too late to influence the elections, so that these
had to be addressed to the convention itself when it first met. Their
demands rested on the proposition that James's tyrannical and unlawful actions had dissolved the government, that is destroyed the
constitution itself. The radical conclusion was that this dissolution
left the nation free to construct a new frame of government, making
whatever changes it thought fit. Such a unique task must necessarily require a larger and more widely-based representative body than
a regular Parliament: although they did not use the term, the radical
Whigs were proposing a constituent assembly.[52] By calling for a free
Parliament, elected in the usual forms and on the existing fran-

chises, William had anticipated such demands in his declaration. Moreover he and his supporters carefully avoided saying that James's policies had overturned the constitution—although their continuation would have done so. One Williamite manifesto proclaimed that religion, liberties, and properties had been "about to be rooted out"; and a prominent supporter asserted that church and state had been "brought to the point of destruction," but actual destruction had been prevented by William's intervention.[53]

The basic principle that guided the convention in making the settlement can best be described as conservationist. Its purpose was to ensure "for time hereafter," for the benefit of posterity, the continuation of those rights which were the possession of the nation. It was therefore axiomatic that the settlement must accord with the known laws and ensure their preservation and perpetuation.[54] Even most radical Whigs thought that changes should be relatively restricted to the alterations of the balance of governmental powers between the king and Parliament, and to changes in the responsibilities of certain categories of public officers. Few thought it possible or desirable to attempt a total reconstruction of government, parliamentary representation, and the administration of the law such as the Levellers had proposed in the late 1640s. Nevertheless some ingenious constitutional projects were advanced in a number of pamphlets and radical Whigs attempted to lobby the convention.[55] From a conservative point of view—and most Whigs as well as all Tories in the convention can be regarded as conservative-minded— there was a real danger of these pamphlets and popular demonstrations gaining momentum, habituating people to the discussion of new ideas and heightening political consciousness at least among Londoners. This fear of the resurgence of radical ideas and influences provided a cogent reason for pressing on with an early settlement of the constitutional issues that faced the convention.[56]

In this context "conservative" means those who regarded political or constitutional change as not only undesirable but also futile, in the sense that imposed changes could never be permanent: like the changes which James had tried to impose they would be arbitrary and incompatible with the ancient constitution. Therefore they expected the convention to restore the constitution which James had invaded. It should be brought back to "its first and purest original, refining it from gross abuses, and supplying its defects."[57] It was not for the convention to enact structural changes. Only by renewing the constitution according to its fundamental principles could a durable settlement be achieved.

The convention took the Petition of Right as its precedent. The situations in 1628 and 1689 were broadly similar in that there had been a period in which liberties had been invaded and claims made for the royal prerogative which would put the king and his servants outside the bounds of the law. One MP wished to go back to a much earlier situation, proposing a new Magna Carta, a comprehensive statement in statutory form of the rights of the nation, including a delimitation of those of the monarchy. His proposal met with disapproval; he was told "not to launch into such a sea," and certainly the enactment of such a complex measure would have been impossibly time-consuming, technically difficult, and divisive in its effects, as it is difficult to see how Whigs and Tories could have reached the necessary agreement.[58] Instead it was a former Leveller, John Wildman, who cited the Petition of Right as indicating the way to proceed, declaring that at that time "the Commons refused to have new laws, but claimed what they demanded *ab origine.*"[59] Consequently the convention proceeded by declaration. It did not enact rights in the form of a regular statute, because there was no cause to do so; the rights which were specified in the Declaration of Rights were ones that did not require statutory enactment because they had always belonged, of right, to the nation and its institutions. However the claim in the Declaration, that it was solely concerned with "vindicating and asserting" ancient rights and liberties, does not bear examination: many of its articles were directly related to issues that had arisen since 1660.[60]

≺ IX ≻

The Declaration of Rights concentrated on reaffirming rights which were the general property or possession of the nation, and particularly of Parliament as its representative institution. In the first draft, the Heads of Grievances, a number of additional matters were listed on which legislative action was contemplated. Many of these directly concerned the rights of individuals and proposed protective action, for example against abuses in the levying of taxes and in legal proceedings.[61] These were omitted from both the Declaration and the Bill of Rights, not because a parliamentary oligarchy began to think it safe to be able to dispense with popular support, but because these proposals added up to an impossibly complex program of legislation which could not be enacted in a single session. Areas of concern as the militia, overlong parliaments, an independent judiciary, and legal procedures were to be the subject of later legislative attention, but the Declaration concentrated on the rights of Parliament itself. It specified that the consent of Parliament was necessary for all changes in the laws and for the maintenance of a standing army in peacetime, and that its grant had to be obtained for all forms of taxation. Parliamentary proceedings should be free, as must be elections, and parliaments should meet frequently.[62]

In contrast to the generally conservative character of the constitutional settlement, the barring of Catholics or any successor married to a Catholic represented a major innovatory element in the Bill of Rights. This could not be justified in terms of the ancient constitution and customary law. As one MP had to admit, "There is nothing in statute or common law against a popish prince," and the historical fact that constitutional liberties had existed before the Reformation embarrassed Whigs.[63] The justification was pragmatic. It had been "found by experience" that having a Catholic sovereign, or one married to a Catholic as all four Stuart kings had been, was incompatible with the preservation of liberties.[64] This prohibition represented a repudiation of the divine right principle of an indefeasible, that is humanly unalterable, right of succession. From another angle it can be seen as a reversal of the principle that governed ancien régime Europe, according to the formula applied since the Augsburg settlement of 1555, *cuius regio eius religio* (the religion of the ruler determines that of the kingdom). By legislating to ensure that the sovereign and his or her consort must be of the same religion as the subjects, that is of the Church of England established by law, Parliament added emphasis to the restricted or limited character of the English monarchy. As Howard Nenner shows, sovereignty after 1688 was located in the king (or queen) in Parliament, and the rights which institutions and individuals possessed did not depend on the Crown. But in matters of religion the ruler had to follow the faith that originated in a statute: even today the sovereign and his or her consort, and heirs and their consorts, are the only lay persons compelled to be Anglicans.

The Revolution of 1688–89 can therefore be seen as a decisive victory for the office theory of monarchy, a defeat in one country for the proprietary theory (and practice) that otherwise prevailed in the ancien régime kingdoms of Europe.[65] In his declarations from exile James continued to use the language and concepts of proprietary monarchy in calling on his subjects to return to their allegiance. It was not just a linguistic convention when James referred to "our" Parliament, laws, and judges. It conveyed the meaning that all rights operated by royal concession, at his pleasure or discretion, because they originated in past royal grants. Similarly James used the same language in trying to convince European monarchs, Protestant as well as Catholic, that the success of the Revolution represented a threat to the institution of monarchy itself.[66]

Jacobite propagandists constantly argued that William, like Oliver Cromwell earlier, would as a usurper inevitably rule in an arbitrary and tyrannical fashion.[67] The Revolution did bring about a profound change in the relationship between sovereign and nation, but in the opposite direction to that predicted by James. This was produced by revising one of the oldest authentic constitutional documents, the coronation oath, which was based on the eleventh-century formula of Edward the Confessor. The Coronation Oath Act substituted very specific promises for those which previous sovereigns had sworn; these had been mainly concerned with the maintenance of the privileges of the clergy and contained only vague undertakings to respect the "rightful customs" of the nation. By the new act William and Mary, and all their successors, had to take an explicit oath to govern "according to the statutes in Parliament agreed on, and the laws and customs of the same."[68] A further promise helped to reconcile Tories to the Revolution: sovereigns had to promise to maintain "the protestant reformed religion established by law." The Tories overcame Whig resistance to the inclusion of the last three words, and by doing so secured the Church of England against statutory change for over a century. George III cited this oath as justification for his implacable determination to block repeal of the civil and religious disabilities imposed by the tests and penal laws on Catholics.[69] In striking contrast to the specific promises required of sovereigns, the oaths which office holders and clergy had to take were purposely made more general: they had only to swear to be "faithful and bear true allegiance" to William and Mary. The new sovereigns were intentionally not described as rightful sovereigns.[70]

The formulation of this new and pragmatic form of oath did much to make it possible for the vast majority of Tories, and a considerable majority of Anglican clergy, to accept the new regime since they were obliged to give it no more than de facto recognition. In addition a great deal of intellectual ingenuity was expended by Tory writers to reconcile support for the Revolution, and acceptance of William and Mary, with the divine right theses to which they had committed themselves so explicitly and enthusiastically in 1679–83 and 1685.[71] Tory participation in the Revolution and the influence which the party exerted in the convention proved to be absolutely crucial in determining the character of the settlement and in ensuring general acceptance of the regime. In a negative sense it made it certain that the outcome would not include the legal establishment of religious freedom. Early in the convention Whig pressure led to a statement in the preliminary Heads of Grievances, of "effectual provision to be made for the *liberty* of Protestants in the exercise of their religion."[72] The Tories, however, grudgingly conceded only the so-called Toleration Act of 1689, which did not confer rights on Dissenters but merely gave them exemptions from the penal laws.[73] Nor did they receive equality of civil rights; the Corporation Act was not repealed. However, toleration went further than most Tories wanted. The bishops had suggested that a measure of indulgence should be given to Dissenters, but they had specified that it should be approved by the Church's own representative body, as well as by Parliament.[74] That would have ensured a narrow measure, and in the convention the Tories argued that the Toleration Act should be temporary and probationary.[75] An act which tacitly accepted the permanence of organized dissent seemed to pose a potential danger to the integrity and privileges of the Church.

The act changing the coronation oath acted as a barrier to any fundamental change, giving the Church a security for its rights which survived almost intact throughout the eighteenth century. The Revolution reestablished the principle and practice of the interdependence of church and state which James had dislocated in 1687–88. Although several hundred clergy refused to take the oaths to William and Mary, and as Non-jurors broke off communion with the majority which did,[76] most Tories accepted a new interpretation of the ways in which divine right principles should apply. This was later proclaimed authoritatively by the most influential Tory cleric of the period, Archbishop John Sharp, who disconnected divine right principles from their formerly exclusive attachment to the personal and indefeasible right of the monarch and his or her heirs. He proclaimed that obedience was due to "our rulers, whether in one or in many," and that this was enjoined by Christ and the law of nature. His argument reflected a permanent change in the character and direction of Tory political thought. God had not prescribed any particular form of government; therefore obedience was due to those who constituted authority—the king, Parliament, and those appointed to administer the laws.[77]

Tory acceptance of the settlement deprived the Jacobites of mass support; consequently they could be contained by the use of statutory methods of control, although in Ireland and Scotland extraordinary and harsh methods had to be employed. William's ministers obtained from Parliament statutory suspensions of Habeas Corpus for specified periods. They also resisted proposals for changes in the procedures used in treason trials.[78] The arguments provoked by these proposals concerned principles and issues that still lie at the heart of debates about public security and the rights of the individual. Whigs who became ministers objected that by giving those accused of treason a genuine opportunity to prepare and conduct a defense they would weaken and endanger the state, "rendering treason more difficult to be punished than before." Nevertheless in 1696 Parliament passed the Trial of Treasons Act, which gave accused persons the assistance of counsel, permitted defense witnesses to give evidence on oath, and required corroboration between prosecution witnesses. This act ended the manipulation of legal procedures to procure convictions that had been practiced by all previous regimes during the century. The rights of the individual were no longer willfully and systematically disregarded when they conflicted with those of the state, whereas in other kingdoms (and also in Scotland and the Dutch Republic) the prosecution still possessed formidable advantages, including use of evidence extorted by torture.[79]

< X >

Although the radical Whigs failed to initiate major constitutional and institutional reforms, the Revolution did lead to a transformation in the way in which government was administered. The executive arm represented by the monarch and his ministers and officials was fenced within bounds set by the law; the executive accordingly became dependent on the active cooperation of Parliament and the political nation. There could never again be any possibility of the Crown dispensing with annual sessions of Parliament, as had happened in 1629–40 and 1681–85, or of a monarch trying to remodel the political nation.[80]

Realization of the fundamental change in the relationship between Crown and Parliament which the Revolution had achieved came as a brutal shock to William himself when a determined majority in the Commons, confident that it had overwhelming support in the country, forced through the disbandment of most of the army which William had raised to fight the war of 1689–97. The political crisis of 1698–99 over disbanding proved to be the first and greatest test of what were known as Revolution principles. The constitution permitted William to defeat the bill for disbanding the army by dissolving Parliament or exercising his royal veto, or to delay it by proroguing the session. Alternatively he could have encouraged the court majority in the Lords to reject the bill, as Charles II had done in order to defeat the exclusion bill in 1680. The instigator of the moves for disbanding, Robert Harley, was not greatly exaggerating when he described any of these actions by the king as amounting to a dissolving of the government. William would certainly have precipitated a total break with the Commons. Charles had not been deterred, knowing that he could continue to rule without parliamentary cooperation; William knew that he could not carry on the government if he irrevocably alienated the Commons and its supporters in the nation.[81]

Ultimately William had to accept the disbanding bill. This humiliating acceptance by a king of his dependence on a representative institution is inconceivable in any other European monarchy in the century before 1789. Standing armies, with the bureaucracies necessary to administer and supply them, occupied a central position in the absolute monarchies of the seventeenth and eighteenth centuries and, even later, the autocracies of the nineteenth. Armies provided ancien régime monarchies with their main *raison d'être;* and they came under the exclusive control of kings, czars, and kaisers until as late as 1917 and 1918. In England the Bill of Rights left the army under royal control, but its very existence in time of peace depended on parliamentary consent, and its size and cost had to be agreed on with Parliament in order to obtain the necessary financial provision.[82]

An equally conclusive proof of the transformation which the Revolution effected in the relationship between governments and the governed can be found in the attitudes displayed by the exiled James. In his declarations he varied the terms which he proposed to impose after regaining his kingdoms, revealing his belief that rights could be granted, confirmed, amended, or withdrawn at his pleasure.[83] In the private memorandum he composed in 1692 for the future guidance of his infant son, James emphasized the importance of respecting property rights, of governing within the laws, and of reestablishing full liberty of conscience.[84] However he outlined drastic changes to the forms of government in order to eliminate the dependence of the Crown on the voluntary cooperation of subjects. Keeping the treasury always in commission, with a salaried secretary playing a central and continuous role, would prevent the emergence of a chief minister. Salaried bureaucrats were to be maintained in all other main departments of state. Revealingly, the key ministerial office in future was to be a new one, a secretaryship of war, invariably to be held by a Catholic.[85] This was modelled on the French office which the Marquis de Louvois had held as minister of war; but—unlike the French—the forces which James intended to reestablish were not designed for foreign wars (against which James warned his son), but for internal security.[86] The army was to act as the main prop of the restored legitimate monarchy; its loyalty was to be ensured by recruiting officers and men as far as was possible from Catholics.

Household posts at Court which brought their holders into contact with the royal family were also to be reserved for Catholics. French models influenced a reform of local government which would bring it under increased direct royal control. It was no longer to depend on men who possessed influence in their own right. Salaried lord lieutenants, similar to the lieutenant governors of French provinces, would supervise local administrators, and a new corps of officials similar to the ubiquitous *intendants* were to be given a legal training at royal expense to make a special study of the royal prerogative in order to use its powers in their executive and supervisory functions. James's assumption that a restored monarchy would survive only with the maintenance of a Catholic professional army and an expanded bureaucracy shows that he envisaged a form of absolute government and believed that only Catholics could be capable of unshakeable loyalty. Clearly both ideas reflected his experiences in 1688, but they also testify to the gap that was to widen between the Jacobite exiles and changing conditions in England. They could not comprehend the changes produced by the Revolution, taking no account of the enlarged part of Parliament in political processes, or of the practical restrictions imposed on sovereigns, ministers, officials, and MPs by public opinion, organized interest groups, and the parties.[87]

When John Somers wrote that the government settled after the Revolution was legal, not arbitrary, and political, not absolute, he was paraphrasing the formula used by Sir John Fortescue in the fifteenth century.[88] But in the next decades political came to mean party-political. William's initial attempts to establish mixed administrations of Whigs and Tories quickly foundered, though he always consciously attempted to make use of advisers who were not tied to parties. The bitter party warfare between Whigs and Tories, which had no parallel in any other country, was intensified by the frequent general elections required by the 1694 Triennial Act, which put a maximum limit of three years on the life of a Parliament. Administrations which were predominantly Whig alternated with those dominated by the Tories.

The persistence and bitterness of party divisions made many people fear, or in the case of the Jacobites hope, that the rage of party passions would undermine the regime established by the Revolution. However parties assumed a representative character: each embodied the interests and opinions of local and family connections, mercantile companies, socio-economic groups, and even colonies. The critics of Sir Robert Walpole as minister—Bolingbroke and his associates—deluded themselves in the 1720s by thinking, or arguing for ulterior purposes, that parties could be dispensed with, and that party activities represented a form of corruption.[89] On the contrary, wide participation in party activity, in elections as well as within Parliament, was seen as differentiating the free Briton from the passive and supine subjects of the absolute sovereigns of Europe, and radical Whigs never lost sight of the need to extend the franchise and so increase the number of participants in the political process. In 1743, when it became clear that Walpole's fall would not produce an alteration in the character of politics, Edward Spelman commented: "in all free governments there ever were and ever will be parties." He added: "parties are not only the effect, but the support, of liberty."[90] More tentatively Benjamin Franklin concurred at a time when citizens of the new United States realized that party divisions were beginning to emerge: such party divisions "will exist wherever there is liberty, and perhaps they help to preserve it."[91]

< XI >

William's long-term objective in intervening in England in 1688 was to gain control over British resources for use in the impending war against France. Of course he was also vitally concerned to preserve his own and Mary's rights, but the Revolution proved to be the most decisive success in the mission which he assumed of protecting the liberties of Europe from French hegemony. William and a very small but far-sighted minority of those who rallied to him saw a conjunction between the urgent need to form the strongest possible coalition against France and the equally critical need to defend and preserve the constitutional liberties and religion of England and Scotland.

Most English politicians and at least a section of the public expected the Revolution to be followed by a war against France, but hardly anyone had any realistic conception of what a war would involve. In its early stages, with Louis providing James with armed assistance in Ireland and threatening an invasion of England, the war proved to be a defensive fight to maintain national independence; the Revolution settlement did not become totally secure until William extracted de facto recognition from Louis as part of the Rijswijk peace settlement of 1697. But a long war of attrition, involving eight hardfought and ruinously expensive continental campaigns, brought about fundamental and irreversible changes in government and in the relationship between government and nation. In a wide historical perspective it is arbitrary to make any separation of the Revolution of 1688–89 from the war which followed.[92] Far from being a bloodless coup, the Revolution was in crucial respects only a beginning, the start of a long-drawn process of change enforced by the demands of major wars fought on the Continent as well as at sea. Some Tories saw this from the first, and tried to limit English commitments.[93] They argued that naval and colonial campaigns were the appropriate and potentially rewarding ways of fighting the war, whereas military campaigns in Europe must require fiscal and governmental changes and innovations.

What was nothing less than a revolution in government followed the Revolution, with the emergence under the stress of war of what has been called the "fiscal-military state."[94] This involved vast and totally unforeseen increases in the number of officials employed by government, a correspondingly large increase in both direct and indirect taxation, the institutionalization of public credit, and what was to most contemporaries a frightening growth of national indebtedness. England became the most efficiently taxed country in Europe, largely because taxes were levied by officials appointed and supervised by central government. Such a degree of centralization had been experienced in England only once during the rule of the Long Parliament and the Commonwealth. Then it had provoked almost universal resentment: the crucial difference in the years after 1688 was that the increase in the effective authority of the central government was matched by a corresponding increase in the degree of its accountability.

All measures had to be agreed by Parliament, and the sovereign and all governmental officers recognized that even in the middle of a desperate war they had to keep within the bounds set by the laws. During the critical 1690s administrations accepted the need to submit annually a state of the army and the navy to Parliament, setting out in minute detail proposed strengths for the next year, so that the Commons in particular should scrutinize it and decide how many ships, how many regiments of cavalry and foot, were required and how they should be costed.[95] At the end of each year during the 1690s the accounts of money actually expended became subject to examination by the increasingly expert public accounts commission nominated by the Commons by secret ballot.[96] Consequently the increases in the machinery of government and in expenditure did not have the effect of increasing the independent power of William's administrations; on the contrary they increased its practical dependence on the continuing cooperation of the political nation.[97]

Recognition of the mutual obligations which connected government with the governed can be seen in one particularly sensitive area, the institution after 1688 of what proved to be a permanent land tax. Although never popular, it was accepted because it represented the discharge by the wealthier sections of society of their duty to support governments over whose policies the political nation had a measure of control.[98] In other words they paid for their privileges, whereas in France most of the aristocracy possessed the privilege of exemption from the direct tax, the *taille*. Ministers had to accept that taxpayers had a direct interest in the rates at which the land tax was levied and formed judgments on the reasons given for increases or for its maintenance at high levels. The land tax embodied the principle of an essential interdependence between government and the political nation and contributed substantially to the achievement of political stability.

The war also made William and his administrations dependent on the new "monied interest," the bankers, financiers, and rentiers whose services proved to be crucial. By advancing loans and transferring money overseas in very large amounts to finance the army and the navy, and to pay subsidies to the allies—a new experience for English governments—they enabled William to contain the French in a war in which the finances of the hostile powers played as decisive a part as the opposing armies. These financial interests, whose security was greatly enhanced by the statutory establishment of the Bank of England, were totally committed to the success of the regime set up by the Revolution: a Jacobite restoration would mean the repudiation of William's debts. A symbiotic relationship developed between the government and those who possessed liquid forms of wealth. Each came to rely entirely on the other.[99] This relationship raised new questions, which are still present in the late twentieth century: about the connections between wealth and power, of how governments should be prevented from governing in the interests of sectional groups at the expense of what became known as the national interest, and of how to detect and then prevent increasingly sophisticated forms of corrupt influence.

≺ XII ≻

Jacobites naturally tried to exploit the distress and discontent caused by William's war, and they went further in accusing him not only of favoring his fellow-countrymen but of introducing corrosive Dutch principles and practices into England.[100] By contrast classical Whig historians like Macaulay and the American historian-diplomat John Lothrop Motley linked the Dutch revolution against Philip II of Spain in the sixteenth century with William III's intervention in England, fitting them into a teleological scheme as "a chapter in the great volume of human fate."[101] There were certain similarities in that those who acted against Philip and James were consciously resisting royal innovations which they believed were intended to undermine their customary rights in order to enable these sovereigns to rule as tyrants.[102] The Dutch abjuration of 1581 was legitimated by the thesis that princes were created by God for the welfare of their people. If they attempted to reduce their subjects to slavery (a word also used frequently in England in 1688–89) the latter had the right to repudiate royal authority. Consequently most English opponents of the Stuarts throughout the century admired the Dutch Republic as the only free state in continental Europe and advocated imitating certain of the key practices that distinguished it from other major states.

English admiration for the Dutch was not unqualified. First, it was Dutch practice that made a favorable impression and not their governmental system or theories. The Dutch constitution did not lend itself to imitation. Its foundation document, the Union of

Utrecht (1579) was little more than a mutual defense treaty between sovereign provinces, each with its own elected stadholder as executive officer (although William III held six of the seven), and its own representative body, a States. The Republic itself had no single executive officer; the States General was composed of mandated deputies bound to follow instructions given them in advance by their provinces. There was no supreme court for all the provinces. The justification for this decentralized system of government lay in its entrenchment of the medieval rights and liberties of the provinces and their constituent cities, but in times of crisis such as the Anglo-Dutch wars brought it resulted in weaknesses that the English had exploited. Significantly when the union between England and Scotland was being negotiated in 1706–7 no real consideration was given to a federal system.[103]

Although the individual liberties of Dutch citizens did not have formal constitutional guarantees, in practice Dutchmen enjoyed much greater freedom in their everyday lives than their English contemporaries before the Revolution. The Dutch Republic had a reputation for religious toleration, but this was not based on any right or constitutional principle. By law all officeholders had to belong to the Reformed Church. But in practice adherents of other faiths, notably Jews and even Catholics, could worship, although the latter had to do so privately. Attempts by militant Calvinist clergy to interfere in secular affairs were blocked by city magistrates. Municipal and provincial authorities rarely acted with any promptness to suppress newssheets or pamphlets and books—unless these attacked themselves—but no principle of freedom of expression or of the press existed. There were no impediments to immigration and emigration, and naturalization was relatively easy. Freedom to trade existed, with the admittedly important exceptions of the East and West Indies companies.

The common factor behind all these practices was the concern of all forms of authority to facilitate economic activity. The diplomat Sir William Temple described the Dutch system of government as one appropriate for rest but not for motion. It was for essentially defensive purposes, to protect the nation's commercial position. Interest provided the bond that held state and society together.[104] Until the 1690s much of Dutch foreign policy and all fiscal policies were geared to promoting the dominant interests in commerce and banking. English observers concluded that this significantly contributed to the superior performance of the Dutch economy, but it brought with it long-term disadvantages. Office, influence, and power became permanently concentrated in a self-perpetuating oligarchy. The dominance of existing interest groups retarded the emergence of new interests. Innovation was discouraged, risk-taking declined. There was no operation in Dutch public affairs of the dynamic processes of renovation, renewal, and reconstruction that characterized the Restoration of 1660 and the Revolution of 1688–89 in England.[105] When William II died in 1650, just after the failure of his attempted absolutist coup, his regent opponents simply left his stadholderships unfilled, making no attempt to explore ways in which a federal system could be made to function more effectively. Similarly in 1672 William III did no more than purge his opponents in the magistratures, making no attempt to widen the basis of representation and participation in the city and provincial administrations. The final outcome of this immobilism was the economic and political stagnation of the so-called Periwig period covering most of the eighteenth century and the revolutions that brought it to an end.[106]

The resemblances between trends towards oligarchy in the Dutch Republic and developments in late seventeenth-century England were obvious to many contemporaries. Many came to fear that the Revolution might have secured only the forms but not the substance or reality of constitutional liberties. First and most obviously, money was being used systematically to extend the influence of administrations. Lord Treasurer Danby had shown in 1673–78 that the multiplication of offices, pensions, and sinecures could be used to build working majorities in Parliament.[107] The expansion of government necessitated by the war gave William's ministers similar opportunities, which they did not neglect: the title of the "Officers' Parliament" was given to the Commons elected in 1690, which ministers seem to have expected to retain for the duration of the war. The wealthy also used their money to play an increasingly dominant part in elections to the Commons, particularly in borough constituencies, driving out the middling gentry who could not afford the escalating costs. Money defeated the attempt by "country" MPs to curb outside intervention in borough elections by imposing a maximum life of three years on any Parliament, and for the same reason the later statute to impose property qualifications so as to exclude dependents or clients had little practical effect.[108] Magnates bought up constituencies when opportunities presented themselves. Country elements fought a long but losing battle against ministerial and magnate influences until their worst fears were realized by the long-term success with which Walpole constructed and manipulated working majorities of placemen and dependents. According to his enemies he finally achieved what James II had vainly attempted to secure, a submissive Parliament which gave him arbitrary power.

Second, men possessed of new forms of wealth used their influence to further their own individual or sectional interests.[109] Special interest groups worked at Westminster to influence governmental policies, engaging in intensive lobbying and using the press to influence opinion in general. But this influence should not be exaggerated. Neither the financial nor the trading and manufacturing interests possessed the kind of dominant influence deployed for over a century by the Amsterdam regents. They were only one component in the combination of interests which coalesced in the years of Whig supremacy after 1714. But they were the most visible because they were newly influential and intrusive, and suspect because of their international connections. Furthermore the practices which brought spectacular wealth to a few seemed likely, as was demonstrated by the first great speculative boom and collapse—the South Sea Bubble— to corrupt wide sections of society as well as the administration and Parliament.[110]

Before 1688 politicians and demagogues opposed to the court found in anti-popery the cause that legitimized their position and behavior, enabling them to mobilize popular prejudices against a detested minority. The Revolution put an end to this opposition strategy; accusations of corruption provided a substitute. Systematic use of corrupt practices allegedly made arbitrary government a practical proposition. Those who accepted inducements and bribes ceased to be free themselves and would therefore connive at the destruction of the nation's liberties. Accusations of corruption were difficult to refute and easily aroused popular indignation at several levels—emotional, rational, and constitutional. Of course many of those who made generalized and specific charges of corruption were

actuated by ambition and cynically denounced ministers for practices which they had formerly used themselves. But corruption was
a reality, undermining the integrity of Parliament and subverting liberties in more subtle and therefore more dangerous ways than the
blatantly absolutist designs of James II.[111]

≺ XIII ≻

The Scottish revolution of 1688–90 and the revolution in Ireland
(1688–91) took very different forms from that in England. Until the
Union Treaty of 1707 Scotland remained an entirely separate kingdom, the only connection being that England and Scotland had the
same person or persons as sovereigns. The Scottish revolution reflected very different political and religious traditions and can be
directly related to the conflicts of 1637–51.

In Scotland religious ideology provided the main motive force in
1688–90 as in 1637–49.[112] The establishment of a fully reformed
church or kirk provided the unifying cause which made it possible
to combine aristocratic factions, a passionately committed clergy,
the minor gentry, and townsmen and peasantry. The concept of a
covenant gave permanent form and embodiment to this union. The
National Covenant of 1638 was a compact between the Scottish
people and God; it brought together in its subscription all sections
of the nation, it maintained continuity with the Reformation by reaffirming earlier declarations, and it bound not only those who subscribed but future generations to keep it inviolable.[113] This had two
longer-term consequences that differentiated developments in Scotland from those in England. First, the National Covenant provided
such a coherent and convincing justification for actions taken to
resist royal policies that there was no parallel in Scotland to the
process of intellectual fermentation in England that after 1640 produced radical political, religious, social, and economic ideas and formulas. Second, the covenant committed its subscribers to the defense of principles and practices that were totally reversed after
1660, when a fully episcopal government of the Church was established for the first time. Only a minority remained actively committed to the covenant, but the legitimacy of the restored monarchy

and its governing agents in Scotland faced repeated challenges, armed rebellions in 1666, 1679, and 1685, and a long guerrilla campaign by the Cameronians.[114] For many of those who took an active part in the 1688–90 revolution, particularly at the popular level, their actions were a continuation of these earlier struggles.

Scottish government after the Restoration can only be described as absolutist, first in practice under the duke of Lauderdale and then also in principle under James. A relatively large standing army had to be employed actively in enforcing the laws. The single-chamber Scottish Parliament was converted into an obedient instrument: in 1681 under the direction of James as royal commissioner it passed the Succession Act.[115] This declared that the Crown passed by hereditary right according to "the fundamental and unalterable laws of this realm," and that no "difference in religion . . . nor act of parliament made or to be made, can alter or divert the right of succession." The Parliament called after James's accession passed a number of repressive statutes that were brutally enforced: the death penalty could be imposed on persons attending conventicles, while absence from church services could be punished with fines or deportation. Further acts gave government officers legal immunity to cover behavior in their official capacity and declared the king to be constitutionally absolute, due obedience to his commands without reserve.[116]

Not only did repressive and partisan government provoke more violence during the Scottish revolution of 1688–90 than England experienced, but a partisan settlement simply reversed the previous position, subjecting the previously dominant Episcopalians to repressive treatment. In strongly Presbyterian districts crowds "rabbled" the conforming clergy.[117] The Scottish convention abolished episcopacy and established a Presbyterian church but did not concede even limited toleration to those of other faiths. The constitutional settlement was equally partisan, making no attempt to reach compromises. The Claim of Right declared that James had invaded the fundamental constitution, altering it from "a legal, limited monarchy to an arbitrary, despotic power," and "inverting all the ends of government." As a result of his actions James was declared to have forfeited the throne, and a long list of his actions was declared unlawful.[118]

A civil war had already broken out when the Claim of Right passed and the throne was offered to William and Mary. James's partisans could mobilize against them a rising based on the potent principle of loyalty to the person of the monarch. Having governed Scotland in 1680–82, James was well placed to appeal to sentiments of loyalty as well as to exploit the resentment against Presbyterian dominance felt by Catholics and Episcopalians.[119] Consequently for the next sixty years the government of Scotland had to be based on superior physical force, bribery, and patronage. The revolution in Scotland did not significantly enlarge political or religious forms of freedom. Like their predecessors before 1688, governments responded to rebellion and disaffection with harshness: in the 1690s as in the 1680s suspected conspirators were tortured; the notorious massacre of Glencoe was designed to intimidate clan chiefs who were trying to equivocate.[120]

≺ XIV ≻

The revolution in Ireland still has a controversial impact in the late twentieth century: in a divided island its events retain symbolic significance. In the seventeenth century Ireland was constitutionally a separate and, unlike Scotland, subordinate kingdom. The Parliament at Westminster could legislate for Ireland, although it contained no Irish peers or members. The English as well as the separate Irish Privy Council had to approve bills before they could be introduced in the Dublin Parliament.[121] These constitutional provisions reflected the status of Ireland as a kingdom acquired by conquest, and (together with the right to appeal from Irish to English courts of law) they acted as a guarantee for the maintenance of what was known as the English interest in Ireland. By this was meant both the general interest of the kingdom of England (for example in matters of trade) and the local interest of the governing class in Ireland, composed of officials and English and Protestant landowners and their dependents.

James initiated a fundamental change in the government of Ireland when he appointed the earl of Tyrconnel as lord deputy in 1686. He was an old associate, a Catholic, head of the most prominent Old

English family, the Talbots, and a formerly active lobbyist for dispossessed Irish landowners.[122] He used his authority to catholicize
the army, to remodel the urban corporations, and to admit Catholics
into civil offices. These developments enabled him to hold almost
the whole of Ireland for James in the first months of 1689. When
related to the English revolution of 1688–89 the resistance which
Tyrconnel organized for James in Ireland can be characterized as a
counterrevolution.[123] It represented an affirmation of loyalty to a
sovereign who had been deprived of his other kingdoms by violent
usurpation: the Act of Recognition passed by the Dublin Parliament
which assembled in 1689 directly repudiated the English Declaration of Rights, refuting its theses with a restatement of divine right
principles.[124] The Jacobite movement also embodied a resurgence of
an older form of loyalty, to the traditional Catholic faith of the
majority of the Irish nation. This legitimized the war in the eyes
of the majority, although James maintained religious toleration for
Protestants.[125]

The essential socio-economic differences between Ireland and
England were particularly apparent in the character of the Jacobite
leadership in 1689–91. By contrast with the civilianized English aristocracy and gentry, their Irish counterparts were still a largely
militarized class habituated to the profession of arms. But by contrast with the Scottish aristocracy and Highland chiefs who rallied
to James, few of the Irish still retained feudal or tribal influence on
a significant scale; the Cromwellian conquest and large-scale expropriations of land had weakened the old connections. They had also
driven Irishmen into military service overseas in Spain, France, and
the Dutch Republic, whereas the Scottish aristocracy had officered
the armies of Charles II and James.

The Jacobite counterrevolution which went down to defeat in
1690–91, and in such decisive fashion that no serious Jacobite
movement ever materialized again within Ireland, did in some respects assume the character of a national movement. The Jacobite
Parliament made Ireland a separate and equal kingdom, passing acts
that declared English statutes to have no effect in Ireland and abolishing legal appeals from Irish to English courts. It also proposed to
overturn the land settlement that had been imposed after 1660 and
which had, with favored exceptions, largely confirmed the expro-

priation of Catholic landowners that had followed the Cromwellian conquest.[126] This gives a sharp insight into the main characteristic that, apart from religion, most clearly differentiated Ireland from England. In England property rights were inseparably connected with political and personal liberties and the rule of law. Political rights gave protection to property rights. Possession of specific types and amounts of property entitled owners to exercise active political rights. By contrast in Ireland property rights derived largely from recent acts of conquest, and their maintenance depended on the continued possession by their owners of military as well as political power—the Protestant aristocracy was as militarized as their Catholic counterparts, serving in an army that before 1685 and after 1689 had as its principal task the maintenance of the status quo. Consequently not only was Ireland in constitutional terms a kingdom subordinated to England by act of conquest, but most of the land titles of the individuals who constituted the English interest derived from conquests and the expropriations and plantations that followed and consolidated them. In 1689–91 the combatant parties, Williamites and Jacobites alike, expected that their victory would be followed by a new application of the same principle, either to confirm and extend, or entirely to reverse, previous acts of expropriation.

The issue of expropriation inevitably complicated the settlement of the Jacobite war. The last stronghold surrendered in October 1691 on articles of capitulation, the so-called Treaty of Limerick. General Ginkel, on William's behalf, promised that the articles would receive royal confirmation and that William and Mary would endeavor to obtain their confirmation by Parliament also. One of the articles gave protection to the estates of those who surrendered at Limerick. This provision infuriated William's Irish partisans who had been expecting a general round of expropriations and made it unthinkable that a future Irish Parliament (composed exclusively of Protestants) would confirm the articles promising a continuation of the position of the Catholics in Charles II's reign (which in fact Parliament proceeded to erode by a new series of penal laws). It was still less likely that any further security would be given, as promised, to Catholics.[127]

The revolution left Ireland a defeated country ruled by a minority, the so-called Protestant ascendancy, in the interests of England. Survival in a war for English independence against the threat of French domination required the suppression of Irish independence. William's dependence on the Protestant minority to garrison the conquered country made it impossible for him to curb their anti-Catholic attitudes or veto their penal legislation. He was also unable to prevent the English Parliament passing measures of economic discrimination against Ireland. In the longer term the revolution perpetuated the process by which England and Ireland became locked into sets of intractable problems. Tyrconnel's temporary domination of most of the country made the Protestants of three provinces realize that their own survival depended entirely on support from England, but once the Catholic majority ceased to be passive (at the end of the eighteenth century) their privileged position became ultimately untenable. By contrast the Scots-Irish in Ulster held their own in the defense of Derry, founding a militant tradition that still survives.[128] In Ireland, unlike England, potent and living myths associated with the events of 1688–91 still provoke bitter controversies and inspire destructive violence.

≺ XV ≻

Those responsible for the Revolution of 1688–89 justified their actions by invoking posterity, claiming that the liberties and religion of unborn generations were now safeguarded for all time. Inevitably, with the passage of time perspectives changed and Revolution principles became subject to reinterpretation. Walpole and other ministers of the first two Georges regarded the Revolution as a completed achievement and, as Kathleen Wilson shows in her chapter, their complacent satisfaction still suffused the orthodox or "establishment" celebrations of the Revolution in its centenary year. Mainstream Whigs claimed that since "modern liberty" was guaranteed by a "modern constitution" there was no need for further changes or reforms. Radical Whigs whose influence expanded in the 1770s and 1780s vehemently dissented, laying emphasis on the inadequacies of an uncompleted Revolution settlement. It was only at this stage, a century after the Revolution itself, that a general and lively ideological debate developed about the nature and implications of

THE REVOLUTION IN CONTEXT

Revolution principles, shortly before a wider and more prolonged debate began over the ideology and practices of the revolution in France. However she also shows that a radical Whig tradition had continued ever since 1688–89 to propound a dissenting interpretation of Revolution principles, which at times exerted considerable influence at a popular level.

The immediate success of the Revolution in 1688–89 depended largely on its pragmatic and non-ideological character, which enabled Whigs and most Tories to combine for a sufficiently long time to complete it. However when set in widest perspective, and certainly by comparison with the later French and Russian revolutions, this absence of ideology and theoretical formulations may seem to diminish its significance and reduce it to an event of only local and period importance. In the past John Locke's *Two Treatises of Government*, published in August 1689, would have been cited as a refutation of any such depreciation. It is now clear that the *Two Treatises* exerted comparatively limited influence during Locke's own life and very little during the months of the Revolution itself. As we now know, the *Two Treatises* was mostly written a decade earlier in the starker context of the exclusion crisis that polarized opinion between Whigs and Tories, and in his years of exile after 1683 Locke continued to be associated with the most militant radical Whigs.[129] It was published too late to influence the main constitutional debates in Parliament, although it may have helped to prevent further delay to the passage of the Bill of Rights. Moreover when it did appear the radical Whigs had failed to stimulate an ongoing and popular debate which would have given Locke's arguments an immediate relevance and perhaps provoked the same support for radical reforms that the Leveller tracts had enlisted in the 1640s.

In a passage of his original text that reflected the first Whigs' fears of a coup by Charles II, Locke argued that a king who used force to disperse a Parliament, or his prerogative to prevent it sitting, was in effect defeating the objects for which government had been originally established, and that this was tantamount to making war on his people.[130] He also perceived that a danger existed of a legislature acting under royal directions to use its powers "to injure or oppress the people" and in a passage added in 1688 explicitly condemned James's attempt to obtain a pre-engaged Parliament as being "as

great a breach of trust, and as perfect a declaration of a design to
subvert the government, as is possible to be met with."[131] Had James
actually assembled a subservient Parliament, or been able to organize serious resistance to William and to crush the provincial risings, a situation would have been created in which Locke's arguments would have had immediate and compelling relevance; but in
practice both William and the convention were able to act as if the
constitution had been threatened but had not been overthrown.

Locke intended the *Two Treatises* to be far more than a manifesto for political action. He wrote so as to establish the true nature
of the origins, institutions, and purposes of government; to expose
the fallacies on which divine right theories were based; and to convince his readers that all future study of government and politics
must follow his exposition of the nature of human understanding
and rational knowledge. In private correspondence Locke was extremely critical of the compromise by which Tories could swear allegiance by the de facto formula because it ensured the survival of
what he regarded as the totally erroneous divine right principles
which he had refuted.[132] The compromise ensured that when a further provision had to be made about the succession, because of the
failure of William, Mary, and Anne to produce heirs, the Act of Settlement (1701) like the Bill of Rights was an entirely pragmatic measure concerned with specifics. It concentrated on aspects of William's conduct of government that had already attracted criticism
and legislated to prevent any future repetition under the Hanoverians.[133] The preamble to the Act of Settlement described its provisions as being an extension of those contained in the Bill of Rights
and supplied the same rationale: both statutes were the product of
experience, and of reflection upon experience—in 1689 of attempts
to subvert the constitution, in 1701 of governmental abuses.

As a second stage of constitutional revision the Act of Settlement fell far short of the constitutional mechanism which Locke
implicitly favored in the very last paragraph of his second treatise,
where he propounded the possibility that a constitution should be
subjected to periodical revision and, if judged to be advisable, reconstruction by the "society" that had originated it.[134] Like Pym in
1628, Locke envisaged processes of renewal and reconstitution. In
his thesis revision should be undertaken not just when an executive

or legislative assembly behaved arbitrarily, but as an essential and regular (if periodical) method of ensuring that government served the purposes for which it had been originally instituted.[135]

The partial constitutional reviews of 1689 and 1701 have never been formally repeated, although the increase in the power of the British executive stimulated discussion during the 1970s and 1980s of enacting a new bill of rights, in effect a written constitution. However the one clear advantage of an unwritten constitution is its flexibility, its capacity to respond to change if those in positions of authority see, or can be made to see, a need for change. This is what happened, although unevenly and in stages, intermittently, during the long eighteenth century that ended in 1828 with repeal of the tests and penal laws, and in 1832 with the Reform Act, passed by Lord Grey. Significant changes did occur in many areas of public life—the law, the press, religion—and these changes provide main themes for chapters in this volume. A conjunction of various forms of change provides the context to the Revolution, but of course the tempo of change did not slacken after 1700. In many areas of life it intensified and became continuous. Britain was the first country ever to experience such continuous processes of rapid and major change, social, economic, and intellectual. Britain as the first industrial nation and world power was the first to experience, and to have to adapt its life to, the processes of modernization that have made the developed nations what they are in the late twentieth century.

In the last analysis it is the relationship between the Revolution and this process of modernization that makes the developments of 1688–89 have much more than local or period significance. It created a governmental system and political culture that was able in a number of pragmatic and intermittent responses—in the form of legislation, judicial judgments, and debates that changed public attitudes—to adapt to changes of a magnitude that had never been experienced before anywhere and to avoid major internal convulsions of violence or social breakdown. The Revolution dismantled what may very generally be described as the Stuart variant of the ancien régime systems prevalent in continental Europe. Thereafter a process of change and adaptation could take effect, although often belatedly and at lengthy intervals, and in an entirely unsystematic fashion. The contrast with France—the second modernizing nation—is revealing. Because of its inability to adapt, the ancien régime suffered dismantlement in ideologically-motivated processes of revolutionary change. These affected all aspects of life and had a direct impact on every single individual. Revolution provoked counterrevolution; Jacobinism provoked a systematic ideology of reaction. Divisions were further deepened by revolutionary (and counterrevolutionary) violence, an integral feature from the beginning. The speed with which the Revolution was effected in England, and the ignominious collapse of James's position, meant that no tradition of violence and repression was established in England— although Scotland continued to be a divided nation until after 1745, and Ireland is still one at the end of the twentieth century. The ideological compromises of 1688–89, illogical though they were, absolved Englishmen from having to treat fellow countrymen in any numbers as traitors. Liberty did not have to advance, as she does in Eugène Delacroix's celebrated painting of 1830, across a mound of corpses of slaughtered compatriots.[136]

Most of the participants in the Revolution of 1688–89 were reacting against the subversive policies introduced by James. They did assert that they were serving the interests of posterity but, as the conservative Edmund Burke realized a century later, they did not seek to dictate to their descendants the pattern of their lives. They simply assumed that future generations would live in much the same fashion as themselves and hold the same values. Their object was not to impose irreversible changes but to prevent arbitrary changes. They can be depicted as men of limited horizons. But they realized and put into successful practice a principle that is absolutely basic to any concept of freedom: that governments exist and operate for the benefit of the governed, and not of the rulers, and are equally bound by the rule of law.

Crown, Parliament, and People

JOHN MILLER

IN THE LATER SEVENTEENTH century Englishmen believed that they were freer than most Europeans. Parliament (which notionally represented every Englishman) gave them a share in law-making and a forum in which to press for the redress of their grievances; the procedures of the common law courts, and especially trial by jury, protected the individual's liberty and property against encroachments by either his fellow citizens or the state. Concepts of "freedom" or "liberty" nevertheless varied. Some in the seventeenth century already talked of them in terms of inherent natural human rights. Most, however, adhered to an older usage, in which "liberties" were privileges belonging to individuals or (more often) to groups.[1]

The most basic were legal rights, such as trial by jury, enjoyed by every subject, although the legal position of women and minors was inferior to that of men. Political rights were much more exclusive. The right to vote in parliamentary and municipal elections was restricted to males, usually property owners, and often to small self-perpetuating oligarchies. Most exclusive of all was the right to be summoned to the House of Lords, enjoyed only by holders of English peerages and the bishops. The right, in most towns, to practice a particular trade or to take part in municipal government was confined to a comparatively restricted group of craftsmen and traders, possessing the "freedom" of their town or craft guild which gave them rights denied to other citizens. Municipal and other corporations (including colleges and universities) had been granted (usually by the Crown) the right to a measure of control over their own affairs: here "freedom" meant immunity from outside intervention. In short, there were numerous different types of "freedom" in seventeenth-century England, with people of substantial wealth and high social rank possessing far more "freedom" than the poor and humble. The dominant groups in society, indeed, saw "freedom" mainly in negative terms: defense of the persons, property, and privileges of all subjects against invasion by the Crown, and also defense of the interests of the propertied against possible assaults by the propertyless.

Seventeenth-century political theorists argued that the origins of these English "liberties" were lost in the mists of antiquity. They had developed slowly over the centuries, enshrining the cumulative wisdom of many generations and exemplifying God's especial favor to the English nation.[2] The powers of kings and the rights of subjects had evolved in a symbiotic relationship, with the boundaries between them marked by law—ancient customs, acts of Parliament, and such constitutional statements as Magna Carta and the Petition of Right. The traditional constitution depended for its proper working on the king's voluntarily keeping within certain limits. The early Stuarts' persistent failure to observe such limits drove the Long Parliament elected in 1640 to seek to restrict the king's power. Some accused Charles I of violating the "fundamental laws": broad general principles which were held to underlie the constitution but had not been formally stated in any specific law. Their precise nature (like "the spirit of the law") was always open to debate: Charles I forced his subjects to articulate more clearly what they meant. Used to seeking guidance in the past, in custom and statute, many accepted that new circumstances necessitated new measures. Nevertheless, they tended to see innovation as being essentially conservative in intention, restoring the integrity of the traditional constitution.[3]

By 1641, however, many believed that more drastic innovations, which could not be justified by an appeal to the past, were needed to guard against future misrule. Subsequently, parliamentarians had to justify taking up arms against their king, which by existing law was treason. It seemed that, contrary to the assumptions of the ancient constitution, the powers of the Crown and the rights of the subject were no longer compatible. Parliamentarian theorists now argued that, in the last resort, the latter should take precedence over the former. They invoked the law of nature (especially the right of self-preservation) and based Parliament's right to resist the king on its representing the people. Such arguments had their dangers. In talking of subjects' rights and in claiming to represent the people, parliamentarian leaders left themselves wide open to charges that Parliament should, but did *not*, respect subjects' rights—it often used arbitrary methods to win the war—and that it did not truly represent the people. Thus the 1640s saw the emergence of two new lines of argument. First, an explicit claim that in the last analysis the king's rights should give way to those of the subject, as set out by Parliament. Second, a more radical claim (articulated mainly by the Levellers) that Parliament itself should be restricted, by immutable "fundamental laws," and made more responsible and responsive to the people, through frequent elections on a much wider franchise.[4]

The attempt in 1660 to restore a consensus did not last. Many came to see Charles II, and still more James II, as threatening English liberties and religion and, specifically, Parliament and the legal system. James's attempts to rig parliamentary elections created a real danger that the Commons might cease to be in any sense representative and become a mere assembly of royal nominees, passing laws to enhance the king's power and undermine the rights of the subject and voting whatever taxes the king demanded. Furthermore under James the judges interpreted the king's powers so broadly as to enable him effectively to abrogate laws without reference to Parliament. Thus while neither Charles nor James claimed a *right* to tax or legislate at will, there seemed a real danger that they were attempting to do so in practice.

Contemporaries contrasted England's "mixed" or "limited" monarchy with the "absolute" monarchies which existed on the continent. In these, the king was the sole legislator and director of the government; all interests were subordinated to his. The outstanding example of such a monarchy was France, the most powerful state in Europe. Despite the very real differences between the monarchies of France and England, many Englishmen in the period 1660–88 feared at times that England's government was becoming more like that of France. Although unfounded or exaggerated, the fact that people acted upon these fears meant that they had a real impact on events: perceptions can be more influential than reality.

In this chapter, I shall consider the growth of fears for liberty, property, and religion, starting with the relative consensus following the Restoration and moving on to the growing political polarization of 1673–85 and then to the way in which James II's behavior united his subjects against him. I shall conclude with a discussion of the constitutional settlement of 1688–89, its significance and its consequences. I shall suggest that if "liberty" was indeed "secured" in 1688–89, this was the product not so much of a long-term struggle to weaken the monarchy and subject it to Parliament (although some had long sought to do so), as of an exasperated recognition that the only way to ensure that monarchs ruled responsibly was to deprive them of any opportunity to do otherwise. The picture was complicated by the fact that "liberty" could be seen as threatened by popular revolution as well as by royal "tyranny," raising the question of whose liberty should be secured, against whom, and how? The developments of these years, and especially of the 1680s, were complex and dependent on the interplay of diverse forces, and their outcome was far from inevitable.

≺ I ≻

The Cavalier Parliament elected in 1661 declared null and void all legislation which had not received the royal assent, sweeping away the ordinances which the Long Parliament and its successors had passed but leaving in place the acts of 1641 which abolished Charles I's fiscal devices (notably ship money) and the prerogative courts of Star Chamber and High Commission. The king could now raise money only in ways approved by Parliament and Englishmen would possess all the rights accorded by the common law. The 1641 legislation had, however, left most of the king's basic powers unscathed. He was still to formulate policy, at home and abroad; to choose his ministers and officials. His exclusive right to command the army, navy, and militia was confirmed in 1661. He was free to call and dismiss parliaments at will.

The effect of new legislation after the Restoration was to extend the king's powers. An act against "tumultuous petitioning" limited the number of signatures which could be collected without the permission of someone in authority and restricted to ten the number who could present a petition. All who served in the militia had to swear that it was unlawful to resist anyone bearing the king's commission, which some saw as a dangerous extension of royal power and diminution of the rights of the subject.[5] Whereas the Triennial Act of 1641 had required that Parliament should meet at least once every three years for a minimum of fifty days (and had established a mechanism to summon it if the king failed to do so), a new act in 1664 dispensed with both the minimum duration and the mechanism. Finally, the Licensing Act of 1662 for the first time gave the Crown statutory powers to censor the press and to control printing.

The men who made the Restoration settlement were ready to trust Charles II with powers with which the Long Parliament had been unwilling to trust his father. At first they had no great reason *not* to trust Charles II, and the experience of the 1640s and 1650s, and continuing rumors of rebellion, made it seem urgently necessary to establish a strong monarchy, so that the king could thwart any renewed bid for power by the radicals who had usurped authority. But there was no desire to return to the status quo ante 1641. The Commons thwarted an attempt to give the king sweeping, permanent powers over the personnel of municipal corporations.[6] Charles did not secure Parliament's approval for a standing army: MPs preferred the militia, officered by country gentlemen like themselves.[7] Most striking of all, the Commons defeated all Charles's attempts to prevent the reestablishment of the Church of England on traditional lines.[8]

Thus far we have talked of laws, of acts of Parliament. But laws need to be enforced and Charles I had shown only too clearly how they could be misused. Some way had to be found to ensure that the king should rule as his subjects thought he ought, and the way was through Parliament, which brought grievances to the king's attention, suggested remedies, and passed laws to deal with new problems. With the restoration of monarchy came the restoration of Parliament in the traditional form, which (however inequitable the electoral system might be) was far more representative of English opinion than the Commonwealth assemblies of the 1650s. This did not mean that there was now to be "parliamentary government," with Parliament taking a leading role in decision making, as Parliament did not want to govern. Most MPs did not aspire to become ministers. Most accepted that they had obligations to their constituents and saw the Commons as representing the people of England (everyone except the peers). But each MP should make up his mind on each issue according to its merits: MPs were not mandated delegates. Few had the expertise, time, or inclination to become involved in administration at the national level. Government was a burden which they were happy to hand back to the king, reserving the right to advise and to criticize his conduct and that of his ministers.[9]

The central problem was how to ensure that the king would be able to govern effectively and that Parliament should meet regularly and have some prospect of the king's heeding its advice and complaints. The key to resolving this problem lay in the royal finances. Since the legislation of 1641 it was no longer legally possible for the king to raise money except in ways approved by Parliament. The convention accepted that the king should be granted a revenue for life, which was intended to be sufficient to cover the normal peacetime costs of government. The yield of the taxes which Parliament voted fell well short of its estimates, but when the king complained the Commons failed to increase the revenue.[10] A king who was chronically short of money would have to call Parliament frequently and pay some heed to its wishes. At times, indeed, the Commons threatened not to vote money unless specific demands were met.[11]

The Restoration settlement in effect went a good way towards restoring the traditional balance between the powers of the Crown and the rights of the subject. Parliament met every year until 1672. Charles, aware of what had happened to his father, usually kept within the law, as it was generally understood. Even so, Charles's relations with Parliament between 1660 and 1671 were not always harmonious. The most important source of disagreement was religion. In the 1660s, although both Commons and king saw religious diversity as politically dangerous, they disagreed as to how best to remove that danger. Charles, overestimating the strength of the Dissenters, thought it better to allow them a measure of indulgence rather than goad them into revolt. The Commons tried to eliminate them through repressive legislation and enacted a series of persecuting statutes, culminating in the Conventicle Act of 1670. Following

Charles's assent to this act, the sessions of 1670–71 were unusually harmonious and constructive, showing that the traditional ideal of cooperation between king and Commons could still become reality. Yet when Parliament next met in 1673, it was in an atmosphere of suspicion and rancor, which persisted for the rest of the reign. What had gone wrong?

≺ II ≻

The key to this abrupt change in the political atmosphere—much remarked upon by contemporaries[12]—lay in the reappearance of anti-Catholicism at the center of the political stage. Fear and hatred of popery was one of the most widespread and powerful forces in seventeenth-century England. Since the Reformation, Protestantism had become bound up with national identity. The Catholic church was alleged to rest upon a historically unsound claim to authority and to enforce superstitious and unscriptural practices, designed by popes and priests to increase their profit and power. Papal claims of a right to depose "heretical" rulers challenged emergent ideas of national sovereignty, making Catholic subjects appear potential traitors to Protestant monarchs: they were in a sense aliens, subjects of a foreign power. This potential became reality with murder plots against Elizabeth and the Gunpowder Plot (1605), but when Charles I embraced a form of Protestantism which many found alarmingly similar to Catholicism and simultaneously made assaults on liberty and property, this led to the identification of Catholicism and absolutism, "popery and arbitrary government."[13]

Fear and detestation of Catholicism continued to be expressed in political terms; it was "founded on politic and temporal interest," as a prop for monarchical power; "Popery in great measure is set up for arbitrary power's sake."[14] Catholic rulers and priests joined in an unholy alliance: the king backed up the clergy's authority, the priests kept the people ignorant and slavishly obedient. Thus an authoritarian church and an authoritarian form of government buttressed one another and both were inimical to liberty, religious and political. Although only about one percent of England's population, Catholics were widely believed to be far more numerous; and the

number of peers and gentry among them gave them a disproportion-
ately large political profile and influence.[15] From 1672, a combination of circumstances made anti-popery *the* dominant theme in
politics. In that year Charles declared war on the Protestant Dutch,
in alliance with the Catholic absolutist Louis XIV of France. He issued a declaration of indulgence whereby, using his ecclesiastical
prerogative, he allowed Dissenters to worship publicly, suspending
the recent acts against them, and Catholics to worship privately in
their homes. Finally, it became clear that Charles's brother, James,
duke of York, had become a Catholic. As Charles after ten years of
marriage had no legitimate children, there was a prospect that if he
died first England would have its first Catholic ruler since Mary I,
execrated in Protestant annals as "Bloody Mary."

From the time the Cavalier Parliament reconvened in 1673, there
were fears that James, and probably Charles, planned to impose
"popery and arbitrary government" with the help of Louis XIV. Then
in 1678 a disreputable but ingenious adventurer called Titus Oates
produced a long, involved tale of a "popish plot" to murder the king.
Circumstances—a mysterious murder, incriminating letters in the
possession of James's former secretary—gave added credibility to his
story. Panic swept the nation and minds were focused on what
might have happened had the plot succeeded and James become
king. The upshot was a campaign to debar James from succeeding to
the throne, in what became known as the exclusion crisis.

Between February 1679 and March 1681 there were three general
elections (the first since 1661). Each produced a Commons in which
the majority favored James's exclusion. Three exclusion bills were
brought in: one was resoundingly rejected by the Lords, the others
were aborted when Charles dissolved Parliament. Charles opposed
exclusion because he saw it as a threat to the monarchy and to himself, but he behaved cautiously, proposing limitations on a future
Catholic king (which would probably have proved unenforceable)
and even hinting that he might agree to an exclusion bill if the terms
were right. But the Whigs persisted in trying to force exclusion on
him and by doing so divided the nation more deeply than at any time
since 1660.[16]

The Whigs mobilized support among the people in an effort to
intimidate the King and Lords into agreeing to exclusion. Their ar-

gument against James was simple: "When he (as all Popish kings do) governs by an army, what will all your laws signify? You will not then have Parliaments to appeal to; he and his council will levy his arbitrary taxes and his army shall gather them for him."[17] It was better to infringe one man's rights than that the whole nation should suffer. Faced with Charles's resistance, they argued that his obligation to do what was best for his people should lead him, in such a matter of life or death, to comply with the nation's wishes as expressed by the Commons. The Whig case was in itself powerful, and it was originally couched in essentially defensive terms: exclusion was necessary for the preservation of liberty and Protestantism. Charles's opposition drove the Whigs to argue, however, that he should subordinate his wishes and judgment to those of the Commons in matters where, legally, he should have had a free choice. This was not easy to justify in terms of precedent and forced the Whigs to rethink their ideas on the constitution much as their forebears had done in the 1640s. Some moved towards the idea of kingship as a trust. Others avoided such novelties and concentrated on a more traditional claim that the king should do what was in his people's best interests. Most Whigs focused on the relationship of king and Commons, energetically mobilizing support outside Parliament, but except for the radical Whigs they avoided discussing the relationship between the Commons and "the people," engaging in fundamentally peaceful and lawful activities—petitions, pamphlets, elections. Only after the defeat in 1681 of the parliamentary campaign for exclusion did the Whigs resort to conspiracy or take to the streets— but on a smaller scale, and with less violence, than in 1640–42.[18]

Despite the relative lack of actual violence during the exclusion crisis, the Tory opponents of exclusion saw the Whigs as ambitious demagogues attempting to strip the king of his rightful powers, exploiting anti-popery and exciting the ugly passions of the mob. Like Charles, they suspected that exclusion would prove only the first stage in a concerted plan to start a new civil war to overthrow monarchy and church. They claimed exclusion would be unjust, depriving James of his birthright without trial. More questionably, they claimed that it was illegal, that the succession could be determined by God alone and that it was not in Parliament's power to change it, despite the fact that Parliament had endorsed changes in the succession in 1399, 1461, and 1485 and had legislated on the subject under the Tudors. To these constitutional divisions were added others over religion. With Dissenters emerging as conspicuous supporters of exclusion and the Anglican clergy its most vociferous opponents, religious and political antipathies reinforced one another.

By early 1681 these antipathies, exacerbated by polemical pamphlets and vicious electoral contests, had created divisions reminiscent of those of 1642. The crucial difference was that Charles II, unlike his father, had not been driven out of London and retained full control of the government of England, Scotland, and Ireland. He was thus able to exploit the backlash against Whiggism to create the opportunity to establish the authoritarian, even "absolute," regime which the Whigs had sought to prevent. Most accounts of Charles II suggest that he lacked the temperament, or the energy, to set out deliberately to create an absolute monarchy: "A king of England who is not slave to five hundred kings (Parliament) . . . is great enough," he said.[19] The most pragmatic of kings, Charles had as first priority survival, not bringing England's government into line with the latest continental fashion, exemplified by Louis XIV.

With French subsidies he could survive financially without Parliament, but his reassertion of royal authority depended mainly on the support of the Tories. They too believed that the Whigs had sought to overturn the existing order, by challenging the king's lawful powers and undermining the independence of Parliament. Tories regarded the mass petitions organized by the Whigs as unwarrantable challenges to the king's legitimate freedom of action. The Tories condemned the Whigs for organizing instructions from electors to their MPs mandating them to support exclusion, thus infringing each MP's duty to make up his mind on the merits of the case. The Tories bitterly resented the way in which the Whig majority in the Commons browbeat the minority by expelling MPs who questioned the veracity of the popish plot or promoted abhorrences. The Whigs launched impeachments against ministers and judges for giving advice or rulings unacceptable to the Whigs. The charges included treason, and their definition of treason was alarmingly elastic: indeed it was argued that treason was whatever Parliament declared it to be.[20] In practice the Whigs did not push impeachments to a conclusion: their aim was to intimidate ministers and judges. Within the Commons they sought, by persisting with inquiries into the plot, to maintain a sense of panic (much as the parliamentary leader John Pym had done in 1641–42). Those who defended James's claim thus laid themselves open to charges of favoring popery. Unable to question openly the anti-Catholic assumptions upon which the case for exclusion rested, the Tories were forced onto the defensive. The Tories deeply resented the Whigs' open support for the Dissenters, condemning the latter as both heterodox and disobedient.

Thus while the Whigs claimed that only exclusion could save English liberty, the Tories saw the greatest threat to liberty as coming from the Whigs. The preservation of liberty and property depended on the maintenance of order, which the Whigs' tactics seemed designed to undermine. "Arbitrariness," remarked one Tory, could be "more in the people than in the king." "There cannot be a more false illusion," wrote another, "than it is to suppose that what power the crown lost was so much liberty gained by the people." Such themes were constantly reiterated in Tory loyal addresses in the years after 1681 and were a central motif of the declaration in which Charles justified dissolving the second and third exclusion parliaments. He complained of the Whigs' unreasonable and subversive conduct, concluding: "Who cannot but remember that religion, liberty and property were all lost and gone when the monarchy was shaken off and could never be revived till that was restored?"[21]

In rallying to the king and his brother, the Tories (like most royalists in 1642) chose the lesser of two evils. They saw the movement for exclusion as "that specious pretence of freeing us from a successor which, let the worst happen as they suggested, would not be so fatal a consequence as what they intended us."[22] They accepted James's assurances that if he became king, he would respect the law and protect the church; and if he died before Charles, the question would not arise. Despite later Whig claims, few Tories believed in unfettered monarchy; they trusted that Charles and James would respect the interests and principles of their "old friends" and uphold the old constitution and maintain an ordered liberty under the law against the threat of subversion and chaos.

However the Tories advanced claims and supported actions which would later prove an embarrassment. They claimed that Parliament could not alter the succession because the hereditary transmission of the right to rule was ordained by God. Faced with an apparent threat of popular revolt, Tories argued (conventionally enough) that, as the powers of kings came from God, resistance to kingly authority could never be justified: if a king maltreated his subjects, they should accept that maltreatment with the same fortitude as the primitive Christians under the pagan Roman emperors. Some Tory historians questioned the historical basis of the reciprocity of rights and duties which many saw as the keystone of the ancient constitution. They showed that parliaments and many laws had their origin in the royal will, with the implication that what the king had given he could also rescind.[23]

Such arguments appeared to make sound political sense in the early 1680s, when the first priority seemed the restoration of respect for authority in church, state, and society; but they left hostages to fortune. Sometimes Tory writers and preachers did not think through the implications of what they were saying, sometimes enthusiasm led them to accord more power to the king (and fewer rights to subjects) than in retrospect was to seem wise. Similar developments can be seen in the area of law enforcement. As the political nation became polarized, partisan passions influenced the execution of justice. Tories were enraged by the refusals of Whig magistrates and juries to prevent electoral violence and intimidation and to enforce the laws against dissent. In normal circumstances justice should be impartial: if impartiality was impossible, however, Tories preferred that the law should be biased in favor of authority and order. "'Tis now come to a civil war," one wrote, "not with the sword but law, and if the king cannot make his judges speak for him, he will be beaten out of the field."[24]

The judges were always royal appointees, but they were not overtly political appointees until the exclusion crisis, when Charles pressed his judges to endorse measures which to some seemed legally dubious. In December 1679 he issued a proclamation which, in effect, treated all petitions to him for Parliament to be summoned as "seditious" and illegal. A second proclamation, in May 1680, ordered the suppression of all unlicensed newsbooks and pamphlets, even though the Licensing Act had lapsed in May 1679. Judges who would not endorse and enforce such measures were removed and the bench became increasingly Tory.[25] Charles also purged obviously

Whig JPs from the commissions of the peace and chose Tory sheriffs in the counties to empanel Tory juries. He "expressed his sense that there is no dallying now and that there ought to be made a clean sweep of such kind of men whose principles are averse to the government."[26]

The king and the Tories showed little scruple about the way in which they used their new-found control of the central law courts and of law enforcement in the shires. Dissenters were prosecuted under a variety of laws, including those originally aimed against Catholics. Individual Whigs were prosecuted under the libel laws and condemned to pay damages far beyond their means; as they could not pay, they stayed in prison. In treason trials, judges accepted definitions of treason which many thought went well beyond the letter or spirit of existing law. In fact, seventeenth-century judges usually sought a conviction in treason trials, as they felt that the security of the state was at stake,[27] but in the highly partisan atmosphere of the 1680s, the victims of their severity raised cries of "illegality" and "persecution." They were to have an opportunity for vindication and revenge after the Revolution.

It was easy for Charles to give the Tories control of the machinery of justice at Westminster and in the shires because he appointed the judges and JPs. Most corporate towns, however, possessed charters which gave a measure of jurisdictional autonomy, with elected members of the corporation exercising some or all of the powers of county JPs. Often urban magistrates were reluctant to enforce the laws against dissent: Poole prided itself on its "true Protestant juries."[28] Most frustrating of all, from Charles's point of view, was London. Its Whig sheriffs, elected on a broad franchise, empaneled Whig juries which routinely acquitted Whigs and Dissenters. When a packed grand jury threw out a treason charge against the Whig leader, the earl of Shaftesbury, Charles complained bitterly of this "denial of justice."[29] He decided to mount a legal challenge to London's charter, through an action of *quo warranto*, asking "by what right" the City enjoyed its liberties. In the summer of 1683 the charter was declared forfeit on the grounds that the City had exceeded its legal powers. It was now to be governed by commissioners whom the king appointed and could remove at will. By-laws for the City were now enacted, not by an elected common council, but by the king. The autonomy of England's greatest and proudest city had been broken.[30]

In the case of a few provincial towns his law officers had to bring similar actions, but most boroughs surrendered their charters and petitioned for new ones. Often in the past towns had sought a succession of new charters, amending (and usually extending) the corporation's powers, in response to changing circumstances. The difference now (again stemming from the depth of political divisions) was that the surrenders were usually partisan maneuvers, designed to strengthen and perpetuate Tory influence. Sometimes Tories within the corporation organized the surrender, but often it owed much to the pressure of neighboring Tory peers and gentlemen. Most new charters followed a standard pattern, naming the first members of the corporation and empowering the king to remove any members in future, enabling the king to determine who held municipal office, now and in the future. The aim of the new charters was not to destroy municipal self-government—some extended the towns' privileges—but to exclude "ill men" from office.[31]

The divisions opened up by the exclusion crisis were by no means confined to the political elite. Political consciousness went well down the social scale and was nourished by partisan outpourings from the pulpit and in the press. The measures of the "Tory reaction" won much popular support, which was strengthened by the revulsion against the Rye House plot (1683), a widely-publicized design to kill Charles and James. Several leading Whigs were executed for treason; grand juries presented Whigs as disaffected and called for the stricter enforcement of the laws against Dissenters; the homes of "suspect" persons were searched for arms. The Whigs became increasingly demoralized. Many made their peace with the court.

In the early 1680s the power of the Stuart monarchy reached its zenith, but neither by drastically extending the Crown's prerogatives, nor by enlarging its machinery of coercion. The crucial point was that, after the exclusion crisis, a large section of the nation joined the king in crushing their common enemies. Beneath the Tories' exaltation of authority and obedience, however, lay the tacit assumption that it was in the royal interest to uphold the interests of church and Tories. They saw hierarchy and subordination in church, state, and society as indissolubly interdependent. Unless the king backed the church in its efforts to produce conformity, it could not effectively support the monarchy. He must respect personal liberty and property rights, and satisfy Tory expectations of office, if they were to serve the Crown and defend it against its enemies. The reservations underlying Tory loyalism were not spelled out: there seemed no need since James's actions and words demonstrated his commitment to the Tories. However, these reservations were none the less real for being tacit, as became all too apparent after James became king.

≺ III ≻

James's accession to the throne in February 1685 brought changes in the style and direction of government. Where Charles was duplicitous, inconstant, and subtle, James was in many ways straightforward, steady, and naive. He said what he meant and divided the world into polar opposites: good and bad, loyal and disloyal. James craved certainty. Almost the caricature of the army officer he once was, he believed all questions could be answered if one could find where authority lay: it then remained only to obey it. While Charles lived, James was an obedient subject; when he became king, James expected subjects to show the same obedience to him.

James's view of monarchy was authoritarian. "I thank God," he wrote in 1692, "it yet has no dependency on Parliament, nor on nothing but God alone, nor ever can be and be a monarchy."[32] By this he meant that kings should reach decisions free of pressures from parliaments or subjects. The idea that God created the monarchy and that kings answered only to God was commonplace, shared by many Tories. It did not imply that the king could override or change the law without consent; nor did James, at first, suggest that it did. "I know" he declared at his accession " . . . that the laws of England are sufficient to make the king as great a monarch as I can wish; and as I shall never depart from the rights and prerogative of the crown, so I shall never invade any man's property."[33] Honor and conscience obliged him to rule according to law and to respect the principles of natural justice. It remained to be seen whether his views of law and natural justice matched those of his subjects.

James was diligent and conscientious, capable of strenuous measures. His rigid attitude to personal loyalty and habit of dividing people and counsels into "good" and "bad" made him unwilling to tolerate much diversity of opinion among his advisers. Under James, the inner ruling circle became narrow. By late 1686 James had been persuaded that many Tories, especially his brothers-in-law, the earls of Clarendon and Rochester, were primarily concerned with the interests of his heir presumptive (his daughter Mary) and her husband (William of Orange), rather than with his own. Tory office-holders were dismissed, Tory magnates ceased to attend the Privy Council. The Earl of Sunderland and the Catholic zealots insinuated that it would be fatal to allow Anglican moderates to talk him into compromises: the fact that they could propose them, indeed, cast doubts on their loyalty. Thus James came to believe that he would achieve his ends if only he held firm.[34]

James declared at his accession that the laws were sufficient to make him as great a king as he could wish, but that did not mean that he thought the monarchy was as strong or secure as it should be. Events had made him all too aware of its vulnerability: the civil wars, the exclusion crisis, the Rye House plot, Monmouth's rebellion in the summer of 1685. Since, in James's eyes, its enemies were so strong, the Crown needed to be stronger. In the exclusion crisis, he thought, "matters were carried to such a head that the monarchy must either be more absolute or quite abolished." After the Rye House plot he urged Charles to seize the opportunity to "revive his authority and to put himself into a position where he no longer needs to fear his enemies."[35] Monmouth's rising gave him a chance to expand his army and he kept up most of the new units once the rebellion had been quickly defeated. He tried to mold the army into a fully professional force, loyal directly to himself and divorced from civilian society. Meanwhile he ran down the militia, whose mediocre performance against Monmouth he ascribed not to military incompetence (the most likely cause) but to disaffection.[36] Inclined to equate criticism with disaffection, he saw a large loyal army as essential for his security.

The fact that James had firm views on authority and obedience and was unlikely to be deflected by considerations of prudence from doing what he thought was right did not make it inevitable that his reign would end in disaster. Had he continued to uphold the Tory interest, it would not have done so. Instead, he committed himself to policies which ran into almost universal condemnation by his subjects. James, however, seemed to go out of his way to give credibility to their fears of popery and arbitrary government. How far were these fears justified?

To contemporaries popery and absolutism were inseparable. For James, whose conversion had been the most important experience of his life, God had preserved him in order to promote true religion and had placed in his hands the powers he needed to do so, but those powers were primarily means to a higher end. He could win immortal fame and discharge his duty to God by bringing England back into the Catholic fold. James believed that the truth of Catholicism, so obvious to him, would become obvious to all if only Catholics could compete freely with Protestants. They were prevented from doing so by penal laws that prohibited all aspects of Catholic activity and test acts that excluded Catholics from Parliament and public office. James sought to have these laws repealed by a Parliament, so that people would no longer be inhibited from becoming Catholics. If that were done, he believed that England would become predominantly Catholic, even, he was reported as saying, in as little as two years.[37]

Many Protestants suspected James of sinister designs. To them, Catholicism depended on the sort of coercion that Louis XIV was using to dragoon the Huguenots into conversions. James did not intend to use such methods. He disapproved of persecution for conscience's sake, although he was ready to coerce those whose religious activities posed, in his eyes, a threat to the state, and who used antipopery as a cover for sedition. However, the opposition he encountered in his search for repeal led him into extending his powers, which served to confirm preconceptions about the link between popery and absolutism.

At first James continued Charles's policies, retaining his ministers and calling a Parliament, which had a substantial Tory majority in the Commons. In return he was voted Charles's revenue with additional supplies for the fleet and to suppress Monmouth's rebellion, which left him financially independent for the rest of his reign. But MPs showed no readiness to repeal the penal laws and test acts. Instead they complained that Catholics had been commissioned as

army officers, and some hinted that this indicated a royal intention
to follow the French example of using the army to force conversions
to Catholicism. Enraged by Tory distrust, James prorogued Parliament on 20 November 1685. It is unlikely that James ever planned
to use his army to convert his subjects, not least because the officer
corps remained mainly Protestant throughout his reign; but most of
his subjects believed that royal absolutism could be established in
England only through use of a standing army. Moreover the circu-
itous method which James used to enable Catholics to hold commissions showed that he was actively seeking ways by which existing laws could be effectively abrogated even before he could obtain
their repeal by a Parliament. Technically James did not break the
Test Act of 1673, which required officers to make a declaration re-
nouncing Catholic beliefs within three months; James recommis-
sioned them just before the three months expired, which clearly defeated the intention of the act.[38]

Although James shared the Anglican and Tory belief in social
hierarchy and political obedience to sovereigns instituted by God,
he promised to support the church only because its principles "are
for monarchy." He did not regard it as a true church and if its members ceased to behave loyally, that protection would be withdrawn.[39]
Conversely he now argued that Dissenters were not naturally seditious, but had been driven to disobedience by Anglican persecution;
there was therefore no reason why they should not enjoy his favor.
Like the Catholics, they were a persecuted minority. By using the
dispensing and suspending powers to relieve them he could also free
the Catholics from their legal disabilities.

The extended use of a prerogative power to dispense with statutes—traditionally employed selectively to temper the rigor of the
law in the interests of justice—in order to suspend entire groups of
statutes raised complex issues. In his simple, direct way James saw
no difference between dispensing with the law in individual cases
and suspending the operation of statutes.[40] For him it was enough
that the judges had upheld the legality of the dispensing power in
the case of *Godden v. Hales* (1686), although six of the twelve judges
had been changed beforehand.[41] In James's view it was against the
law of nature for a king to be deprived by the test acts of the services
of loyal Catholic subjects, nor did he see why he should be bound by

laws which, unlike those protecting persons and property, were (in his eyes) contrary to the principles of natural justice. So he proceeded to dispense Catholics and Dissenters from the penal laws and test acts, and then suspended the former, pending their repeal by Parliament.

James saw these legal issues as straightforward. But whereas the law purported to offer an objective definition of legality, James's view was subjective, based on his own very personal sense of what was just. Here he resembled Louis XIV, who claimed the right to override laws for the public good and argued that kings, unlike subjects, could not justify their conduct to God merely by showing that it was in accordance with law.[42] Here was a breadth of discretion with which few Englishmen would willingly trust any king, especially one who seemed inclined (by religion and temperament) towards absolutism and showed clear favoritism towards Catholics. In the words of a strong Tory and future Jacobite: "If the king can dispense with the laws at his pleasure, Westminster Hall [where the judges sat] may be shut up and the statute book burned."[43]

If his subjects were alarmed by James's use of the dispensing power, he saw it as a temporary expedient: the need for it would disappear once Parliament repealed the penal laws and test acts. After interrogating individually most of the members of the 1685 Parliament about their attitude to repeal, he realized that most would not do as he wished. He dissolved Parliament and set out to secure a very different Commons. JPs were asked whether, if elected, they would support repeal and would vote for pro-repeal candidates. Many answered ambiguously, but of the non-Catholics who gave a definite answer, twice as many answered in the negative as in the affirmative.[44] Faced with this additional evidence of Tory hostility to repeal, James replaced most of the refusers with a mixture of Catholics, compliant Anglicans, and Dissenters.

The relatively disappointing response of the county JPs did not materially affect James's electoral strategy. County electorates were too large to be bribed or intimidated, so James concentrated on the boroughs, which returned the great majority of MPs. Here the signs were more propitious. Whig electoral success in the exclusion crisis had shown the strength of dissent in many boroughs: hence the new charters of 1681–85, designed to break their influence. James set out to reverse the Tory purges, reinstate the Dissenters, and reap the same electoral rewards as the Whigs; he recruited many of Shaftesbury's electoral agents, who exploited the toleration James offered to the Dissenters.[45]

In pursuing this strategy, James used the powers granted by the charters of 1682–85 to remove members of corporations at will; he also nominated their replacements, although the charters gave him no power to do so.[46] Many boroughs proved uncooperative. Bristol took six months to obey an order to receive sixty-five new freemen. Bedford's corporation refused to say how it would vote, as the franchise was in the whole body of the inhabitants. Corporations were purged as many as four times and some received new charters in 1688 which, unlike those granted earlier, gave the king the right to appoint as well as remove members of the corporations. His agents canvassed vigorously, distributed royal propaganda, and where legitimate methods failed fell back on force and fraud. Electorates were reduced by cutting the size of the corporation or body of freemen; in garrison towns, soldiers were enrolled as electors.

James doubtless saw little difference between his electoral methods and the electoral techniques used by the Whigs in 1679–81 and the Tory exploitation of the charters in 1685. Yet there was a vital difference. Tories and Whigs had wide popular support. James did not; relatively few Whigs and fewer Tories supported his campaign. The Dissenters' response was mixed. Many, especially the richer and more influential Presbyterians, viewed James's conduct with suspicion. Some still hoped for a single national church, but even those who did not were wary of anything offered by a Catholic king. While most Dissenters embraced the liberty which James granted, few were ready to pay the price he asked, the repeal of the test acts, which would allow Catholics into positions of power. Their reluctance was increased when William and Mary assured them that they would still enjoy toleration after James died.

To dismiss James's electoral campaign as doomed to failure would be simplistic. Some contemporaries feared that it might succeed. If it had, the king's "bare authority" would have counted for more than the wishes of any significant section of his people, and Parliament would have ceased to be in any sense representative.[47] However, the situation was transformed in June 1688 by the birth of

James's son. Hitherto he had been working against time, knowing his immediate successors would probably undo much of what he had tried to do for the Catholics. Now he could proceed more slowly, as he had a Catholic heir to continue his policies. Indeed his son's birth made him even more confident that God was with him.

By then James had alienated all but the most blindly loyal or self-seeking Tories by his assault on their hard-won monopoly of religious life. The clergy's disillusionment began when James ordered the bishops to suppress anti-Catholic preaching. When this had little effect, he set up an ecclesiastical commission to discipline the clergy. It suspended Henry Compton, the most politically minded of the bishops, from his see of London for refusing to punish one of his clergy for an anti-Catholic sermon and deprived the fellows of Magdalen College, Oxford, for refusing to elect James's unqualified nominee as president: most of their replacements were Catholics. The episode aroused great controversy, not only because of the religious implications, but also because James was seen as attacking property rights without due process of law: a college fellowship was widely seen as the equivalent of a freehold in land.[48]

Still more contentious was a declaration of indulgence issued in April 1687, which deprived the Church of its established status. It was now to be just one denomination among many. To the many who believed that without a single church there could be no national unity, no guarantee of social order, no maintenance of Christian orthodoxy, this was a bitter blow. Moreover, despite James's professions of impartiality and claims that Catholicism would prosper in fair competition, he tried to suppress anti-Catholic sermons, actively promoted Catholic propaganda, and used the ecclesiastical commission to harass the Anglican clergy. In appointments to office, he favored Catholics (and to a lesser extent Dissenters) at the expense of Anglicans. Clerical suspicions of James's intentions doubtless owed much to anti-Catholic prejudice; but his actions did much to make those suspicions credible.

James's order, on 4 May 1688, to read a second declaration of indulgence in their churches completed clerical disillusion. They were being asked to publicize, and by implication to endorse, an act of questionable legality which would destroy the church as an established church. The great majority failed to read it. The archbishop of Canterbury and six of his colleagues petitioned the king that the clergy should not be required to read the declaration, on the grounds that it was "founded upon such a dispensing power as hath often been declared illegal in Parliament."[49] James reacted furiously, especially when the petition was printed and circulated, prosecuting the bishops for seditious libel. The trial, from his point of view, was a disaster. The judges failed to prevent discussion of the dispensing power, although the plea that an alleged libel was true was no defense in law. Worse, one of the judges went out of his way to condemn it: "If this be once allowed of, there will need no Parliament; all the legislature will be in the king." Amid massive popular rejoicing, the jury acquitted the bishops.[50]

The seven bishops' trial epitomized James's regime. He alienated the most loyal of his subjects: five of the seven later refused to swear allegiance to William and Mary. The trial, which was widely reported, discredited the dispensing power. By taking this stand on the pronouncements of Parliament and making gestures of goodwill towards dissent, the bishops successfully countered James's bid for dissenting support. But if his regime suffered a rebuff, it was not on the verge of collapse. James still had a large, apparently loyal army. As in 1640, any serious challenge to the regime would have to come from outside.

≺ IV ≻

William's decision to invade rested on two unfounded assumptions: that James wished to cut Mary out of the succession and that he had a close alliance with Louis. News of the queen's pregnancy and the Catholics' confidence that she would produce a son aroused suspicions of an intended fraud which the child's birth merely seemed to confirm. Like many Englishmen, William chose to treat the baby as "suppositious." Diplomatic uncertainties and bad weather delayed William's departure, but at last he set sail, landing at Torbay on 5 November.

In the last months of 1688 James's self-confidence collapsed. Everything went wrong. Instead of helping him (as James expected) Louis became embroiled in an extremely bloody war on the Rhine.

When William landed, English notables joined him, including James's protégé John Churchill (the future duke of Marlborough) and Princess Anne. Northern magnates appeared in arms; London erupted in anti-Catholic riots. Perplexed, James turned to the Tories, who proved reluctant to resume their offices and repel the invaders: as one remarked "some would think one kick of the breech enough for a gentleman."[51] Instead they urged James to press ahead with elections for a "free Parliament," but James argued that elections could not be free while a foreign army was in the country. The Tories—not least the bishops—were insistent, for if a Tory Parliament were elected, it could then force James to reverse all that he had done since 1685, leaving in place a solidly Tory regime.

William's justificatory declaration was designed to appeal to both Tories and Whigs. It ignored Whig complaints about the Tory reaction of 1681–85 and focused on the abuses of James's reign, which had been resented by both parties; it also stated that William's sole aim was to secure a free Parliament, exactly what the Tories wanted. Contemporaries, especially Whigs, liked to depict 1688 as a revolution in which most of the nation (except for some Tories) rejected "popery and arbitrary government." Conversely, some eighteenth-century Whigs were concerned to stress the orderliness of the Revolution, the lack of violence, because if it was accepted that there *had* been wide popular involvement in the Revolution, this might seem to legitimate subsequent popular challenges to the established order. In fact both Whigs and Tories sought, through press and pulpit, to mobilize wide popular support in 1688. Already pamphlets produced in both England and Holland had warned the Dissenters against accepting James's indulgence.[52] Moreover, much disinformation was disseminated, through the press and by word of mouth: that James had a secret alliance with Louis, that he was bringing over thousands of French or Irish soldiers to butcher his Protestant subjects. Most pamphlets created alarm rather than direct popular action: an exception was the spurious *Third Declaration of the Prince of Orange*, which stated that the papists intended to put London to fire and sword and ordered that all Catholics should be disarmed; any found in arms, or in office, were to be killed. Following this declaration, the lord mayor ordered the disarming of all Catholics in London: a group of citizens had warned that if he did not they would do it themselves.[53] Popular action against Catholics, however, had begun even before William landed, with riots in London against Catholic chapels.

Until early December there was little sign of autonomous popular action outside London. When northern peers took up arms (ostensibly to forestall the papists) they did not issue a general call to arms. Elsewhere magnates and gentlemen called out the militia and sought to calm fears of papist attacks and the Irish.[54] For a few days just before and after James's flight, however, it seemed that the traditional rulers might lose control. When James fled he made no provision for the continuance of ordered government—indeed he went out of his way to leave things in confusion, throwing the great seal into the Thames. There were riots in London: Catholic chapels and houses were plundered and gutted. Meanwhile the few Irish units in James's army were dismissed and set off for home. This gave rise to wild rumors that the Irish were coming to fire and plunder, to kill man, woman and child; these rumors spread as far afield as Berwick and Cornwall. Fear of the Irish allowed the authorities in London a breathing space in which to reestablish order, but popular action against Catholics continued elsewhere: chapels were smashed, homes plundered, priests beaten. As in most early modern riots, the targets were highly specific and seen as legitimate: Catholic chapels and Catholic office-holding were illegal. Only in a few places, notably Bury St. Edmunds, did plunder and violence threaten to become indiscriminate: even there, order was soon restored.[55]

To see the Revolution as the work of a few aristocrats would thus be misleading. A wide cross-section of people was kept informed of events and of the issues at stake (not always accurately), by rumor and the press. Many were involved in some form of action, even if this meant only staying up all night in case the Irish came. On the other hand, to stress popular interest and participation in the Revolution is not to imply that there was a distinct "popular" position in 1688, but rather that similar concerns were shared by a broad social spectrum. The focusing of fear and hostility on small "alien" minorities—Catholics and the Irish—helped to maintain a broad measure of unity. Only sporadically did elite control and law and order threaten to break down: often aristocrats were able by their mere presence to reassure the worried populace and restore calm.[56]

However, the extent and severity of the disorders alarmed members of the elite: "everyone is in great frights and wish for the Prince of Orange's coming, to quiet things."[57] Awareness of the fragility of elite control put pressure on peers and gentlemen of all shades of political opinion to reach a quick settlement (even if this meant compromising their principles) in order to preserve the existing social and political order. As one peer recalled, "the rabble" could have become the masters "if the beasts had known their own strength."[58] Although it is far from clear that "the rabble" *wanted* to be "the masters," the important point was the fear which the disorders inspired among the elite. Whatever their differences, Whig and Tory leaders could agree on the need to concentrate on the issue of the subjects' relations with the Crown, rather than with the distribution of power among the different orders of subjects. As a result, those who saw in 1688–89 an opportunity to transform the relationship between Parliament and people were given little chance to influence the settlement that ensued; claims in the convention that the Commons did not in fact represent "the people" were brushed aside.[59] People of all social ranks helped to drive out James II; but the Revolution settlement was shaped by the traditional ruling elite in Parliament, not by popular pressures from outside.

<< V >>

The Revolution of 1688–89 has often been seen as bipartisan. In the sense that both Whigs and Tories took part it was; but as events unfolded, the differences between them became more visible. Although not all Tories were slaves to principle, many suffered real problems of conscience. Having committed themselves so unequivocally to non-resistance and the hereditary succession, they found themselves aiding and abetting acts of resistance which led to the expulsion of the rightful king. To make matters worse, William seemed less than friendly towards the church. Tories tried to keep alive James's theoretical claim to the Crown in order to vindicate their principles, but they failed, because the need for a quick settlement meant that William was in a position to force his acceptance as king. But he could not do so openly: his declaration committed him to proceeding through a free Parliament; and a naked usurpation would destroy much of the support, or acquiescence, which had facilitated his progress. Moreover his allies in the European war which had already started, many of them Catholics, would be alienated, especially after he had assured them that he did not aim to depose James. His many opponents in the Dutch Republic had long accused him of having monarchical ambitions, so for all these reasons, William was careful at each stage to solicit invitations from various groups of Englishmen. It was "by invitation" that he successively invaded, came to London, took over the civil and military government, and called a convention, fulfilling his promise of a free Parliament. When the convention met, William exerted covert but effective pressure to elicit an invitation to become king. The Tories obstructed him but succumbed at last to *force majeure.*

Whig attempts to claim a monopoly of credit for the Revolution and of power under the new regime failed. While the elections to the convention, which met on 22 January 1689, produced a Whig majority in the Commons, the Tories had a majority in the Lords. This meant that overtly partisan measures were unlikely to get through both Houses, so the Whigs needed to cast their proposals in terms which the Tory peers might accept. William had no wish to be wholly identified with one party. Experience of the Whig exiles (mostly radicals) led him to see Whigs as crypto-republicans, whereas the Tories (despite their attachment to James's title) were in his eyes good friends to monarchy. However, many Tories held "country" principles that led them to join with Whigs fearful that William might seek to become absolute. Besides those actuated by ambition, many Tories took office in order to defend the church and to avoid being at the mercy of the Whigs.

The Revolution settlement represented a lowest common denominator. Two main issues had to be settled: who was to occupy the throne and upon what terms? A few Whigs asserted that James had been driven out by force and that "the people" could "new form themselves again, under a government yet to be chosen."[60] Most argued that he had given up his crown, either through misgovernment, or by deserting his people; he had deposed himself.[61] To place all the onus on James not only made it easier for Tories to accept a change of ruler but also excluded "the people" from the process. If James had left the throne vacant, the convention could claim that it was merely making good the vacancy, resolving a problem that was most unlikely to recur. Thus the element of innovation was minimized and the Whigs could stress their wish to keep things "as near the ancient government as can be."[62]

Against Whig proposals that the Crown should be offered to William and Mary, Tory peers proposed, first, that William and Mary should be proclaimed regents for James; then, that the Crown had passed to Mary as next heir. They did not actually envisage James's return. Both Houses passed a resolution that "it hath been found by experience to be inconsistent with the safety and welfare of this Protestant kingdom to be governed by a Popish prince," which showed clearly that neither Whigs nor Tories wished to be ruled by James or his infant son. Subsequent claims by Tory peers that to declare the throne "vacant" would make the Crown elective may have been designed to prevent William's being made king in his own right and to safeguard the hereditary claim of Mary and Anne. The Tories thus sought to salvage from the wreckage some part of the principles to which they had committed themselves so forthrightly in the early 1680s.[63] They were partly successful. Mary was declared queen regnant, although without the executive power, which was vested wholly in William. Moreover, the transmission of the succession was to follow strictly hereditary lines—first Mary's children, then Anne's, then any William might have by a second marriage. The oath of allegiance was amended so that Tories would not have to recognize William and Mary as "rightful and lawful" monarchs.

The settlement of the Crown in 1689 was pragmatic and in many ways messy: by leaving the question of William and Mary's *right* to the throne unclear, it was possible to view the change of ruler in different ways. Some Whigs claimed that it vindicated Parliament's right to determine the succession and that henceforth monarchs derived their right to rule from Parliament. This claim was given a greater plausibility by the clauses on the succession in the Act of Settlement of 1701. By then as it was clear that Anne would leave no children to succeed, the act laid down that after her the Crown should pass to the electress of Hanover, the nearest Protestant claimant, and her descendants.[64] In Whig eyes this showed that it was now Parliament, not divine hereditary right, which determined who should rule. Having found Catholic rule totally unacceptable, the Tories adapted their commitment to the hereditary principle by restricting it to Protestants and from 1701 to Anglicans. Besides these partisan positions—the denial of legitimism and the claim that it survived but in exclusively Protestant form—most people accepted the change of ruler as a necessary remedial action forced upon the convention by James's irresponsibility. Exceptional circumstances had led to some adjustments in the succession; experience had shown the need to exclude Catholics.

In retrospect many saw the Revolution as vindicating the principle that kings existed for the good of their people. Parliament's disposing of the Crown might seem to strip it of its aura of majesty, but reverence for monarchy had never depended solely, or even primarily, on reason and logic. That it should have continued after 1689 would seem odd only if one assumes that the seventeenth century saw a conscious struggle to subject the monarch to Parliament. In fact, the monarchy and its powers were accepted as both necessary and useful, drawing their validity from God and prescription. The king was, for these very reasons, obliged to use his powers for his subjects' good: if he did not (as James I had said) he was a tyrant.[65] Subjects suspected the Stuarts of misusing their powers to the detriment of liberty, property, and religion, and in self-defense were driven to limit the king's ability to harm them, either by defining particular powers more narrowly, or by excluding from the throne those—Catholics—who they believed would inevitably abuse their power. If this involved innovation (which often they strenuously denied) the underlying motive was defensive. The fact that some kings abused their powers did not discredit the institution of monarchy.

Of all the Stuarts, James II misused his authority the most grossly; so besides settling the succession the convention wished to ensure that such abuses could not happen again. A Commons committee with a Whig majority drew up a list of "Heads of Grievances," which combined specifically Whig grievances from 1681–85 with others from James's reign that affected both parties. On 4 February the Commons divided the heads into two groups: those which would require fresh legislation and those which were said to restate existing law. The reasons were pragmatic. New legislation would take time and a speedy settlement was essential. Moreover, both

William and the Tory majority in the Lords would probably oppose any attempt to impose drastic new restrictions on the Crown. The Commons therefore concentrated on items which would not require legislation and incorporated them into the Declaration of Rights, which, after some amendment by the Lords, was read to William and Mary just before they were offered the Crown.[66]

In deciding whether the Declaration was simply a restatement of existing law or broke new ground, one needs to bear in mind the complexity of English law, the subjective element in contemporary perceptions of "legality," and the distinction between the letter and the spirit of the law. Can something which is technically justifiable, but seems at variance with basic principles of justice, be seen as "legal"? Conversely, should a provision which defines a royal power more narrowly in order to bring it into line with the broadly accepted principles of the constitution be described as "innovatory"? This inherent ambivalence made it possible for contemporaries, and historians, to interpret the Declaration in different ways. It was clearly part of a process whereby, during the seventeenth century, Parliament sought, intermittently, to define certain powers of the Crown more narrowly and so to restrict them. The motivation behind these restrictions varied. Radical Whigs claimed as a matter of principle that the king's prerogatives should be substantially reduced, to make him more responsive to the wishes of Parliament and the people. Others saw these restrictions as being forced on Parliament by the Stuarts' misdeeds and sought to keep them to a minimum. They were concerned only to repair what was obviously amiss. However many probably did not think through the implications of what they were doing but reacted to problems as they arose: pragmatism was a central feature of the Revolution. Interpretation of the motives of the men of 1689, and whether one emphasizes the extent of these restrictions or of the Crown's surviving prerogatives, are ultimately matters of individual historical judgment.

The Declaration's constitutional provisions break down into three main groups. One dealt with the misuse of the law courts, mainly in 1681–85. The condemnation of excessive bail and fines, as a means of keeping people in jail without legal redress, accorded with traditional legal thinking. So did the prohibition of "cruel and unusual punishments," such as the sentence imposed on Titus

Oates for perjury: because perjury did not carry the death penalty, he was sentenced to a series of floggings which was intended to kill him but did not. Another article required that jurors should be duly empanelled and that those serving in treason trials should be free-holders. Existing law was not clear on the last point, but it was in line with the basic principle that a defendant should be tried by an impartial jury of his peers and by due process of law. The Declaration also condemned the odious practice whereby the king granted away the fines and forfeitures, to which accused people might be condemned, before they came to trial; this practice had been condemned by medieval statutes and denounced as illegal by distinguished lawyers. This first group of provisions, then, sought to reassert the integrity of the legal system, which had so often been perverted for political ends in the 1680s. Where there was clarification of disputed points, this was in line with the spirit of existing law.[67]

Three articles related to Parliament. The statement that elections ought to be free referred to James's attempt to pack Parliament; Whigs might also see it as applying to the Tory triumph in 1685. Another article stated that Parliament ought to meet "frequently," but no specific frequency was prescribed. The assertion that "freedom of speech and debates or proceedings in Parliament ought not to be impeached or questioned in any court or place out of Parliament" was less vague. It related to the prosecution of a former Speaker for licensing a "seditious" tract. The Commons had long claimed freedom of speech; the clause constituted an attempt to consolidate, and perhaps extend, an established right which had recently come under attack—limited innovation on broadly traditional lines.[68]

Most articles reaffirmed the letter, or at least conformed to the spirit, of existing law. The prohibition on levying money, except as granted by Parliament, restated a central feature of the constitution. It referred to James's levying the excise in the first weeks of his reign, before Parliament met; Parliament had retrospectively legalized his action. The claim that the ecclesiastical commission had been illegal was questionable. An act had abolished the Court of High Commission in 1641, but the ecclesiastical commission's powers were more limited and it was doubtful whether it was a court.[69]

On the issue of the dispensing and suspending powers it had long been accepted that the king could dispense with statutes in particular cases, in the interests of justice. The judges had ruled in *Godden v. Hales* that the king could dispense with statutes as he judged necessary. Some of them had reservations about this ruling and others became alarmed when James interpreted it so broadly as to render some acts of Parliament inoperable and to suspend others altogether. This might be justified as a logical extension of existing law, but it was totally at variance with its spirit and with the fundamental principle that laws could be made and unmade only by acts of Parliament. The judges told James he could not dispense with the 1678 Test Act in order to allow Catholic peers to sit in the Lords.[70] In the convention Tories and Whigs agreed that no king could be trusted with a suspending power. On the dispensing power there was less agreement. The Lords were prepared to condemn it only "as it hath been assumed and exercised of late." Later it was laid down that it could be used only where explicitly allowed by statute.[71]

The convention also stated that "the raising or keeping a standing army within this kingdom in time of peace, unless it be with the consent of Parliament, is against law." The king's right to command all forces by sea and land had been firmly restated by the 1661 Militia Act, and the Cavalier Parliament had not attempted to prevent Charles from maintaining a few thousand soldiers scattered in garrisons which posed little threat to liberty. A large force drawn together in the environs of London was a very different matter. It posed the greatest possible threat to the liberty of the subject and the integrity of Parliament. By this innovation the convention sought to protect England against such a threat in the future.[72]

When the Declaration was turned into a statute, the Bill of Rights, later in 1689, provisions were added requiring future rulers to take an oath to maintain the Protestant religion and forbidding any member of the royal family to marry a Catholic. Of those of the heads which were not included in the Declaration, the Toleration Act of 1689 went some considerable way to provide for "the liberty of Protestants in the exercise of their religion." The demand "that the too long continuance of the same Parliament be prevented" was met by the 1694 Triennial Act. This provided that there should be a general election at least once every three years, thus limiting the king's power to call and dismiss Parliaments at will. The 1696 Trial for Treasons Act provided greater safeguards for defendants. The Act

of Settlement, besides settling the succession, gave judges security
of tenure: no longer could the king dismiss them for giving unacceptable rulings. It also declared that a person impeached by Parliament could not escape trial by pleading a royal pardon and limited
the prerogative in other ways, not envisaged in 1689, which reflected experience of William's reign. No future foreign king could
engage in war for the defense of his foreign territories without Parliament's consent; foreigners were to be ineligible to hold offices, sit
in Parliament, or receive grants from the Crown.[73]

Even after these changes the king, in theory, retained his fundamental prerogatives. He still formulated policy, at home and abroad,
and made civil, ecclesiastical, and military appointments. And yet,
from 1689, his ability to use these powers became more and more
severely circumscribed. William III and his successors found it increasingly difficult to use their acknowledged powers to the full because of the financial settlement. In terms of revenue, William's position was far weaker than that of his predecessors. He inherited
some revenues from James, but others had to be granted afresh by
Parliament. The Commons could curb the king, as MPs clearly perceived, by failing to vote him enough money.[74] He would then have
to keep coming to Parliament for more money and the Commons
could if it chose insist that he redress grievances before they granted
it. Moreover, his financial dependence on Parliament was hugely increased by the vast cost of the war which was the direct consequence of William's accession: indeed, the wars of 1689–97 and
1702–13 were both, in a sense, wars of the English succession. By
the end of William's reign, Parliament was meeting each year and
voting detailed, itemized estimates for the army and navy, which
gave it a chance to scrutinize and to influence government expenditure and policy in a way that had never been possible before.[75]

The Revolution and the wars gave Parliament a new permanence
and the financial power to impose its will on the king if it chose.
During the critical 1690s the Commons repeatedly extorted concessions by "tacking" conditions to money bills; the king had to choose
between agreeing to the conditions and losing his money. Often William was forced to make concessions which he thought dangerous
or unjust: he had to disband most of the army at the end of the war
and to rescind grants of Irish land to Dutch officers. He did not

tamely surrender—indeed he used his veto more than any of his Stuart predecessors—but financial need set limits to his resistance. William and his successors learned to adapt to a post-Revolution order. They realized that they had to tailor their policies to fit the expectations and prejudices of Parliament. Their ministers, who had to pilot through money bills and defend royal policies in Parliament, were still more conscious of this need. Again and again, when pressing the king to take their advice, they stressed that it was imperative to avoid trouble in Parliament; but these ministers had some assets in electoral and parliamentary management which their forebears had lacked. The royal revenue, the armed forces, and the administration all grew during the wars, creating additional patronage which could be used to buy support in Parliament. This led their critics to claim that they (and especially Walpole) had destroyed the integrity of both Parliament and the electorate through bribery. There was some truth in this, but if early Georgian parliaments offered less open opposition to the Crown than those of Charles II or William III, this owed much to ministers' skill in avoiding measures which would antagonize the Commons majority.

To a historian of the seventeenth century, parliaments under George I and George II seem strangely calm and harmonious. Money bills sailed smoothly through; the Commons no longer (as in the 1660s and 1690s) demanded to scrutinize the Crown's accounts.[76] But the relative absence of the conflict which had been so common in seventeenth-century parliaments did not mean that there was an absence of constraint. Rather, awareness of Parliament's financial power led kings and ministers to impose constraints upon themselves. Wise kings had always taken their subjects' wishes into account: now the need for Parliament's support, or at least acquiescence, made this essential. This was evident in what emerged as the most important prerogative in the eighteenth century, the making of foreign policy. Kings needed Parliament to pay for their foreign policy so they had to take its wishes into account. The Act of Settlement imposed the first statutory restriction on royal control of foreign policy by stating that a foreign king could engage in a war to defend his homeland only with Parliament's consent; but the constraints created by the need to work with Parliament restricted the king far more.[77]

The Hanoverians, because of the need to work with Parliament, operated in practice within tighter constraints than the Stuarts. Nor were these constraints confined to Parliament. When the Whigs gained power in 1714 they used a mixture of private Whig money and government patronage to gain control of enough borough seats to give them a constant majority in the Commons, but this did not mean that they could ignore opinion "without doors." Even in constituencies where the electorate was small and venal its support could not necessarily be taken for granted. In a society with a vigorous political press, it was altogether impossible to exclude "public opinion" from politics: hence the care taken by ministers to get across their point of view in government newspapers. On several occasions politicians seriously misread the public mood and were forced to change their stance by the sheer force of public opinion: in the 1733 excise crisis, with the clamor for war with Spain in 1739–40, and in 1753–54, when Parliament repealed the Jew Act (which had earlier passed with little controversy) because of the public outcry it provoked.[78] Despite the anomalies of the electoral system, despite the prevalence of "corruption," despite the fact that the Commons was an imperfect reflection of the "national will," it was not a total sham and the possibility of revitalizing its representative role had not been destroyed.[79]

The Revolution of 1688–89 was in many ways muddled. It was shrouded in ideological confusion, partly because men were pushed by circumstances into actions which ran counter to their principles, partly because the need to avoid outraging William and the Tory peers and the fervent desire to prevent radical change led to a fudging of issues and an avoidance of divisive arguments. But this does not mean that the Revolution was not of great importance for the history of liberty, in England and elsewhere. Later generations saw it as the cornerstone of their liberties—an MP referred to the Bill of Rights as "our original contract" as early as 1690[80]—and used it to validate their claims for greater liberty. Their view of the Revolution might be historically dubious, but that did not make it any less influential: myth can be more powerful than reality, not least because it is usually less complicated.

Moreover, when all allowances are made, James II had posed a real threat to the English constitution. If James had no grand strategy for subverting English liberty or for destroying Protestantism by force, he had great assets when it came to trying to put those policies into effect—wide-ranging prerogatives,[81] a largely cooperative judiciary, an adequate revenue, and an enlarged standing army. Had he been able to make good his conception of the dispensing power, he would have been able to override laws at will. Had he succeeded in his efforts to pack the Commons, Parliament might have become a rubber stamp, giving the illusion of consent to legislation and taxation without the reality—a more insidious threat to government by consent than his father's attempt to rule without Parliament altogether. Moreover, the birth of his son created the prospect not only of a Catholic successor but of an ongoing Catholic dynasty. In time, new generations would grow up who had known no government but that of a Catholic king. Those who, in retrospect, saw 1688 as a delivery from popery were essentially correct. Those who saw it as a reassertion of English liberties against the threat of absolutism had at least a plausible case. Those who depicted it as a triumph of Whig libertarianism against Tory authoritarianism did partisan violence to the truth.

Liberty, Law, and Property:
The Constitution in Retrospect from 1689

HOWARD NENNER

IN THE HISTORY OF modern freedom something of critical importance happened in the seventeenth century to the idea of liberty. An older notion of liberties as grants from the king, and in certain circumstances revocable by him, was transmuted into rights of the people that were immune from the monarch's recall. Vulnerable feudal franchises, even when strengthened by continuation over time, had never before been securely beyond the king's reach. They only became unassailable by the nation's denying that they were, or ever had been, in the disposal of the Crown. By 1688–89 individuals' liberty had become their property, inherited from their English ancestors and safeguarded by their English law. No matter that the older view of liberties had a greater claim to historical and legal accuracy, that royalists had a greater purchase on reality in claiming that "the people owe all their liberties, franchises, charters and immunities . . . to the bounty of former kings."[1] The achievement of the Revolution of 1688–89 would be largely the victory of what had become the new orthodoxy. Nor was this merely polemics in the service of politics. By 1689 a disposition of mind had become fixed in which the security of the subjects' liberty, law, and property was to be a condition of the monarch's right to rule, the yardstick of the government's right to exist. The wish, which had been father to the thought, had come to be an article of constitutional faith.

◄ I ►

The emergent belief that liberty meant something more—or even something other—than the aggregate of concessions from a long line of kings proceeded from a myth about the origins of political society. And it was not exclusively a Whig myth. The Tory earl of Danby, commenting in 1689 on all that had recently transpired, wrote that the people had claimed their

liberty and property, according to their ancient laws and customs, not as a gift, but as a right inherent in themselves, and never transferred, aliened, or conveyed to any king, but declared, recognized and confirmed to them by many.[2]

What is striking about this assertion of the subjects' liberties is that it signalled more than just a shift from what Chief Justice Matthew Hale (the most respected constitutional lawyer of the Restoration period) had identified as contractual concessions from the king in return for financial support.[3] It was also a major escalation in constitutional thought from the argument that concessions from earlier monarchs had matured through centuries of use into irrevocable rights. Once it could be established that these rights were never dependent upon kings because they had always belonged to the people, a critical conceptual divide would have been crossed. There would no longer be a need to worry about the king's challenge to liberty in *quo warranto* proceedings or his threat to established religion through the use of the *non obstante*. What the king had never possessed, and therefore never granted, could not be in his power to revoke.

Liberty then, for the most part, came to mean those rights which had been granted by God to his people and which had never been surrendered by them to their kings. The subjects' heritage existed independent of the favor of kings. It was in keeping with the Protestant argument that Christ, who had disowned an earthly kingdom, had left that kingdom to all Christians, not—as the Catholics would maintain—to Peter and his successors.[4] What the people did with their kingdom, what they chose to give away and what they chose to keep, was for them to decide. An anonymous pamphleteer, writing at the time of the settlement of 1689, put the matter in what had become increasingly familiar language: "That power which the people reserveth from the soveraign is called liberty."[5] He then went on to remark that at the institution of government it had not even been necessary to specify "our goods and heritages" as being expressly reserved. Control over one's own property was deemed to be so fundamental a liberty that each individual's retention of that control, subject only to "judicial process," was tacitly understood.

The people did have certain liberties which had been expressly granted by kings; but the seventeenth-century inclination was increasingly to see such grants as declaring and confirming antecedent liberties, not creating new ones. The interpretation of Magna Carta was a conspicuous example of this bias. Sir Robert Atkyns, who had been dismissed as a judge in 1680, but was about to be re-appointed, writing in 1689 against the continued use of the royal dispensing power, echoed earlier commentators when he insisted that although "this statute of Magna Charta run in the stile of a grant from the king," the concessions it contained "were the common laws and rights of the people before."⁶ Simply stated and widely believed was the idea that those rights that were basic and inviolate were those for which the people were obliged to no one but God.⁷

To assert the existence of an inviolable liberty in the people was not in the end sufficient to preserve that liberty. Polemicists, politicians, and lawyers needed to go further. They implied but did not yet elaborate a theory of inalienable rights. That would come in the eighteenth century, principally as part of the American experience. Yet what they did suggest was almost as extreme, and certainly adequate to their own revolutionary purpose: we are, by right of inheritance, the possessors of a property in our liberty which, though it could have been alienated to kings, never was. Consequently, those kings and their successors are barred absolutely from taking it away. The effect, however, was the same and for that reason met with the same challenge. As Robert Sheringham contended, in a royalist apology anticipating the Restoration, the inescapable outcome of the idea of the people's inalienable rights and the companion notion of rights that had never been surrendered was popular sovereignty, the investing of the people with "supream jurisdiction over all magistrates."⁸

Sheringham captured more than a royalist disposition of mind in 1659–60. His denunciation of the idea of popular sovereignty caught the national mood. But a generation later all had changed. A nation still not ready for popular rule was nonetheless prepared for a turn in that direction. It was prepared to abandon the idea of sovereign rights being "so inseparably annexed to . . . [the king's] royal person by the laws of the land, that they cannot be separated from him."⁹ The people's rights might not be inalienable, but neither were the king's. Even more important, by the time of the Revolution royal rights were not only to be thought of as expressly alienable, they were also to be regarded as constructively voidable by the king's "illegal" acts. The specific message was that any monarch who infringed the rights that the people had reserved unto themselves was at significant risk of forfeiting his own right to rule. Although no king would consciously intend to forfeit the throne, the "law" could still intervene and construct such an intention from his wanton political behavior. This was to be the accepted and comforting fiction of 1689. The people's "concessions," it would be asserted, "cannot extend farther than for their own preservation, and when that ceases, the grant determines."[10]

These were some of the legal patterns of thought that were to shape political vocabulary—and political action as well—through the autumn and winter of 1688–89, and because they proved sufficient to the task of ridding the nation of James II it was unnecessary to go any further toward establishing a right of revolution. The king in 1688–89 would not need to be deposed by his subjects. That in effect had been done before in the case of Charles I, but in the decade that followed 1649 a government conceived in regicide and nurtured on republicanism and military rule proved to be politically unworkable. It was not a path to be traveled again, nor did it have to be. All that would be called for was a constitutional interpretation that allowed James II to be dethroned by his own actions and the consequent operation of law. The unintended result of the king's "tyranny" was to be the loss of the king's throne.

In the Convention debates on the vacancy of the throne, a knowledgeable lay constitutionalist, Sir Thomas Lee, the very model of a country MP, put a significant rhetorical question. He wished to know "whether upon the original contract there were not a power preserved in the nation to provide for its self in such exigencies?" The answer Lee provided was simple and portentous: the estates of the realm had reserved to themselves the power "to make provision in all times, and upon all occasions, for extraordinary cases and necessities."[11] The implications of that rendering of the constitution went well beyond the settlement of the succession. In addition to disposing of the king's crown the estates were effectively challenging the king's legislative prerogative. By the end of 1689 that challenge had been made good. Both the suspending and the dispensing powers were gone and little more was heard of the king's holding, in the reservoir of sovereign power, the prerogative right to respond to legislative necessity. This was not to suggest that the need for an extraordinary legislative power had disappeared, only that the power had now been appropriated and transferred to king-in-Parliament. Henceforth king-in-Parliament, not the king alone, would be the ultimate arbiter of necessity and the effective custodian of the law.

≺ II ≻

The rhetorical conjunction of liberty, law, and property was not unique to the seventeenth-century era of Restoration and Revolution. Neither was it reserved to anti-Stuart sensibilities alone. Charles I, in his speech from the scaffold in 1649, insisted that the conduct of government was the province of the king, but he readily conceded that the people's "liberty and freedom consist in having of government those laws by which their life and their goods may be most their own."[12] This liberty he claimed to have respected. Similarly, Charles II and James II, in turn, repeatedly gave assurances that they would never invade their subjects' property.[13] And as long as those assurances seemed credible the balance of liberty and prerogative would likely be maintained. "While kings are a protection to liberty, property and religion," one writer observed, "the world is naturally prone to flatter them."[14] He might have added that their subjects would continue to obey them.

   James II's fall can usefully be seen in these terms. Having despoiled his subjects' legally established religion, and having wantonly violated their sense of liberty and property, James had forfeited his right to their continued allegiance. It was asserted that under James "liberty and property, the birth-right of every English man, were rendered meer titulary things."[15] Certainly that analysis accorded with the June 1688 invitation to William of Orange, the prince's own declaration of reasons for his descent into England, and the Guildhall declaration of the Lords in December. The assembled lords, calling on William to assume temporary direction of the government, were looking ahead specifically to the convening of a free

Parliament "wherein our laws, our liberties and properties may be secured."[16] And once the work of the Convention was done, William could be offered joint possession of the Crown as a mark of the nation's gratitude.[17] He could be rewarded for having restored the English to what Daniel Defoe proclaimed was most dear to them, the "enjoyment of our liberties and properties, secured to us by the laws of the land."[18]

It is testimony to the importance of property that in Restoration debates on religious toleration, a property argument was invariably invoked. Catholics, who were suspect by every legal and political standard, could be vilified not only for their faith, but for their supposed disregard of this most prized element of the English inheritance. By 1689 it could simply be assumed that an "affection for popery" led to "the loss of English liberty and property."[19] Catholics, however, were not the only threat to an Anglican hegemony. So too were dissenting Protestants who would not be accorded relief from the penal laws. Royal attempts at a prerogative Declaration of Indulgence had failed and the 1673 Test Act had placed limitations on their holding office under the Crown. And here again the debate turned on the question of property. Those who supported the Tests were able to satisfy themselves, if not their opponents, that the legislation did "not disturb . . . [the king's subjects] in their estates and possessions"; nor did it "deprive them of the liberty of their persons."[20] The Dissenters' properties and persons were accordingly seen not to be at risk. Yet what *was* believed to be at risk was the property of Parliament in the laws it had passed. While all laws are properly said to be the king's, Robert Atkyns observed, the Lords and Commons having had a hand in making those laws, receive "a propriety and interest in them once they are made."[21] This was the view that would prevail in 1689 when the suspending power was condemned and the dispensing power allowed to die. Laws, when made, were to become the joint property of those who made them, and were henceforth not to be altered or repealed except by consent of all the property holders involved.

The defenders of Anglican orthodoxy against popery and Protestant dissent were not alone in appropriating the property argument. If Anglicans were to point to their established religion as being a property protected by law, the Dissenters' reply was scarcely less persuasive. As Charles II was obliged, and had expressly vowed, to be mindful of everyone's property, it was alleged that this undertaking could only be kept by an indulgence to all Dissenters. The duke of Buckingham, the self-proclaimed champion of toleration, paid fulsome homage in 1675 to the importance of that idea, equating property in the instant case with liberty of conscience. "My Lords," he said,

there is a thing called property (whatever some men may think) that the people of England are fondest of. It is that they will never part with, and it is that his Majesty has promised to take particular care of. This, my Lords, in my opinion, can never be done without an indulgence to all Protestant dissenters.[22]

Aiming toward the same result, Sir Robert Howard, an office-holder who expressed country sentiments, made an alternative use of the property arguments during the 1673 debates on the Declaration of Indulgence in order to minimize the effects of religious toleration. He questioned how its extension to other Protestants could be seen to invade, or even threaten, established property rights, that is "life, liberty and estate."[23]

The likely answer, as demonstrated repeatedly in the debate on the suspending and dispensing powers, was that contemporaries believed just as strongly that they had a property in their laws; and as their religion was by law established, its exclusive privileges could not be abridged except by Parliament. This, as much as any violation of religion, is what Gilbert Burnet meant in 1687 when he attacked James II's first Declaration of Indulgence as an invasion of property.[24] It is also what commentators like Atkyns meant at the time of the Revolution when they maintained that "the law is now on our side, and our religion is become part of our property."[25] Property had become much more than estates or corporeal possessions. The word, highly charged in seventeenth-century political usage, had come to mean an Englishman's vested and unassailable rights.

Burnet called "the first branch of property . . . the right that a man has to his life."[26] That much seemed unexceptionable; and although there were obvious limitations upon how one might dispose of that property, and the lengths to which one might go to protect it, the dominion that each individual was presumed to exercise over his or her own life and liberty allowed in some circumstances for that property to be transferred by contract or deed. This was the secular underpinning for much of the law regulating marriage. Despite the tendency to safeguard a married woman's interest in her own estates, the woman herself was for particular purposes to be regarded as her husband's possession. She had voluntarily transferred herself to his dominion, so that if she were guilty of sexual infidelity, it could be seen not only as a violation of God's commandment, but an infringement of her husband's property as well. "The husband," Matthew Hale affirmed, "hath a propriety in the body of his wife by the matrimonial contract, which was in her power to give up."[27]

The assertion of property rights was equally important to the issue of monarchical succession. In this regard the history of the decade from Exclusion through Revolution is also the story of the Stuarts' attempt to preserve their property in the Crown. It was widely accepted that Charles II held the Crown by heritable right from his father, and by the applicable rules of hereditary descent was expecting to pass that property to the duke of York, his presumptive heir. James insisted during the years of the Exclusion Crisis that he could not legally be divested of his right, not even by an act of Parliament. But the royal patrimony, preserved in 1685, was to be undone only four years later. The prince of Orange, who in 1689 was no better than fourth in the Stuart line of succession, nonetheless succeeded jointly to his father-in-law's throne. By the rules of inheritance he had no legal right to the property of the Crown, and even if James were understood to have abdicated and the prince of Wales to be no more than a fraud, the Crown should have descended to Mary alone. In an attempt to preserve the integrity of the property concept it would be asserted by some that the royal estate did descend to Mary and because she was married the estate passed properly to her husband's dominion and control;[28] but this assertion was not particularly persuasive. By most readings of the Revolution settlement, the presumption of the Crown's corresponding to a heritable estate in land had been severely shaken.

Nevertheless, the Stuart claim to an indefeasible property in the Crown did not die quickly. The Jacobite cause would survive the Revolution by more than fifty years. William would continue to be unacceptable to those who believed that only James, because he "hath the best right, can make us the best title to what we have or want."[29] The Stuarts would continue to insist that their property be restored, adding that until this was done no man's right to property could be secure. The settlement of 1689 had translated William and Mary to the English throne, yet despite all the appearances of a move to an elective monarchy the pretense persisted of the Crown as a heritable estate.

It would be a mistake, therefore, to view the undoing of James II as a defeat for the contemporary importance of property. Across the seventeenth century the idea had developed of the Crown as a forfeitable estate. That idea had exploded into reality with the king's trial and execution in 1649, and it was now come again forty years later. What had happened in 1688–89 was the revival and acceleration of a process begun in the 1640s, the practical transformation of the Crown from an estate in fee to an estate in trust. It was not a new idea. Kings had long been willing to acknowledge their crowns as a trust from God for the benefit of their subjects. What they had not before been required to contemplate was a trust that had been created by the people rather than by God. The result, by 1689, was that the property issue was resolved in favor of the subjects and their new sovereigns, while the legitimate Stuart claim began to languish and eventually died. Tory scruples and Jacobite legitimism would prove to be no match for the view of monarchy asserted periodically throughout the century and ultimately made good at the Revolution: "a king is not for his own but his subjects' sake only; and we have in truth rather title . . . to him, than he to us."[30] This remark by a prophetic observer could be no more than a bold hope in 1679. Ten years later it had come stunningly close to the mark.

< III >

English men and women versed in the fundamentals of the common law appreciated the importance of proving title. There could be no secure right to any property without being able to show whence that right had come. This, as has already been suggested, was why the right of inheritance, and especially of inheritance from a past beyond the reach of memory, had to be protected. In a seventeenth-century view of basic rights, life, liberty, and estates—all of which were the subject's property—were inherited from an ancestry so remote in time as of necessity to be undocumented. As a result, and despite the invoking of protection from the "ancient constitution," these rights were politically vulnerable.[31] The law, therefore, became everything—the agency by which the inheritance was passed, the weapon by which it was defended from the king, and, not least, an integral part of the inheritance itself. The English had title to their laws; and the laws, in turn, gave them title to all that they valued.[32] William Petyt, the antiquarian and keeper of the official records in the Tower, reported this attitude as being so essential to the English political culture that kings as well as people held the nation's laws "in great estimation, and reverence, as their best birth-right."[33] Charles I, in particular, had "published to all posterity that the law was the inheritance of every subject."[34] But in this regard it would be William of Orange, understandably, for whom the most praise would be reserved. Addressing the prince in December 1688, Sir George Treby, shortly to become speaker of the Convention, commended him for having "preserved our dearest interests ... our laws; which are our ancient title to our lives, liberties, and estates; and without which this world were a wilderness."[35]

Treby's image of a world without laws was consonant with Thomas Hobbes's depiction of the state of nature; and whereas Hobbes may not have made many converts to his vision of secular absolutism, his assessment of unregulated liberty was shared widely among his contemporaries. "The generality of us," according to Jeremy Collier, moralist and non-juror controversialist, are by nature "weak, deceitful and turbulent creatures," which was why all civilized society needed rules.[36] It was a recognition of freedom not only needing to be protected by law, but also having to be bounded by it.[37] The marquis of Halifax, in his *Character of a Trimmer*, was especially mindful of the problem, calling specifically upon the law for the subduing of humanity's perverse wills and the binding up of its "unruly passions."[38] People, because of their natures, had to be protected from each other—and also from themselves.[39] The question, then, became one of balance, how to weigh the subject's right to liberty and property against the magistrate's obligation to rule.[40] The practical answer was not easy to achieve, as is evident from the periodic attempts throughout the seventeenth century to adjust the balance of government. In theory, however, it was the law that would provide the answer. On the critical issues of liberty and property the law would mediate and determine disputes among subjects and between subjects and their king.[41]

The difficulty with the theory was that it left a number of troublesome questions unresolved. Most significant of these were who would make the law and who would be designated to interpret it.[42] Also of interest was whether the law, or any part of it, was immutable, and therefore beyond the dominion of the king alone, or even of the king-in-Parliament. This, perhaps, was the most intriguing theoretical question, although in practical terms the one that proved to be the least important. Until the seventeenth century there was no part of the law, not Magna Carta itself, that was regarded as fundamental in the sense of being irrevocable and unalterable.[43] Then, in 1610, came Lord Chief Justice Coke's dictum in *Dr. Bonham's Case* (which concerned the College of Physicians acting as judges in a matter concerning its own rights) that "the common law will control acts of parliament, and some times adjudge them to be utterly void."[44] Like many of Coke's pronouncements, this was seemingly without foundation, and it was ignored until invoked in 1765 by the Massachusetts Assembly to declare the Stamp Act void. Whether Coke meant to be advancing a principle of judicial review or, as some modern commentators have suggested, merely an argument in support of strict statutory construction,[45] is open to question; but it is clear that the idea of judicial review had significant political appeal and was certain to be heard from again.[46]

When, in 1677, the earl of Shaftesbury was committed to the Tower by order of the House of Lords, he sought relief by a writ of habeas corpus in King's Bench. Shaftesbury argued, albeit unsuccessfully, that the courts of common law had the right to judge an order of the Lords "that is putt in execucion to deprive any subject of his libertye"; indeed, they could judge any act of Parliament and find it "void if it be against Magna Charta."[47] This fundamental law argument was also available to defenders of the Stuart succession, who argued that James's expectation of the Crown could not be defeated by statute, appealing to a simple fundamental law position that Parliament could not alter the succession, could not deprive a royal heir of his patrimony; and concluding that "if such an Act should pass, it would be invalid in itself."[48]

The importance of immutability and judicial review notwith-standing, there was a more basic issue underlying the idea of funda-mental laws and constitutions: which laws, which constitutions, which values, were to be regarded as fundamental? For awhile it seemed as if the critics of an expanded prerogative would try to hold the line against the monarchy by appealing to Magna Carta. Shaftes-bury's argument in his habeas corpus matter is an illustration in point. Yet by 1688–89 the rhetorical shield of Magna Carta was no longer enough. However mythic it had become, the great charter was still vulnerable to interpretation as a grant of liberties from a medie-val English king; and if it had been granted by one king it might conceivably be revoked by another. In the search for fundamentals something better was needed. In one way or another what was re-quired, and what would emerge from the events of 1688–89, was the simple, although no less mythic, belief that "when a free people did enter into a contract and gave up their liberty on certain conditions, it was called a limited government, and these conditions the funda-mental laws."[49] That, in effect, was what fundamental law had come to mean: not the grant of power, but the *reserve* of power that enti-tled the people to challenge their king. Even if the Lords were reluc-tant to conclude that James had "abdicated" and that the throne was "vacant," there would be no quarrel with the premise of the Com-mons' resolution that James had "endeavoured to subvert the con-stitution of the kingdom" and had "violated the fundamental laws." In the elaboration of constitutional values, what was fundamental, and inviolable by the king except at risk of the forfeiture of his au-thority, were those stipulations agreed to at the time of the original contract.[50] This construction by no means addressed all of England's outstanding political problems. The identification of basic rights was still open to interpretation and disagreement; but in the Declaration of Rights the Convention came as close as it was able to suggesting what a common understanding of these fundamentals might be.[51]

The rhetoric of fundamental law had only a small effect on the seventeenth-century understanding of how law was or ought to be made. For the most part, politicians and jurists alike recognized that the positive law of England, although forged in custom, could be originated, altered, and repealed in Parliament. In the same way that Coke had confused the issue by suggesting the possibility of judicial review, he underscored the corollary idea that statutes were generally recognized as declarative of the unwritten common law. But even Coke had appreciated the role of Parliament in creating law. "Of Acts of Parliament," he wrote unambiguously in his *Fourth Institutes*, "some be introductory of a new law";[52] and that jurisprudential assertion would be echoed and amplified without dissent throughout the century.[53] By and large there was little if any question about Parliament's wide-ranging legislative function, but Parliament was asked to exercise its legislative function responsibly. Matthew Hale, for one, acknowledged that the "laws of men . . . [were not] fixed and unalterable," but he pleaded for any changes in those laws to be approached "with greate prudence, advice, care and upon a full and cleare prospect of the whole business."[54] The same caveat could be issued with regard to the constitution, because it, too, might be altered upon cause. This, understandably, would be a much more sensitive and difficult undertaking, as was evident in the failed attempt at Exclusion; but by the time the Revolution was over and the Settlement fully underway, the leading Whig lawyer John Somers could remark without explanation that the constitution, although it "be as good as possible for the present time, none can be good at all times."[55] Laws and constitutions had come to be seen as something other than institutions of God, something other than ends in themselves. They were instruments of human creation, for the regulation of human behavior, in the service of human needs.

≺ IV ≻

The acceptance of law as accessible to change left open a further question of vast significance: by whose authority would change be made? For those who inclined toward the virtues of royal absolutism it was appealing to embrace the idea that law was made by the king alone, and that to speak of the authority of Parliament meant only that the Lords would be asked for advice and the Commons for assent. This had been the royalist political theorist Robert Filmer's interpretation of the law-making process,[56] but it was very much a minority and outdated view. By 1660 the principle that the legislative function resided in king-in-Parliament was no longer at issue. The king might still, in formulaic terms, be said to enact the laws, but, as

Matthew Hale explained, "there is a certaine solemnitie and qualification of that power, namely the advice & assent of the two houses
of parliament, without which no law can be made."[57]

This judicious and balanced opinion would be endorsed by politicians and theorists of all political persuasions; but in another place
Hale edged dangerously, perhaps inadvertently, toward more uncertain ground. In reiterating his observation that law was created by
king, Lords, and Commons, he spoke of this authority as having issued from "the original or fundamental law bounding monarchy."[58]
The chief justice offered no further analysis, or even a suggestion, of
what would happen if the king or either house violated this fundamental boundary by attempting unilaterally to make or alter law;
but even before the Convention met, in early January 1689, the Revolution was already being read as an extension of Hale's remark.
James II, one writer charged, had set out to abrogate the laws without the consent of the people assembled in Parliament; consequently the king had subverted the foundations, the very fundamentals, of the government, and the government was thereby dissolved.[59]

This theme would become increasingly familiar in the interregnum between James's flight to France and the offering of the Crown
to William and Mary. Even if the political nation was not prepared
to contemplate the dissolution of the constitution, the consequence
of which would have been the lapsing of all civil rights, it was nonetheless ready to hold its delinquent king to account for having violated the fundamental law. For Englishmen who believed that the
constitutional illegality of the suspending power, at least in ecclesiastical matters, had been settled when Charles II was obliged to
withdraw his Declaration of Indulgence in 1673, the issuing of a new
Declaration by James was tantamount to "a subversion of this whole
government."[60] Charles had assured the Commons that he did not
"pretend to the right of suspending any laws wherein the properties,
rights, or liberties of his subjects are concerned."[61] The Commons
replied by telling the king that he did not have the authority to grant
toleration unilaterally when the effect of that would be the "inter-
rupting of the free course of the laws and altering the legislative
power, which hath always been acknowledged to reside in your
Majesty and your two houses of parliament."[62] Charles backed down
but did not concede the principle; and this retreat did not deter

James from reviving the suspending power. He was prepared to suspend the Act of Uniformity, all the penal laws, and probably both Test Acts. His two Declarations of Indulgence embodied the royal interpretation of prerogative power, a belief that the king on his own could effectively repeal an act of Parliament. Although James intended suspension only as a temporary measure and stated his explicit expectation of a statutory repeal of the offending laws to follow in a Parliament meeting no later than November 1688, his attempt to employ a suspending power, particularly in furtherance of his objectionable religious politics, was seen to be subverting the law-making function that resided in king-in-Parliament alone.

Curiously, 1688–89 would provide a resounding echo of 1641–42. In the same way that the Civil War had been precipitated by Parliament's issuing a militia ordinance, and thereby taking it upon itself to make law without Charles I, a half century later James II would be seen to have subverted the constitution in his disregard of the Test Acts and the penal laws. He would be charged with having excluded Parliament from the legislative process by dispensing and attempting to suspend the law on the authority of his royal will alone.[63] In both periods the integrity of the law-making function of king-in-Parliament had been breached, and damage done to the very fabric of the constitution itself. The similar crises of 1641–42 and 1688–89 spoke to the recurring belief over the span of the century that excluding any one of the necessary participants in the legislative process was "a direct subversion of our government, the chief fundamental of which is, that the laws should be made by the king and parliament."[64]

It is not difficult to understand why legislation as the exclusive preserve of king-in-Parliament was considered to be fundamental to the constitution of government. Any alternative, especially one that afforded a significant edge to the king through the unregulated use of the dispensing power, would be a potential danger to the rule of law. It would mean, as Shaftesbury alleged in 1675, that the laws would be "but rules amongst our selves during the king's pleasure";[65] and, as Daniel Defoe added retrospectively in 1689, "it would have rendered all laws in England not only uncertain and insecure, but utterly needless; nay altogether ridiculous."[66] The manifest fear was of the king arrogating to himself so much control of the law, principally through the dispensing power, that his subjects would hold their property no longer as of right, but merely as "tenants at will."[67] It is little wonder, then, that in the opening lines of William's declaration of reasons for coming to England, the citing of the kingdom's "laws, liberties, and customs" having been "openly transgressed and annulled" is linked directly to the evils of the dispensing power, and that the power is uncompromisingly condemned.[68]

James's actions caused a growing chorus of condemnation throughout his reign. In response to the king's increased use of the *non obstante* in aid of Catholics, he was exhorted repeatedly to respect king-in-Parliament's exclusive dominion over all aspects of the legislative process. Altering and repealing the law, even in respect of its application to a few people, was alleged to be no less than making the law, and therefore an infringement of king-in-Parliament's legislative right.[69] For some critics the monarchical dispensing power was understood simply not to extend to any corner of the common law,[70] while for others it was especially objectionable because it violated Bracton's dictum that the king was under the law,[71] or because it was seen to be a breach of the king's coronation oath to maintain the law.[72] The common thread of these complaints was that the dispensing power was an unwarranted extension of the prerogative, a subversion of the constitution, and an affront to both law and reason. By 1689 it was no longer politically acceptable that "he who hath but a share with others in the making of a law . . . should have the power by himself alone to dispense with the law."[73]

In truth, the dispensing power had a long and respectable history. Even in early 1689, after James had fled to France and the Revolution had been nearly secured, the common law judges were still persuaded that there had been ample precedent for its regulated use.[74] In fact, the most compelling argument for the *non obstante* was that "it was never doubted but that the king had always a power of dispencing with penall laws in particular cases," which was why the Declaration of Rights, largely at the Lords' insistence, went only so far as to condemn the dispensing power as "it hath been used of late."[75] There would always be the need to mitigate the effects of the law in those cases where the inflexible application of a given law might not be in the interest of individual justice or the common good. As the court reasoned in the 1674 case of *Thomas v. Sorrel*, when dispensations issued as far back as the reign of James I were challenged citing the authority of Coke, "there is an impossibility of foreseeing all particulars, and some may be of necessity or profit to be dispensed with."[76]

Nonetheless, if the king were authorized to dispense with the application of any law to a given individual or, what was worse, to suspend the operation of a law so that it would apply to no one, it was feared that he would be effectively empowered to abrogate any legislation of which he disapproved. Yet what made James's prerogative powers especially menacing was that they were being used in furtherance of an obnoxious religious design. Had the dispensing power not been used to advance Catholics to office, it is more than likely that any protests against its use would have been muted, if heard at all.[77] As it was, however, the more James was willing to resort to his prerogative, the more would Englishmen perceive their religion, their estates, their liberties, and their laws to be imperilled.

A critical point was reached in 1686 when King's Bench upheld the dispensing power in the case of *Godden v. Hales*, brought collusively to vindicate the king's prerogative right. *Thomas v. Sorrel* had sustained the use of the *non obstante* in matters concerning the king alone, matters which did not affect the common good. The rationale behind the court's holding was that the king could not be precluded from use of his prerogative in those areas where the public had no demonstrated interest and where no individual could show injury as a result of the king's action. *Godden v. Hales* endorsed that holding and specifically affirmed the application of the dispensing power to the Test Act. James, at his pleasure, was privileged to disregard the Test in individual cases, and thereby to elevate Catholics to civil and military office.

But *Godden v. Hales* did something more. In that case Chief Justice Edward Herbert implied that the *pro bono publico* test would afford no practical restraint on the dispensing power because it was for the king alone to decide when he would use it. The effect of that dictum was to dismiss Chief Justice Francis North's earlier arguments in *Thomas v. Sorrel*. North had insisted that the monarchical dispensing power in matters touching upon the public interest was to be regarded as a power in trust, not to be employed merely at the pleasure of the king, but only "upon consideracion of circumstances." The argument was grounded in the premise that all subjects had an interest in any law made for their government or for the common good. They had a property in those laws which was not to be given away by the king as if it were his own land or treasure. Laws *pro bono publico* were a common inheritance, not the king's alone.[78] *Thomas v. Sorrel* was ultimately decided on narrower ground, but North's view of the dispensing power as a personal trust was negated by Herbert's dictum. The legal result of *Godden v. Hales* was that the public could make no claim to an interest in enforcing the Test Act and, as to any other statute, had no way to challenge a king's decision that the statute did not touch anyone's interest but his own.

Godden v. Hales was the last judicial pronouncement in the matter before the Revolution, but it in no way foreclosed the dispensing power as a political issue. Royal apologists claimed that the matter was settled because James had done all that he could by submitting the question of the dispensing power to the judges who had upheld it.[79] Herbert had concluded his dictum in *Godden v. Hales* by asserting that the dispensing power was "not in trust given to the king, but tis the antient remains of the crown, which never was nor can be taken from him."[80] The argument was familiar, indeed identical to that advanced in support of those rights of the people that, having been inherited from an ancient past, could not be revoked or abridged by an earthly authority.[81] This, in fact, was precisely what William's declaration referred to when it accused the judges of "declaring that this dispensing power is a right belonging to the crown; as if it were in the power of the twelve judges to offer up the laws, rights, and liberties of the whole nation to the king."[82] The Revolution, then, would be a contest for the preservation of patrimonies, either the king's or the people's; and because James's actions had made them seem to be incompatible and ultimately irreconcilable, only one could be sustained.

≺ V ≻

The Revolution of 1688 reopened the mid-century question of whether the practical constraints of the law could be applied to the king as well as to his subjects. Halifax's Trimmer believed that "if the will of a prince is contrary either to reason itself or to the universal opinion of his subjects, the law by a kind restraint rescueth him from a disease that would undo him"; [83] yet that was more in the nature of wishful thinking than of political reality—and certainly contrary to the experience of Charles I. Charles had been brought to trial precisely because the restraint of the law was seen to have failed. It was far from certain that Charles was guilty of the charges brought against him, but the army's Remonstrance of 1648 had gotten it absolutely right when, in calling for the trial of the king, it observed that "the having of good constitutions, and making of good laws, were of little security or avail, without power to punish those that break or go about to overthrow them." [84]

In respect of their emblematic value, the 1648 Remonstrance and the 1660 trial of the regicides marked the beginning and end of a failed constitutional experiment. In 1648 the army's Remonstrance signalled the radical vision of a polity in which rulers could be made to answer for their own malfeasance. Consistent with that vision, Charles I was held publicly to account for the alleged illegality of his rule. He was destroyed, as Cromwell had promised, with the crown still on his head. Charles Stuart had not been deposed and murdered, but had been tried and executed as king of England. Monarchical government was abolished soon afterwards. Yet twelve years later monarchy was restored, and with it the constitutional maxim that the king can do no wrong. In 1660 that meant a king effectively unreachable by the law. It is a matter of "plain and true law," Orlando Bridgman declared as president of the court trying the regicides, "that no authority, no single person, no community of persons, not the people collectively or representatively, have any coercive power over the king of England." [85]

In his concern to repudiate regicide Bridgman may have sounded more of an apology for absolute monarchy than he intended, but he expressed the new mood of non-resistance and passive obedience to monarchical authority. The idea that the king could do no wrong did not have to mean that the king was above the law, and for the most part never did mean that; [86] but it did signify the legal truth "that he hath no peer, & cannot be judged." [87] That was why, according to a universal understanding of the constitution, the king always acted of necessity through his ministers. [88] They, not he, were to be held to account for any wrongdoing. The law's protection of the king even went so far as to make it impossible for him to authorize any wrongdoing. Any illegal act of the government was either assumed to be unauthorized or, in Hale's more sophisticated analysis, deemed simply to be null and void.[89] If the law would not permit the king to do wrong, it could only mean that anything the king commanded that was illegal, would be of no effect. In one way or another, then, the maxim served as a shield to protect the king from others, and also from himself.

The Revolution and Settlement of 1688–89 signified the falling away of that shield. For the second time in the century, the sovereign would be held to an accounting for his misrule. The maxim that the king *can* do no wrong would be turned to mean that the king *should not be allowed* to do wrong.[90] In what was slowly becoming an acceptable perception of the constitution, it would no longer be possible to save the king by sacrificing his ministers. Despite the labored pretense that James had abdicated, the emerging constitutional reality was that kings accused of fundamental malfeasance, that is, of having violated their subjects' inherited right to liberty and property, were themselves at risk of having their own property, their crowns and their right to rule, forcibly taken away. The Tory earl of Nottingham was one who saw it coming and who was appalled at the prospect. He feared that if the Commons' resolution of 28 January were to carry the Convention, "then adieu to the maxim of the kings not doeing wrong, and we may have recourse to that other of *respondeat superior* [let the master answer for his servant's actions], as a more effectual satisfaction."[91] It was a stunningly accurate perception because it implied the permissible destruction of a monarch whose title to the throne, certainly at his accession, was beyond question. The critical distinctions, however, were that this time, unlike 1648–49, the king would escape with his life and the monarchy itself would survive.

≺ VI ≻

Those who believed in the desirability of a more efficient and, thus, a less restricted royal government were of the opinion that the prerogative ought not to be unduly restrained. Petyt identified this position with Filmer and condemned it as an unwarranted assault on the rights of the subject. He charged that it made the prerogative "a preheminence in cases of necessity above and before the law of property and inheritance."[92] Hale, reacting to Hobbes, had been similarly troubled that if the king's prerogative were to be unregulated it would mean that "all his subjects properties depend upon his pleasure."[93] As a theme, this balancing of property against prerogative gathered force with the 1675 bill for a non-resisting test, which would have required all members of Parliament to subscribe an oath declaring the illegality of any resistance to royal authority. The oath was intended to prevent any legislative move to alter the existing form of government in church or state. Central to the opposition against it was Shaftesbury's insistence that the proposed test might subordinate the subject's property to the monarch's will. A subject would not be able legally to prevent his property being wrongfully seized by someone acting with the king's commission.[94]

The defense of property against the encroachments of the prerogative was to be a passionate political concern of the 1680s; it would lead to the assertion, once the Revolution had succeeded, that resistance was legally justified when property was illegally threatened.[95] If the subjects' rights, widely conceived as their inherited interest in life, liberty, estates, and the law itself, were assaulted by the king, the subjects were privileged—indeed enjoined—to resist.[96] Jeremy Collier, the non-juror whose sympathies were wholly alien to a right of resistance, appreciated nonetheless that "oppression is apt to make wise men mad," and that "nothing touches them so much to the quick, as the breaking in upon their properties."[97] And, in religious terms calculated to appeal to those who took it seriously, it was argued that the Anglican principle of passive obedience was now out of date. Passive obedience, although suitable for primitive Christians who "had no liberty, and desired no property," was no longer appropriate to modern English Protestants who "possess estates, and have a need to entail them on our children."[98] The logic of that argument may not have been sufficient to offset deep-seated Anglican scruples about non-resistance, but the use of a property-centered discourse was still likely to have been persuasive. Certainly when the conjunction of religion and property was apprehended more directly, as in the turning out of the president and fellows of Magdalen College, Oxford, there was no doubt in most minds that those who had been dispossessed had been illegally deprived of their freeholds.[99] Nor were the implications of the ouster lost on the nation at large. The radical Whig propagandist Robert Ferguson concluded that once the Magdalen ejectments had taken place "we could no longer be said to have properties or inheritances, but what we possessed was precarious, and held by no other tenure but that of court pleasure and connivance."[100]

The Magdalen College case excited passions precisely because the outcome touched so directly on the several components of liberty as broadly defined. The ejectments obviously threatened religion, but in ways which were more immediate they menaced law and property as well. At issue were the proper uses of the monarchical dispensing power and specifically the king's authority to dismantle freehold estates outside of a court of record without recognized processes of law. When the presidency of Magdalen fell vacant in 1687 the king called for the election of Anthony Farmer, a recent convert to Catholicism and a reprobate of somewhat longer standing. It was one of James's more conspicuous political mistakes. The college's statutes restricted the presidency to a "man of good life and reputation"[101] who was, or had been, a fellow of Magdalen or New College; because Farmer met neither test of eligibility, the fellows resisted the nomination. And when the king did not respond to a request for a more suitable nominee the fellows proceeded to the election of their own choice, John Hough. The result, which took several months to unfold, was that Hough's election was voided by the Ecclesiastical Commission; Samuel Parker, bishop of Oxford, was installed as president; and the fellows of Magdalen, ultimately refusing to submit to Parker, were themselves "deprived and expelled."[102]

By his efforts James managed to enrage the sensibilities of the broader political community. Neither the fellows of Magdalen nor Hough, their elected president, submitted quietly to what they and their contemporaries regarded as the illegal seizure of their estates. John Hough's position was especially clear and incisively to the mark. "I cannot," he said, "be deprived of my freehold but by course of law in Westminster Hall"; and in a slightly earlier rhetorical flourish he had embellished the point by protesting that he was the only man "who was ever deprived of a freehold, wherein he was legally invested, and of which he was quietly possessed, without being summoned or heard."[103]

The echoes of the Magdalen episode reverberated loudly: Burnet reported that the nation "looked on all this proceeding with a just indignation. It was thought an open piece of robbery and burglary, when men, authorized by no legal commission, came and forcibly turned men out of their possession and freehold. . . . [T]his struck at the whole estate, and all the temporalties of the church."[104] Significantly, the response to the dispossessing of the president and fellows was excited more by James's assault on their property without due process of law than it was by his undermining of their religion. In William's catalogue of grievances against the Ecclesiastical Commission, high on the list was the charge that it had dispossessed the Magdalen fellows "without so much as citing them before any court that could take legal cognisance of that affair, or obtaining any sentence against them by a competent judge."[105]

It is especially instructive of the issues in this case that Chief Justice Herbert, who had earlier delivered himself of the infamous dictum in *Godden v. Hales*, denied in this instance that the dispensing power extended to the subject's freehold property. As a member of the Ecclesiastical Commission in 1687 Herbert believed that the election of Hough to the presidency of Magdalen was regular, and he dissented from the majority by voting against incapacitating Hough and the ejected fellows from any further ecclesiastical preferments.[106] Herbert later wrote that whereas he supported James's right to dispense in particular cases involving "penal laws of a publick nature . . . yet [the king] cannot dispense with laws which vest any the least right or property in any of his subjects."[107] James's challenge to the Anglican control of education, of which his scheme for Magdalen was a conspicuous part, had brought about a telling transmutation. What had been conceived in the counsels of the king as ecclesiastical and educational policy had become in the mind of the people a campaign in contempt of their property and law.

< VII >

The gathering fear, translated into larger terms, was of the advance of royal absolutism. This led to the outpouring of legal argument against later Stuart ecclesiastical policy, and specifically against Charles II's and James II's attempts to make that policy on the strength of the prerogative alone. The fear was that somehow the prerogative would be allowed to escape into an uncontrolled territory of absolute power. "Prerogative royal & souverain authority are terms already received & knowne," went one criticism of James's 1687 proclamation for liberty of conscience in Scotland, "but for this absolute power as it is a new terme, so those that have coyned it may make it signify what they will."[108] The warning was a reminder of the difficulties inherent in bringing the prerogative under control, difficulties that Matthew Hale had pointed to earlier. Hale had affirmed the proposition that monarchical power in England was "not absolute & unlimited, but bounded by rule & law";[109] yet he appreciated nonetheless that "in some points the government *is* absolutely monarchical . . . wherein the king hath absolutely and alone power to do as he pleaseth."[110] The problem was to identify and circumscribe those areas in which an unregulated prerogative might operate.

It was of little comfort that a careful distinction might be drawn, that the word "absolute," when applied to the English monarchy, was "to be understood not in respect of laws, but of tenure,"[111] signifying only what Henry VIII's Parliament had meant in its sixteenth-century pronouncement that "this realm of England is an empire."[112] That distinction and that assurance were not enough. By the late seventeenth century the monarchy's independence of popes and emperors was no longer at issue, and absolute monarchy had come to signify something else entirely. It was therefore appropriate that George Lawson's treatise *Politica Sacra & Civilis* appear in a second edition in 1689. "An absolute monarch," Lawson had written, "hath a full power over his subjects goods and persons, . . . so that the people have neither propriety in their goods, nor liberty of their persons."[113] Lawson had identified a new centrality of meaning in the word absolute, and he adumbrated in 1660 what a generation later would become the political nation's greatest fear. Prompted by that fear, Petyt insisted that "the king of England hath no prerogative, but what the law of the land allows him";[114] and many others voiced much the same opinion.[115] The alternative was to acknowledge the prerogative as being in the monarch's sole dominion and control, a danger at any time, but particularly so under a Catholic king.

The public perceptions of this later Stuart threat were distinguished from the earlier fears of Charles I by the cumulative realization that after two civil wars, an extended dissolution of the monarchy, and a Restoration era in which Parliament's voice was frequently heard, the prerogative of kings was still largely unrestrained. The critics of an extended prerogative knew that in order to protect the rule of law the prerogative would have to be subject to effective limitation. Specifically, it would have to be transformed from an irresponsible monarchical instrument to a regulated, even if still largely undefined, department of the law. Merely to insist that the prerogative *is* law was not enough.[116] "We must not," Danby warned, "presume a prerogative, and then conclude it law, but first find the law, and by it prove the prerogative."[117] It was a critical distinction, but even with Danby's point conceded there was still no agreement on locating the boundary between government and property, between the king's sovereignty and the subject's liberty. Not only did prerogative need to be subsumed under law, but some general test of appropriate use had to be established. Here, too, Danby was right on the mark in characterizing what only the Revolution and Settlement would be able to achieve. "Interpretations of law," he wrote, "ought rather to favour liberty and property, than prerogative, because the benefiting of the subject comes nearer to the end of the government, than the excessive honouring the prince. . . . And when we have found the prerogative, it must be measur'd by what the publick good will bear."[118] This was the test, the rule *pro bono publico* that had been invoked periodically throughout the century but which, until 1689, was without effect. Not until the suspending and dispensing powers were dismantled and the legislative sovereignty of king-in-Parliament assured would the prerogative be harnessed to a rule of law and made to operate for the public good.

That tension between liberty and property on the one hand and prerogative on the other was dramatically prefigured in the events of the spring and early summer of 1688. In the case of the *Seven Bishops*, the last constitutional crisis before William and revolution descended on England, the nation witnessed a contest appropriately described by the Presbyterian observer of contemporary events Roger Morrice as a test of wills—the "prince's private will and pleasure against his legal and incontrovertible will," by which Morrice meant law as enacted in Parliament.[119] In another frame, of course, the contest was just as much a collision of political wills, the king's against the bishops'. In April 1688 James issued a second Declaration of Indulgence, ordering it read on two successive Sundays at every Anglican service in the realm. His purpose was to discomfort and disrupt the established church. Either the clergy would comply, and by reading the Declaration to their congregations acquiesce in the royal policy of toleration; or, in apparently rejecting toleration, drive a deeper wedge between themselves and the dissenters, leaving the latter nowhere to turn but to the king. Another more likely possibility was that the Anglican clergy would be divided in its response, but that too would have served the king's purpose.

What James failed to calculate was that the church would join issue on the suspending power, not on toleration and the encroachments of popery as the king had expected. Over the course of several meetings in May Archbishop Sancroft and six of his bishops decided to petition the king to excuse them from distributing and reading the Declaration. The petition recorded their loyalty to James and insisted that they were not moved by "any want of due tenderness to Dissenters," whose cause they asserted ought properly to be "considered and settled in Parliament and Convocation." Yet the crux of their protest was that the Declaration "founded upon such a dispensing power as hath often been declared illegal in Parliament . . . is a matter of so great moment and consequence to the nation, both in Church and State, that your petitioners cannot in prudence, honour or conscience . . . make themselves parties to it."[120]

The bishops' petition was immediately and widely publicized with the result that the king's order to read his Declaration in churches throughout the realm was widely ignored. By mid-June James's suspending power in matters ecclesiastical had been thoroughly repudiated by the established church. James wanted to see the bishops punished for raising "a standard of rebellion," but he had learned something from his earlier mistakes and resisted the temptation to use his Ecclesiastical Commission. He chose instead to go to King's Bench so that he might destroy his enemies by the common law. King's Bench was the appropriate court for a charge of seditious libel; it was also an intelligent political choice. Common law judges who sat at the king's pleasure, and who had been moved about or dismissed when necessary in order to provide the right decision in politically sensitive cases, had demonstrated as recently as 1686 in *Godden v. Hales* that the dispensing power was safe in their hands. This time, however, the judges proved to be more sensitive to law than to politics.

There were several lessons to be read in the trial and acquittal of the seven bishops. In the first instance the judges properly attempted to decide the case on the narrowest legal grounds. For awhile it seemed that the matter might end with the failure of the prosecution to prove publication in the county of Middlesex, but when that obstacle was overcome the focus shifted to the necessary elements of libel. John Somers argued for the defense that there was nothing in the bishops' petition that was false, malicious, or seditious, and "because the intent was innocent" the petition could not be construed as a libel.[121] Two of the four judges, Holloway and Powell, responded favorably to that argument, while Allibone and Chief Justice Wright were prepared to denounce as a seditious libel any publication that "shall disturb the government, or make mischief and stir among the people."[122] Most important in respect of legal procedure was that the court chose not to decide the matter itself, but rather to submit what was a clear question of law to the determination of the jury. The result was a verdict of not guilty.

If there had been any doubt before, the *Seven Bishops Case* settled the important question of the right outside of Parliament to petition the king, and by so doing extended the uncertain boundaries of the subject's freedom of expression. Yet in its implications for politics and the constitution much more than the limits of seditious libel had been implied. Despite the studied refusal of the court to decide the legality of the suspending power, that issue remained at or near the surface of the trial throughout the proceedings; and when on the morning of 30 June the bishops were acquitted, the verdict was read by the nation at large to be a curtailing of the king's prerogative and the repudiating of his efforts to take unilateral control of the law. Specifically, it was now understood that in matters ecclesiastical the king could not suspend the operation of an act of Parliament. As Justice Powell had warned, suspending an ecclesiastical law was only one step removed from suspending any law whatever, and "if this be once allowed of, there will need no parliament; all the legislature will be in the king."[123] It was an especially bold statement coming as it did from one of the king's judges, and there was no surprise when the next day Powell was dismissed. But politically it was too late. The king's position, as expressed by Allibone, that "it is the business of the government to manage matters relating to the government; it is the business of subjects to mind only their properties and interest," was reminiscent of Charles I's final definition of "true liberty" as consisting not in governing, which belonged to the king, but in living under those laws which preserved their lives and goods.[124] If there was political merit in that argument in 1649 it had all but vanished forty years later. The broader teaching of the *Seven Bishops Case* was that the people do have a property in their religion and their laws—and by extension in their government—and that that property was not to be touched by the king, except that it be done in Parliament.

< VIII >

It was not enough simply to elaborate theories about the higher value of the public good in the hope that this would lead to an acceptably bounded monarchy. There also needed to be a way of making the king, if necessary, forfeit the office and dignity of his crown. To this end Charles I had been charged in 1648 with having "traitorously and maliciously levyed war against . . . parliament and . . . people."[125] Because that charge had led directly to Charles's execution, the possibility of a king's treason would be slow to regain currency once the monarchy was restored. The nation, disposed to expiate its sin of regicide, in 1660 renewed its commitment to nonresistance and passive obedience, and through most of the Restoration this national memory and sensitivity to the excesses of 1649 provided a formidable base of Stuart support.

By 1688 some way was needed again to make a delinquent king accountable to the kingdom represented in Parliament. One answer was to construct a crime of treason against the state and to allow for the possibility that the king himself might be guilty of that crime.

This was Danby's approach;[126] others spoke to the possibilities of treasons against the government,[127] the constitution,[128] the Crown,[129] the realm,[130] and the people,[131] all of which might be committed by the king. In the end, the Convention did not accuse James explicitly of treason, although the Commons resolution came as close as possible to that accusation without calling it by name. Nor was James ever tried for any of his alleged crimes. The unanticipated ease of the Revolution had resulted in the sudden departure of one king and the immediate availability of another. With some difficulty, but to great effect, it was pretended that James had abdicated and that the throne was vacant. For politicians eager to consolidate their success and to convince themselves that they had done nothing wrong, the issue of their king's treason—or, more painfully, their own—conveniently did not have to be faced.

What the politicians did have to face were both the causes and the consequences of a king's forfeiting his throne. Without an admission that James had somehow relinquished the estate and dignity of the Crown, whether by abdication or desertion, he would still be king. Not that that option was without merit or appeal. A motion to establish a regency for James, necessarily implying that he remained in possession of the throne, failed to carry the House of Lords by only three, or possibly two, votes.[132] That defeat, however, did not point automatically to the resolution of all remaining political and constitutional issues. Yet once it became clear that kingship would this time be retained, that James II was no longer acceptable as king, and that a legally plausible transition would have to be made to a new monarch, the focus of the political nation could immediately be shortened to the critical question of forfeiture. The conclusion, at least in respect of James's being deposed, was certain; only the legal justification for that conclusion had now to be provided—and agreed upon.

In all that followed there was an implicit assumption at work: kings who, by definition, are obliged to provide basic services to their subjects cease being kings once those services are at an end. Curiously, the fundamental difference between an obligation proceeding directly from God and one derived constructively from the private law of contract or trust, was for this purpose relatively unimportant. What counted was the conviction that the king be

obliged to protect his people; to provide for their good order; to safeguard their liberties, their estates, and their religion; and to govern
them according to their laws. If he failed to do all or most of these
things, and quite possibly even if he failed to do any one of them, he
would be seen to have forfeited his right to rule. As these were the
functions that defined a king, his failure of performance would mean
the forsaking of his throne. It could therefore be argued that continued allegiance to James was neither required nor proper as the king
was no longer willing or able to protect his subjects and "preserve
them in their persons and their estates and in all their ancient legal
securities."[133]

The polemical literature on this subject, understandably tentative and ambiguous in the early years of the restored monarchy,
gathered strength and conviction from the Exclusion Crisis through
the Revolution. From 1679 to 1681 the principal constitutional
question was whether the duke of York could be deprived of his anticipated inheritance of the crown. Those Whigs who answered the
question in the affirmative, and whose respect for inherited rights
was certainly the equal of the Tories, drew a distinction between the
inheritance of a private estate and the patrimony of the office of the
Crown. The latter, they argued, carried with it the vast responsibilities of government, and especially the preservation of religion. As
James could not be expected to meet those responsibilities, he ought
not to be permitted to come to the throne.[134] This, of course, was an
argument in anticipation of a problem, and therefore without the
force of the allegations made a decade later when James, as king, had
realized the exclusionists' fears. By 1688 the prospects for a Catholic
hegemony had improved dramatically. James could therefore be accused unequivocally of leading the nation to popery, and the expectation voiced that he be allowed to suffer accordingly.[135]

This was to become the characteristic way of viewing the Revolution and of distancing it from the repudiated excesses of civil war
and regicide. Conspicuously ignored in 1688–89 were the claims
that a sovereign people had the right to judge and dethrone its king
and that it was privileged to remake the government to a different
constitutional taste.[136] In fact, the Convention's constitutional posture throughout its proceedings and deliberations was consistently
one of forbearance. At a time of unprecedented political crisis, and

with an extraordinary opportunity to effect radical change, the assembled Lords and Commons chose to do less rather than more. Not
only did the Convention avoid any suggestion of a renewed republicanism; it even denied that in placing William on the throne it was
rejecting hereditary monarchy.[137]

Later histories in the Whig canon would celebrate the wisdom of
this revolutionary minimalism even though it had meant a number
of missed opportunities. But at the time of the Revolution some contemporaries were particularly concerned that the settlement be
made more secure than it had been in 1660. In this way they could
hope to avoid a recurrence of those problems created by the imperfect reordering of affairs at Charles II's restoration.[138] Not that it
would be easy. The Convention of 1689 was itself an imperfect child
of the Revolution. It had not been called by the king and was constitutionally without any legal power other than what it unilaterally
chose to claim. As Heneage Finch warned his fellow commoners,
they were an assembly unlawfully met, and with an authority "too
scanty to be able to make a new king."[139] Yet rather than respond to
that objection, the Convention chose simply to get on with its work
and to avoid all questions that touched on the matter of sovereignty.

Nowhere in the Convention's reported proceedings were there
any discussions of this larger issue of sovereign power, of its possibilities as well as of its limitations. The members simply would
not respond to the suggestion, received from at least one quarter,
that they seize the main chance, that they recognize in the Convention possibilities of power infinitely greater than any Parliament
possessed. "A parliament makes laws for the administration," they
were advised, "but the people as in a community make laws for the
constitution."[140] The pamphleteer and novelist Tobias Smollett, taking a longer view from the middle of the next century, would express
similar regret that "they neglected the fairest opportunity that ever
occurred, to retrench those prerogatives of the crown to which they
imputed all the late and former calamities of the kingdom."[141]

Yet at no point had that been the perceptible mood of the Convention. Instead of assuming responsibility for its own destiny, the
political nation chose to depict James, rather than itself, as the principal actor in the unfolding political drama. Even William was relegated to little more than a supporting role. "When a king ceases to

govern by law," went one account reaching for a level of universal truth, "he ceases to be a king: And this was the case of King James, before the Prince of Orange landed."[142] Ironically, it was James who had effectively deposed and "unkinged" himself.[143] By choosing to rule by his will rather than by law, he had made the supreme political sacrifice: by operation of law rather than by the nation's will, he was seen to have forfeited the Crown.

The rhetoric, and ultimately the reality, of the Revolution bore witness to the fundamental value of the liberty and property of the subject, protected by law. If there had been any doubt before, every monarch after 1689 would be on notice that a violation of those fundamentals, and of the constitution that was seen to express them, put the throne significantly at risk. The new political reality was that kings who invaded their subjects' property would be liable to the forfeiture of their own most prized possession, the Crown itself—an eye for an eye, a tooth for a tooth, property for property. At the Exclusion Crisis, and again at the Revolution, it was argued that the king's estate in the Crown had, at all costs, to be protected; otherwise no man's property or liberty was secure: "for by the same authority they dethrone King James, disinherit the Prince of Wales, and alter the lineal succession, they may, without any formality of laws, do the like to any particular person of what degree soever."[144] But by 1689 that argument no longer worked. Obviously property was not to be esteemed any the less; rather by a vastly important exchanging of places, the security of the subject's property, instead of the monarch's, was made the standard of the quiet and good order of the kingdom. It was also as if the political philosopher James Harrington's vision of the proper foundations of government had finally been realized. In clear Harringtonian echoes, a commentator on the Convention reckoned that the disjunction between power and property had brought the nation to its present pass. "The constitutions of our government," he observed, "placing the dominion in the king, whilst the property is in the people, does in this commit a sort of violence upon nature, in separating thus the soul from the body, the power from the possession."[145] In a nation where the balance of property had shifted from king to people, the balance of power was expected to follow in train.

There was a further conceptual option for devaluing the king's property. In addition to subordinating it to that of the subject, it could also be downgraded from an estate in fee to a property in trust.[146] By this construction the Crown and the government might still be regarded as in the king's possession, yet a possession controlled by the conditions of the original trust instrument. The result would be to transform the monarch from a sovereign ruler into "the supream officer, and a kind of high reeve of the nation";[147] and while monarchy might still be regarded technically as an estate, it would in effect have become an office, "not in property, but in care."[148] The only remaining question would be whether the king, as trustee, would forfeit his office upon any default in his trust obligations. Reasoning by analogy from the private law, Serjeant Holt (soon to be chief justice) would argue in the Convention that an act contrary to a trust was a disclaimer of that trust, to which Nottingham responded that although the trustee might be held to account, the trust itself was not necessarily dissolved.[149]

James II was ultimately deprived of his crown; and in the end all the Convention's scruples, however compelling, were subordinated to the demands of necessity and the persistent invocation of the subjects' fundamental rights. The anonymous *Essay Upon the Original and Designe of Magistracie*, although going further than would ultimately be necessary, captured one of the components of the prevailing mood. The "property of the subject," it maintained, "hath ever been the eye sore of monarchs, tho he [the subject] has as just a claim to it, as these have to their crowns, and whoever goes about to subvert it dissolves the constitution, and forefaults his own title."[150]

As it happened, the Convention never did cross the divide of a dissolved constitution, and never had to. A careful adjustment of their perceptions allowed Lords and Commons to hold James's threat to the constitution to be sufficient to warrant the forfeiture of his throne. As long as that threat was understood to mean the king's contempt of the law through his "open invasion of liberty and property,"[151] James's "having endeavoured to subvert the constitution of the kingdom" would prove to be enough. "For only he who governs according to law is a king, he that endeavours to subvert the law, is none."[152]

The Revolution and Settlement of 1688–89, for all its strained conservatism, was an agent of rapid acceleration in English political rhetoric. From a prolonged early emphasis on the obligations of subjects, there was a shift in the seventeenth century to a greater concern with their rights. That shift was not completed in 1689, but by that time it could be asserted unselfconsciously that "the law prefers the peace and order of the polity before the particular rights even of the king himself"; [153] or, as Danby had put it, "the benefiting of the subject comes nearer to the end of government than the excessive honouring the prince." [154] Whether instituted of God or created by compact or trust, kingship and government were to be regarded for no purpose other than the public good, "the quiet and prosperity of the commonwealth." By this accounting, James could properly be repudiated and the people's allegiance transferred to William. It was William who could secure the nation's law, liberty, religion, and property, while James, quite plainly, could not. Kings henceforth were to rule by laws made, altered, and repealed in Parliament only, and the fundamental rights of subjects, their liberty, and their property, could not be abridged by any claim of prerogative alone. *Salus populi suprema lex*, by virtue of the Revolution's success, had become the measure of monarchical right.

From Persecution to "Toleration"

GORDON J. SCHOCHET

An universal Toleration is that *Trojan Horse*, which brings in our *enemies* without being seen," Edward Stillingfleet proclaimed in 1680 in his *Mischief of Separation*, one of the most famous and polemic sermons preached during the Restoration.[1] Stillingfleet, high church Latitudinarian and dean of St. Paul's, was no friend of religious dissent and saw in it the potential undoing of the Anglican establishment and therefore of England itself. Despite the fierce opposition the sermon created—countless attacks and defenses were published in the months following its delivery—his views were widely shared and were merely the current anti-Dissenter contribution to a dispute that had been raging throughout the reign of King Charles II. Not since 1660 had the prospects for toleration looked so good, as Stillingfleet and those of his persuasion well knew; but again, as so many times in the past, hostile forces prevailed. The situation was soon to change.

On 11 December 1688, James II took a series of actions that were construed later as amounting to having "abdicated the government," thereby leaving the throne "vacant," in the words finally settled upon by the convention of 1689. A few months later, the "representatives" of his former subjects, now meeting in the convention-turned-Parliament, barred Roman Catholics from succeeding to the English throne and adopted what has since been known as the Act of Toleration. The act provided nothing for Roman Catholics but granted a limited but legislatively unprecedented degree of freedom from penalties to most dissenting Protestants. However, the penal laws were not repealed and the Test and Corporation Acts were still in place: they would remain for over a century as official obstacles to full membership and participation in English society for non-Anglicans.[2] James's hasty and not altogether voluntary departure and Parliament's acceptance of even limited toleration were closely related; my aim is to tell and explain part of the story (or stories) that preceded their occurrence.

< I >

The religious settlement that reestablished traditional hierarchical Anglicanism at the Restoration left England a sharply divided nation and provided the legal basis for the sectarian conflicts and parliamentary and church policies of persecution that characterized the reigns of Charles II and James II. Basically, there were four distinct groups, each with its own objectives and political status. The Church of England regained control but its dominance and power were derived from its official position.

Outside the Church were two groups of Protestants. The first and most significant of them were the Presbyterians, most of whom wished to be reincorporated into the Anglican church. They had always been inclined toward the idea of a unified, national church but preferred that religious discipline be enforced at the parish level and wanted modification of the episcopacy. For example, a cleric later ejected as a Dissenter wrote in 1660 that "Multiconformity of Religion" was not compatible with the contentious character of the English nation, and that toleration would be seen by those in authority as a potential threat and, consequently, by its beneficiaries as insecure.[3] Some church and parliamentary leaders were sympathetic, but many others were not. Much political agitation during the Restoration period centered around attempts to find acceptable forms of comprehension, as this policy was called, whereby the Presbyterians could be restored to membership in the established church.

Beyond Presbyterianism were the separating denominations, the major ones being the Independents or Congregationalists (who were doctrinally akin to the Presbyterians), the Quakers, and the Baptists; there were as well, numbers of minor and extremist sects. These groups viewed religious organization in terms of "gathered churches."

They could not accept the structure either of a national episcopacy or of ruling synods—to say nothing of Anglican doctrines—and wanted legal recognition without penalties for their existence outside the official church.

Even further removed were the Roman Catholics, feared and reviled by Nonconformists, members of Parliament, and Anglicans alike. Charles and James, on the other hand, were sympathetic to Roman Catholicism. Charles's posture probably stemmed less from religious conviction than from his political ties to Louis XIV and from loyalty to Catholics for their support during the Interregnum; James, on the other hand, was known to be a member of the Church of Rome from the mid-1670s.

The widely shared presumption was that there was a continuing plot emanating from Rome to restore papal authority over England. A rare call for toleration for Catholics, made by Henry Stubbe, a violently polemical writer and associate of the philosopher Thomas Hobbes, required as a condition for the possession of this freedom, "denying the *Popes* power in any way in Temporals, to *depose Magistrates*, to *dispose of lands*, of the *civil obedience of subjects.*"[4] The belief in the existence of a papal conspiracy was fueled by the fact that virtually every toleration scheme advanced by the Crown provided relief for Roman Catholic recusants as well as for Protestant Dissenters. Parliament, however, was generally unwilling to accommodate either papist or Dissenter, although there was a persistent parliamentary voice in support of the latter throughout the period. The Church was divided: some Anglican leaders were understanding of the Catholic position and were hostile to dissent; others were worried about the papist threat and joined the search for a way of bringing the Presbyterians back into the Church; while still others refused to contemplate any concessions and were intolerant of all non-Anglican sects.

The arena of religious discussion throughout the reigns of Charles II and his brother was even more complicated than this account would suggest, for it was not always a simple matter to distinguish dissenters from conformists or even Catholics from Anglicans. Partial or "occasional" conformity to Anglican ritual by dissenting Protestants was not unusual, and so-called "Church-Papists" were relatively common. So far as can be determined, there were slightly more than 93,000 Nonconformists in England and Wales in 1676, barely 4 percent of the total population. Roman Catholics were supposedly a mere 0.5 percent of the population, numbering approximately 12,500.[5] Despite these small numbers, which represented the hard core of consistent adherents, they were considered dangerous and were feared by many clerics and politicians.

Close to the political center of all these issues until his death in 1683 stood Anthony Ashley Cooper, better known as the first earl of Shaftesbury. And wherever Shaftesbury stood, nearby was his secretary, member of his household, advisor, and confidant, John Locke. Shaftesbury and Locke are among the central characters of this tale—one, the political genius of the age, the other, one of its greatest minds; one, the creator of the prototype of the modern "political party," the other, the author of what subsequent ages have come to regard as one of the *loci classici* of modern political thought, the *Two Treatises of Government.*

The Locke of this story, however, is the author of the *Epistola de Tolerentia*, published in Latin at Gouda in April or May of 1689, just as Parliament was about to pass the Act of Toleration. It was soon translated by the self-confessed Socinian William Popple and has been known since by its English title, *A Letter Concerning Toleration.*[6] Locke's *Letter*, without question, is one of the great works in the literature of religious liberty. The relation of religious dissidents to the political order—the legitimate extent of magisterial authority over religious practices—engaged Locke's attention throughout his adult life; it was the subject matter of his earliest sustained writing (at least the earliest that still exists), of five other essays, of numerous journal and notebook entries and manuscript fragments, and of the tract on which he was working at the time of his death in 1704.[7] This issue was also an important but not explicitly defined part of the *Two Treatises*, for it was a subject that had an important place in English politics throughout the Stuart era.[8]

Locke's doctrinal and principled justifications of religious toleration stand in sharp contrast to the arguments based on expediency that were usually offered in support of policies aimed at providing relief for Dissenters. Both Charles in 1662 and 1672 and James in 1687 and 1688 defended their declarations of indulgence with appeals to the peace and economic needs of the kingdom, rather than to the "rights" of Dissenters or the nature of one's relationship to God.

< II >

To talk of the political and social entitlements of religious dissidents in seventeenth-century England is inevitably to enter into the polemical domain of "church history." And to assert that their standing outside the established church was itself "political"—or at least had a substantial if not irreducible political component or impact—is to suggest that the Anglican Church and its history must themselves be seen as "political."

The very basis of Restoration Anglicanism was political. Political sermonizing was a regular feature of church life. "Royal Martyr" sermons, delivered every 30 January and published with black mourning borders, taught passive obedience and nonresistance, as did other explicitly political sermons, such as those preached before the opening of assizes, on 5 November and other fast and thanksgiving days, and on the 29 May anniversary of the restoration of Charles II. These sermons invariably derived the duties to obey civil authority and to live peaceably and quietly from Biblical passages. The implicit presumptions were that the survival of temporal sovereignty required the support of an established church (as in "No bishop, no king") and that the inculcation of religious principles was alone capable of holding people in due obedience to their civil authorities.

This tradition stretched back at least to the two Tudor homilies on the subject, the *Exhortation concerning Good Order and Obedience to Rulers and Magistrates* of 1547 and the 1570 *Homilie against Disobedience and Willful Rebellion*. Indeed, prior to the Civil War, the network of authority and control that the church maintained in England was hardly rivaled by that of the civil society. Much of that organization had been destroyed in the 1640s, and the attempt to reestablish authority and to reinstitute respect for it in and after 1660 was seen as necessary for the establishment of temporal authority.

In this respect, 1688 and the Act of Toleration would eventually usher in a far greater change than was appreciated at the time or than is generally recognized today. In the end, "toleration" was not simply about religious beliefs and practices but about a loosening and eventual severing of this tight bond between the temporal and spiritual realms. The long-term effect of so-called toleration was that the state had to discard its dependence upon its own exclusive church as a primary means of fostering attitudes and habits of political obedience.

"Toleration" did not possess so precise or singular a meaning in late seventeenth-century England as it appears to in the twentieth century. It was used casually and variously to mean almost *any kind* of relief from the penalties imposed upon Dissenters from the established church, from indulgence-granted exemption from penal laws, through incorporation into the Church of England by means of comprehension, to statutory legitimation of non-conformity.[9] Of religious liberty per se—that is, of the *right* of all people to practice their religion without interference from the civil authorities and without any consequent loss of social or political status—we read very little. Religious liberty, so conceived, implies that all denominations would be on an equal footing, a position that hinted of disestablishment, a minority position in the 1640s and 1650s and politically inappropriate after the Restoration. There were, on all sides, references and appeals to liberty of conscience, but these appear to have had varying and imprecise meanings.

Locke came closer than any one else to calling for full and genuine religious liberty (though he did not use the term) in his insistence that the magistrate had no legitimate power over religious structures, practices, and beliefs except where a paramount issue of public good was at stake.[10] But even Locke insisted upon the maintenance of a Christian community, and he would have excluded from membership Roman Catholics (because they retained allegiance to a foreign authority, the pope) and atheists.[11] The unfolding of the practice of religious toleration and liberty is complex. The histories of English sectarianism and nonconformity show that religious groups or sects rarely began their lives in pursuit of toleration. Requests for toleration were often the last refuge of a group that initially claimed an entitlement to *dominate* on grounds of its religious rectitude. Separation into a distinct denomination came at

a conceptually (and often historically) later stage, representing a
need to withdraw from the contaminating effects of worshipping
with the sinful majority and, in some cases, to "gather" into separate congregations of "visible saints." It is difficult to believe, however, that the separating groups would not have preferred to reform
and control the established Church of England.[12]

Political and religious officials in Restoration England, alarmed
by the prospect of internal divisions along religious lines, feared that
such divisions would lead to the utter disintegration of society. It
was not simply the presumption that because civil and spiritual authority had the same basis in God's law, weakening of the church's
status would lead to a corresponding undermining of the state. That
was certainly part of it, but even more important were the belief
that the propagation of error would mislead the people and the
fear that religious divisions would provoke disturbances. Indeed,
one of the more interesting—if somewhat convoluted—arguments
made against toleration in the 1660s and 1670s was that the widespread social disruption caused by the existence of religious diversity would necessitate an undesirable increase in the state's powers.
As Roger L'Estrange, a particularly polemical Anglican, wrote in
1663, religious freedom would create the equivalent of war, and
there would have to be "a *Standing Army*, upon necessity to keep
them [the dissenters] Quiet. For in *This Town*, a *Toleration* of *Religion* is *Cousin-German* to a *License* for *Rebellion*: and at best, 'tis
but *One* Ill that procreates *Another*."[13]

We have very little sense of the psychological dynamics of religious persecution, for we tend to regard it from the vantage of its
victims rather than from the perspective of the enforcers. But it is
essential to comprehend the mentality of persecution if we are to
understand the religious situation in the seventeenth century. From
the establishment vantage, there are, in fact, two sets of sound reasons in favor of a policy of suppressing religious diversity and heterodoxy and containing dissent. One is religious, the repression of
"heresy"; the other is social, the preservation of the social and political order.

Religious beliefs are deeply held convictions about the nature
and meaning of virtue, right, and salvation. There is little of greater

significance to a religious person than his or her sense of relationship to God and understanding of what God demands. It is not in the nature of such convictions to allow room for the toleration of diversity or, as it perceived from this perspective, error. Toleration would mean permitting and perhaps even condoning the existence of beliefs and practices that denied the validity of one's own convictions about the most sacred and important of principles and allowing all who held the false beliefs to condemn themselves to eternal damnation.

Moreover, there are sociological and anthropological grounds for presuming that in a relatively traditional and integrated society widely shared religious beliefs are fundamental parts of the psychological make-up or constitution of the individual members. It is profoundly difficult for people to give up such beliefs or to accept the proposition that they are any less important than they had thought. Weakening, threatening, or in any way jeopardizing those beliefs could have seriously disturbing consequences. The anticipated responses to such possibilities are firm resistance in the form of irrational defenses of the old beliefs and rabid attacks on the new, offending ones. Widespread personal and perhaps even societal disintegration are further possibilities.

It is no less the case that shared religious beliefs are important parts of the underlying fabric that holds societies together. Because they are so significant and mysterious on the personal level—and quite apart from religions' conventional claims to exclusive, authoritarian, and authoritative possession of God's truth and of being obliged to follow one's duty to do God's work—there is great comfort and psychological value in knowing that one holds one's religion in common with others. When those beliefs, the mystery they enshrine, and the membership in a religious body they produce are all identical to those of the larger social order, the society itself is strengthened by the sense of harmony and community that is created. The union of church and state—the resolution of divine mystery in the civil order—is one of the most powerful political forces in the world. And it is at its strongest where there is no religious diversity.

Much of this sociological wisdom was implicitly recognized by opponents of toleration and religious liberty in seventeenth- and eighteenth-century England, who were certainly familiar with the recent religious civil wars on the Continent. Hobbes blamed the English Civil War on the democratization of religious beliefs, saying that debates on religious issues in the political arena had made unresolvable issues of private conscience into matters of public record.[14] The future bishop of Gloucester William Warburton used unmistakably Hobbesian arguments in 1736, in urging the retention of the Test Act. Religious diversity in the state, he held, would destroy the unity that is essential to political stability.[15]

≺ III ≻

The restoration of Charles II entailed more than the mere reestablishment of the pre-Civil War Church of England and the return of episcopacy. For many people who were forced to surrender an unprecedented degree of doctrinal and practical religious autonomy, the reestablishment of Anglicanism did not involve the exchange of one liturgy for another or even a return to the conditions prior to the Civil War; for in that earlier period there had been virtually no insistence upon the autonomy of personal religious judgment. Large numbers who could not accept the conditions imposed by the reinstituted Anglican discipline were excluded from membership in the established church and, consequently, from full membership in secular society as well. But although Anglicans regarded them as having separated themselves by their refusal, many Presbyterians continued to work for a settlement that would enable them to reenter the Church. However, after 1662 they found themselves in a novel position, outside the Church and in company with divergent and conflicting sects who were all voluntary separatists.

The reestablishment of Anglicanism destroyed the relative religious freedom that had been enjoyed under Cromwell. Its loss threatened to drive Noncomformists into a resolute and societally dangerous opposition. Anglicans appreciated this possibility, but they regarded Nonconformists as factious and potential rebels and their religious principles as politically subversive. The so-called Clarendon Code was designed to impose the Church's religious and social discipline on Dissenters, but it actually increased the opposition to the established church of those who remained outside it. The Restoration may have signalled a return to stability; but although the desire for that return was widespread, the potential for large-scale disruption lay just beneath the surface. It was a potential that was to be exploited on all sides during the next thirty years.

From the perspective of the government and established church, it was clear that something had to be done about so substantial a body of people who were no longer incorporated into the official structure but continued to live in the society. The dissenting ministers and teachers were regarded as having excluded themselves by obstinately persisting in their errors and refusing to accept the conditions for membership in the restored Church of England. The Anglican presumption was that those outside the establishment would quickly be induced or coerced into reuniting with the Church on its terms. Otherwise, because they were not members of the established church, the Nonconformists would be cut off from religious discipline and control. True, they remained under the scrutiny of traditional magisterial authority; but that authority was not reenforced, as it was for Anglican confessors, by the Church.

Government and church officials were troubled about this loss of control; the tracts and parliamentary debates of the period frequently express concern about the "anarchy," "heresy," and "schism" of nonconformity, which bred disobedience to the state. And the Dissenters were attacked because they bred "sin," "heresy"—especially Socinianism—and "lawlessness" among themselves and provided bad examples for the weaker Anglicans. There was already considerable opposition to Nonconformists in 1660, and significant persecution preceded Charles's return in May.[16] Venner's rising in January 1661—when a handful of religious enthusiasts terrorized London for three days—confirmed beliefs about the dangers to be expected from Dissenters. It ended hopes for the toleration of Anabaptists, Quakers, and Fifth Monarchists and strengthened the anti-Dissenter sentiments of the Cavalier Parliament.[17] Additionally, there were reports of plots and intended insurrections by Nonconformists throughout the first half of the 1660s. Hatred and distrust of the Dissenters, a wish to punish them for the Civil War and particularly Charles I's murder, and a desire for revenge were dominant passions the first years of the Restoration, despite the promises of conciliation that had been made. For some people, however, "anarchy," "schism," and the rest may also have been rhetorical masks covering other motives such as the quest for political power, anxieties about the loss of control, uncertainties about the state of the world and one's place in it, and inabilities to accept diversity.

Whatever the reasons, the *perceived* issue was real and required attention: what shall be done with the Nonconformists? The ideal solution from the perspective of some Anglicans was to include them within the established church. This policy of comprehension was widely advocated from time to time. It would have eliminated the public significance and disruptive force of all the doctrinal disputes, as well as the social and political problems of there being a significant part of the population beyond the reach of the Anglican communion. In order to accommodate people who "scrupled" at current practices, comprehension would have required changes in Anglican ceremonies, liturgical practices, and organization and so could only have been instituted by parliamentary legislation that had the endorsement of the leadership of the church—acting perhaps through convocation—and of course, approval of the sovereign. Proponents of comprehension therefore engaged in searches for a form of church government and to a lesser extent for a body of doctrines and rituals that both sides could accept.

An early consequence of this search was the re-opening, in 1659, of the old debates over "indifferency." What practices and forms had God commanded as *essential* to salvation, and which had been left to human discretion by divine silence and therefore *indifference*? The former were not to be compromised, whereas the latter were construed as matters of convenience or custom or simply were parts of the external public order about which people could not scruple. The *theological* distinction was itself hardly questioned, but differing *political* conclusions were drawn from it, and there was disagreement about precisely what was indifferent and what was essential. Episcopal government, for instance, had great historical and symbolic significance to the Church of England, but it was theologically "indifferent" because Christ had not prescribed a specific structure for his church. To the Independents and a good many Presbyterians, on the other hand, episcopacy was rejected because it derived from human rather than divine authority and was believed to interfere with or contradict God's will. So strong a position meant that some of the nonconforming sects ultimately rejected all non-Biblical authority.

All this is relevant to theological disputation and is *internal* to religion. It is precisely the stuff from which reformations, counter-reformations, heresies, and schisms spring. It is of profound public consequence where there is an established church or prescribed form of worship that is enforced by the civil magistrate. In that case, dissenters from the establishment are not free simply to withdraw and organize their own denominations or congregations but can be forced to conform or face civil penalties.

The issue dividing Dissenters and Anglicans in Restoration England was two-fold. First, there was the series of specific theological questions about whether something was in fact essential or indifferent. The other, and more important, matter was whether the civil magistrate could enforce conformity once it was declared that some feature of Anglican doctrine or theology was indifferent, which in turn raised the prior question of the legitimacy of magisterial imposition in religious affairs in general.

Among the most important issues in contention were what the Dissenters regarded as the "papist" practices of Anglicanism. These included the holidays observed, the forms of prayer, kneeling at communion, the presence in churches of the cross, the use of the sign of the cross in baptism and the ring in marriage ceremonies, the vestments worn by ministers, and other "idolatrous" tokens, which had in fact been taken over from Roman Catholicism, purportedly to reconcile the laity in the early years of Queen Elizabeth. Objections to episcopacy and the structure of church government and to episcopal ordination of ministers represented to Anglicans a rejection of the ministry and a failure to understand its character and functions. The Church of England saw itself as having returned to primitive Christianity, to the practices and traditions of the early church, and therefore that it was in fact the Catholic church in England, purified of corrupt and inappropriate historical accretions. In this respect, episcopal ordination was of crucial importance, for it allowed the Church of England to claim direct and unbroken descent from the apostolic church of Peter and also provided a means of validating and maintaining continuity with the pre-Reformation church.

These disagreements placed the greatest obstacles in the way of comprehension, for what was essential and therefore uncompromisable to the Church—ordination and episcopacy—was indifferent and therefore dispensable to some Dissenters. And what the Church of England saw as indifferent and therefore subject to temporal intervention—such as the manner of worship, priestly garb, and observation of the sabbath—all, according to Presbyterian doctrine, touched matters about which God had issued specific commandments and which were therefore immune from human determination. The only workable compromise seemed to be the permissive one of allowing those whose beliefs would not sanction their engaging in certain practices that the church regarded as indifferent anyway to follow their personal "consciences." That was the position of the group within the Church later known as Latitudinarians. Generally regarded as advocates of naturalism and reason in religion and supporters of the "new science," Latitudinarians are usually viewed as religious moderates who supported the comprehension of Presbyterians and the toleration of most other Protestant sects. Not troubled by the attenuation of religious uniformity, they believed that an inclusive church was more important than a thoroughly uniform ritual.[18] Blocking that compromise was a pair of responses from stricter Anglican apologists. First, any attenuation of the catholic nature of the Church was altogether unacceptable. It was this position that ultimately stood in the way of comprehension. Second, if something was indifferent, there could be no objections to its being uniformly imposed by the Church and to having that uniformity enforced by the magistrate.

Locke's *Two Tracts* of 1660–61 were a contribution to the indifferency debate in reply to the anonymous *The Great Question concerning Things Indifferent* (1660), which argued for a wide area of indifferency in which the magistrate had no legitimate business meddling. Locke, on the other hand and in a manner that is generally taken to vary considerably from his later writings, argued that precisely *because* of their indifferent status, these practices could be regulated and *imposed* by the civil magistrate.[19] This very diversity of practices was destructive of the civil order necessary for peace and stability, many anti-Dissenters argued, and when God left the determination of things indifferent to human choice, the intention was to allow each civil society to choose for itself, *not each person, con-*

gregation, or sect. Thus, the doctrinal, religious disputes between Anglicans and Nonconformists were seen to be irreconcilable in their own terms and were made political and given over to the magistrate for resolution.

An excellent illustration of all these difficulties is provided by Edward Stillingfleet in his *Irenicum,* apparently written on the eve of the Restoration and published six months later. Stillingfleet, later bishop of Worcester, developed an ingenious answer to the Nonconformist argument that the primitive church had been organized congregationally and that the episcopal hierarchy was a later incursion of the Romanist church that the Church of England was wrong to perpetuate. His investigations revealed the ancient status of bishops and episcopacy as well as of synodical rule. The actual structure of church government was thus a matter of indifference despite the contrary insistences of Independents and some Presbyterians and was therefore legitimately subject to magisterial regulation. The history and needs of England demonstrated the preferability of the episcopate. Presbyterians and Anglicans were divided on issues of structure and governance, which were matters of indifference. Because history and practice were on the side of the episcopacy, Presbyterians were obliged to accept it and could do so without offending or fettering their consciences, which remained free even though "authority" over them was necessarily surrendered.

Arguments that are very close to those of Stillingfleet's *Irenicum* were incorporated into Restoration Anglican attitudes. Their presence reveals a number of persistent and fundamental features of establishment thinking and underscores the political rather than the theological nature of Anglican attitudes toward dissent. Presbyterians and Independents (unlike Quakers and Baptists, with whom there was no possibility of reconciliation) were rarely accused of heresy. Their religious crimes were "error" and sometimes "schism"; and while heresy was generally regarded as an inevitable consequence of schism and the ensuing lack of ecclesiastical discipline, Dissenters were invariably regarded as fellow Protestants, not the harbingers of the dreaded Anti-Christ that some sectarians saw in the Church of England. Theologically, all the conflicts that the Church saw between itself and the Dissenters—except for ordination and episcopacy—were matters of indifference. In this, the Church showed its general inability (probably shared by most Latitudinarians as well)—or unwillingness—to understand and take seriously the position of Dissenters on indifferency. Merely labelling something indifferent did not make it so, and large numbers of Dissenters continued to believe that many of the Church of England's practices were heretical, which justified their continuing separation. This was a matter of deep and important religious conviction and principle. On this level, at least, Dissenter and establishment apologists argued past each other, the one appealing to theological principle, the other to political convenience and expediency.

To Locke the entire issue of indifferency was irrelevant, for as he put it in a 1667 "Essay concerning Toleracon" that he did not publish, it ultimately came down to the personal judgment of each individual about what God required in the true way of worship:

> ... in religious worship noething is indifferent for it being the useing of those habits gestures &c wch I thinke acceptable to god in my worshiping of him, however they may be in their own nature perfectly indifferent, yet when I am worshiping my god in a way I think he has prescribed & will approve of I cannot alter omit or adde any circumstance in yt wch I thinke the true way of worship.[20]

From this it followed, for Locke and others who believed as he did, that the magistrate had no power over so-called indifferency; his task was simply to preserve civil order. So long as individuals were not disturbing the public peace (thus Roman Catholics could be excluded, for their allegiance to the Pope made them suspect even if they appeared to live quietly), they should be free to live and worship as they pleased. The strict, high Anglican response to this position was that religion by its nature is a public matter; because of the inescapable taint of original sin, people were not and could never be free agents. Locke, on the contrary, presumed that people were both rational and fallible and that because the magistrate was equally fallible he was no more able than anyone else to protect the population against error.

Throughout, there was a widely shared acceptance of the principle that personal conscience neither could nor should be coerced; but it was never clear precisely what conscience was and certainly no agreement about its political status. Sometimes called "judgment" or even "intellect," conscience was generally regarded as a fundamental and irreducible personal guide to right and wrong as well as the fount of one's deepest and most sacred convictions. In seventeenth-century England "liberty of conscience," for the most part, had religious connotations. It generally referred to one's entitlement, within certain limits having to do with order and public peace, to hold and act upon religious convictions that were contrary to the established practices.

In neither religion nor politics was conscience generally asserted to be an infallible guide; it could err, as the conflicts among claims of conscience clearly showed.[21] The troubles of the recent times, according to enemies of the Nonconformists, were the result of confusion of the fact that consciences were materially and morally uncoercible with a presumption of their sanctity and a consequent insistence upon liberty of conscience.[22] This doctrine simply could not be admitted into the established church; but allowing those who preached it to remain both outside that church and unregulated would reintroduce the chaos of the Commonwealth and Protectorate period by permitting the spread of schismatic, heretical, and disloyal doctrines that would mislead and corrupt the masses of the people. There was a saving factor, though, for conscience could be "informed" and "instructed" without being violated, and the "will" could be "engaged" while that instruction was taking place. It was a doctrine that had a respectable lineage in the Church of England, going back at least to Richard Hooker's injunctions to Puritans in his *Laws of Ecclesiastical Polity*. Incorporating the Dissenters into the establishment was therefore to be desired; if they refused to come along, they must be penalized—not for their erroneous consciences but for the threats they posed to the civil peace—and induced into submission.

Again, Locke's words are instructive. In 1660–61, when advocating the right of magistrates to impose practices that fall into the category of indifferent, Locke distinguished between liberty of the judgment and liberty of the will. The former exists when judgment is not required to agree that something is "in its own nature necessary"; this is liberty of conscience. Liberty of the will exists when assent to an action is not required. Locke's conclusion was that all laws, civil and ecclesiastical, those concerning divine worship as well as civil life, "are just and valid, obliging men to act but not to judge," and so "unite a necessity of obedience with a liberty of conscience."[23]

≺ IV ≻

Charles envisaged comprehension in his Worcester House Declaration of October 1660. At Breda, the previous April, he had committed himself, with some qualifications, to something distinctly different, a parliamentary indulgence that would guarantee "a liberty to tender consciences." He did this by promising that "no man shall be disquieted or called into question for differences of opinion in matter of religion which do not disturb the peace of the kingdom," and he affirmed his readiness to achieve this in an act of Parliament.[24]

It is difficult to say precisely what Charles had in mind in this Breda declaration. Certainly he was sympathetic to Roman Catholicism even then and not particularly receptive to Presbyterianism; he included Catholics among those whose differing religious views "do not disturb the peace of the kingdom."[25] The Worcester House Declaration, however, seems to have ignored the ends proffered at Breda and did not mention Catholic or Protestant separatists. It was aimed at the Presbyterians. Endorsing the need for "unity and peace of the Church," Charles called for modifications in Anglican ceremonies and the exemption without penalty of Protestants from practices *within the established church* they found objectionable.[26] The desire to include moderate Presbyterians within the Anglican church was shown by his offer of bishoprics to some of their leaders. Only Edward Reynolds accepted; the refusals by the others—including the powerful, outspoken, and often offensive Richard Baxter—were critical, for the absence of a significant Presbyterian voice among the bishops has been blamed for the failure to preserve the unity of the Church of England.[27]

The next year, a conference of episcopal leaders of the Church and a number of Presbyterians met at the Savoy. After several months of debates between uncompromising bishops and intransigent Presbyterian ministers, the Savoy conference ended without reaching agreement, which left the reestablished episcopal discipline firmly in place and marked an important step in the effective exclusion of Presbyterian Dissenters from the Church.[28] In the preceding months, numbers of ministers who during the Interregnum had not been ordained by the traditional laying on of hands by bishops had submitted to reordination. The practice was an affront to many Presbyterians, who refused to condone this rejection of the legitimacy of their ministries; but reordination was legally institutionalized in the 1661 Act of Uniformity, becoming one of the major stumbling blocks in all subsequent attempts at comprehension. That denial of the validity of Presbyterian ordination, along with the requirement of assent to everything in the *Book of Common Prayer*, was one of the final and most fateful blows to Presbyterian hopes.

The Savoy conference and all subsequent attempts at comprehension failed because the presumed costs were too high for either side to pay. It has been suggested that the Anglican bishops were insincere and devious and that their strategy in the period 1660–62 was to wear down the Presbyterians with promises and prolonged negotiations. Meanwhile Parliament nullified all legislation adopted without royal assent between 1641 and 1660; the king began to appoint bishops; episcopacy was reestablished as the legal government of the church although bishops were at first still excluded from the House of Lords; and the internal government of the Anglican church was resumed by a revived convocation. The Savoy conference appeared to be a deceitful show of good faith. If it had made any significant proposals, they could have been overruled by the reinstituted convocation and by the Cavalier House of Commons, which was already initiating a policy of persecution.[29]

The general but mistaken expectation of the reestablished church throughout the Restoration period seems to have been that persecution would so weaken dissent as eventually to cause it to disappear. It was a presumption with historical warrant, for policies of sustained persecution had succeeded in containing and eroding, if not altogether eliminating, Catholics in Elizabethan England. "Tolerating" Dissenters, on the other hand—and equally allowing Presbyterians to flourish within the church—would only encourage

their continued existence and growth while undermining the establishment itself. The constant presence of this view in much parliamentary and Restoration thinking helps to explain the treatment of
Dissenters. Parliament ignored the king's desires for accommodation, telling him that the Breda declaration was no longer binding.
Instead it passed a series of repressive statutes against dissenting
religious activities and against Dissenters' holding office.[30]

As severe as these strictures—subsequently known as the Clarendon Code—were, with the important exceptions of the prohibition of office-holding by non-Anglicans, they did not attempt
overtly to restrict *civil* entitlements. Nothing was said about the
franchise, about jury service, and about civic membership in general. There is only one known instance in which Dissenters were
specifically denied the vote, a 1677 by-election in Berwick.[31] The
situation was vastly different in colonial Massachusetts. In 1642,
Thomas Lechford, a disgruntled Anglican lawyer, upon returning to
England after three years in Massachusetts, wrote of his former
home:

None may be a *Freeman* of that commonwealth, being a Societie or Corporation, named by the name of the *Gouvernor, Deputy Gouvernor*, and *Assistants of the Massachusetts Bay in New-England*, unless he be a Church
member amongst them. None have a voice in election of Gouvernors, Deputies, and Assistants; none are to be Magistrates, Officers, or Jurymen,
grounded on Petition, but *Freemen*. The Ministers give the votes in all the
elections of Magistrates. Now the most of persons at *New-England* are not
admitted to their Church, and therefore are not *Freemen*, and when they
come to tryal there, be it for life or limb, name or estate, or whatsoever,
they must be tryed and judged too by those of the Church, who are in a sort
their adversaries: how equall that hath been, or may be, some by experience,
doe know, others may judge.[32]

However, it is more than likely that a substantial number of the
franchise disputes in England in this period were grounded in religious differences.[33]

The sequence of events during 1662 dramatically revealed the
divergence between the king's religious position and that of the
dominant Anglican majority in Parliament. Charles gave his assent
to the Act of Uniformity in May. This originated with a bill initiated
and drafted by the Commons, not the Crown, which had been introduced before the Savoy conference ended in failure. At a late stage
the Commons rejected a proviso inserted in the Lords to give ex-

plicit confirmation to the king's power to dispense in ecclesiastical matters, which would include its provisions. The act required Presbyterians to seek reordination, to "assent and consent" to everything contained in the revised *Book of Common Prayer*, and it gave all clergy until 24 August to meet its requirements. Three days earlier, acting at the request of some Presbyterians whom he had encouraged, Charles asked the Privy Council to postpone its enforcement. Vehement opposition from Gilbert Sheldon, bishop of London and in practice leader of the Anglicans, forced him to abandon the suggestion. Sheldon argued "that the State and Church would never be free from disorders and disturbances, if factious men could extort whatever they desired, by their impudence and importunity."[34] Consequently the act went into effect, and nearly 1,000 clergy lost their livings; more than half were Presbyterians.[35]

Despite this defeat Charles persisted with attempts to honor his Breda declaration. In December he issued a "Declaration in Favour of Toleration," which also proved to be futile. "Maintenance of the true Protestant religion" is secured, he said, and the "Uniformity of the Church of England in discipline, ceremony and government" is settled. Addressing the Act of Uniformity, the king promised to seek from Parliament "some such Act . . . as may enable us to exercise with a more universal satisfaction that power of dispensing which we conceive to be inherent in us"; his commitment specifically included Catholics.[36] Parliament had not been in session when the declaration was issued, but when it reconvened two months later, the Commons swiftly expressed its undisguised hostility. In the process, it articulated a theory of representation that suggested a doctrine of legislative supremacy: those who asserted that the Breda declaration still had effect had

put their right into the hands of their representatives, whom they chose to serve for them in this parliament: who have passed, and your majesty consented to the Act of Uniformity.—If any shall presume to say, That a right to the benefit of this Declaration doth still remain, after this Act passed; it tends to dissolve the very bonds of government; and to suppose a disability in your majesty, and your houses of parliament, to make a law contrary to any part of your majesty's Declaration, though both houses should advise your majesty to it.

Standard arguments against indulgence were repeated: that it would "establish schism by law," that it would "increase the sects and sectaries: whose numbers will weaken the true Protestant profession" and would lead to a "general Toleration," and that it would "be so far from tending to the peace of kingdom, that it is likely rather to occasion great disturbance . . ."[37]

In 1664 Parliament passed and the king signed the original act against conventicles, unauthorized meetings of Dissenters, described by the Speaker as "seed-plots and nurseries" of conspiratorial activities, under pretense of religious worship.[38] In 1665 the Five Mile Act passed, barring ejected ministers from living in places where they had formerly officiated or which returned MPs. Despite the obvious sentiments of Parliament, Charles encouraged the introduction of a bill granting indulgence for liberty of conscience, which would have given both Dissenters and Catholics exemption from the penal laws in return for an annual payment; this encountered such strong opposition that it never came to a vote.[39]

The prospects of relief being given to Dissenters improved in 1667. That year witnessed an increase in the number of tracts and pamphlets published dealing with the status of religious dissidents. Clarendon's dismissal as chancellor in August, and the impeachment launched against him in November, opened up the possibility of a more conciliatory policy towards Dissenters.[40] His fall and exile represented a major defeat for the bishops, whose influence at Court was to remain depressed until Thomas Osborne, earl of Danby, emerged as their champion in 1674. The king had taken an active part in destroying Clarendon's power, and it seemed likely that the second duke of Buckingham, a champion of toleration, would become the leading minister.[41] He and his associates became involved in the plans being made by a group of Presbyterians to introduce a comprehension bill.[42]

Some word of the negotiations became public in mid-September, and some of the proposed provisions were alluded to in pamphlets, together with discussions about likely parliamentary reactions. One anonymous tract asked Parliament for "moderation in the business of Religion, first seriously debated, and then prudently concluded, in an Act of *Accommodation* between the *Conformist* and *Non-Conformist* that are sober in their principles, and Indulgence toward others who are so in their lives: So far I mean as ever it will stand with the Rules, both of Civil and Religious Prudence, and the good

Order of the Land."[43] To which a Cavalier veteran, Thomas Tomkins, replied, "In variety of worship the one must needs reckon the other Erroneous, perhaps impious; and then how lamentably must that Country be divided, whose inhabitants think themselves as bound to love God as to hate one another." Why weaken the monarchy, he asked, where "the Church is already so settled and hath a great dependence on the Government, and the Government hath a standing influence on it?" It is "no kindness to the *Monarchy*" to substitute for a regulated clergy, a ministry that is dependent upon the people.[44] The only contemporary accounts of the plans are to be found in Richard Baxter's autobiographical remains and a lengthy manuscript that Thomas Barlow (later bishop of Lincoln) compiled and bound as a preface to a collection of comprehension and toleration tracts he assembled in 1667–68.[45] There is no mention of the proposal in the Parliamentary debates for 1667, for, as Barlow, noted, the bill was never "brought into ye House though Col: [John] Birch intended it, and once faintly offered it, but (dispaireinge of success) sate down."[46]

After much negotiation and redrafting, a later version officially surfaced and was finally introduced in February 1667/8.[47] That second proposal also included indulgence provisions to permit "such Protestants as cannot be comprehended under the public Establishment . . . [to] have liberty for the Exercise of their Religion in Public." It would have required the registration of the names of all who were granted this indulgence and declared that "every one admitted to this liberty [shall] be disabled to bear any public office."[48] In his speech opening the session on 10 February, Charles urged Parliament to "beget a better union and composure in the minds of my Protestant Subjects in matters of Religion; whereby they may be induced not only to submit quietly to the government, but also cheerfully give their support of it." Nonetheless, the bill was defeated, and the king was urged instead to enforce the laws against conventicles more strictly.[49]

At this point, the earl of Shaftesbury, still merely Lord Ashley, enters and transforms the story. While there is no direct evidence to link Shaftesbury to the fall of Clarendon or to the comprehension schemes of 1667–68, it is reasonable to believe that he was on the periphery at least of the latter.[50] In July 1667, John Locke became a member of the Shaftesbury household, and in the same year he composed—and made three further and revised copies of—his manuscript "Essay concerning Toleration." Internal references make it clear that the "Essay" was intended as a contribution to the pamphlet debates of 1667–68. The careful and numerous revisions, the importance of the subject to Shaftesbury, and the later history of both men invite the conclusion that the "Essay" was conceived as Shaftesbury's contribution to the cause of comprehension.[51] The failure of the 1667–68 plans marked the temporary end of attempts to obtain legislative relief for Dissenters, but Nonconformists and their supporters were certainly not satisfied, and Charles was again looking for some way around Parliament and the Clarendon Code as early as 1670. About that time Shaftesbury presented to Charles a Memorial arguing that because the Conventicles Act only made dissenting worship illegal if more than a certain number were present and because the public peace would not be disturbed, it would be lawful for changes to be made, by implication by the king himself, although Shaftesbury ambiguously referred to "Your authority in Parliament."[52]

What Shaftesbury presumably had in mind was that Charles should dispense with the penal laws. English kings had long possessed a dispensing power, the legal ability in individual cases to set aside the operation of specified laws similar to, but legally and qualitatively different from, an entitlement generally to suspend the operation of specified laws. The dispensing power was never defined or precisely limited, but its existence was hardly questioned either. What were questioned were the extent of the power to dispense and specific instances of its exercise. In the end, it was the very sort of practice that would conflict with the growth of what is today called constitutionalism, and its exercise could easily and dangerously approach suspension. Among the areas of greatest potential difficulty were dispensations that were directly contrary to expressed and recent parliamentary acts such as, in this instance, the Clarendon Code, and suspension of laws that defined or limited monarchical authority.[53]

Charles's reaction to Shaftesbury's paper is not known, but we may surmise that he was at least reluctant to apply his dispensing power to the penalties against Dissenters, for there is among the Shaftesbury papers a 1671/2 manuscript in Locke's hand on that

very subject. Entitled "Concerning his Ma⸃y Supreame Power Ecclesiastical Established by the Laws of this Kingdome at this present
time in their full force and vigor," it is an historical and legal justification of the supreme power of the sovereign, as head of the
church, over all the laws governing ecclesiastical matters. That
power included the ability to suspend and dispense with laws touching church affairs. The unavoidable inference was that Charles was
legally entitled to exercise this power.[54]

Charles issued a Declaration of Indulgence on 15 March 1672 in
which he specifically included Catholics; he "declar[ed] our will and
pleasure to be that the execution of all and all manner of penalties
in matters ecclesiastical, against whatsoever sort of nonconformists
or recusants, be immediately *suspended*, and they are hereby *suspended*."[55] The inclusion of relief for recusants was part of the king's
commitment from the still-secret Treaty of Dover, for his declaration implicitly recognized and legitimated the presence of Catholic
priests in England.

Parliament was not in session in 1672, but when it did recon-
vene, it vigorously attacked Charles's declaration, which had been
in force for nearly a year. Defending it in his speech at the opening
of the new session on 4 February 1673, the king virtually threatened
Parliament, saying, "I shall take it very ill to receive contradiction
in what I have done. And, I shall deal plainly with you. I am resolved
to stick by my Declaration."[56] The Commons replied two weeks
later and did not hide its displeasure: "We find ourselves bound in
duty to inform your majesty that penal statutes, in matters Ecclesiastical, cannot be suspended but by act of Parliament."[57] On 24 February, Charles answered that he was "very much troubled" at having
caused such an unprecedented outburst and emphasized that he was
not claiming a right to suspend laws concerning the properties,
rights, and liberties of his subjects or to alter the doctrine or government of the Church.[58]

After just two days more, the Commons insisted that the king
was "very much mis-informed" about the nature of his prerogative
rights, "since no such power was ever claimed, or exercised, by any
of your maj.'s predecessors."[59] Charles wisely avoided escalating the
developing constitutional struggle. While Parliament was considering a bill against the growth of popery that became the first Test Act

and constituted a direct response to Charles's declaration, he submitted to the pressures and withdrew it. He did not, however, renounce his claim to a royal dispensing power. In the period that the penalties had been suspended, more than 1,500 dissenting ministers and chapels were licensed, a result that added to the problems of the established church.[60]

While this was going on, the Parliament was considering its own limited toleration proposal, a "Bill for Ease to his maj.'s Protestant Subjects who are Dissenters, in matter of Religion, from the Church of England." This sharp but temporary reversal of policy by the Cavalier Parliament suggests that the objections to Charles's declaration had at least as much to do with legal jurisdiction as with the treatment of Nonconformists.[61]

Apparently making his own political point, Charles adjourned that session of the Parliament before the Lords could hear a report of a conference with the Commons on the Bill—but not before, as Andrew Marvell observed in retrospect, he had accepted the Test Act "in exchange for [votes of] money" to carry on his war against the Dutch.[62] The Test Act forced Catholics from office, effectively destroying the current ministry. The new minister, Thomas Osborne, later earl of Danby, inaugurated a return to Anglican principles and policies. One apologist attacked the "two idols" of liberty of conscience and toleration, developing arguments based on the high Anglican (and Hobbesian) distinction between conscience and will. Dismissing pleas for liberty of conscience, he contended that conscience could not be forced; the power of authority could only reach externals, and therefore laws and regulations that were necessary to the safety of society could be enforced without infringing upon people's consciences. "To suspend *Penalties* is the ready way to make the Rulers undervalued and contemned; their *Laws* slighted and reproached; to cause the Offender to grow insecure, impudent and not ashamed; to make the heart of the Righteous *faint*, and the hands of the Weaker strengthened." Moreover, it would "involve the whole Nation confusedly to run into an Universal *Licentiousness*, upon hope of *Impunity*."[63]

Danby, an unyielding opponent of toleration, by championing and mobilizing the beleaguered bishops in the Lords provoked claims that he was reviving the Laudian church. This was perceived by Danby's critics as not far removed from popery. Fear of Catholicism now threatened to eclipse indulgence for Protestant Dissenters among the concerns of Shaftesbury and his future associates. Shaftesbury, who had been removed from the government, became ever more critical of the Crown's policies (even though he continued to defend the 1672 declaration as the correct policy for that time). It was becoming increasingly probable that James, who was now known to have converted to Catholicism, would succeed Charles on the throne if he outlived him. Catholics were allegedly growing more influential at the court, and there were charges that high Anglicans despite their show of zeal against them supported "Romanish" practices.

These fears and suspicions were expressed in Shaftesbury's 1675 *Letter from a Person of Quality*. This described debates in the Lords in April and May 1675 on the "Bill to Prevent Dangers which May Arise from Persons Disaffected to the Government," which proposed a new test to prevent alterations in church and state, and would have made it impossible to adopt either comprehension or indulgence. In substance, the *Letter* was a statement and defense of Shaftesbury's opposition to the bill as yet another step toward arbitrary government, and it is an important indication that Shaftesbury's anxieties during the exclusion controversy about the impending state of English politics were not the products of an immediate anti-papist hysteria or political opportunism.

The *Letter* spoke of an "*Invasion of the Liberties and Priviledges of the* Peerage," asked "whether Armes in any case can be taken up against a lawful Prince," and described the movement toward "*Arbitrary Government.*"[64] It opened with an attack on the "*Great Church Men,*" who through "a Project of several Years standing," are attempting "to *make a distinct Party* from the rest of the Nation of the High Episcopal Man, and the Old Cavalier, who are to swallow the hopes of enjoying all the Power and Office of the Kingdom." Further, they are attempting "to *have the Government of the Church Sworne to as Unalterable,* and so Tacitly owned to be of Divine Right," and they "declare the Government absolute and *Arbitrary,* and allow Monarchy as well as Episcopacy to be *jure Divino,* and not to be bounded, or limited by humane laws."[65] Shaftesbury saw the persecution of Dissenters by the court and bishops as linked with their sympathy for popery and arbitrary government. Under such a government "propriety" and liberty would not be secure but would depend upon one's professed religious beliefs and the whims of arbitrary rulers who would not appreciate the inseparability of their own and their subjects' interests.[66]

A few months later, Shaftesbury again attacked the doctrine that monarchy was *jure divino* before the House of Lords, saying that the principle "hath not been long here," and attributed it first to Archbishop Laud, then to Manwaring and Sibthorp, next to Sanderson, and to proponents of the Clarendon Code.[67] In fact, Danby had begun to persecute Catholics as part of his attempt to strengthen the Anglican establishment, and the 1675 Test Bill was part of that policy. Nonetheless, Shaftesbury's cause was taken up in 1678 by Andrew Marvell, but it was as good as lost even when it began.

Early in 1679, while the first exclusion Parliament was beginning its sessions, Shaftesbury had Thomas Stringer, a member of his household, draw up a document entitled "State of the Kingdom." In this memorandum, James was cited as the agent behind a definite design to establish arbitrary government in England. Danby, it was believed, had come very close to succeeding in his attempts to make Charles an absolute ruler; the failed "Bill to Prevent Dangers" of 1675 had been but one—albeit the crucial and most dangerous one—instrument in that policy. The Duke's interest in Danby's and the "Great Church Men's" program was easily explained: in order to succeed peacefully despite his religion, James had to see that his brother was firmly established as an absolute ruler:

The Duke of Yorke . . . dreames of nothing but his Brothers Crown, ever since Doctor Morley and his Brethren of the Jure Divino Episcopacy did designe to make him King: When his Elder Brother had as they thought revolted to the Scotsh Presbytery . . . To secure the Crowne, and a Party to himself att home and abroad; and that the Pope might not dispense with a Divorce to his Brother, he hath declared himself of the Popish Religion, of all others the most contrary to the Interest of England, and which must certainly either loose him the Crowne, or weaken the Nation, soe as the Governm⟨t⟩ will not be worth the haveing. . . . His Interest and designs are to introduce a Military and Arbitrary Governm⟨t⟩ in his Brothers tyme; which can only secure a man of his Religion, a quiet possession of his beloved Crowne.[68]

If Shaftesbury still believed that Charles could be separated from the' influences of his ministers and of James, the next few months were to prove him wrong, as the policy of exclusion brought Shaftesbury into direct conflict with the monarch.[69]

The strong objections to a Catholic successor, the great and widespread fears of a possible return of the Catholic church, the contrived and well-manipulated hysteria of the "popish plot," and Shaftesbury's genius in turning the question of the sovereign's religion into a constitutional debate over the relative powers of king and Parliament in the exclusion parliaments all should have increased the likelihood of political success. In the end, the exclusionists were out-maneuvered by Charles, who, after all, held the power to dismiss the Parliament.

Relief for Dissenters remained a live issue in the three exclusion parliaments, which were sympathetic to the cause of Dissenters. Toleration thus remained a specter to be exorcised by high churchmen.[70] It was during one of the prorogations of what was to become the second exclusion Parliament that Edward Stillingfleet returned to the fray with his famous *Mischief of Separation* sermon. Adopting a position on human nature that was precisely the opposite of Locke's and condemning individual judgment as superficial, self-interested, or fickle, he attacked toleration, as we have already seen, as "that Trojan Horse" that under "the pretense of setting our Gates wide enough open, to let in all our friends" would ultimately give England over to its enemies and destroy all religion. Sectarian enthusiasts would be the gainers from toleration. So far from exposing the folly of their beliefs, it would lead to others becoming infected by them, and divisions, disputes, and conflicts would increase. Ultimately religion itself would sink into contempt. Weary of contention, men would even submit to papal tyranny, if only "because it pretends to some kind of unity."[71]

Stillingfleet is generally numbered among the Latitudinarian advocates of comprehension, a reputation that seems to be based upon his 1660 *Irenicum*, but even there, the conditions under which he was willing to admit Presbyterians to communion were strict and narrow. His conception of comprehension seems to have been based more on coercion than on the compromise and accommo-

'dation that characterized the positions of other Latitudinarian divines such as John Wilkins and John Tillotson. In fact, a number of indulgence and comprehension measures—containing explicit anti-Catholic provisions—were proposed to and considered by both houses of the Parliament after the Lords had rejected the 1680 exclusion bill, but the king adjourned the session before final action could be taken.[72] Stillingfleet specifically attacked these measures and the idea of *"a general Indulgence for* Dissenters" in the preface to his *Unreasonableness of Separation*, published the next year partially in defense of his sermon.[73]

Stillingfleet may have been somewhat ahead of his contemporaries, for it soon became evident that hostility against Dissenters was increasing and once again threatened to surpass anti-Romanism in its intensity. However, in the short life of the third exclusion Parliament the comprehension and indulgence bills from the previous parliamentary session were revived, many of the provisions resembling those of the abortive 1667–68 proposal. Perhaps the net, long-term result of all this was the initial formulation of the idea of a limited indulgence that Tory moderates and Whig supporters of the Dissenters would eventually pass in the Toleration Act of 1689. For that act was, in fact, a slightly revised version of the ill-fated indulgence bill from the exclusion parliaments and was introduced by a Tory, the earl of Nottingham.[74] But long before that event occurred, the involvement of Whig proponents of toleration and exclusion in conspiracies resulted in the penal laws' being strictly enforced, especially in London, and dissent severely persecuted.[75]

Persecution continued into the early years of the reign of James II. The anti-Dissenter impetus came from the Crown.[76] This was an interesting reversal of positions, for in the past it had been Parliament that had rejected the king's calls for Protestant unity and blocked his attempts to relieve Nonconformists from the penal statutes by insisting upon their vigorous enforcement. But in 1680–81 it was Charles who thwarted parliamentary efforts. It would remain for James to reassume the monarch's accustomed role in this regard. Rebuffed by the Tories and churchmen in his schemes to advance the causes of his fellow Roman Catholics, James turned, in 1687, to that least likely source, the Nonconformists. Like Charles, he offered an indulgence that extended to Dissenters and Catholics. The

1687 declaration of indulgence suspended all penal laws, giving Catholics full equality of rights in matters of religion, including public worship. James justified his action by saying that constraining conscience and forcing people "in matters of mere religion" was not only contrary to his inclination, but went against the interest of government by damaging trade and provoking emigration.[77]

The plan alarmed moderate churchmen, who feared both the encouragements given to popery and the possibility that James might acquire the support of the Dissenters and in fact some offered their public thanks, including a group of London Presbyterians.[78] The marquis of Halifax, who had helped defeat exclusion, was deeply suspicious of the Declaration, which he saw as intended to advance the interests of Catholics without giving real security to the Dissenters. He warned the latter that "this alliance between Liberty and Infallibility is bringing together the two most contrary things that are in the world. The Church of Rome doth not only dislike the allowing liberty, but by its principles it cannot do it."[79] In reply Henry Care, a former Whig turned Catholic apologist and author of *English Liberties*, weakly and irrelevantly claimed that there was no understanding between the Dissenters and the Catholics.[80]

The next year, in a maneuver that was designed to force the hand of the Church, the king reissued the declaration and ordered that it be read in all the parishes in the country.[81] High churchmen had objected to the indulgence for Nonconformists, and moderates were fearful of the use of the royal prerogative on behalf of popery, but the Church had been relatively silent about the indulgence. As previous chapters have described, the new order was generally disobeyed, which brought James into open conflict with the leaders of the church. Archbishop of Canterbury William Sancroft, a strong supporter of royalist ideology,[82] and six of his fellow bishops objected to the king's order to have their clergy read the declaration and argued that it was based on the suspending power and therefore illegal. Their petition to James was published—although not by them—and they were charged with seditious libel. The famous trial—and acquittal—of the seven bishops[83] created a political rift between James and the Church and helped to establish an unprecedented cooperativeness between the Church and at least the wing of the Presbyterians who wanted comprehension. The short-term prospects for a

genuine comprehension were probably better as a result of the declaration than they had been throughout the Restoration period, but
that was soon to change.

≺ V ≻

The final episode in this tale is the granting of legislative indulgence
to substantial numbers of Dissenters in the passage of "An Act for
Exempting Their Majesties' Protestant Subjects Dissenting from the
Church of England from the Penalties of Certain Laws" (the so-
called Toleration Act) in May 1689.[84] Apart from revisions drafted
by Nottingham its provisions were similar to those contained in the
unsuccessful indulgence bills which had been introduced in the exclusion parliaments. It did not provide general toleration or confer
unencumbered citizenship on Dissenters but merely gave them exemption from penalties contained in the Clarendon Code and earlier
penal laws. However, these were not repealed, so that the position of
Dissenters continued to be implicitly precarious. On the other hand
the Commons rejected a proposal to restrict the bill to a short term.
In arguing for this a leading Tory, Sir Thomas Clarges, said: "This
Bill establishes a sort of bill contrary to the Church of England. I
would therefore have it temporary and probational. I cannot foresee
what it may reach to, therefore I would have it for seven years only,
and to the end of the session of the next parliament."[85]

The so-called Toleration Act was less important from the Tory
angle than the unsuccessful comprehension bill which accompanied it. Anglican leaders had opposed previous proposals for comprehension, but they supported this bill because of the restrictions
they had written into it. The bill envisaged revisions of the prayer
book, but these would have to be approved by convocation, the
representative body of the Anglican clergy. Its almost certain unwillingness to accept major changes would ensure that any concessions would be insufficient to satisfy the majority of Presbyterians.
The latter wanted changes that would enable all Dissenters "that
were comprehensible" to re-enter the Church. They saw the provisions of the bill, according to the Presbyterian diarist Roger Morrice,
as designed to preserve the Church on its "old, little, narrow foun-

dation," and it forced them to accept the Toleration Act instead.[86] In doing so they finally surrendered their hope of reuniting with the Church, and also excluded themselves from holding governmental and military offices under the Crown. The possibility of Whig Dissenters becoming eligible for offices was raised by William in March 1689. This alarmed the Tories, who faced the prospect of losing offices and powers if either a comprehension bill passed, allowing Dissenters whom they identified as Whig auxiliaries to become Anglicans and so make themselves eligible for office, or, if the oaths were altered as the new king wished, to "leave room for the Admission of all Protestants that are willing and able to serve."[87] Consequently the Tory leaders resolved to obstruct both the comprehension and indulgence bills, reviving allegations about Dissenters as "obstinate, unreasonable and factious" to justify their action.[88] They allowed indulgence to pass, but William had to withdraw his initiative.

This chapter in part has examined some of the questions surrounding toleration of religious dissidents from the perspective of the establishment—the government and the church. In establishment terms, the questions would have been resolved into a single query: What can be done about so substantial and obstinate a group of people and the potential threat they present? Somehow the Dissenters had to be controlled and their threat contained.

The Nonconformists, on the other hand, insisted that their views were Biblical and therefore had God's sanction; thus, they claimed the entitlement—indeed, the duty—to go on believing and praying according to their consciences and as witnesses to the truth. They were not to be intimidated by the established civil or religious authorities in this. Some of these groups would have gone further than merely demanding their own right to exist; they would have destroyed the established church as the heretical Anti-Christ they saw it to be and replaced it with their own structure. Others would have been content merely to have been left alone.

The only possible source of resolution was the government and its established church. It is ironic, by twentieth-century standards, that the agency that felt threatened by the existence of nonconformity in the first place also acted as the authorized decision-maker. Rather than the neutral or disinterested arbiter we might expect to mediate in a conflict between competing religious views, the judge was one of the interested parties.

The official attitude was hardly one of conciliation, and it was complicated by growing fears of Roman Catholicism. One of the difficulties was a failure to devise an equitable and acceptable scheme of leniency for Protestant Dissenters that would not apply with equal force to the papists. The problem, of course, was that neither James nor Charles wished to exclude Catholics; both used the device of granting relief to Dissenters as the means of lessening the burdens on papists. Anti-Catholic sentiments were aggravated by suspicions about Charles's motives and the belief that he, much of his court, and a significant part of the church's leadership were sympathetic to Roman Catholicism and actually accepted it as a true if corrupt church. The Catholicism of James, while he was heir presumptive, was the source of a large part of that anxiety. When, after succeeding to the throne, he granted exemption from the penal laws to Catholic as well as Protestant Dissenters in the 1687 Declaration of Indulgence, James confirmed the suspicions that many had harbored for years.

During the 1670s Parliament's attention had been turned from Protestant Dissenters to Roman Catholics, but this new concern stemmed not so much from the status of Catholics outside the Church of England as from the related fear of having a papist on the throne. By late 1688, what had earlier been dreaded was now a reality. We know the results, and we end as we began, with the temporal association of the expulsion of the Catholic James II (and the disqualification of any Catholic or of anyone married to one from the succession) and the adoption of an act finally granting some relief from the penal laws to most Protestant Nonconformists.

This however leaves unanswered questions and a puzzle: How did this happen, and what did it mean? How did this so-called toleration become possible? There is little to suggest that attitudes had changed drastically or that a mere shift in the number of parliamentary members sympathetic to legislative indulgence could have brought about so significant a reversal of policy, a movement from official persecution to official indifference.

It is equally unlikely that attitudes toward non-Catholic Dissenters were softened by the relief felt at the end of the immediate threat posed by James II or by hopes for Protestant unity. The roles of William and Mary ought not be neglected. William himself was raised in an atmosphere of toleration and was taught that a ruler should promote as much religious freedom as was consistent with one dominant church. Catholics were excluded by Dutch law from governmental positions, but otherwise the prince was deeply committed to religious liberty.[89] When his and Mary's opinion about the English penal and test laws was sought by an agent of King James's, they replied:

That no Christian ought to be persecuted for his Conscience, or be ill used because he differs from the publick and established Religion: And therefore, They can consent, that the Papists in England, Scotland and Ireland be suffered to continue in their Religion, with as much Liberty as is allowed them by the States in these Provinces; in which it cannot be denied, that they enjoy a full Liberty of Conscience. And as for the Dissenters, Their Highnesses do not only consent, but do heartily approve of their having an entire Liberty for the full Exercise of their Religion, without any trouble or hindrance.

They went on to endorse repeal of the penal laws so long as *"those Laws remain in their full vigour by which the R. Catholics are shut out of both Houses of Parliament, and out of all publick Employments, Ecclesiastical, Civil and Military."*[90] In short, they opposed repeal of the test acts and defended their position with the claim that merely keeping Roman Catholics from public employment did not persecute them "on account of their Consciences" but was "no more than a securing the *Protestant Religion* from any Prejudices that it may receive from the *R. Catholics.*"[91]

The character and content of rule and authority are rarely reversed other than as the result of successful revolution, by changes in the beliefs and value structure of the dominant group. It is doubtful that the views of the new king and queen could have caused an alteration. Changes of that magnitude are brought on, usually, by a change in the group itself, and it is precisely that sort of change that William and Mary did not accomplish, as the negative response to the king's call for the admission of "all Protestants that are willing and able to serve" to offices in the state showed.

Moreover the continuing second-class status of Protestant Nonconformists long after 1688 suggests that very little had actually

changed. Yet the door had been opened to considerably larger
changes in the fabric of society than any anticipated at the time; the
dominance of the Church of England had been preserved, but at a
very heavy price. "The Church in Danger," Burnet's *Pastoral Letter,*
the "occasional conformity" controversy, the Schism Bill, the Sacheverell affair, the "Bangorian Controversy," Warburton's *Alliance* (to
name only a few of the illustrative highlights of the following half
century) all point in the same direction.

In terms of changing value structures, 1688 does not qualify as a
revolution. A rethinking of principles on religious issues did not occur. The driving forces behind the passage of the Toleration Act were
expediency and political calculation. Thus, the shift in policy does
not appear to have been so drastic, and the puzzle is not so difficult
to solve. "Toleration," so called, was simply the next means at hand
to control and contain Protestant nonconformity. Comprehension
had proved impossible to achieve; persecution had not worked; and
genuine religious liberty was unacceptable. Indulgence was all that
remained. But it was a narrow parliamentary indulgence that repealed none of the persecuting statutes; it merely granted limited
exemptions from some of their penalties without conferring full,
participating membership in English society upon non-Anglicans. It
was not a principled recognition of a "right" to religious liberty,
however much its unintended consequences may have moved Britain in that direction. The aim was not to benefit the Dissenters but
to preserve and protect England and its established church. Many
believed that nonconformity would be absorbed into mainstream
Anglicanism and that it would die out as a result of toleration.

The beneficiaries of the Toleration Act certainly desired and de-
served a fuller and more genuine freedom. They had to settle for
what they were given. It was more than they had been offered since
the Declaration of Breda.

This paper has grown out of work on John Locke's writings on
religious toleration, the research for which has enjoyed the generous
support of both the Research Division and the Fellowship Division
of the National Endowment for the Humanities, Rutgers University,
the Folger Institute of the Folger Shakespeare Library, and of course,
the Center for the History of Freedom of Washington University. I

am especially indebted to Henry Horwitz, James Jones, Howard Nenner, and Lois Schwoerer among my colleagues at the Center, as well as to Francis Greene, Roberta Kozlowski, Tim Harris, and John Spurr for their assistance and advice. As usual, Louise Haberman's counsel and wise judgment improved many of my arguments.

It has not been possible to discuss most of the relevant materials that were published since this paper was completed in 1989, but I should at least refer to the recent collection bearing the same title as this essay: *From Persecution to Toleration: The Glorious Revolution and Religion in England*, ed. Ole Peter Grell, Jonathan Israel, and Nicholas Tyacke (Oxford, 1991), in which see especially the contribution by Mark Goldie, "The Theory of Religious Intolerance in Restoration England," Chap. 13.

From Toleration to Religious Liberty

R. K. WEBB

IN 1681 THE REV. THOMAS BURNET published the first two books of his *Sacred Theory of the Earth*. Biblical but not narrow in his quest for authority, scientifically informed, magnificent in conception and style, he was in Basil Willey's words, "a kind of prose Milton thirty years nearer to Addison." Burnet saw the earth as we know it as the product of a vast catastrophe. The whole globe had been a paradise, but when its smooth and regular crust was cracked and a universal deluge released upon a sinful world, "the whole fabrick brake, and the frame of the Earth was torn in pieces as by an Earthquake; and those great portions or fragments, into which it was divided, fell down into the Abyss, some in one posture and some in another."[1] Contemporaries might well have borrowed that language to describe what happened to religion in England in the period between 1662 and 1689, when dissent was thrust from the Church into a confused and threatening future.

≺ I ≻

The Burnet metaphor was not of course exact. The religious unity of the country before 1640 had masked bitterly divided views on doctrine, ceremonies, and governance and the two decades of the Civil War and Commonwealth resembled chaos more than order. But the Restoration seemed none the less catastrophic for the confusion that preceded it and most Anglicans wanted to restore a world that never was. Indeed, the warmest spirits among them favored drastic measures to enforce the unity they saw as essential to a Christian society in both its ecclesiastical and its political aspects.

In their eyes, it was to be yet another condemnation of the Revolution of 1688 that it confirmed, rather than mended, the shattered state of English religion.[2]

The new religious settlement brought no marked increase in liberty, in either theory or immediate result. Parliament conferred on the Dissenters a narrow indulgence that only gradually evolved in common parlance into "the toleration." Even the alternative of comprehension would have been an ungenerous accommodation of only a part of nonconformity. The existence of dissent on bare, and some feared revocable, sufferance for at least a generation was scarcely surprising at a time when some still living could recall the part played by sectaries in the trial and beheading of Charles I and the tyranny that followed, and when Englishmen heard these events preached about each year on 30 January, the anniversary of the king's execution. On the other hand, some of the more committed Dissenters felt that they had been rudely ejected from a promised land, and for well over a century their descendants drew political ambitions and language from the ideals of the Commonwealth.[3] These vivid and conflicting historical memories were complicated by the general conviction that whatever happened was the dictate of God: the ways of divine providence were difficult to interpret as they had been manifested in the past and were impossible to predict for the future.

The Revolution forced the Church to reckon with new occupants of the throne and with the altered terms on which they held their title. Not many churchmen embraced the changes immediately but most came uneasily around, convinced perhaps by compelling interpretations of what had happened in 1688 or by the stability and probable permanence of the new regime. About four hundred clergymen could not bring themselves to violate either their oaths or the doctrine of divine right and non-resistance that had carried such conviction to Anglicans during the Restoration; unable to swear allegiance to the new monarchs, they went into the ecclesiastical wilderness as the Non-jurors, with Archbishop Sancroft, primate since 1677, at their head. A church already in schism as a result of the Uniformity Act (1662) faced a new division, losing a significant portion of its leadership at a crucial moment. In consequence, successive archbishops of Canterbury—John Tillotson (1691–94) and

Thomas Tenison (1694–1715)—not only had to work from a base narrowed in both force and outlook but faced a steady barrage of criticism from the Non-jurors, safe in their principled impotence. Moreover, Anglicans and Dissenters alike were often the pawns or victims of politicians playing a decidedly secular game; indeed, though the parties that emerged in the Church after the Revolution reflected profound differences in mental habit, spiritual inclination, and experience, their first precipitation owed more to civil than to ecclesiastical politics.

In this weakened state, the Church had to engage in an agonizing process of definition: what, in these changed circumstances, was the Church? what were the dissenting sects? what doctrines or tests best secured internal cohesion? and how did the Church and the sects relate to each other and to the state? This task had to be accomplished against the insistent imperatives of politics and at a time when radically new ideas were threatening the very basis of the Christian dispensation. It is through these successive attempts at definition, in theory and practice, that the gradual transition from indulgence to a real measure of toleration can be traced, though practice, as always, lagged well behind theory. Moving beyond toleration to broader notions of religious liberty had to wait for nearly a century.

The extremities of the religious settlement were addressed in two boldly devised statutes through which Parliament responded to severe challenges posed in the 1690s. On the one side lay the old concern about Catholicism, a point on which the church and popular prejudice were at one. Following the Treaty of Ryswick, which in 1697 ended the war into which William III had taken England against Louis XIV, some of the Catholic refugees who had fled to the Continent after the departure of James II returned, bringing with them priests whose number was no doubt multiplied in popular imagination. The result, in 1700, was a new addition to the long list of penal laws against Catholics, one more than a little reminiscent of recent statutes against papists in Ireland. The act offered a hundred pounds to anyone who would prosecute to conviction "one or more Popish Bishop Priest or Jesuite" for saying mass or exercising any other priestly office, while it sought to prevent perpetuation of the Catholic laity by fining Catholics who sent children abroad to be educated, by depriving Catholics of the right to purchase estates, directly or through a trust, and by providing that if Catholic owners of, or heirs to, estates refused the oaths of loyalty to William, inheritance would pass to the Protestant next of kin. The act was supported by Gilbert Burnet, the Whig bishop, "notwithstanding my principles for toleration, and against all persecution for conscience sake." Papists, he was sure, would necessarily be "ill subjects to a protestant prince," the more so when a Catholic pretender threatened.[4] But the act remained a dead letter. Such drastic steps were not really needed, given the stationary or declining state of Catholicism in England, and the established church was left to assert its essential difference from Rome in a flood of sermons and treatises.

A far greater threat was posed by the twin specters of heterodoxy and unbelief, which appeared first in a revived Socinian movement and then in a new controversy over Deism. Criticism or rejection of the Trinity—that central, profound, and troubling Christian doctrine—had been scattered about the Continent in the sixteenth century, from the Spaniard Michael Servetus in France, to the Sozzini in Italy and later in Poland, to the reformed churches of Hungary and the tolerated ferment of the Netherlands. The generally acknowledged initiator of the English Socinian movement in mid-century was John Biddle, a Gloucester schoolmaster who arrived at his anti-Trinitarian views (as many of his countrymen were to do over the years) by study of the Bible, reinforced only later by reading in Faustus Socinus. Removed from his school in 1647, Biddle was repeatedly imprisoned or banished by Parliament, Cromwell, and Charles II. Biddle's principal disciple was Thomas Firmin, a wealthy mercer and philanthropist, who collaborated on a series of Unitarian tracts that set off alarm bells among churchmen at the end of the century, especially as defenders of orthodoxy themselves risked falling into heresy in their zeal to refute such monstrous ideas.[5]

While the Unitarian controversy quickly died down, the Deistic movement, which entered a new phase when its most notorious adherent, John Toland, published *Christianity not Mysterious* in 1696, continued in rude strength for at least half a century. Deists argued that the moral order was determined by, and discoverable from, the laws of nature laid down by a benevolent God and that revelation and the panoply of organized Christianity were needless, even dangerous superfluities. Churchmen could not leave such a contention unanswered. One possibility lay in using the secular courts, but although some major figures were brought to trial, the law in England seems to have been preoccupied chiefly with village atheists, though never with the violence visited in Scotland on Thomas Aikenhead, an eighteen-year-old boy executed in 1697, in what under even the sterner law of that country was recognized at the time as a gross miscarriage of justice.

In the furor that followed the publication of Toland's book, however, a worried Parliament petitioned William, and the king responded with a ringing proclamation against heterodoxy. In 1698, Parliament passed the so-called Blasphemy Act, directed really against apostates, those who had been educated in the Church and who then by writing, teaching, or "advised speaking" maintained that any person of the Trinity was not God, or that the Christian religion was not true, or that the Old and New Testaments were without divine authority. The penalty for a first offense was loss of eligibility to hold office; a second offense could bring denial of access to the courts and three years' imprisonment. But here, as with the Catholic threat, the law only bared its fangs. The statute allowed a very short time after the offense for lodging a formal complaint, and a similar limitation came to apply to bringing the case to trial, thus assuring that the act would never be applied. The common law provided sufficient remedy and judges over a couple of centuries seemed eager to reiterate the dictum of Lord Chief Justice Hale in 1676 that "Christianity is parcel of the laws of England."[6]

It appeared, then, that any effective assault on highly-placed heterodoxy had to be mounted from within the Church, as excommunication—the severest penalty that Church courts could impose on laymen—lost its effectiveness after 1689. The failure of the Church's leaders to discipline heterodox clergy gave a powerful impetus to the arguments advanced in 1697 by Francis Atterbury in *A Letter to a Convocation Man* for the revival of convocation. The lower house of convocation could then become a sounding board for the parochial clergy, whose militancy was fuelled by personal experience of problems created by the legalization of dissent and the disturbance of the simple faith of their parishioners by heterodox ideas. Some even thought convocation could serve as a court in which heretics might be tried if the church courts had failed to act. The bishops were reluctant to confer such an opportunity on inveterate critics and had genuine doubts about the legality of some of the claims advanced for the powers of the institution. Their position was strengthened by the demolition of Atterbury's historical arguments by William Wake, then rector of St. James's Westminster and a future archbishop of Canterbury, and by Edmund Gibson, who later became bishop of London. But the real weakness of convocation was that after the oral agreement between Archbishop Sheldon and Lord Clarendon (1664), which had given Parliament the power to tax the clergy, there was no need to summon it. Consequently it met only once—disastrously in 1689—between 1664 and 1701.

The politically dictated revival of convocation in 1701 gave Atterbury the forum he wanted for the clergy and for himself, but the institution did not display the practical effectiveness that its advocates had expected. Its attempt to censure Toland as a dangerous heretic was lost in the general conflict between the upper and lower Houses; and the 1711 attempt to censure and try William Whiston for Arianism, which had already led to his being dismissed as professor of mathematics at Cambridge, also failed. The final clash came in 1717, with the attack on Benjamin Hoadly, then bishop of Bangor and the very model of a Whig and Latitudinarian bishop, for preaching that the truth and efficacy of religion were matters for private judgment and that, under the titular and non-interventionist headship of Christ, there was no justification for a visible church empowered to determine orthodoxy and to excommunicate, or even for its hierarchy. To check the mounting assault on Hoadly, the Crown prorogued convocation before business could be transacted. This act was repeated yearly, with one futile exception in 1741, until 1855. But if Hoadly's sermon and the ensuing "Bangorian Controversy" were the occasion for the suspension of convocation, a more fundamental cause was "the open scandal of its internal dissensions."[7]

≺ II ≻

By 1720, then, the Church had repeatedly distanced itself from Rome and had tried, ineffectually, to combat an assumed threat from heterodoxy—both challenges from tiny minorities whose danger loomed far larger in perception than it did in immediate actuality. The church was more successful in asserting its distinctiveness and prerogatives when contending with the much larger minority of Dissenters. Churchmen were unanimous in asserting the necessity of Christian unity and saw separation (and the toleration that flowed from it) as an unfortunate and perhaps temporary expedient, inescapable for those in the gathered churches but surmountable for others by reasoned argument and the passage of time.

A major political consequence of separation was the practice of occasional conformity. Some Dissenters attended services in the parish church out of sentimental attachment or as a way of clinging to the idea of a national church, even though they were excluded from it. But a practical reason for the custom lay in those provisions of the Corporation Act of 1661 and the Test Act of 1673 which required anyone holding office to take communion in the established church; the taking of communion by men who were not regular attenders at Anglican services thus became the means of qualifying for office in violation of the spirit if not the letter of the laws, and some enterprising London clergymen brazenly set themselves up to provide the requisite certificates. To those with truly scrupulous minds, occasional conformity was abhorrent as a profanation of the sacrament for political ends; and the emerging high-church party was determined to prohibit it. The Whigs were sufficiently beholden to their dissenting constituencies to secure the defeat in the House of Lords of bills against occasional conformity in 1702, 1703, and 1704. But in 1711, weakened by an election the previous year and needing dissident Tory support in their attack on the impending peace of Utrecht, the Whigs abandoned their old obligation and accepted a somewhat milder bill. For seven years thereafter, the Occasional Conformity Act made a Dissenter who attended a conventicle after qualifying for office-holding in an Anglican church liable to a fine of £40 and disqualification from office until he had conformed without attendance elsewhere for a year, during which communion must be taken three times.

A second Tory and high-church campaign was mounted against the dissenting academies, those institutions that had arisen as alternatives to the grammar schools and to Oxford and Cambridge, which after 1662 demanded subscription to the Thirty-nine Articles.

Taking both lay and divinity students, the academies were training grounds for future generations of dissenting ministers and congregational leaders. Educationally conservative in their early years of precarious existence, they have an imposing reputation in educational history that was earned largely in the eighteenth century. In the heated imaginations of high churchmen, they were nurseries of sedition. Charles Leslie, one of the most vituperative of the Nonjuror publicists, saw their sole purpose as "the education of youth in all the poisonous principles of fanaticism and faction, and to debauch them with the corrupted maxims of republicanism"; while Henry Sacheverell, the notorious high-church preacher, denounced them as seminaries "wherein *Atheism, Deism, Tritheism, Socinianism,* with all the *Hellish Principles* of *Fanaticism, Regicide,* and *Anarchy,* are openly *Profess'd,* and *Taught,* to *Corrupt* and *Debauch* the *Youth* of the *Nation,* in all *Parts* of it, down to *Posterity.*"[8] In 1714 the Schism Act passed by a handsome margin in the Commons, though by a mere seven votes in the Lords, where five bishops formally protested its passage. Thereafter, all schoolmasters were required to hold an episcopal license which in turn demanded a sacramental test and entire abstention from dissenting worship. That Queen Anne died on the day the act was to come into force, with the consequence that it was never applied, entered into dissenting consciousness as a divine judgment. Both the Occasional Conformity Act and the Schism Act were repealed in 1718, though the delay of four years after the Hanoverian succession and the decision of Archbishop Wake, one of the protestors in 1714, to oppose repeal showed that toleration even among sympathetic churchmen remained strictly limited.

The first impression that comes from an overview of the high-church initiative in the generation between 1689 and 1718 is one of fundamental weakness. Their more extreme partisans could briefly attract wide popular support with the reiterated cry of "the church in danger," the best instance being the lionization of the shallow and intemperate Sacheverell. On 5 November 1709, in St. Paul's Cathedral before the lord mayor of London, Sacheverell preached a sermon excoriating in carefully calculated language the "false brethren" who put the Church in peril—not only Dissenters and Latitudinarians but low churchmen and Whig politicians—and seemed to question the very foundation of the Glorious Revolution. The Whig government incautiously launched an impeachment against Sacheverell but could obtain no penalty beyond a three-year suspension from preaching and the public burning of the offending sermon. In the rioting that punctuated Sacheverell's trial early in 1710 and the demonstrations that followed, a number of dissenting meeting houses were attacked and burned. But the steady constituency of such hotheads was small, and in the long run their tactics were self-defeating. Still, as secular needs sometimes served ecclesiastical purposes, the period of Tory ascendancy from 1710 to 1714 produced the Occasional Conformity Act, the Schism Act, an act for the construction of fifty new churches in London, and the extension of toleration to Episcopalians in Presbyterian Scotland, where, suppressed since the Revolution, they had displayed marked Jacobite leanings.[9]

The Church itself offered obstacles to the high-church agenda. Latitudinarianism persisted, and, while the bishops offered a range of political and theological coloration, they were generally sympathetic to the idea of limited toleration and prudential in their policy.[10] If in the practical world the Whigs were less powerful stays of the dissenting cause than Anglican myth allowed, those obligations had still to be reckoned with, while the anti-church and even anti-Christian tendencies of some of the more advanced Whigs were only an extreme formulation of a more generally diffused anticlericalism. In addition, lay control of many ecclesiastical appointments and the jurisdictional patchwork of the countryside inhibited the imposition of any monolithic standard.

A slow deposit of preferences, assumptions, and reactions during the first half of the eighteenth century nevertheless justifies the view that one can trace through the years of the Whig ascendancy the emerging rationale, and to some extent the reality, of a confessional state.[11] It is perilously easy, because of the violence and opportunism that emerged in the high-church campaign in Anne's reign, to overlook the extent to which those chiefly responsible for the Church were concerned for her welfare, prerogatives, and place in both the divine economy and civil society. Wake's preoccupation with the concerns and prerogatives of the Church quickly cost him his influence within the government on policy and appointments;

in this he was succeeded by Gibson, but he in turn lost power. Gibson had long been denounced by high-church and even moderately Tory clergy for his service to Sir Robert Walpole, whose brilliant, cynical manipulation of the machinery of politics kept him at the pinnacle of power for two decades. But successive appointments of Whig bishops only masked Gibson's determined opposition to Latitudinarians, which alienated him from the court; while his jealous defense of the Church's interests led him to oppose dissenting efforts to secure repeal of the test and corporation acts in 1732–33 and to obstruct the Quakers' tithe bill of 1736. It was the latter that brought the growing tension between Gibson and Walpole into the open, robbing the bishop of his role as the government's ecclesiastical adviser and ruining his prospects for translation to Canterbury.[12] If two such consummate scholars and cautious ecclesiastical statesmen as Wake and Gibson could sacrifice their political power and advancement to their prior loyalty to the Church, how much more distress and alienation can one imagine among the concerned, fearful, and less cosmopolitan occupants of country rectories?

Yet the Church was not immobilized by fear or prejudice. That same half century saw a dramatic alteration in the forms of church defense, a change that can be measured by comparing two works famous in their time. The most authoritative early statement of the claims of the Church was *A Discourse on Church Government*, published in 1707 by the Rev. John Potter, chaplain to the queen and later archbishop of Canterbury. Equally inimical, as an admiring Victorian editor saw it, to the pretensions of Rome and the democratic spirit that had paralyzed the Church since the Reformation, Potter's book "breathes the spirit of that primitive age when the church of Christ was still governed by truth and principle,"[13] truth and principle that Potter set out to recover for his own time. The church was not, he argued in contrast to Locke, a voluntary society resembling "a society of philosophers, where many useful and excellent truths are taught; but no man is obliged to come into it, or to continue in it." Rather, it is a divinely mandated institution, as is evident from the testimony of Scripture and in the organization of the primitive church. It must function as an organic whole, from which no subordinate part can be removed without suffering death. Potter used the apostolic equality of bishops to undercut Roman claims of papal primacy; and he also insisted, against the Quakers and religious radicals, that the visible church was necessary, as was the need for public support of its hierarchy and priesthood. All this was argued with a wealth of learning and a sense of authority that flowed naturally from a church Potter saw at the center of things. To that church and the form of Christianity it espoused there could be no legitimate alternative in England.

A generation later, in 1736, a country rector, William Warburton—a lawyer by training, a *littérateur* by preference, and a future bishop of Gloucester—published *The Alliance between Church and State; or, The Necessity and Equity of an Established Religion and a Test Law, demonstrated from the essence and end of Civil Society, upon the fundamental principles of the Law of Nature and Nations.* All nations throughout history, Warburton insisted, have found an established religion necessary; like Potter, he was seeking its grounds and limits. He assumed a division of powers—civil society is concerned with the body, religious society with the soul—but each is defective without what the other can offer, and so the two freely negotiate an alliance or union. The magistrate desires the alliance because he knows that, without the restraints of religion, men would run wild; the Church, however, can moderate passions, enforce morality, bring about greater reverence for the magistrate, and, by assuring the purity of religion, secure the identity of truth and utility. Moreover, linkage with the Church would spare the magistrate the awkwardness of an independent religious society that might (like the Quakers or other religious radicals) oppose defensive war or magistracy itself, or (like the Catholics) advocate celibacy and asceticism, or (like the Catholic religious orders) create powerful bonds between clergy and people that could be used to draw vast wealth to the Church.

In return, the Church gets security and a settled income, jurisdictional authority for the "coactive power" of its courts ("coercive power" in subsequent editions) for the enforcement of morality, and a share in the legislature through the seating of its bishops in Parliament. The Church's terms are modest. It asks neither for great wealth or honors, nor for the help of the state in forcible conversion: there is to be a toleration within strict limits set by the existence of a test law, the requirement that all without distinction contribute to the upkeep of the established church, and the denial of public maintenance to dissenting ministers. Indeed, in the transactional ethos that permeates the *Alliance*, the existence of a test law, by preventing parliamentary or administrative challenge to establishment, is both the price and the guarantee of toleration; and so the Dissenters, though they might act otherwise, had every reason to be grateful for its existence.

Warburton insisted that though he might illustrate from English example his account of the alliance was based "solely on the contemplation of nature, and the unvariable reason of things"; that the law of nature was so perfectly mirrored in English institutions as they had emerged in the eighteenth century was a happy accident—a contention that has resulted in a certain bemusement among scholars. Nevertheless Warburton's alliance, viewed coldly, looks more like a submission than a treaty between equals. Moreover the universalist premises of Warburton's book ironically leave the magistrate to define the Church as merely the largest of the religious societies in his dominions. Accordingly, the truth the established church will maintain is relative; there is not even any assurance that its religion will be Christian, let alone Anglican. Yet Warburton's argument managed to carry conviction for the better part of the century.

Warburton would surely have seen little difference between his view and Potter's view of the church and the place of dissent, but the mode of argument, and some of the consequences, come from a different world. Potter supported his case with biblical texts that set out God's commands and Jesus's expectations, and by expounding the early Christian polity as it could be deduced from biblical accounts of the activities of the apostles. For Warburton and his readers, authority lay not so much in the Bible as in the self-evident force of abstractions like contract, self-interest, utility, and happiness. Accordingly, liberty plays an increasingly important part in successive editions of Warburton's book. In all of them security for the temporal liberty and property of men is seen as the end of civil society, but Warburton also refers (in the first edition of 1736) to "a general Spirit of Liberty" that "has began [sic] to prevail," and that has changed the public cry from the Church in danger—less and less persuasive as religion lost influence—to fears about violations of the law of nature and danger to civil rights. In the second edition of

1741, Warburton rebutted his critics on several heads—the appropriateness of his theorizing, the legitimacy of religion's serving a state "founded on the Principles of the natural Rights and Liberties of Mankind," and a proper assessment of liberty. "We live in a Time when the Principles of Public Liberty are well understood," he declared, but the danger lies in the overreaching that comes from licentiousness. He concludes with a long quotation from Francis Hare, lately Bishop of Chichester, warning against "this *boundless* Liberty . . . which hath laid waste Religion far and wide and hath spread thro' all Ranks of People a Contempt for every Thing that is *sacred* . . ."[14] In the third edition, seven years later, Hare's cautionary words had been dropped, and Warburton maintains that the general spirit of liberty "hath prevailed," and that the charge of violating the laws of nature has receded, leaving the universal cry the danger to civil liberties.

By the fourth edition in 1766, Warburton had been moved to a yet wider view of liberty by Jean-Jacques Rousseau's contention that Christianity meant slavery. Warburton's appeal is to St. Paul: "Where the spirit of the Lord is, there is Liberty." True, Paul was alarmed by the threat to Christianity arising from the belief of some early Christians that civil slavery was dissolved by simple conversion; and he ordered his restive coreligionists to abide by their callings, yet "ye are bought with a Price; be ye not servants [or slaves] of men," a text that, in Warburton's gloss, places so high a value on the dignity of human life bought with Christ's passion that the redeemed must never rest content with slavery when "without violating the established rights of society, it is in their power to become free." The liberty enjoined by the gospel is, then, civil as well as religious, and must bring both freedom of enquiry and free exercise of conscience in its train: a grand and elevated mind, a sublime sentiment, a consciousness of the dignity of our nature, which alike follow from the gospel and the spirit of the Lord, "will ever be pushing us on to the attainment and preservation of those CIVIL RIGHTS, which we have been taught by reason to know are ours; and which we have been made to feel by experience, are . . . the most indispensable to human happiness." This argument, potentially so corrosive of the exclusive church polity Warburton was at pains to defend, marks a considerable advance on Potter and Hare or on Archbishop Wake's lament in 1728 that the country was "so afraid of the least tendency to persecution, that we cannot bear the least restraint. It is a sad case that we cannot keep in the middle way, and allow what is fit to be published, or may be read without reproach, but at the same time both restrain and punish what is openly blasphemous and tends to the ruin of all religion and indeed of all respect for every thing that is either pious or serious." [15] But Warburton's ambition remained the creation of "a State of *sober* and *perfect Liberty*," and he drew back from any possible extreme conclusions. As fruits are at their most perfect when nearest to decay, he says, so liberty is subject to abuse, and he turns from Paul to Peter to remind Christians that (another transaction) they received their liberty in exchange for becoming servants of God, a relationship that must be reflected in obedience to earthly masters—fear God, honour the king. The complacency of Tillotson, the calm assumption of Potter, and the unease of Wake had been reconciled and triumphantly raised to a principle. [16]

≺ III ≻

Dissenters lagged behind the Church in attempting to define their place in the English religious scene. Confused and fearful that they might again be plunged into proscription and repression, they had to locate themselves not only against the Church (and of course Rome) but against each other; and it is hardly surprising that, practicing their religion on no more than sufferance, they should resort increasingly to the language of rights.

The Presbyterians were the largest segment of dissent; their ministers made up nearly sixty per cent of those who took advantage of the indulgence of 1672, and it has been calculated that in the early eighteenth century, the 637 Presbyterian congregations in England were only slightly less than the number of Quaker meetings but were three times as numerous as Congregationalist (also known as Independent) or Baptist congregations. The total dissenting strength was almost 340,000, something over six per cent of the whole, though there was considerable regional variation. [17]

Presbyterian strength in numbers, however, masks the damage

done to them during the Restoration. Although the Quakers had been the greatest sufferers from persecution, they seemed collectively to thrive on it, strengthened by their belief in the "inner light." Congregationalists and Baptists—separatists and sectarians—also gained cohesion during the persecution; a toleration was the dispensation that fitted best with the tendency to exuberant variety inherent in the gathered churches. But the Presbyterians, wedded to the ideal of a national church, were certain that, if their preferred means of governance by presbyteries and synods was unobtainable, some modification of episcopacy and liturgy could bring about a comprehensive establishment in which they would assume a rightful place. Instead, the Act of Uniformity was far more restrictive than they could have expected and the hostility and ill-treatment they experienced forced them increasingly into the congregational mold of the gathered churches, whose Calvinism they shared but whose discipline and insistence on testimony to experience they were far less likely to impose on their members. Moreover, they had lost some of their ablest leaders after 1660: the aristocracy and gentry deserted them almost completely, and over time many sons and daughters of Presbyterian families were to defect to the establishment.

The centrifugal forces that hampered dissenting unity almost from the moment of public recognition of the right of dissent to exist were illustrated by the rapid collapse of the attempt to establish the "Happy Union" of London Congregationalists and Presbyterian ministers in 1690–91,[18] and in the Salters' Hall controversy in 1719. The Unitarian and Deistic storms that had so shaken the Church at the end of the seventeenth century had left dissent, isolated as it was, relatively untouched; but sensibilities were sharply challenged by the publication in 1712 of Samuel Clarke's *Scripture-Doctrine of the Trinity*, an exhaustive collation of every biblical text that might bear on the question of the Trinity. Clarke, the rector of St. James's Westminster, concluded that true divinity, self-generated and independent, was to be ascribed only to God the Father: though the Son is divine and pre-existent, that existence, like His power, is derived from the Father; the Holy Spirit, also a creation of the Father, is subordinate to Him in all things and to the Son in most. Therefore only the Father is a proper object of worship. As Clarke was recognized as one of the ablest theologians of his time, the position that the eighteenth century came to know as "Arian" could scarcely have had a more authoritative exposition, and it troubled orthodox Dissenters as much as Anglicans.

The Salters' Hall controversy grew out of the eager interest of some Exeter Academy students in Clarke's book—students who had already been secretly in touch with Whiston, the Cambridge Arian. They were found out, and by 1716 doubts were widespread about the orthodoxy not only of the academy but of the ministers to the three Presbyterian meetings in the town. When a clear statement on the Trinity was demanded from the most prominent of the ministers and he replied with an evasive sermon and a plea for toleration, and when further efforts to resolve matters got nowhere, the question was referred to the London ministers, a traditional appeal of recognized weight. When the ministers met at Salters' Hall, a proposal to accompany the requested advices to Exeter with a declaration for the Trinity was lost by 57 to 53. But the moderator of the meeting assured the Exeter Dissenters that the advices came from men sound on the question of the Trinity, and scholars since have supported that judgment, arguing that if the Trinity had been truly at issue, the vote would have gone the other way. What the division was really about was the self-sufficient authority of the Bible, open to individual interpretation without the aid of creeds or other human formulations: one observer caught the point in a much-quoted comment that "The Bible carried it by four." Benjamin Hoadly's summary was characteristic—the meetings at Salters' Hall, he said, marked the first time since the apostles that a meeting of divines had carried a question for liberty.[19]

Longstanding divergences between Presbyterian and Congregationalists persisted. The Presbyterians continued to drift not only toward Arianism but toward Arminianism, the rejection of Calvinistic predestination. There were other differences as well. Although Presbyterians were by then congregational in organization, the internal structure of their congregations tended to be hierarchical rather than democratic. Moreover, they tended to set ministers apart from their congregations, in keeping with the tradition of a learned ministry, and worried that virtually anyone who could gain a congregation and a license could set up as a minister—hence the much greater value Presbyterians placed on the practice of ordination. Then, too, Presbyterians seemed to opt instinctively for breadth as against narrowness: they were more willing to meet and discuss across boundaries; they displayed a greater worldliness that extended to such minor secular pleasures as dancing, wine, and card playing; and their usually greater wealth and higher social position were evident in their architecture. Daniel Defoe observed that in Ipswich the Presbyterian meeting house was "as large and as fine a building of that kind as most on this side of England, and the inside the best finished of any I have seen, London not excepted," while the Independents' chapel, handsome and new though it was, was "not as gay or so large as the other."[20]

These distinctions did not, however, lead at once to a basic fracturing of dissent. Members of a congregation of one inclination frequently attended the chapel of the other, while in many smaller towns a single dissenting chapel ministered to all persuasions. So long as theological considerations were muted or suppressed, diverging tendencies remained only tendencies, and prudence as well as taste was served by the preference of the time (shared with Anglican Latitudinarians) for sermons on "practical" moral subjects.

Down to about the middle of the century, Dissenters maintained this posture of uneasy accommodation. Outwardly, they obtained a wider, if still measured, toleration, bounded, as most Anglicans insisted, by the basic laws—the Act of Uniformity, the Corporation Act, the Test Act, and the Toleration Act. Acceptance of toleration was easier for Anglicans because, as Wake had recognized in opposing the legislation of 1718, dissent appeared to be shrinking in numbers.[21] In time the law became more expansive, though not fundamentally so. Leaving aside the special provisions made for the Quakers, the principal legislative increase in toleration is usually thought to have come through the indemnity acts passed fairly regularly (not, as is often said, annually) from 1726—acts generally taken as forgiving failure to take the sacrament to qualify for office under the Test Act and the Corporation Act. In fact, the indemnity acts were aimed at reconciling the Corporation Act, which required taking communion within a year *prior to* election, with the Test Act, in which the requirement was within three months *after* entering office; thus the indemnity acts benefited primarily Angli-

cans.[22] That Dissenters held office prior to 1828 in impressive numbers is, then, due less to the indemnity acts than to a statute of
limitations (in effect) contained in an act of 1718 dealing with corporations. Although the fine for holding office when unqualified
was set at a draconian £500, the six months allowed for prosecution
came to be seen as a limit after which prosecution was not to be
undertaken.[23]

The granting of toleration brought the Dissenters themselves
into action to protect what they had gained and, possibly, to extend
it. Here pride of place belongs to the Quakers. Quakers were admitted to the benefits of the act of 1689, though some had argued that
they, like the Catholics and the Unitarians, should be excluded:
their refusal to swear oaths made them suspect, and the advice and
support given by their great leader William Penn to James II had not
been forgotten. In the committee on sufferings—established in 1675
to help well-disposed authorities to moderate the persecutions and
to bring cohesion to isolated groups of Quakers through the sharing
of experience—the Quakers had a weapon of considerable defensive
importance; they could not only influence the modification or rejection of bills in Parliament, but when something favorable was done,
bring it to the attention of their congregations and muster electoral
support for their friends; they could also guard against prejudicial
administration of the laws.

The first successful Quaker agitation was mounted to soften the
statutory requirement in the act of 1689 to take oaths, a matter on
which Quakers took the biblical text "Swear not at all" literally.
Mustering influential support brought success early in 1696, with
an act allowing Quakers to affirm in all circumstances when oaths
were required, though they were still excluded from giving evidence
in criminal cases, serving on juries, or holding government office.
The act was renewed in 1702 and made perpetual in 1715, after
which a new campaign culminated in an act of 1722 that reduced
the wording of the affirmation to a simple declaration, with no reference to the "presence of Almighty God," a phrase that had troubled some Quakers and in defense of which the Church fought a
bitter but unsuccessful battle. The extraordinary political sophisti-
cation which the Quakers had developed was not uniformly successful. A bill instituting relief from prosecution for non-payment of

tithe passed the House of Commons in 1736 but was defeated in the Lords, where the powerful opposition of the bishops was brought to bear.

The other dissenting denominations followed at some distance behind the Quakers, both in initiating political action and in the success that attended it. Despite their theological differences, a deputation of Presbyterians, Congregationalists, and Baptists joined together to present addresses to the sovereign and from the early eighteenth century a loose grouping of metropolitan ministers emerged; but only in 1727 did the three boards of London ministers agree to formal creation of the Protestant Dissenting Ministers of the Three Denominations, with a joint committee for regular business. In October 1732 laymen were brought into planning for the repeal of the Test and Corporation Acts, and the new body came to be known as the Dissenting Deputies. Although the Deputies failed to get those acts repealed, they did remarkable service in dealing with local grievances—unjust persecutions, magistrates who denied registration to chapels, the refusal of parish clergymen to allow Dissenters to be buried in churchyards, and even disputes within congregations. Although in time the divisions within dissent were to shatter them, the Deputies were an important unifying element in the eighteenth century and a means of assuring some reality in detail to a grudging policy of toleration.[24]

In 1748, Archbishop Thomas Herring, who came from a dissenting background, wrote that "nothing in the world is more contrary to my judgment of things than to make alterations in our establishment, of which in some sense the toleration act is a part; and what I am determined to stick to, is the support of these two in conjunction. I think philosophy, Christianity, and policy are all against changes."[25] A delightful revelation of the temper of an age about to pass away, the archbishop's remarks reiterated the nearly unanimous view of early eighteenth-century Anglicans that, while toleration had an agreed place, that place was to be kept within narrow limits—a view not yet compromised by Warburton's tentative resort to the language of liberty. But the scope of toleration had increased over the years since 1689, even though this was more *de facto* than *de jure*.

Some credit must be given to the general inclination of the

Whigs who dominated government in the generation after 1715, though they were as determined as Herring to avoid fundamental change. Local culture and tradition had varying but important effects. There was, for example, a strong dissenting presence in the London corporation. These were the years, moreover, when provincial society was beginning to enter into its greatest age in the reign of George III; and in at least parts of provincial England, as well as in London, dissent played a part out of all proportion to its numbers in the population as a whole. Local variations were the rule. Over against London or Bristol had to be set Anglican Liverpool; the key role played by Dissenters over a century of municipal life in Nottingham was certainly not replicated in the utterly Tory corporation of neighboring Leicester. In Bridport, where Dissenters were given a notable presence on the corporation when James II reconstructed it in 1687, membership in the corporation came to be concentrated in a single congregation, which by the end of the century was thoroughly Unitarian.[26]

Though the incidence of dissenting political power, like the pattern of petty discrimination, might vary from place to place, the visual evidence that survives in the chapels attests to the nearly universal presence of an aware and confident dissent. A few congregations can trace a continuous history back to 1672 or even earlier, but most originated in 1689 or the years immediately after. Some early congregations met in houses or barns or in former chapels-of-ease put at their disposal. The buildings erected immediately after the Revolution bespeak an understandable uncertainty and fear, given memories of recent persecution; their modesty testifies to humble beginnings and their form to prudence. In rural areas and small towns, chapels built to resemble farm houses are still to be seen, in Knutsford (1689) and Dean Row (c. 1690) in Cheshire, for example. The similarly domestic meeting house in Macclesfield (1690) is tucked away behind other buildings, difficult to find and hard to approach through narrow passageways; the grand chapel at Ipswich (1700) admired by Defoe is nevertheless recorded as having a peephole, while Lydgate Chapel at New Mill in Yorkshire (1695) is said to have been built on a slight rise so that during divine service a lookout could be kept against the advance of a mob. And physical attack was not the only fear: the trust deeds of some con-

gregations contained provisions for disposing of their assets should
toleration be revoked. By contrast, the chapels built after 1720 proclaim security and prosperity alike. They are large, prominently
placed, and lighted by broad windows by then less likely to be broken. They were, moreover, instantly recognizable as chapels, with
their boxy classical shapes and their orientation to a long wall rather
than a chancel at the east end, to emphasize the centrality of
preaching.[27]

In 1645, in what is now Atherton, in Lancashire, a small brick
chapel was built on land belonging to John Atherton, a squire so
benevolent and supportive that no one thought about a lease. Dissenting worship continued there throughout the Restoration and
into the new century. Then, in 1715, the minister, "General" James
Wood—the grandson of a minister ejected in 1662 and the son of a
minister "silenced" in 1662 and imprisoned in 1670—raised a vol-
unteer force that fought successfully against the pretender at the
Battle of Preston, an act never forgiven by Richard Atherton, a fif-
teen-year-old Jacobite who would soon inherit the estate. When he
reached his majority in 1721, Atherton turned the congregation out;
two years later he had the chapel consecrated as the first Anglican
church in the neighborhood. But the evicted congregation raised a
large, handsome, elegantly appointed meeting house, Chowbent
Chapel, that testifies not only to prosperity but to proud defiance.[28]
Chowbent is a useful symbol for early eighteenth-century dissent:
distinctive, secure, accepting of and willing to defend its place in the
constitution of church and state, devoted to the ruling dynasty, and
supportive of a government whose principles it shared and whose
practices it understood. In the words of Edmund Calamy, Dissenters
acknowledged

a conscientious Subjection to the Government they live under (be it in
one Form or another) to be the Duty of all Christians: and pay such Deference to the Magistrate, even in Ecclesiastical Matters, as to be ready
to give him Satisfaction, that they take no Methods that are destructive
to Civil Peace. Nor have they any Notions opposite to Absolute Passive
Obedience and Nonresistance, but such as are common to them with the
best Friends both to the Government of King *William*, and the Protestant
Succession.[29]

Consistently with these words, Philip Doddridge, perhaps the most
respected and influential Dissenter of his time, helped raise a force

in 1745 to fight another pretender. The Warburtonian transaction
had been completed.

≺ IV ≻

Toleration and religious liberty were terms used more or less inter-
changeably in the decades after 1689. Historians since have tended
to follow that practice: thus A. J. Carlyle, writing in 1924, insisted
that, in principle if not in all details, "the victory of toleration is
marked by the Toleration Act of 1689."[30] But, as I have tried to argue,
principle, like God, may be in the details.

The catastrophes that created the religious situation in the late
seventeenth century were succeeded by a period of subtler change
that brought toleration closer to reality by the middle of the eighteenth century. The transition from toleration to liberty, from civil
religion to a glimmer of true ecumenicism, from monopoly to market is founded on fundamental change that may once more be illuminated by a geological metaphor, drawn not from a long-dead clergyman but from modern plate-tectonic theories. What faults, then,
may be discovered beneath the surface of the Warburtonian land-
scape? There were, I think, three: a devotional shift in English religion; the tension between faith and reason; and the emergence of a
new intellectual style.

The Warburtonian synthesis was soon threatened by powerful
new impulses to piety and pastoral concern. Even though we should
remember that Georgian churchmen, whatever their limitations in
the eyes of their Victorian successors, had their own serious standards of churchmanship and cure of souls, no formal religious organization has been able to absorb or withstand a sweeping pietistic
movement without the danger of breaking, and such a moment came
to both the church and dissent in the middle of the eighteenth century. Fifty years earlier a burst of enthusiasm for spreading the Gospel
both inside and outside England had given rise to the Society for the
Propagation of the Gospel, the Society for Promoting Christian
Knowledge, the charity school movement, and individual or group efforts within the church for the intensification of faith and the reformation of manners.[31] The Non-jurors, austere and untempted by
power, produced an ethos and a literature of devotion, of which

William Law was the presiding genius, while within the high-church wing of the Establishment, small religious societies, groups of like-minded friends, and devout members in isolation sought through prayer, self-examination, and mutual reinforcement to lead truly holy lives. None of these movements or organizations disappeared; but as so often happens, the vital force lessened, what had been exceptional became routine, and, no doubt discouraged by the failure of their example, individuals turned in even more upon themselves. William Law ended in mysticism.

From the 1730s, however, a new current of devotion and piety flowed with increasing strength. It came in part from the impact of continental pietistic movements, notably the Moravians. It was spread by the revivalism and field preaching that had begun in Wales as early as 1714 and that, with almost incalculable results, was taken up in England by George Whitefield and John Wesley in the great Methodist movement. Methodism, in contrast to Calvinism, was committed to the Arminian view that no one was shut out from salvation for all eternity; but among the other Dissenters, still largely Calvinist, and even among the Methodists themselves, the preoccupation with the drama of sin and salvation led to a rebirth, or re-emergence, of attitudes reminiscent of Puritanism. The Church had been negotiating a difficult but well-charted passage between the Scylla of superstition and the Charybdis of enthusiasm; now confronting a new, unalloyed enthusiasm, Anglicans reacted uncertainly and sometimes violently. Wesley himself was repeatedly set upon, and Methodists became regular targets of mob action, frequently at the instigation of clerical opponents.[32] Many Dissenters felt the same distrust of enthusiasm, but among them, too, a new spirituality and evangelism reversed the decline of the early part of the century. The Independents gave dissent perhaps its greatest encouragement in the new piety, through the preaching and writing of Philip Doddridge, especially his *Rise and Progress of Religion in the Soul* (1745), and the magnificent and moving hymns of Isaac Watts. In numbers, if not in immediate influence, the Presbyterians were the losers: some Presbyterian congregations disappeared and others split (usually to the benefit of the Independents), in almost every instance mirroring distinctions in wealth, education, and social position.

The second great fault system was an increasingly irreconcilable clash between faith and reason. A succession of intellectual triumphs could be ascribed to the exercise of unfettered reason, Newton's physics and Locke's psychology prime among them; encouraged by such examples, the spirit of inquiry spread and a crisis of authority spread with it. But the conflict cannot be understood in the confident simplicities that the Victorians invoked in their talk of warfare between science and religion: the reality is riddled with exceptions and ambiguities. There was, for example, a rational piety of great profundity and force: the passionate devotion to Christianity of that consummate rationalist Joseph Priestley was incomprehensible to his philosophical admirers on the Continent, and to some in England, while his preoccupation with eschatology (questions concerned with divine judgment and eternal damnation) has continued to trouble scholars, though in him, as in most adherents of rational religion, these seeming opposites were entirely integrated. On the evangelical side, it is possible to find religious experience that can rightly be equated with mere simple-minded assertion or with the overwhelming force of experience; but in the hands of Bishop Joseph Butler, who as a pupil at a dissenting academy had corresponded with Samuel Clarke, the testimony was far more subtle. For him, the book of nature was there to be read, but the difficulties inherent in the exercise were analogous to the difficulties of revelation, a hurdle to be surmounted only with the aid of faith. Neither pure reason nor blind credence swept the field in England.

The conflict of Evangelical and Latitudinarian within the Church is well enough known not to need attention here. I select, rather, two instances from dissent, both from Independency, to illustrate the subtle interplay of reason and faith. In one case, the result was a kind of paralysis of will; in the other, a paradoxical advance in the spirit of liberty.

The principal dissenting chapels in Leeds were Call Lane and Mill Hill. Though the former was Independent and the latter Presbyterian, they had a long history of cooperation. When Call Lane was being built in 1691, both congregations worshipped at Mill Hill, and exchange of pulpits remained a regular feature of congregational life. Members went to both places of worship, even though Mill Hill followed a heterodox path.

Joseph Ryder, a master clothier and a devout man of very ordinary intellect, was forced to confront his understanding of the Bible with the insistence of Thomas Walker, the minister at Mill Hill, for a free rein for reason and full liberty of judgment. Surely, Ryder wrote in his diary in 1748, there must be some rule to apply in a disagreement to find which party is wrong. Of a sermon toward the end of 1751, he wrote, "To hear the doctrines which our pious forefathers suffered for, but not only so, such doctrines as the Scriptures, in my apprehension of things, appear clearly to hold forth—in a manner confuted—it gives me great concern." In 1755, when a visiting preacher at Mill Hill recommended charity for those who differ from us, Ryder wondered "how all things can be right." When works were named as the condition of God's acceptance he commented: "Free mercy through a Redeemer is what I have put my confidence in," while another member saw this as taking the crown from the head of Jesus and putting it on the minister's own. Ryder did not take much part in disputes about the imputed righteousness of Christ and about the Trinity, for which a friend rebuked him; but, he said, "I consider if one is not duly furnished with convincing arguments, I rather choose to say little than to make ill words on questions such as the greatest divines cannot bring down to our reason, being above reason."

Ryder was unsettled in other directions as well. When a Baptist minister baptized several people in the River Aire in 1760, Ryder noted it as "a transaction unknown at Leeds to the greatest part of the inhabitants, if not to all . . . Sects and parties we have now in great numbers, and everyone perhaps think themselves to be right. What may be the issue of all is known only to God." When he first encountered a Methodist, in 1745, he was shaken by the idea that perfection was attainable in this life, "a doctrine which I was never before taught—neither do I find any ground to take it in." When he disputed with a Methodist woman some months later, he found her uncharitable, censorious, and unaccountably proof against "the calmest reasonings on my part." Repeatedly, he refused to go hear George Whitefield for fear of being deceived or "unhinged," and when he dared to try in 1766, he simply could make nothing of it: "What may be the issue of this new scheme in religion, God only knows." If pluralism is a precondition of tolerance, it was certainly to be found in Leeds. Ryder became tolerant by default—and was very unhappy about it.[33]

The second example concerns the dissenting academies which spread themselves across a spectrum. The most important of them, Doddridge's academy in Northampton, gives us a key insight into the interplay of piety and reason. All the instruction at Northampton was in English, a practice at only one academy before 1689; and while the tactic assured that the level of classical learning in the academies would not equal that of the universities, it also made recent writing readily accessible for teaching and discussion. Though he did not originate the method, Doddridge scrupulously laid competing theological interpretations before his students, encouraging them to make up their own minds. Doddridge's intellectual and religious model was the seventeenth-century divine, Richard Baxter, that "meer Catholick" advocate of a church (as against a sect) in which all men might unite; but in Doddridge a transition is underway from Catholic to catholic, where the typography encapsulates the history of fifty or a hundred years of intellectual life. Doddridge's methods and temper were bequeathed to successor academies, notably that established at Daventry in 1752, a year after Doddridge's death, at which Joseph Priestley was the first pupil to be enrolled. There in the divinity classes authors were read on both sides of every issue, and discussion covered "every question of much importance, such as Liberty and Necessity, the sleep of the soul, and all the articles of theological orthodoxy and heresy," with the tutor, Caleb Ashworth, taking the orthodox side and the subtutor, Samuel Gray, the heterodox side in an atmosphere of freedom and good temper. It is worth pointing out, too, that the larger chapels usually had more than one minister, often of different generations, so that the pulpits might speak pure Geneva in the morning and pure Westminster (Clarke's Westminster) in the afternoon.[34]

But there is more to be learned from Doddridge than his instinctive openness. In the dispute over the decline of the dissenting interest provoked by a pamphlet published in 1730 by Thomas Gough, a young Dissenter who later conformed, Doddridge made a vital contribution in his *Free Thoughts on the Most Probable Means of Reviving the Dissenting Interest*, published the same year. Gough had argued not only for inculcating greater awareness of the grounds for dissent but for fewer congregations and higher ministerial salaries, less disputation, more education and refinement, more gentleman-liness. But Doddridge would have none of Gough's urging that dissent be made more like the Church—a fight on that ground would never be won. The Dissenters, he maintained, must be taken as they are, deeply serious and moved by the meaning of the gospel scheme whose doctrines they feel working in their souls, "experimental subjects" that they want to hear dealt with seriously and tenderly. No pastor could abandon nine tenths of his people, so he must modify his liberty of expression to appeal to them; to be acceptable, the dissenting preacher "must be an evangelical, an experimental, a plain and affectionate preacher," a prescription Doddridge followed in the pulpit, in his congregation, and in his writings.

But, as the methods and results of his academy should lead one to expect, the ultimate end of preaching seems to be broader than many, then or now, might accept. Doddridge might reject "clandestine and hypocritical methods" of preaching liberty in order to undermine it, but he saw a clandestine purpose in preaching an evangelical, experimental faith. If religious experience can lead to bigotry and intolerance, then the fortress must be taken by sap, not storm. When the humbler members of the congregation hear the preacher advancing "a truly spiritual and experimental strain," yet in the rational and graceful manner "agreeable to the younger and politer part of our auditory," then they will not listen to seek out heresy but will put a favorable construction on ambiguous expressions and try to find as much orthodoxy as they can. And even if they suspect the worst, they will hope that "age and experience will perfect what is wanting; and that God will reveal it to us in his own time." Handsomely treated, free from hearing attacks on their "darling notions," certain that the great concerns of religion are being zealously pursued, their affection will grow, "and thus their bigotry will gradually wear away, till perhaps they come at last to embrace those more generous notions, from which they would at first have started back with horror." In Doddridge, evangelism for orthodox concerns was joined with evangelism for rational and liberal notions of Christianity, with a prudential eye for inherited prejudices, innate capacities, and congregational majorities. So sensitized, the experienced preacher not only could command all of his flock but might, in time, by subtly calculated methods, educate them.[35]

Doddridge's piety, not the less serious for its prudence, brings us to the third fault, related to evolving modes of piety and reason but, I believe, distinct from them: it has to do with what might be called intellectual style. To appreciate this shift in sensibility and mode of discourse requires a prior appreciation that something was happening to the conception of truth. Truth as correctness, with respect to creeds or to institutional mandate, appears to have been at an increasing discount,[36] but truth as consonance was flourishing—on the one side consonance to searing religious experience, on the other consonance to law as it was increasingly perceived to rule both nature and society. But neither of these notions was conducive to the widest conception of liberty. The foundation for that lay in the idea of truth as something never to be attained—in this world, at least—as a *terminus ad quem*, as an object of pursuit in which we can be sure of increasing approximation, of successive probable truths, without certainty of a final closing. Here was the opportunity, indeed the imperative, for debate and advocacy. This view was no monopoly of the rational Dissenters. It was an Anglican who proclaimed that "Science of all kinds is progressive; like the human mind of which it is the object, it shall never arrive at perfection upon earth; never can it be said this is all a man shall know. Christianity has this in common with other sciences; every age adds something to the discoveries of the preceding, and the counsels of God are deep and impenetrable enough to excite all the talents of mankind to the end of time."[37]

The censoriousness and lack of charity that so troubled Joseph Ryder in his encounter with the Methodist woman were to be found in areas far removed from her sort of experiential religion; by the end of the century a style that had been sedulously cultivated over a couple of generations was under attack. A number of scholars have recently called attention to politeness as a key ingredient in the culture of the early eighteenth century. By the middle and latter part of the century, however, the word candor has risen to a new prominence, and a cursory look at the eighteenth-century *Short-Title Catalogue* will confirm the increasing use of that word, or words related to it, in the publications of the time. But candor was coming to mean something more than the definition given by Dr. Samuel Johnson in his *Dictionary* (1747). The sweetness of temper, purity of mind, openness, ingenuity, and kindness that appear as definitions were, of course, qualities proclaimed or sought by all those candid inquirers and candid friends scattered across the fields of controversy. Today, however, our principal understanding of the word is a definition given in the *Oxford English Dictionary*: "freedom from reserve in one's statements, openness, frankness, ingenuousness, outspokenness," the first citation being to the pseudonymous pamphleteer Junius in 1769. The way was being opened to the preoccupation of nineteenth-century radicals with the "publication of opinions."[38] Here, then, was the making of a true marketplace of ideas, for which John Stuart Mill was to write the *summa*—not *On Tolerance*, but *On Liberty*.

◄ V ►

The place of Joseph Priestley in the history of science is of the first importance. He is scarcely less important in the history of English religion, standing as he does at the beginning of the continuous denominational history of English Unitarianism, a movement which, though a tiny remnant today, had immense social, political, and theological importance through much of the nineteenth century. A polymath of surprising range, even in a century noted for omnivorous intellects, he was the preeminent spokesman for rational, radical dissent, and no one was a more eloquent apostle for religious liberty.

An Arian from his student days at Daventry, in the 1770s Priestley took up Unitarian theology and polemics in earnest, with startling effect, but the controversies we shall examine here had less to do with Unitarianism than with dissent, less with theology and more with denominational and general politics. To be sure, Priestley's views on these matters were deeply rooted in his commitment to rationalism and to demystification as essential to a right understanding of Christianity, both historically and philosophically. More immediately important, however, was his experience as a tutor in languages and belles lettres at the Warrington Academy between 1761 and 1767.

At Warrington he struck out in a new direction with his famous lectures on English history, general history and policy, and the laws and constitution of England. His *Lectures on History and General Policy*, given at Warrington but not published until 1788, explains his early career as a controversialist. For gentlemen who would take an active part in civic life, Priestley thought, no more relevant or liberal mode of instruction could be found than history, especially when tied to civil policy, "such as the theory of laws, government, manufactures, commerce, naval force, &c. with whatever may be demonstrated from history to have contributed to the flourishing state of nations, to rendering a people happy and populous at home, and formidable abroad," the science of government being incomparably the most important of these. This explains why Priestley was engaged and depressed by political developments in the reign of George III. In his characteristically precipitous way he had already made the transition to the oppositionist stance that his fellow Dissenters were coming to more gradually, particularly as tensions with the American colonies mounted to war.[39] Against this background of increasingly troubling domestic politics, Priestley was led to think, by a succession of publications, that the damage inflicted by the king and his ministers on civil liberties was to be paralleled by a new attack on religious liberty, awakening memories of the legislative assaults on dissent of 1710–14.

In 1769 Priestley attacked the famous jurist, Sir William Blackstone, who, in the last volume of the *Commentaries* (1769), had maintained that nonconformity, whether by mere non-attendance or through "mistaken or perverse zeal," was an offense against the established church. Blackstone seemed to Priestley to be branding dissent as a crime, in startling contrast to a widely welcomed decision by the House of Lords in 1767, in which Lord Chief Justice Mansfield, the leading legal authority of the second half of the century, had praised the exercise of conscience, insisted that nonconformity cannot be criminal under natural law, and given the widest possible sweep to the Toleration Act. In reply, Blackstone apologized for a certain lack of caution and emphasized his support of conscience and toleration, but also reminded his attacker of the undoubted existence of the unrepealed criminal statutes touching on dissent. Priestley continued to deplore the suggestion of disloyalty and warned that it was "actually considered by many persons, as a notification to Dissenters, in what light they were considered by those who are now in power."[40]

The first major work of controversy, however, was the *Essay on the First Principles of Government*, published in 1768. The book is predominantly an argument about religious liberty, but the main discussion is marked by a thoughtful, fascinating, and original speculation about politics. The essay begins with a discussion of government, the great instrument of society's progress toward the perfection of the species, which Divine Providence in its beneficence has decreed. To attain the partial good that government, and government alone, can accomplish, men unite into society, abandoning a portion of their liberty, which is thus divided into two kinds: political liberty, the power to hold office or to choose those who do, and civil liberty, "that power over their own actions, which the members of the state reserve to themselves, and which their officers must not infringe." To some extent, the form of government is immaterial, but collective action is not in all instances superior to individual action. Where numbers can help individuals, then political society may appropriately intervene; but numbers are of little help in the managing of one's domestic affairs, while in the discovery of truth, it is invariably individuals who are called upon to assist the multitude. Education must be left to individual initiative; this allowed Priestley to incorporate earlier attacks on proposals for a uniform system of education, which struck him as Spartan rather than Athenian and smacked of the Schism Bill, "the most odious measure of the most odious ministry that ever sat at the helm of the British government."

Religion is the most important question setting bounds to civil government. The happy countries have been the tolerant ones, and the only alliance that can exist between religion and civil policy is the magistrate's equal protection of all forms of religion, any other "alliance between church and state" being only "the alliance of different sorts of worldly-minded men, for their temporal emolument." Indeed, Warburton appears to have posited a wretched bargain for the Church—in exchange for a protection it would probably have got anyhow, he subjected it to secular dictation in its own affairs. To be sure, ecclesiastical tyranny, like all other evils, is permitted by "the Divine Being, for wise and good ends . . . but he has given us a power to oppose them, and to guard ourselves against them . . . He makes use of men, as his instruments, both in establishing and removing all these abuses in ecclesiastical governments."

Priestley proposed some drastic changes in the established church, virtually abandoning the Thirty-nine Articles, making clerical stipends equal or proportional to the duties involved, removing the clergy from any role in civil affairs. But above all, toleration should be made complete, extending to Catholics, Deists, atheists, or whatever. Here, as he promised in his preface, he went well beyond Locke, though he was certain that, had Locke lived into the age of George III, he would have abandoned any restrictions on toleration. Priestley was, of course, sure that the Unitarianism he was bound by the very existence of religious freedom to propagate would ultimately carry off the victory, but he was quite willing to believe that at some distant time Unitarianism in its turn could be proved wrong, as might Christianity itself.[41]

In 1769, Priestley published *A View of the Principles and Conduct of the Protestant Dissenters with respect to the Civil and Ecclesiastical Constitution of England*, to demonstrate to the country at large that Dissenters were loyal subjects and that the pluralism they represented was productive of civil benefit. Later that year, in *A Free Address to Protestant Dissenters, as Such*, he set out to force Dissenters to "think and act in a manner worthy of their profession," to make that profession known in all its implications, and to lead those who hold it to *"rejoice that they are counted worthy to suffer shame* in so glorious a cause." The boldness of his hectoring provoked fears that the "precipitation, inattention to real life, and vehemence of temper" in Priestley's polemics might endanger the toleration that had been achieved, because this came "partly through the present state of our laws, and partly through the wisdom and mildness of administration." Further progress should be made, not by frontal assault, but "by mild and gentle methods, and by gradual and almost imperceptible steps." Priestley's slashing reply to this criticism was not an appealing performance, and the quarrel has importance only for an incidental result. In these publications of 1768–70, Priestley used various forms and combinations of the words religion, truth, liberty, virtue, and learning. After complimenting Priestley on his services to "truth, virtue, and religion," one critic complained about "the manner in which the Dissenting interest was continually represented . . . as the cause of truth, religion and liberty," a phrase "extremely vague and indeterminate," which, for want of precise ideas, might be taken to mean that those goods were to be found only among Dissenters, a claim both wrong and arrogant. But Priestley, delighted with the phrase, insisted that the triple cause was rightly associated with dissent. On 14 September 1786, Dr. Thomas Barnes, minister of Cross Street, Manchester, dedicated the new Manchester Academy "to TRUTH! to LIBERTY! to RELIGION!" This dedication was reaffirmed by Principal James Drummond in his opening address to Manchester College in 1885 and again in 1889 when the College moved to Oxford where, in 1891, the words were placed in stone over the doorway of the new buildings. The identification of truth, liberty, and religion became a rhetorical commonplace, and Priestley's certainty of their ultimate victory was to be found everywhere among the Unitarians—in ministers and laymen alike—as well as among a few ministers in other dissenting denominations.[42]

Additional arguments in favor of religious liberty may be chosen from the Church itself, in the writings of William Paley, who transmitted the completed moral wisdom of the eighteenth century to the nineteenth. Paley, like Warburton, defended establishments on grounds of utility, the justification as well for the maintenance of a separate class of learned men to interpret and transmit knowledge of the sacred texts. But he called for complete toleration for all Dissenters, including access to office, barring only some instances where political prudence might dictate otherwise, and then, as in the case of Roman Catholics, the restriction should be abrogated as soon as the political occasion for it should lose its force. Though he would make exceptions for ridicule or mockery of religious subjects, he otherwise advocated the widest circulation of ideas, for "truth results from discussion and from controversy; is investigated by the labours and researches of private persons. Whatever therefore, prohibits these, obstructs that industry and that liberty," and all persecution, all intolerance not only disgraces Christianity and vitiates public morals but encourages hypocrisy, hampers the quest for truth, and needlessly violates natural liberty. No one could maintain that Paley and Priestley were at one on all the specifics, but they were far closer on most specifics and (establishment apart) on the principles of liberty than either was to Warburton or even Locke.[43]

≺ VI ≻

"Modern religious liberty," it has been said, "emerges . . . not from the quarrel between Protestant and Catholic but rather from the bitter conflict between Protestant and Protestant."[44] One aspect of that bitter conflict has been the burden of this chapter, and we have seen steadily broader conceptions of religious liberty emerging from it. It is important, however, to remain aware that although theory was steadily advancing, the eighteenth century was not an age when the theory was reflected in a steady growth in liberal practice. Laws discriminating against Dissenters remained unrepealed, except for a concession in 1779 that relieved dissenting ministers of the requirement to subscribe certain of the Thirty-nine Articles. Dissenters could not matriculate at Oxford or take a degree at Cambridge without subscribing. They could be married only in parish churches and burial in the parish churchyard might very well be refused. They were liable for tithes and for payment of church rates for the upkeep of the church building and appurtenances. Beyond the proscription from holding office, whatever the frequency with which it was breached, social discrimination was endemic, though most eighteenth-century Dissenters avoided confrontation and some even developed a sense of inner superiority to those who looked down on them. And the possibility of violence was never far below the surface.

A brief look at the situation of the two most important non-Protestant religious groupings in England reveals the same combination of tentative advance in toleration and dogged, atavistic harassment. Jews were permitted to return to England in 1656, and in the early years of the Restoration a few hundred Jews lived in or near London. With the forging of the connection with the Netherlands after 1688, larger numbers entered the country from that religious melting-pot, and in the early eighteenth century began an influx of Ashkenazim from northern and eastern Europe that soon came to outnumber the largely Sephardic population of seventeenth-century

English Jewry. The right of Jews to practice their religion and to build synagogues had been secured. Their legal capacity to own freehold land, however, was in doubt; while in London—all that mattered until the appearance of Jews in provincial towns in mid-century—they were excluded from freedom of the City and so from the retail trade as well as from membership in the corporation, though at the end of the seventeenth century twelve Jews were permitted to trade on the royal exchange. Like Quakers, Jews faced a difficulty over oaths—often demanded on the New as well as the Old Testament or "on the true faith of a Christian"—but, unlike the Quakers, they were long in getting dispensation, despite some early concessions that allowed them to give evidence and to go to law to recover debts. Jews were nonetheless better treated in England than in most of continental Europe, and many of them prospered.

˙ One of their lesser grievances had to do with naturalization, a cumbersome and expensive process of interest to only a few wealthy immigrants. No one anticipated difficulty when an act was carried in 1753 to remove the requirement of taking the Sacrament from the naturalization procedure; more important was an incidental provision, prohibiting Jews from exercising the right of presentation to livings in the church, that indirectly clarified their right to hold land. The bill went through the Lords without a division and passed the Commons by a handsome majority in a small house. But after the bill's passage a prolonged outburst of anti-Semitic violence, coming on the eve of a general election, forced the government to second thoughts; at the very end of the year, the act, including the provision respecting land, was repealed.

This extraordinary episode, marked by public hatred and political cowardice, essentially put an end to the formal advance of Jewish liberties until well into the next century. But during the reign of George III, the numbers of Jews grew from a few thousand to tens of thousands, and, while many remained desperately poor, the prosperity of some increased spectacularly. Jews gained a wider respect from the English, though less for the intrinsic worth of Judaism than for the worth of Jews as individuals and potential Christians. The evangelical movement, in the Church and in dissent, sparked powerful conversionist efforts which, paradoxically, assumed respect and encouraged it; a resurgent millenarian interest foresaw, sympathetically, the return of the Jews to Israel; and Joseph Priestley advanced as one benefit of Unitarianism that its uncluttered monotheism would make it easier for Jews (and Mahometans) to be brought to Christianity. Alongside growing appreciation of the cultivation and philanthropy of leading Jewish families like the Goldsmids and the Montefiores, the efforts of the prize-fighter Daniel Mendoza to teach boxing to young Jews are said to have ended a series of anti-Jewish outrages.

In the new century, thanks in part to some effective parliamentary champions, legislative progress was resumed, though a horrendous series of medieval anti-Jewish statutes remained unrepealed. Efforts to include Jews in the repeal of dissenting disabilities in 1828 failed, as did attempts at statutory assimilation. But in lesser ways, progress was rapid: a general naturalization act in 1826, without mention of Jews and without significant public notice, accomplished the ends attempted in 1753; freedom of the City of London was opened to Jews in 1830, with municipal offices gradually following; the creation of the University of London in 1826 and 1837 got round the subscription problem at the older universities. In time the single remaining disability of importance was membership in Parliament, unresolved until the 1850s, not quite the last test—an honor reserved to the atheist Charles Bradlaugh in the 1880s—of England's standing as a Christian country.[45]

England's Catholics were also a small minority of the population—perhaps 60,000 in 1641, 80,000 in 1770—but they loomed far larger than did the Jews in the mythology, the polemics, and the fears of Protestants of nearly all breeds. There was good sixteenth- and seventeenth-century warrant for distrust, even hatred, of popery; and pride in military and political victories over the pope and his allies and in the superiority of Protestantism was reinforced by parochialism and prurience. Dark imaginings about monasteries and nunneries complemented the intimations of perpetual treason and underlay both periodic outbreaks of public hatred, from the popish plot of 1678 to the Gordon riots in 1780 to "papal aggression" in 1851, and a sub-literature of perennial appeal.

The geographical distribution of Catholicism was complex, unquestionably more prevalent in the North and on the borders of Wales than in the South, but patchy even in its strongholds. Seven-

teenth-century Catholicism was dominated by the gentry, which led
to clustering around recusant estates and to other interesting consequences—the loss of priestly independence, the high proportion of
priests drawn from the gentry, and the almost exclusively private
celebration of mass, often avoiding chapels even where they existed
in pre-Reformation country houses. A falling away in the last half of
the seventeenth century was reversed after 1700, and a gradual increase in numbers brought a decrease in gentry influence and the
slow growth of denominational characteristics. A far more rapid
transformation began about 1770; not only did numbers rise, but
Catholicism became an urban rather than a rural phenomenon, and
the proportions of poor Catholics rose. All this happened before any
substantial Irish immigration, which was still negligible in the
1780s. By 1820, the two national groups had reached parity and the
English were soon to become a distinct minority, perhaps twenty
per cent of the three quarters of a million Catholics by the 1850s.
This phenomenal growth through the expansion of the immigrant
community rapidly outstripped the administrative capacity of the
discreet missionary organization of vicars apostolic, but, to a remarkable degree, the emancipation of Catholics in England, in both
the broad and narrow senses of the term, was a function of the harsh
political realities across the Irish Sea; from the 1770s British governments made more generous gestures to Catholics than they did to
Dissenters. But popular hostility scarcely abated, and the Gordon
riots in London in 1780, brought on by concessions intended to ease
recruiting of Catholics into the army at a time of military despera-
tion, let loose the worst violence of a violent century.

Taking the old English Catholic community in the eighteenth
century, one is struck by the immense disjuncture between the
treacherous, slippery, violent, and threatening Catholicism of leg-
end and popular prejudice and the quietly devout, demonstrably
loyal reality. Perhaps that reality was guaranteed by the existence of
a savage anti-Catholic penal code; that it was not enforced in the
eighteenth century was no proof that it might not be called upon if
needed. This schizophrenic attitude was clearly present in Bishop
Gibson, who was convinced that Catholics were enemies within,
against whom a steady barrage of propaganda had to be mounted and
over whom careful administrative surveillance was needed, yet
whose commitment to toleration kept him from enforcing the laws

so long as the Catholics remained private and silent. His stern hostility to Catholicism, with its deep historical roots and its nationalistic and xenophobic impulses, survived in strength, in similarly elevated reaches of ecclesiastical and political life, right down to 1829 and after.

Those within the Protestant community who had gone farthest along the road to religious liberty, even though they continued to distrust the papacy and to be troubled by superstitious elements in Catholic thought and worship, were forced by their principles to concede, even to welcome, the open practice of Catholicism and to urge the removal of disabilities. Josiah Tucker, dean of Gloucester, upbraided Dissenters for their inconsistency in opposing Catholic claims, and Joseph Priestley similarly criticized those who petitioned against the act of 1779—passed unanimously in both houses of Parliament to remove some of the statutory discrimination—not only because they were behaving as they argued Catholics behaved toward Protestants in other countries, but because they failed to see that the right course was to oppose zeal to zeal and to open a debate in which Protestant principles would inevitably triumph. Priestley insisted that there was no necessary enmity between Catholicism and liberty—a contention he thought was sufficiently proved by the breakup of Catholic Europe at the Reformation, by Catholic opposition to the Jesuits, by Jansenism, and by the colony of Maryland. Let the Catholics display their religion in its full splendor, he declared; let their processions go through the streets uninterrupted, and then let the good sense of Englishmen determine if they would fall down before a God in a wafer. "I stand in need of liberty myself, and I wish that every creature of God may enjoy it equally with myself. *May his will be done on earth, as it is in heaven;* that is, voluntarily and cheerfully; and may we by our humane, rational, and Christian treatment, triumph over the minds, and not, by the aid of the civil power, over the persons and properties of our deluded fellow-citizens."[46]

The "need of liberty myself," which entailed not only freedom to practice a dissenting religion but civil equality and state neutrality with respect to religion, has not been fully realized in Britain, at least so far as an established church has continued to exist, however much it may be a lame, Erastian episcopacy.

The path to an increased measure of civil equality was not easy.

The 1770s were marked by genuine optimism. But the only victory of the decade was the concession in 1779 that dissenting ministers no longer needed to subscribe thirty-five of the Thirty-nine Articles so long as they would declare their belief that the Scriptures "do contain the revealed will of God," the phrase "whole revealed will" having been significantly deleted following a brief dissenting agitation. In 1732, Thomas Sherlock, bishop of Salisbury, had defended the Test Act as a fitting guarantee that office-holders would be Christian; and he had recalled the behavior of Dissenters in the past century. "However harmless and innocent the intention of the present Dissenters" in their efforts at Repeal, that offered no assurance about the behavior of their descendants. By the 1790s, it seemed to many that Sherlock's foreboding was entirely justified. The failures of the 1770s and Prime Minister William Pitt's abandonment of parliamentary reform after the mid-eighties increased the Dissenters' frustration and, as Priestley demonstrates, heightened their rhetoric and led some to greater involvement in radical and even revolutionary causes. This exasperation triggered a backlash. Dissenters, whose manifest loyalty to the monarchy had been demonstrated at the time of the Jacobite rising in 1745, became newly suspect when they began to emerge as supporters of the American cause after 1775. When the French Revolution threatened Britain with vast social upheaval, "Church and king" became as potent a cry as "The Church in danger" had been at the beginning of the century. The loyalty of all varieties of Dissenters—even those Methodists who on principle remained aloof from all political agitation—was called into question in the 1790s; and the Unitarians, as the most radical of Dissenters in both religion and politics, were pursued with especial vindictiveness. The Birmingham riots of 1791 saw the destruction of the two Unitarian chapels and of the houses of some of the Unitarian leaders, as well as Priestley's library and laboratory. Priestley himself abandoned England for the United States in 1794, and a number of his correligionists joined him, at least temporarily, while many more contemplated emigration from a country in which they feared they could never attain true freedom or even a modicum of equality and security.[47]

Early in the new century a turning seemed to have appeared. Orthodox dissent was going from strength to strength, in faith, in num-

bers, and in organization; the Methodists had, to all intents and purposes, become another denomination (or denominations) apart from
the Church. Presbyterian congregations could still count a few
Arian ministers into the twenties, but by the war's end, these were
absorbed in a Unitarianism that, though small in numbers, still retained vast social, economic, and political importance.[48]

The Dissenting Deputies—headed by William Smith, the posses-
sor of a large fortune who had entered Parliament in the 1780s in
Pitt's interest—were faced with a difficult problem when, in 1809,
Lord Sidmouth, the home secretary, proposed a bill, eventually introduced in 1811, to control the registration of dissenting ministers
by, among other things, requiring testimonials to fitness and settled
congregations. Sidmouth saw the step, with some justification, as
an effort at quality control as well as a damper on radical and blasphemous activity at the fringes of dissent.[49] But on principle, as well
as because of the possibility of prejudicial administration, Dissenters generally disliked Sidmouth's bill and criticized the failure of
Smith and the Deputies to oppose it forthrightly. The government
withdrew the bill and the next year repealed the Conventicle and
Five Mile Acts. Here the Deputies' influence was very strong, as it
was in 1813, when the exclusion of anti-Trinitarians from the benefits of the Toleration Act was done away with.

The immediate post-war years did not favor further dissenting
advance, but in the more peaceable and prosperous twenties the government turned to pragmatic reform; it was only a matter of time
and strategic calculation until the Test Act and the Corporation Act
were repealed. This prime dissenting goal was, however, hostage to
the dominant political issue of the twenties, Catholic emancipation,
presented in increasingly stark relief by the activities of Daniel
O'Connell and his Catholic Association in Ireland and by the polarization of the English parties. In the end, repeal was the first accomplished, in 1828. All office-holders were required to take an oath
against attempting to injure the established church or to interfere
with its privileges, but that seemed not to hamper the growth within
a few years of a serious campaign for disestablishment. The initiative came more from Congregationalists and Baptists than from the
Unitarians, who were thrust out of their leadership of dissent as
a whole, though they continued for a time to dominate dissenting

parliamentary representation and to play an utterly disproportion-
ate role in reformed local government. Catholic emancipation—the
right of Catholics to hold office and to sit in Parliament—was conceded the next year.

The acts of 1828 and 1829, it has been said, marked the end,
respectively, of the Anglican and of the Protestant constitutions.[50]
But many discriminations remained, and the issue of dissent and the
Church, like the issue of church and state, bedeviled political and
social life for the remainder of the century. Still, viewed constitutionally, the acts were the crucial concession of principle. In 1829,
the Unitarian minister, journalist, and radical politician W. J. Fox
preached a sermon in his Finsbury chapel to celebrate the accom-
plishment of Catholic emancipation and the first anniversary of repeal. At last, he argued, law and Christianity were properly linked,
no longer by penalties ringing Christianity about for its protection,
but by the freeing of Christianity to command the law and to influence its form and administration. Religious liberty had been achieved,
not by insurrection or revolution, not by parties or ministers, but by
the "bloodless and glorious conquest of opinion," which would now
force the legislature to assure national prosperity, social harmony,
religious candor, and the advance of theological truth. God's providence—as the spirit of the age, that *machina ex deo* against which
Priestley had seen the tyrant as powerless—had established liberty,
and religious truth would inevitably follow.[51]

A substantial part of this chapter is based on work done at the
Institute for Advanced Study, Princeton, in 1982–83. The section on
Joseph Priestley, also with Princeton origins, was extended as a result of a bicentenary conference at Manchester College Oxford in
1986 and a seminar at the Folger Institute in Washington, D. C. in
1987. I wish to thank these three institutions, as well as the Rev. P. B.
Godfrey, editor of *Faith and Freedom*, for permission to incorporate
portions of the Manchester College paper, published in that journal
and cited here in n. 42.

Liberty of the Press and Public Opinion: 1660-1695

LOIS G. SCHWOERER

CONTRARY TO COMMON OPINION, the Revolution of 1688–89 was not a watershed in the history of freedom of the press. The leaders of the Revolution inherited no well-developed principle of liberty of the press and they did not articulate one. The Bill of Rights, the document that set out the terms of the settlement and laid claim to certain rights, contained no reference to the press. Freedom of the press was not among the ancient rights and liberties of Englishmen: it could not be traced back to an ancient constitution and it had no part in a theory of natural rights. There was, in fact, no theoretical vocabulary at hand that revolutionary leaders might have employed had they been interested in liberty of the press. But, they had no interest in the question. During the months of revolution they themselves had violated the previous government's restrictions on printing, but once in power they imposed those same policies and procedures. And in response to the regulations, as had happened throughout the Restoration era, as the rate of literacy increased and the audience for printed news, polemics, and literature grew, critics of these restraints found ways to circumvent them. At the same time, changes in politics, international affairs, and social and economic conditions that followed the Revolution made it increasingly difficult to enforce press regulations. In 1695, with the central government preoccupied with war and the untimely death of Queen Mary II, Parliament allowed the system that had existed for 175 years to lapse. No theory of liberty of the press accompanied this step, and liberty of the press, as that concept is commonly understood in the Western world today, did not result, but a significant change in the way the press operated did follow.

≺ I ≻

Shortly after the Restoration both king and Parliament sought to repress printed material that was critical of the settlement in state and church. Believing that an unfettered press was the major reason for the real and rumored plots against the government, both turned to procedures and mechanisms that their predecessors had tried for over a hundred years. Within a week of his return, Charles II used his royal prerogative to appoint the veteran Royalist, Sir John Berkenhead, as licenser of the press and by an order in council instructed the Stationers Company to exercise its previous authority to search and seize printed material critical of the government and the church.[1] The use of royal prerogative was a time-honored method of controlling the press. Henry VIII, the first English king to impose restraints on printing, had used proclamations to prohibit the printing of material subversive of his political authority and changing religious policies and to inflict penalties of fines, imprisonment, and death.[2] Thereafter, proclamations and orders in council set out rules for the press, and, although the use of royal proclamations was sharply criticized in the seventeenth century, Charles II and other late-Stuart kings continued to employ them in their effort to manage the press.

Charles's calling upon the Stationers Company to resume its role as the government's enforcement agent also reflected past policies. The company, chartered as a London guild in 1557 by Mary I, received a virtual monopoly over all printing and sale of books in the country in exchange for its cooperation in administering the government's orders respecting press control.[3] To carry out their duties the Stationers were empowered to search for and seize prohibited material and arrest the suspected printer or anyone else who interfered with the search. In other words, the company became the principal agency for implementing the Crown's control of the press, an arrangement testifying to the rudimentary administrative structure of the central government in the sixteenth century.

The printing monopoly enjoyed by the Stationers Company was confirmed and expanded in the early seventeenth century, so that as a corporate body the Stationers controlled the printing of many classes of books, among them Bibles and other religious texts, which were known as the English "stock." In exchange for these lucrative monopolies, the Stationers agreed to disburse money annually to its indigent members and widows and defended their monopolies on grounds of their social welfare projects.

The general practice of granting monopolies provoked fierce criticism in the early seventeenth century; yet in 1621, when James recalled various monopolies, he specifically excepted printing monopolies. Three years later Parliament, following the king's lead, excluded printing patents from the Statute of Monopolies, which had the effect of exempting them from the control of the common law courts. Since the king granted printing monopolies under his prerogative powers, these monopolies remained subject to the Privy Council and (until the Civil War) to the Court of Star Chamber and the Court of High Commission. The practice of granting monopolies to control the press was revived at the Restoration and continued during the late seventeenth century.

Parliament shared with the king a concern to restrain the press. In the Cavalier Parliament a first attempt during the session of 1661 to pass a bill to control the press failed because the Lords insisted that their houses should be exempted from search.[4] The Crown therefore took interim action; it issued a warrant to Sir Roger L'Estrange, a devoted monarchist and active writer and publisher, empowering him to search for unlicensed "pictures, books, pamphlets or papers," destroy them and deface the press that printed them, and proceed against all persons who distributed unlicensed printed material. The warrant also denounced the dispersion of libels in *manuscript* form, especially by "coffee-house men," thus noticing that the new coffee houses in London played a role in exciting interest in public affairs and in dispersing allegedly seditious matter.[5]

In the spring of 1662, the Commons introduced a new print bill. Disturbed by its slow progress, Charles showed the importance he attached to the issue.[6] In an urgent message blaming the "late rebellion in the Kingdom and Schisms in the Church" on the "Liberty of the Press," he declared that next to settling the armed forces, control

of the press "did most conduce to the securing the Peace of the Kingdom." The two Houses responded by completing the bill within a
fortnight and the Licensing Act became law on 19 May 1662.[7] It
marked a significant change in the source of authority of press control; it was the first statutory regulation of the press, apart from laws
passed during the Civil War and Cromwellian interregnum. The
1662 act was still in force at the time of the Revolution.

Charles's blaming the press for the "late Rebellion" was good
politics, but not without reason. The Tudor licensing system had
collapsed when the Long Parliament abolished the prerogative courts
in 1641, which had the unintended consequence of removing the
licensing decrees and practically dissolving controls over the press.
A torrent of printed material poured from the presses. New "diur-
nals" or newspapers featuring domestic and parliamentary news appeared: their number soared from four in 1641 to a high of 722 in
1645 and averaged about 300 in subsequent years to 1660.[8] The number of polemical tracts and pamphlets also grew, from 22 pieces in
1640 to approximately 2,000 in 1642, dropping back to about 1,000
in the next two years. Between 1640 and 1660 the yearly average ran
just under 700 titles, compared with the yearly average of 200 titles
between 1576 and 1640.[9] This material debated political and religious issues, usually in expressly critical terms, as had never before
happened. Precisely who read this material or listened to it being
read will never be known, but certainly it reached downward to
lower-middle and lower classes in London and spread far beyond
the city.[10]

The act passed in 1662 aimed to prevent "the frequent Abuses
in printing seditious, treasonable, and unlicensed Books and Pamphlets," and to regulate printing.[11] The act set up a system of pre-
publication censorship that closely followed the terms of the Star
Chamber decree of 1637, itself indebted to the Star Chamber decree
of 1586, which in turn had drawn upon decrees of 1559 and 1566.
Books were assigned to censors according to their subject: politics
or history to a secretary of state; law to the lord chancellor; religion,
philosophy, and all other works to the archbishop of Canterbury and
bishop of London. The word "Licensed" on a book signified written
permission; the words "With Allowance," oral approval; and the
words "Published by Authority" meant an official order.[12] After

passing the censors a book or pamphlet had to be entered in the Stationers register with a disclosure about its content before it could be printed. The act stated that nothing could be printed that was "heretical, seditious, schismatical or offensive . . . to the Christian faith or to the doctrine or discipline of the Church of England." These complex arrangements testified to the great increase in printed matter, the difficulty in judging its significance, and the determination of the government to outlaw printed material critical of the restored order in church and state.

The act also regulated the printing craft, in effect confirming the monopoly of the Stationers Company. The number of printers, which stood at fifty-nine in 1660, was to be reduced to the twenty master printers of the Stationers Company, not including the king's printer and the printers of the two universities; vacancies, as they occurred, were to be filled by nominees of the archbishop of Canterbury or bishop of London. Each printer had to affix his name to what he printed, post a bond of £300 against unlawful printing, ascertain the name of the author should the authorities require that information, and present a copy to the king's library and to the two universities. The act limited printing in England to London, Cambridge, Oxford, and also York where printers were forbidden to print English stock books. The act confirmed the Stationers Company's power of search and seizure and also ordered that the secretaries of state might issue both general and specific warrants to search places where "they shall know, or upon some probable reason suspect" the presence of unlicensed material. This clause in the act was of enormous importance, for under it the government carried on its "search and seize" operations during the era and into the next century.[13] Vending of books was restricted to members of the Stationers Company or licensees of the bishop of a particular diocese, except for small shopkeepers in and about Westminster who had been in business before 1661, a point that recognized a development in the book trade whose disruption would have certainly caused an outcry.

Significantly for future developments, the act confirmed the printing monopolies granted by royal warrant, thereby reigniting long standing criticism against monopolies, criticism that figured in the decision in 1695 to allow the controls to lapse. It imposed heavy

penalties: suspension from printing for three years for the first offense; for a second violation, total disbarrment from the craft, a fine,
imprisonment, or corporal punishment "not extending to life or
limb."

The act also contained an expiry date of two years. Its inclusion
reflected MPs' dissatisfaction with the bill. Indeed, less than a year
after its passage, in February 1663, the House appointed a committee to review the act (as well as others) and to "hear objections as
shall be against" it, and took the same step in 1666 after renewing
it. Significantly, this review committee was asked to provide for the
"effectual Execution" of the act.[14] But over the next thirty years, despite apparent misgivings, the Licensing Act was renewed at specified intervals without significant change, each time with new expiry
dates, as in 1664 and 1665. In 1679, for partisan political reasons,
Parliament allowed the act to lapse, but in 1685 James II's Parliament revived it.[15] William and Mary's Parliament renewed it for two
years in 1692 and in 1695 allowed it to expire. Each time the act
came up for renewal, Parliament's role respecting the press was also
renewed; this legislative process made it easier than it might otherwise have been for press censorship and controls to lapse.

No one objected to the Licensing Act from 1662 to 1679 on
grounds that it violated the principle of freedom of the press. If the
surviving record is accurate, only John Locke said anything about
limiting the magistrate's power over the printed word. In the course
of an essay on religious toleration written in 1667, Locke agreed that
the magistrate might prohibit the publishing of certain ideas if they
disturbed the public, but he cautioned that he should not do so unless he had "seriously and impartially" concluded that the repression "was really necessary for the peace, safety or security of his
people."[16]

Why was it that no one developed the principle of liberty of the
press? For one thing, there was no traditional principle to evoke; no
one could argue that liberty of the press was an ancient right of Englishmen. Obviously, the printing press itself was a relatively new
invention; it had been in England only about two hundred years.
Any politically conscious person would have known that virtually
from its arrival the central government had claimed control over it.
The only persons who had written at any length about liberty of the

press were the Leveller leaders such as John Lilburne, Richard Overton, and William Walwyn, and the poet John Milton. And not one of them developed an unqualified argument for the principle of liberty of the press. Lilburne excoriated the restrictions that prevented the Levellers from getting their message to the public; but he did not favor the same opportunity for his opponents, calling royalist tracts "Malignant" and objecting to their appearance. Walwyn wrote about the desirability of "freedom of discourse," but also expressed the contradictory belief that opinions "dangerous to the State"—that is, royalist opinions—should be banned in print.[17] Milton's *Aeropagitica* (1644) appealed to the Lords and Commons, flattering them with the thought that they had given the nation liberty, "the nurse of all great wits," and the reason for the outpouring from the press. But now the Long Parliament, by its "licensing and prohibiting," had injured Truth. "Let her [Truth] and Falsehood grapple; who ever knew Truth put to the worse, in a free and open encounter?" "She needs no policies, nor stratagems, nor licensings to make her victorious." However, Milton favored freedom for only a limited number of views and specifically denied that freedom to Catholics, atheists, non-Christians and, less emphatically, Anglicans. Moreover, Milton argued against pre-publication licensing on grounds that "the fire and executioner" would punish those who abuse the liberty to publish, not on the basis of a principle of liberty of the press.[18] Further, he accepted the post of licenser under Cromwell. For all his elegant language Milton believed that although *his* Truth was absolute and perfect, it needed help from the censor to protect it from misguided mankind. In any case, these radical views were, of course, proscribed after 1660.

There was a widespread feeling that the restored monarchy should control printed matter to preserve itself and domestic peace from the threat posed by former Cromwellians. The difference of opinion centered on the best means to do that. Some thought that the procedures of the act were not effective enough. L'Estrange himself asserted in 1663 that the press was *still* actively trying to "engage [the people] in a direct Rebellion" and that the Stationers Company was failing to eradicate offensive material. Claiming that "the whole [book] Trade passes through the fingers of their own Creatures," he declared with manifest exaggeration, that "many hun-

dred-thousands of Seditious Papers ... have passed unpunished."
L'Estrange recommended replacing the Stationers Company as enforcement agent by a new governmental officer answerable to the
king and Privy Council. His proposed officer would restrict the number of presses and printers, rigorously supervise the printers, and
thereby control the number and character of printed pieces. L'Estrange recommended that redundant printers should be induced to
inform on printers suspected of violating restrictions by promising them the next available vacancy in the trade. In effect he would
have turned unemployed printers into spies for the government. He
wanted severe penalties: fines, mutilation, banishment, prison, and
death, depending upon the offense.[19]

Following the lead of the king, who in 1660 had issued a proclamation prohibiting the reprinting of earlier texts that had promoted
tyrannicide (among them George Buchanan's *De Jure Regni apud
Scotos* and Milton's *Defensio Pro Populo Anglicano*), L'Estrange provided a lengthy list of abhorrent ideas to be banned, including the
views that in case of necessity, the two Houses may exercise sovereignty; that the king is one of three estates; and that the people have
the right to resist government.[20] L'Estrange also offered an "index"
of books to be banned, among them *Vindiciae contra Tyrannos* and
Richard Baxter's *Holy Common-Wealth*. Further, L'Estrange recommended against reprinting books, saying that earlier writers
"speak playner and strike homer to the Capacity and Humour of the
Multitude" than recent authors do. He had in mind the tracts and
pamphlets from the Civil Wars that he believed were still effectively
spreading seditious and blasphemous ideas and aimed to reach a
broad public.[21] In sum, he set out a program designed to impose
thought control by rigorously limiting the number of presses and
printers and by tightening the surveillance of the craft.

L'Estrange's idea of creating a new officer to supervise the press
found favor with the king. Tacitly acknowledging disappointment in
the performance of the Stationers Company, Charles in August 1663
appointed L'Estrange, who had recommended his own appointment,
to the position of surveyor of the imprimery under the direction of
the secretaries of state, ordering him to report to the king and Privy
Council. L'Estrange was to suppress all unlicensed printed matter,
including pictures. Charles also empowered him to license books

and tracts that did not already fall to one of the licensers.[22] Messengers of the Press, called "instruments for discovery and intelligence," were appointed to assist him. L'Estrange's new office competed with the Stationers and jealousy between him and the company did nothing to facilitate efficient execution of the act. Yet the company continued as one of the government's agents in press control.

L'Estrange also received from the king a patent for the sole right to print and publish news, and during the next three years he brought out two closely related newspapers, *The Intelligencer* and *The Newes*. Written in a lively style, they provided readers with selected items of news aimed at promoting the government and disparaging its critics. Then, in 1666 following manipulations by Joseph Williamson, at this time an undersecretary of state, L'Estrange's patent was withdrawn. The *London Gazette* became the official government newspaper. Edited by Williamson, the *Gazette* offered a thin diet of royal proclamations, official announcements, and some diluted foreign news, but it remained the only printed newspaper until 1679. Persons wanting to keep abreast of domestic developments had to rely on written newsletters available through subscription at five pounds a year. These newsletters multiplied during the era, one of them lasting until 1689.[23] They illustrate how domestic news might circulate at a time of attempted severe repression.

The court instituted other measures beyond the Licensing Act to try to bring printed matter under control. Using his prerogative powers, the king issued proclamations and orders in council to suppress books, arrest unauthorized printers and persons associated with offensive pieces, and announce changes in policy.[24] Charles also turned to the law to assist in controlling the press. Although the strengthened and expanded law of treason could now be construed to cover printing and publishing as acts compassing the death or removal of the king, Charles used it sparingly. A couple of printers were detained on charges of treason and booksellers were threatened with the charge, but only one printer was brought to trial.[25] That case in 1664 involved John Twyn, in whose shop L'Estrange, now busy about his duties at press repression, had found sheets from a tract entitled *A Treatise of the Execution of Justice,* or *Mene Tekel or The*

Downfall of Tyranny. Written by Captain Roger Jones, a former officer in Cromwell's army, the tract called upon the people to depose and kill Charles II. The government, already alarmed over news of an uprising of Dissenters and Cromwellian soldiers in the north, believed that the pamphlet and the uprising were connected. Scholars differ on whether Twyn's motives in printing the pamphlet were political or economic, but he was found guilty of treason, and, citing the need to make examples and deter would-be-violators of press laws, Lord Chief Justice Sir Robert Hyde sentenced him to be hanged, drawn, and quartered. Charles's successors were also reluctant to employ treason law against printers: for the rest of the century only two men, one under James II, the other during the reign of William and Mary, were convicted of treason for printing offensive material. Treason law was so harsh that apparently it was decided impolitic to use it to punish violations of press restrictions.[26]

The common law of seditious libel was also called upon, but in fewer instances during the Restoration than used to be thought. It has recently been shown that previous historians, not realizing the word "libel" in seventeenth-century usage meant any tract, thought that all trials about a "libel" were based on the law of seditious libel; in fact, most of those trials were based on the violations of the Licensing Act. A seditious libel meant a piece of writing in manuscript or print that defamed the government's policies or personnel, encouraged a breach of the peace or incited rebellion, and contained malice and evil intentions. From the court's point of view, the disadvantage of the law was the necessity of persuading a jury of malicious intent. During Charles II's reign only four trials were based on the charge of seditious libel, and under James II only three, including that of the *Seven Bishops* in May 1688.[27] It was not until after the lapse of the Licensing Act in 1695 that the government leaned heavily on the law of seditious libel to restrain the press.

The government tried to improve the performance of the Stationers, who were required to cooperate with L'Estrange in drawing up new bylaws. New bylaws adopted in 1670 and 1671 followed several of L'Estrange's recommendations but softened others: whereas he had suggested that any stationer who prints an unlicensed item should lose his interest in the English stock, the bylaws called for such a printer to lose his profit from the stock for one year only.[28]

L'Estrange also recommended additional harsh measures, including withdrawal of some of the Stationers' patents, but was frustrated by judicial rulings and court decisions in 1671, 1677, and 1681 holding that the company's original patents were valid and that the king could not issue new patents for the same class of books. These conclusions were of great importance; by upholding the Stationers' right in their existing patents and protecting them against threats from the court to withdraw patents they were a major reason for the company's negligence in fulfilling its obligations as licensing agent for the press.[29] Ordinances passed at government insistence by the company in 1681 and 1683 required that every printed piece show the name of the printer or bookseller, set fines for printing pirated pieces, and ordered that members personally ensure that the title of all forthcoming printed matter was entered in the Company's register.[30] The attempts of the government in trying to make the Stationers more effective were a persistent feature of press control.

< II >

Severe problems attended the Crown's efforts to achieve a compliant press. Self-interest and susceptibility to bribes tainted the men who had the task of monitoring the craft of printing and censoring manuscripts. L'Estrange himself, who more than any other single figure was devoted to the idea of censorship, pursued his own personal advantage in petitioning the king for more money and greater authority. He was not above accepting bribes to overlook an unlicensed press or book and was even said to turn the blind eye "if the printer's wife would but smile on him."[31] The messengers of the press, with responsibility for carrying out the secretary's warrants for search, seizure, and arrest, were also sometimes seduced by bribes.[32] The Stationers wardens were not especially interested in prosecuting printers who violated censorship laws; they were known to warn them of an impending search. However they would prosecute vigorously printers who violated patented printing rights.[33]

The mechanism for censoring material also worked imperfectly. Church officials, the secretaries of state, and the surveyor of the press, who were already burdened with other important responsibilities, often delegated the tiresome and time-consuming work of licensing. Their appointees often performed their work in a perfunctory manner. Sometimes the Privy Council had to turn to the attorney general for an evaluation of a book.[34]

Censors engaged in a cat and mouse game with authors or publishers intent upon getting a manuscript approved. Ruses were devised to deceive the censor. One was to change the text of a book after it had been passed. Another was to craft the text in ways that conveyed subversive ideas surreptitiously: as L'Estrange said, authors who "write in fear of the law are forc'd to cover their Meaning under Ambiguities."[35] For example, radical Whigs during the exclusion crisis invented a code language that enabled them to communicate subversive ideas in words that could be construed in different senses so that it would be difficult to bring a charge. The word "invade" meant that the peoples' rights and liberties had been destroyed, with the implication that the people were thereby released from obedience to the king.[36] A society which practices censorship invites writers to employ strategies, including literary ones, to escape control.[37]

The number of printed pieces in circulation in the Restoration era was enormous. During Charles II's reign the yearly average was between 700 and 1,000 printed pieces and at times of crisis jumped to 2,000 or more. Print runs of pieces varied but ran as high as 3,000 for a popular item. So two million pieces, including 400,000 almanacs a year, is an approximate estimate.[38] These numbers represent a "tenfold expansion" over earlier years and show the magnitude of the problem of censorship.

The succession of exciting events throughout the period inevitably sustained avid interest in public affairs. People were not satisfied by the narrow perspective of the official *London Gazette*. Unlicensed material held much greater interest for some people. Indeed, one observer commented that an official imprimatur damned a book in the eyes of some people, who concluded that the author must be "some dull phlegmatick fellow, who either wanted wit or honesty to vouch himself."[39] Controversies were facilitated by the growth in literacy. Between the Civil Wars and 1714 literacy rates overall increased from 30 to 45 percent for men and from 10 to 25 percent for women; in London the rate was almost 80 percent for men. Illiterates could also become fairly well-informed by hearing tracts read and discussing the issues with others.[40] Foreign ambassadors expressed astonishment over the fact that London watermen talked about politics as they rowed them along the Thames. During the exclusion crisis some porters, almost certainly illiterate, who were drinking at Duke's Place discussed an issue of great importance, the duke of Monmouth's claim to the throne.[41]

Licensed first in 1663, coffee houses rapidly became centers where men from all classes could congregate to listen to and exchange news of domestic and foreign affairs, thus creating a new problem for authorities intent on controlling the press.[42] Tracts were available and prints were often pasted on the walls. As early as 1662 the government expressed alarm over coffee houses; in 1671 referred to them as "nurseries of sedition"; in 1672 issued a proclamation about the increase in "bold and Licentious discourses" in coffee houses by men who endeavor to "create and nourish universall jealouise and dissatisfaction" against the government; in 1673 complained that men sit half the day "talking of news . . . arraigning the judgments and discretion of governors."[43] On New Year's Day 1676, Charles II issued a proclamation closing the coffee houses because "divers false . . . and scandalous reports are devised and spread abroad, to the defamation of his Majestie's government."[44] The proclamation was withdrawn within ten days, the government forced to admit that people simply were not going to obey it. Coffee houses were allowed to reopen, but the keepers had to take the oaths of allegiance and supremacy and to promise to ban all "scandalous Papers, Books or Libells" critical of the government and its people.[45] This stratagem did not work well either. In September 1677 the Privy Council withdrew the licenses of twenty coffee-house keepers, the king expressing anger at them and their clientele "some of them of lewd principles, and some of mean birth and education," who discuss affairs of state. During the exclusion crisis coffee houses were favorite meeting places for partisan political discussions and became identified with the newly formed parties, Tory members favouring Gray's Inn Coffee-house, Whigs, Kid's Coffee-house. L'Estrange fumed in 1681 that "every Coffee-house [is] furnished with News-Papers and Pamphlets (both written and Printed) of personal Scandal, Schism and Treason."[46] On the eve of the Revo-

lution, James II was complaining about the "seditious news" that
was spread in coffee houses and other public places, and in a futile
proclamation forbade people to discuss political affairs by writing,
printing, speaking, or listening.[47]

Members of the book trade—printers, publishers, booksellers,
hawkers—were intransigent in their determination to produce and
market unlicensed material. The number of printers in London who
had set up their presses in defiance of the law was four in 1668 and
ten in 1675, according to contemporary records, and there may have
been, of course, more than that.[48] They practiced all manner of sub-
terfuge, hiding their presses in secret places—behind a bed, "run up
on wheels," in an attic to which the entrance was through a trap
door, "in a shed, in a garden, through an alley 'twixt Long Lane and
Charterhouse Lane." They used false names and code language in
their correspondence. Books were surreptitiously imported and circulated in "Dry-Fatts, Bales, Packs, Maunds, or other Fardells."[49]
Among persons who produced "heretical, seditious or blasphemous" material were Awnsham Churchill (John Locke's printer and
a leading bookseller after the Revolution), Anne and Richard Bald-
win, Elizabeth and Thomas Brewster, Henry Care, Langley Curtis,
John Darby, Richard Janeway, Benjamin Harris, Francis Smith (the
last two Baptists) and the Catholic printer Nathaniel Thompson.
There is no doubt that many were motivated partly by ideology.
Thompson was described as "sowing Dissension and discord among
Protestants" to promote Catholicism and, some said, Toryism.
Darby was described by a near-contemporary as a "true asserter of
English liberties." Smith was overheard to declare when being es-
corted into Newgate Prison that he would "never leave printing and
writing till this kingdom was brought to a free state."[50] But they and
others were also moved by the profit motive, as Baldwin candidly
admitted. Although the income of printers is not available, the price
of printed tracts and books and the number of pieces in circulation
suggest that an enterprising printer could reap a profit by making
available unlicensed material. That Thompson could readily pay the
fines imposed on him and stand bail of £1,000 shows that he made
money.[51] Moreover, apprentice printers violated restrictions because
restraints destroyed their chance of practicing the craft they were
trained in and deprived them of a livelihood. In 1676, a printer, Rob-

ert Everingham, was called before the court of common council of the Stationers Company to answer the charge of setting up an unlicensed press. He said that he had done it "because hee served his time at the trade & for no other reason."[52]

The popish plot and exclusion crisis heightened the partisan uses of the press and brought change in press control. The Tory and Whig parties employed all kinds of printed material—tracts, pamphlets, poems, pictures, and cartoons—in an effort to discredit the other and bring their message to the public.[53] The emergence of parties produced a major change in the legal basis for press control. When the Licensing Act came up for renewal in the spring of 1679 it was allowed to expire. Perhaps some members of the House of Commons were influenced by a tract by Charles Blount (discussed below) that argued on grounds of principle for the removal of pre-publication restraints, but the major reason was the Whig calculation that by freeing the press they could appeal to and enlist public support for the bill excluding James from the succession to the throne. The committee on temporary laws, appointed on March 26, 1679, may have also thought that their failure to recommend renewal of the press law would prevent the king, whose lord chancellor had urged the law's reform and renewal, from proroguing Parliament. But Charles had to prorogue Parliament and then dissolve it in July in order to check exclusion. Thus the Licensing Act and statutory controls over the press lapsed.[54]

Mounting partisan animosity in 1680 led to a further loosening of restraints on the press. The Whigs persuaded the Commons to publicize its votes, a move representing a sharp break with past attitudes about confidentiality of parliamentary affairs. The avowed aim was to correct unauthorized accounts of Parliament's activities and to establish a record of the House's proceedings against the possibility that the king would misrepresent them, as he did later in a declaration of 1681.[55] But the underlying purpose, as in the lapse of the printing law, was to generate popular support for exclusion. The Commons ordered that its votes be printed weekly under the supervision of the Speaker and provided that the order might be renewed each year. In 1681, it ordered printing of proceedings as well as votes. These *Votes of the House of Commons* contained, inter alia, notices of resolutions, petitions, messages to and from the king, and reports of committees—in short, a comprehensive account of the activities (except speeches) of the House. The two orders were implemented by resolutions rather than by standing orders, almost certainly because they were seen as instruments in a partisan contest and not as permanent policy. In other words, these steps did not reflect the principle of freedom of the press. The assumption that the public would buy the printed *Votes* proved correct; "thousands" of copies were sold each week, contributing to the formation of public opinion and intensifying popular interest in political issues.[56]

Less partisan arguments for more relaxed press controls also appeared from all parts of the political spectrum. Francis North, a devoted royal servant and chief justice of the Court of Common Pleas, argued against harsh repression as counter-productive because it provoked public resentment against the Crown and hurt poor printers. Thomas Hobbes let it be known that he regarded the monopoly of the Stationers as a "great hindrance to the advancement of 'learning.'"[57] In his pamphlet *A Just Vindication of Learning: or, An Humble Address to the High Court of Parliament In behalf of the Liberty of the Press, alluded to as possibly influencing the decision on the Licensing/Printing Act,* Blount, a Deist and republican, insisted that the most effective way to counter the popish menace was by a free press, "whereby whoever opposes the Publick Interest, are [sic] exposed and rendered odious to the people."[58] Drawing heavily, but without acknowledgment, upon Milton's *Aeropagitica*, Blount declared that a censored press obstructed learning, offended reason ("the very Eye of God"), insulted the "common people," and "endangered the government." Quoting Milton directly, he wrote, "Truth needs no Policies, no Stratagems, no Licensings to render her Victorious." The licensing system, he maintained, was unnecessary and unworthy of Englishmen; it made the government no different from papists and Mahometans. For all his rhetoric, Blount's commitment to freedom of the press was limited; he justified the removal of censorship on the grounds that anyone who wrote "Scandalous Reflections upon the Government" was subject by current laws to fine and imprisonment.

Another author, William Lawrence, a dissenting minister, condemned a fettered press—"it stops the truth of all intelligence, which is so invaluable a Treasure, and difficult to be got into the

Gates of Princes"—and excoriated procedures that gave to "Spiritual or Temporal Judges Power . . . to have what Law, what Gospel, what Text, what Translation, what Canonical, what Apocryphal, what Scripture, what Act of parliament, what Common law, what Statute, what Religion, what Justice, what Liberty, and what Slavery they please." Yet Lawrence recommended one restraint, a law that would prevent dissentient Protestants from printing or preaching publicly on matters of "Ceremonial dissentiency, or other matter not necessary to Salvation." Such disputes would weaken the unity of the Protestant community in its struggle against the papists and create a situation in which all Protestants would be a "prey" to Catholics.[59] However, these arguments favoring a freer press were isolated and did not develop into a principle of liberty of the press.

The court responded energetically to the lapse of the Licensing Act. The Privy Council met the day after the lapse and, predicting an increase in the number of "seditious Pamphlets," summoned L'Estrange and the masters and wardens of the Stationers Company to attend them to receive "fit Directions . . . against unlicensed Bookes."[60] But deciding on "fit Directions" was no easy matter, and the question of how to control the press in the absence of a statutory law was repeatedly before them over the next two years. Several stratagems were developed.

One step the Council took was to issue on its own authority general arrest, search and seize warrants and specific warrants against a named person or printed piece.[61] Another move was to try to contain the circulation of printed matter by controlling the hawkers who dispersed books. As a result of royal orders the lord mayor of London, the aldermen, and the wardens of the Stationers Company considered the matter in August 1679 and ordered the marshal and constables to bring hawkers before a city official for questioning. The penalty for peddling seditious material was hard labor at Bridewell prison. In October, having ordered the judges to devise an "expedient" to limit the hawkers, the Council, in a softer approach, issued a proclamation offering a pardon to hawkers who reported the name of the bookseller or printer who supplied him or her with seditious material to sell.[62] Neither approach seems to have worked; in December the Council turned to court officers to get rid of hawkers who were plying their trade at the gates of Whitehall.[63] Unli-

censed hawkers continued to appear on the streets of London although a new charter, issued to the Stationers Company in 1684,
provided that only its members could sell books. And in 1687, the
Stationers and other tradesmen created a fund out of which to pay a
private individual who promised to rid the city of hawkers; clearly
he was without effect: at the time of the Revolution hawkers were
so busy that an observer predicted, with evident humor, that they
would become the next city company.[64]

The Council also tried to improve the Stationers performance.
The royal bookbinder, Samuel Mearne, was installed as a master for
1679, and he used his influence to persuade the company to impose
fines for failure to abide by licensing rules. With court encouragement the company drew up supplementary ordinances in 1681 and
1683 imposing fines for violating regulations that had appeared in
the old Licensing Act, such as importing or printing pirated copies.[65] The continued closeness between court and Stationers was revealed in 1684 during the quo warranto proceedings against London
companies. That Stationers was the first to surrender its charter and
the first to receive a new one. The Stationers was rewarded with
clauses (requested by the company) that made membership obliga-
tory for letter-founders and builders of presses, gave royal approval
to the company's register (to reinforce the Stationers' effort to provide a kind of copyright), and limited the binding and sale of books
in London and environs to company members. Charles's successors
continued to depend on the Stationers until the lapse of the Licensing Act in 1695, and the 1684 charter was not replaced until 1933.[66]

When in 1679 the Council asked the Stationers and L'Estrange to
prepare fresh proposals for "regulating the abuses and libertyes of
the Presse," the latter, in an about-face of his earlier attitude, recommended that the printers be incorporated as a separate company,
declaring that "ye Presse may be Regulated this way and no other."
Among his reasons was the one printers had given earlier when they
sought incorporation, namely that the superior knowledge of the
craft that printers possessed made them more effective than anyone
else in uncovering violations of printing laws. As before, opposition
from the Stationers killed the proposal.[67] The most effective step
that the Council took to assure the government's control over the
press was to seek the assistance of the judges, who held their tenure

at the pleasure of the king. Responding in October 1679, the judges ruled that the government could seize seditious and blasphemous papers and jail those persons responsible pending trial. A proclamation announced these points and set up a reward system for informers. At about the same time, Lord Chief Justice William Scroggs affirmed from the bench the power of the law "to punish a Libellous and Licentious Press" and his determination to do just that. Defendants appearing before him on charges relating to the press felt his resolve; for example, Henry Care was imprisoned and denied bail; Francis Smith was sent to jail for selling a tract.[68]

The October legal opinion, however, had said nothing about the unlicensed newspapers that, for the first time since the early days of the Restoration, had begun to appear. Harris's *Domestick Intelligence*, the first genuine newspaper, was on the streets of London on 7 July 1679. Other newssheets followed in profusion. Among them were Langley's *The True Protestant Mercury*, Janeway's *Impartial Protestant Mercury*, and Smith's *Protestant Intelligence*, all of which appeared between 1679 and 1682, all brought out by Dissenters and critics of the government, except for a paper with changing titles that the Catholic Nat Thomspon printed. Even worse from the government's point of view was the appearance of weekly papers of political comment, the most important of which were Henry Care's *Weekly Pacquet of Advice from Rome: or, The History of Popery* and Edward Rawlins's *Heraclitus Ridens*. In sharp contrast to the *London Gazette*, the government's official newspaper, these newssheets focused on domestic events and the issues that were of burning interest to the public. They reported, inter alia, the *Votes of the House of Comons* (after November 1680), news of Privy Council meetings (leaked by one of their "sources"), election returns, news of parliamentary activities such as petitions and addresses and debates (also leaked), accounts of trials, and information about London politics.[69] For a time these papers appeared regularly, incensing the government with their persistent revelations and popularity. With Parliament prorogued the Council asked the judges to consider "how far his Majesty's Royal Power may by law be made use" of in regulating newspapers.[70] Although differences of opinion were reported, in May 1680 the judges handed down the opinion that the king "may by Law prohibit the printing & publishing all News Bookes & Pamphletts of News whatsoever not licensed by your Authority."[71] They grounded this opinion on the idea that unlicensed news tended to breach the peace of the nation, and on the king's prerogative to grant printing monopolies. In a proclamation dated 12 May, the Privy Council announced a ban on all unlicensed newsbooks.[72]

This ruling allowed the government to proceed legally against the authors, publishers, and printers of newspapers. In the trial of Henry Care in the summer of 1680, an extreme interpretation of the royal prerogative over licensing news was expounded from the bench. Citing the recent opinion of the judges, George Jeffreys, at this time recorder of London, declared, "No person whatsoever could expose to the public knowledge anything that concerned the affairs of the public, without license from the king."[73] It would be difficult to find a more explicit statement of the view the Crown held of its legal authority over licensing the news. The ruling radically extended the royal prerogative and alarmed the Whigs. In November 1680, Henry Powle complained that by this decision the judges had made new law and thereby threatened the existence of Parliament, and Whig leaders cited the decision in drafting articles of impeachment against Scroggs.[74] But, acting on this ruling, in November 1682 the government banned the publication of all newssheets except the *London Gazette* and the *Observator*, a new paper published during the crisis by L'Estrange.

L'Estrange's *Observator* was arguably the court's most powerful weapon in the contest for public allegiance. The paper saturated the market, appearing three or four times a week from 13 April 1681 to 9 March 1687. Exploiting the dialogue form to convey news and ideas, L'Estrange hotly condemned the opposition press as responsible for making the "multitude madd." People, he said, were well-disposed if left to themselves, but the press had "Hair'd and Juggled [them] out of their Senses with so many Frightful Stories and Impostures." Significantly, he went on to say that "the Press must set 'um Right again. . . . There's no way in the world, but by Printing, to convey the Remedy to the Disease." He clearly stated his purpose: it was "to encounter the Faction, and to Vindicate the Government; to detect Forgeries . . . Calumnies, and Malice; and to Refute Seditious Doctrines." Using anecdotes, fictional characters, ridicule, humor, and colloquial language, L'Estrange pursued this goal, attacking Whigs, Dissenters, Trimmers, and their friends among pamphleteers, printers, and publishers.[75]

In these various ways, then, the government tightened control over the press; yet it was not entirely successful in restraining it. A dramatic and instructive example of how critics were able to print a tract certain to displease the court and how the court handled the incident at a time when the Licensing Act was not in force is provided by the scaffold speech of Lord William Russell. A leader of the Whig opposition in the Commons from 1678–81, Russell was condemned in 1683 as a traitor for his part in the Rye House plot, an alleged conspiracy to assassinate Charles and James and stage a Whig coup.[76]

Russell, his wife and family, and his political associates regarded the speech as the only means at hand of vindicating Russell's reputation and the integrity of the Whigs. Russell's friends contacted John Darby, a printer known to be sympathetic to the Whigs, delivered the manuscript to him the night before the execution, and ensured that the tract was on sale in the streets "within an hour" of Russell's death on July 21. The very next day 2500 copies appeared in Bedfordshire, where Russell's family estate was located. The *Speech* sold "prodigiously," going through three editions in 1683. There must have been at least 25,000 copies in circulation during 1683.[77]

Russell's *Speech* was offensive to the government because of its criticism of state and Anglican church. Portraying himself as a devout Protestant and Anglican who could not accept "all the heights" of that communion, Russell called on all *true* Protestants to unite "against the common enemy," popery. He characterized himself as an innocent who wanted only to save his beloved country from Catholicism and absolutism, as a martyr to the Whig cause. Crown lawyers had stretched the evidence to make "constructive treason" and had convicted him "by forms and subtleties of law." This was tantamount to judicial murder but Russell ended by forgiving everyone connected with his "murther."

Russell's *Speech* enraged the court. The tract had defeated the king's expectations that by a "show trial" the government would be able to brand the Whigs as a treasonable faction. Accordingly, a swift, well-orchestrated response followed. The Privy Council interrogated people suspected of having a hand in writing or distributing the speech, including Lady Russell, Dr. Gilbert Burnet (an Anglican

cleric increasingly critical of the government), Samuel Johnson
(Russell's chaplain), and the printer John Darby. Darby was given
only a light fine but was warned not to print anything against the
government again.[78] Burnet was so alarmed by the displeasure of the
Council and the continuing "malice" of the court that in September
he left for the Continent.[79] Specifically in response to Russell's
speech and other tracts about the Rye House plot, Charles II ordered
that a declaration be issued describing the conspiracies, summarizing the evidence, and justifying the government's actions.

The government continued to use the press to keep the public
informed about its progress in dealing with the conspiracy, issuing
accounts of the trials and executions, a report on the conspirators,
and an account of the plot under the lurid title *A History of the New
Plot: Or, A Prospect of Conspirators, their Designs Damnable, Ends
Miserable, Deaths Exemplary.* Striking pictures illustrated this
tract—one shows a frog and a mouse "at variance which shall be
king," while over them a kite prepares to swoop down and destroy
both. An explicit moral was drawn: "So factious Men Conspiring
doe Contend/But Hasten their own Ruin in the End."[80] These pictorial details and accompanying explanation suggest that this pamphlet was deliberately aimed at a mass market. The government also
published many tracts directly to refute Russell's *Speech.* By the end
of the year approximately fifty tracts, ranging in style and approach,
were in circulation.

Whatever the view of the court about its prerogative rights over
printing and whatever its efforts to implement that position, the fact
was that the licensing rules were violated, even at times when the
government desired the most thorough-going repression. By the
time of the Revolution, English people were well accustomed to
the public airing in print of political and religious commentary and
ideas that were sharply critical of the government. This background
of experience with the print media was an important part of the
context within which the Revolution unfolded.

< III >

On his accession to the throne in February 1685, James II promptly
took steps to reinstate and strengthen former procedures in control-

ling printed matter. From February 1685 to November 1687, the new secretary of state, Robert Spencer, earl of Sunderland, issued thirty-four orders respecting the press. Among them were orders to reinforce the Stationers Company and to suppress seditious emblems and pictures, an indication of the power of iconographic material.[81] In July 1685 the king's first and only Parliament re-enacted the Licensing Act, giving it an expiry date of seven years. L'Estrange received recognition, being knighted in April and receiving a warrant on May 21 to "exercise all such powers as he formerly did" to regulate the press.[82] However, James encountered a new problem because censors refused to license Catholic books and the Stationers wardens seized Catholic works. James countered by banning anti-Catholic works in the term catalogues, appointing a Catholic to the post of king's printer, and allowing a Catholic convert to operate a press in Oxford. Catholic books began to appear, advertised in the *Gazette*.[83] Like his predecessors highly sensitive to the importance of controlling and interpreting the news, James allowed Henry Care, a former Whig but now a Catholic convert, to print a weekly newspaper, *Public Occurrences Truely Stated*, that provided a pro-government account of events.[84] In a further effort to influence public opinion in his favor, the king instructed his agents in the fall of 1687 to place "books and papers . . . in coffeehouses and houses of public entertainment." In the spring of 1688, the court inspired rumors, commissioned tracts, and dispersed *gratis* quantities of the king's "papers." At about the same time, James issued a "severe" proclamation restricting printing and offered a reward of £1,000 to discover the author of an offending tract, *Reflexions on Mr. Fagel's Letter*, whose purpose was to persuade Dissenters not to credit the king's promises of relief to them. The proclamation also limited the buying and selling of books and specifically prohibited peddlers from selling books. Radical Whig pamphleteers suffered punishment, as in the case of the Reverend Samuel Johnson, who in 1686 was stripped of his holy orders, pilloried, and whipped for writing *A Humble and Hearty Address to All the English Protestants in this Present Army*. In April 1688 a contemporary wrote that "neither art, money, nor pains are omitted" in James's effort to influence public opinion.[85]

As the crisis leading to Revolution deepened in the autumn of 1688, William of Orange and his partisans mounted a massive propaganda campaign; James responded by intensifying his efforts to control the press and to get his own message to the people. The campaign on both sides provides a striking example of the uses of the press in political maneuvering and shows how seriously public opinion was regarded.[86]

William was no stranger to using the press to manipulate public opinion in England. James Johnstone, who acted as his press agent, wrote that if William wanted to keep the "nation in humour [he] must entertain it by papers."[87] With help from others, he spelled out a specific press campaign that was largely followed. Among the recommendations was that a history of the prince and his family be written to praise William's character and administration in Holland; and at least five tracts appeared in the fall and winter of 1688–89 to do just that. Englishmen supplied a draft of a manifesto justifying the intended invasion. Following a careful review of the substance and style of the draft and the resolution of disputes about its content, a "committee" of Dutch and English men prepared the most effectively written tract that appeared in 1688–89, *The Declaration of His Highness William Henry, Prince of Orange, of the Reasons Inducing Him to Appear in Armes in the Kingdom of England for Preserving of the Protestant Religion and for Restoring the Lawes and Liberties of England, Scotland, and Ireland.*[88] Even James's ambassador at The Hague, who abhorred the contents of the manifesto, described its style as "civil and smooth" and warned that it would "gain the people's affections."[89]

The timing and distribution of this piece also occupied the attention of William's servants. To avoid "leaks," William delayed issuing the *Declaration* until just before his invasion. It appeared in English, Dutch, German, and French and was printed in Amsterdam, The Hague, Hamburg, Magdeburg, and Rotterdam. Altogether, twenty-one editions appeared in 1688, eight of them in English. The *Declaration* was distributed from one end of Britain to the other. "Many thousand copies" were sent across the channel to be "consigned to some trusty person in London" for distribution. A password was devised for the prince's agents to protect them from "speaking to any wrong person who brings the papers."[90] Friends of the prince received copies to distribute and bundles of free copies were sent to booksellers to sell at their own profit, a tactic that had been used at the time of the exclusion crisis, harnessing the profit motive to induce sales.

The *Declaration* was not the only tract that William and his friends put into circulation. Printed broadsides were addressed to the English army and fleet. These were short, simple exhortations in which William urged the men to join him in defense of the nation's religion, the point that held greatest appeal, and also of the country's laws, liberties, and properties and promised them rewards if they came in "seasonably." The *Letter to the Army*, according to an eighteenth-century historian, had a "wonderful effect" on the soldiers, in that it persuaded men not to fight for James and to support William in his call for a free Parliament.[91] William's agents also used the press to appeal to Scotland. They published a special version of the *Declaration* addressed to Scotland. It stressed the violations of law that had occurred in Scotland, called for a "universal concurrence" for the prince, and threatened anyone who opposed him.

William took a printing press with him—along with soldiers, horses, and money—as part of his invasion equipment. What better proof could there be of his determination to use the press for political purposes? Within three weeks of his arrival, he was reported to be printing "two gazettes a week," among other papers.[92] William also commissioned Burnet to write pamphlets dealing with questions that were troubling thoughtful Englishmen. Two pieces—one on the problems that would result from recalling James after his flight, and the other on the reason for the king's withdrawing from Rochester—were printed "By Authority." A third, also by Burnet and issued "By the Prince of Orange's special command," undertook to answer a tract from James that disparaged William's manifesto.[93] In each case, these "official" pamphlets reinforced the main themes of the *Declaration* and thereby enhanced its significance.

This material was so consistent in its message and so widespread that no one with the least interest in politics could have escaped exposure to the idea that William had invaded England as selfless deliverer for the purpose of rescuing the nation's religion, laws, and liberties. James II was depicted as a tyrant, bound to Jesuits and Louis XIV, and bent on destroying England's religion, liberties, and law, even to the point of foisting a suppositious baby on the nation.

William's *Declaration* served as a position paper, a basis for discussing solutions to the crisis. It also influenced the solution to the crisis by limiting William's political options. Because of the promise in his manifesto, he felt obliged to refer the solution to the crisis to an elected Parliament. William's propaganda restricted his responses to the Declaration of Rights passed by the convention. The theme in the prince's propaganda that he came only to redress grievances and restore rights and the specific statement that the "only means" to do so was in a Parliament by a declaration of rights made it impossible for William to resist the convention's determination to present their claim. In accepting the Declaration of Rights, William sacrificed his reluctance to restrict—either substantively or symbolically—the powers of the monarch to his need to maintain a public image compatible with his propaganda.

Finally, by asserting that the prince came only to assure the calling of a free Parliament which would settle the national crisis, William's printed propaganda conveyed the impression that Englishmen held the fate of the nation in their own hands. Partly as a result of this perception, a broad consensus of approval for the Dutch prince and his policies (however short-lived that approbation proved to be) was achieved when it was most needed—while the crisis was being resolved. Later, James attributed the defections in his army and the nation to William's propaganda, which made him, he said, "appear as black as Hell." A pamphleteer also referred to "those little stories" circulated in print which "more than anything else alienated men's affections."[94]

The campaign in the press to shape public opinion, then, helps to explain William's success. In addition to printed written material, printed iconographic material appeared. At least forty-nine prints were devised to support William's cause and to appeal to a wider audience than pamphlets and tracts could reach. These prints are amusing and exuberant and those qualities must have delighted and, at the same time, instructed viewers. One of the most appealing was *England's Memorial: Of its Wonderfull deliverance from French tiranny and Popish oppression . . . 1688.* In the center stands a flourishing orange tree—the symbol since 1641 of the House of Orange—obviously signifying the goodness and strength of William. All around is evidence of the dangers England faced and the success of William in repulsing them. In the upper right-hand corner appears the Church of England, plainly awry, about to topple over. Above it is the eye of providence, one ray of which bathes the orange tree and promises, "My blessing shall attend thee every where." Opposite the eye of providence in the upper left hand corner sits a council of devils and Jesuits, one of whom remarks, "This cursed plant [the orange tree] has Sau'd the Heretick Church." Beneath them Louis XIV cuts off the heads of his subjects, plainly illustrating what English subjects might expect from a Catholic king. Near the tree stands James II, looking startled. An orange has knocked off his crown. Although putting pictures in the service of politics was not new in 1688–89—prints had appeared during the exclusion crisis[95]—a greater number were in circulation at the time of the Revolution than ever before.

Polemical playing cards, the forerunners of the comic strip, also effectively presented incidents in the Revolution. Such cards first appeared in 1659, satirizing the Rump Parliament; and others appeared during the popish plot, the Rye House plot, and Monmouth's rebellion. Two packs were printed early in 1689, one of them advertised for twelve pence in the *Orange Gazette*. When the cards are arranged in an appropriate sequence, they provide a pictorial narrative record of events. With their simple figures and short text, the cards could appeal to a very broad spectrum of people.[96]

William's propaganda overwhelmed James's press campaign. James tried in October 1688 to suppress criticism by restricting the circulation of news, commanding coffee houses to keep no written news but the official *London Gazette*, upon pain of forfeiting their licenses and burning seditious books.[97] He banned absolutely William's *Declaration* and the broadside letters addressed to the army and navy. In a proclamation issued on 2 November, three days before the prince landed, the king declared it treason for anyone to read, receive, conceal, publish, disperse, repeat, or hand about any of the prince's printed pieces.[98] Men discovered bringing copies of the *Declaration* into England were arrested.[99] The Privy Council sat the afternoon of the day William landed drawing up a "counter-declaration" which was rushed to the press the next day. Three tracts—*Animadversions, Some Reflections, and Some Modest Remarks*—replied directly to William's manifesto, depicting the prince as a conqueror and disparaging his motives, reputation, and moral integrity.[100] Other tracts reinforced and expanded these themes, as for example *The Dutch Design Anatomiz'd; or, A Discovery of the wickedness and unjustice of the intended invasion*, which stressed the dangers to England's liberties and trade that William's invasion posed.

With James's departure the radical Whigs made intensive use of the press to influence public opinion on behalf of their proposed reforms, arguing for changes in government. To attract a wide readership, they devised attractive titles—such as *A Word to the Wise, For Setling the Government*, advertised their pamphlets in other publications, and left copies at coffee houses.[101] Their main concern was to influence members of the convention addressing some titles directly to them, as for example, *Proposals Humbly offered To the Lords and Commons in the present convention, for Settling of the Government*. One pamphlet, according to its author, was handed directly to members of the convention, while another "was delivered" to the Commons just before an important vote.[102] Tracts were reprinted in *Collections* that appeared on the eve of the opening of the convention on 22 January 1689, the timing surely to make them readily available to members. For example, John Wildman's *Letter to a Friend* was in print by 5 January 1689, and by 18 January it was reprinted in a *Sixth Collection of Papers*.

These radical tracts had some influence on the steps taken in the convention, although there is only one claim that a specific tract changed votes.[103] Sir John Maynard spoke slightingly of schemes being concocted in coffee houses, and another Whig, John Birch, perhaps with such schemes in mind, recommended the drafting of a claim of rights to forestall mob uprisings or pressure on the convention. Arguments in language very close to that of the tracts appeared in debates. For example, remarks about the people having a divine right to their liberties replicate a passage in Robert Ferguson's *Brief Justification*. Public opinion, created in large measure by the press, had an important part to play in the politics of the Revolution. The success of the press effort is reflected in the remark of a hostile critic that the issues had been drawn down to every vulgar capacity.[104] As had happened at earlier crisis points during the century, all sides saw advantages in using the press to reach people outside as well as within traditional elite categories. Critics of the establishment violated the laws, and got away with it, because in 1688 the administrative mechanisms broke. Yet, when these critics became the establishment, they sought to reinstitute the very laws and procedures they had violated.

Although the Glorious Revolution is sometimes credited with bringing about freedom of the press in England, in fact it contributed only indirectly to winning liberty of the press. It is true that some interest was expressed in allowing greater freedom in parliamentary reporting, but that interest did not prevail before the contrary opinion of the majority.

The question of allowing information about parliamentary affairs to circulate in print arose on the opening day of the convention, with the Commons rejecting a motion that the votes of the House be printed. The majority contended that the House should "remain Master of their own Votes (which they could not if Printed)," and preserve the freedom to change their minds and to make concessions to the Lords.[105] A motion to print votes was re-introduced on 9 March, after the convention had been transformed into a legal parliament, but was opposed by at least eight prominent members, all except one Whigs and former exclusionists, who in 1680–81 had favored printing votes and proceedings. They objected that printing the votes violated precedent, revealed actions that seldom were final, involved the two Houses in potential conflict, threatened the freedom of parliamentary debate, and subjected members to the vagaries of the "ballot box."[106]

On the other hand, the printing of votes was favored by a minority which included Whigs and former exclusionists who had almost certainly supported printing in 1680–81. Their main argument was that the people were entitled to know what their elected representatives did. No member in the new circumstances following the Revolution ought to feel intimidated. Besides, Parliament's affairs were freely discussed anyway—but in garbled form—in coffee houses, and an accurate report of them would be assured if the motion passed. At the same time there was political calculation in the move to print votes, namely to enlist popular support for the measures taken by the convention. The motion to print votes lost by a vote of 145 to 180. Although the attitude of the majority was softened by October 1689, when the votes were ordered printed under the supervision of the Speaker, commitment to the principle of confidentiality was rigorously preserved.[107]

Orders passed by the Commons to restrict the public's access to its chamber reflected the same basic attitude. In conformity with earlier precedents, the convention passed five such orders; that it had to do so frequently reveals the difficulties in keeping the public out of the chamber.[108] The Commons was clearly determined to maintain the past practice of excluding strangers. News of parliamentary activities did circulate through gossip, calculated leaks, and unlicensed printed accounts.[109] Members responded energetically to the appearance of this printed material, with invective and heated comment, one member sharply objecting to people who took "notice of our Debates." In the fall the Commons pointedly reminded newsmongers that they were not to reprint parliamentary news in newsletters and other written papers without the consent of the Speaker.[110] The convention and the subsequent Parliament dealt with violations of its "closed doors" policy by searching out and punishing offending authors, printers, and publishers.[111] Subversive material received demonstratively severe treatment. *A Short History of the Convention, or New Christen'd Parliament* impugned the election to the convention, the election of the Speaker, the integrity of the members, and the terms of the settlement. It called upon "Prince" William to bring back "King" James, which so angered members that they ordered the common hangman to burn the pamphlet at Palace Yard, Temple Bar, and the old exchange.[112]

The *principle* of liberty of the press was not in the forefront of anyone's mind during the weeks of the revolution, from the fall of 1688 through mid-February 1689, when the settlement of affairs was under consideration. What was of concern respecting the press was how it could be used to mold public opinion in favor of a particular point of view. The press was an important instrument in the political maneuvering of these months and a vehicle for circulating political ideas. But, neither in tracts or pamphlets nor in the debates of the convention was a theory about liberty of the press advanced. None of the tracts of earlier radicals who had broached the idea— Walwyn, Overton, Lilburne, and Milton—was reprinted in 1689,[113] and the leaders of the Revolution generally wished to distance themselves from earlier radicals. No useable intellectual tradition existed in support of the principle of liberty of the press. Only one pamphlet out of the approximately two thousand tracts and pamphlets that were in circulation during these months dealt with the press: *A Speech Without-Doors*, written by an eccentric publicist, Edmond Hickeringill, which called for a repeal of the Licensing Act. Hickeringill described the act as contrary to common law (because it obstructed the trade of printing) and to the law of God (because God enjoins men not to hide their light under a "napkin"), but his argument had no discernible influence.[114]

Had the men in the Revolution considered liberty of the press important and press control a grievance of the nation, someone would surely have raised the question in the convention debates on the grievances and rights of the nation. But no one could suggest that liberty of the press was an ancient right of the nation; the press was only 200 years old and had always been subject to control by the Crown. Consequently press freedom appears neither in the Heads of Grievances (the first draft of the Declaration of Rights) nor in the final version of the document that was presented to William and Mary on 13 February; nor is it in the Bill of Rights, which received royal assent in December 1689. The Revolution was settled without reference to the idea of liberty of the press.

The new government displayed the same attitude towards the press as previous governments. From October 1689 to April 1695 there were seventeen trials for unlicensed printing.[115] And in June 1693, the charge of treason was brought against the most notorious of Jacobite printers, William Anderton. He stood accused of printing seditious material. Desperate Jacobite tracts, one entitled *Remarks on the Present Confederacy and the Late Revolution*, which called for the nation to rise up in arms against the tyrant William, were found in his shop. The jury, however, was reluctant to condemn Anderton, whose defense was that he did not know the contents of what he was printing. Only after Chief Justice Treby supplied strong arguments did the jury reach a verdict of guilty. Mary II, who was regent at the time, refused to pardon Anderton, and he suffered the dreadful penalties of a convicted traitor.[116] The Anderton case was only the third time in the late seventeenth century that a printer was charged with treason for printing seditious material; it illustrates the instability of the reign and also the seriousness with which William and Mary regarded the power of the press.

Yet, within the first four years of William and Mary's reign, in-

terest in removing the old pre-publication censorship procedures
and the restraints on the press began to surface. Prominent among
the reasons, to be fully discussed in the following chapter, was the
fact that the procedures were largely ineffective. Besides being ineffective, they were costly, time-consuming, and burdensome to administrators. Moreover, printers and others stressed the economic
hardships that press policy imposed on them; railed at monopolies
and the role of the Stationers Company; and praised the advantages
of a free press, including employment for printers, revenue for the
government, and competition to the prosperous press in the Netherlands.[117] In place of the old "liberty" of a monopoly, they wanted a
new "liberty" of the individual printer, publisher, and bookseller.

Political considerations also operated. Jealousy between the two
houses of Parliament furthered progress towards abandoning the old
controls, as did Tory and Whig partisan politics. Licensers came and
went in the post-revolutionary world of parties, with each politically appointed licenser damaging the other party in turn. The political nation needed a free press to keep abreast of developments on
the Continent, in the war, and in finance and business. Young MPs
especially demanded access to such information.[118] But no parliamentary leader argued for the principle of "liberty of the press," and
only a minority endorsed the idea of allowing printed accounts of
parliamentary activities. Scholars and intellectuals also complained
about the government's restrictive press policy. Reflecting their interests, John Locke maintained that the Stationers monopolies low-
ered the quality and raised the price of classical books and caused
"great oppression upon Schollers."[119] Only Blount argued for a press
free of pre-publication censorship in the name of "Truth"; [120] nobody
developed the idea of the press as a "right."

When Parliament allowed the Licensing Act of 1662 to die in the
spring of 1695, the result was a different relationship between press
and government. For the time being pre-publication censorship disappeared. A freer press than had existed before emerged, but the
struggle of the press to achieve independence from the government
continued in different forms.

Press and Public Opinion: Prospective

G. C. GIBBS

AMONG THE CEREMONIES held in 1788 to commemorate the centenary of the Revolution of 1688, the most significant was the anniversary ceremony of the London Revolution Society on 4 November, the date of William III's birth and marriage. This date, chosen in preference to 5 November, the day of William's landing at Torbay, avoided confounding commemoration of the Revolution with that of Gun Powder plot. Further, the inclusion in the Anglican service appointed for 5 November of an exhortation to servants "to be obedient unto their own masters, and to please them well in all things; not answering again" seemed totally unfit for the celebration of the Revolution. During the celebratory dinner forty-one toasts were drunk, inviting attention to a large number of desirable reforms; perhaps because the two toasts were well-spaced, the company was called upon to drink to the press twice. After "The Majesty of the People," "The Glorious Revolution and the immortal memory of our great deliverer, King William III," and "May every succeeding century maintain the principles of the Glorious Revolution, enjoy its blessings and transmit them to future ages unimpaired and improved," came "May the freedom of election be preserved, the trial by jury maintained, and the liberty of the press secured, to the latest posterity." Twenty-seven toasts later, having toasted on the way, among other things, the immortal memory of Alfred the Great; the principles of Magna Carta, the Habeas Corpus Act, and the incomparable Bill of Rights; "the cause of liberty throughout the globe"; and "the example of one revolution to prevent the necessity of another," the company rose to toast "the freedom of the press, the bulwark of English liberty." The society agreed to a public profession of its political principles, "as valid in 1788 as a century before."

This took the form of a tripartite declaration; its third part ran: "That the right of private judgement, liberty of conscience, trial by jury, the freedom of the press and freedom of election ought ever to be held sacred and inviolable."[1]

These happenings in the London Revolution Society on 4 November 1788 provide much that is of interest to students of the English democratic tradition, and of its messianic strain; of eighteenth-century popular culture; and of the historiography and changing political utility of the Glorious Revolution. However, what will strike students of the English press as distinctly odd is the twice repeated claim that liberty or freedom of the press, as the bulwark of English liberty, had been a principle of the Revolution, one of its blessings, and a notion as well-founded in 1688 as it was in 1788. A desire to see a free press elevated into an essential part and safeguard of the constitution was so distant from the reality of events in 1688–89 as well as 1695, the year the Licensing Act lapsed and incontestably the seminal year in the development of a free press in England, as to be virtually invisible. What was much more apparent in those years, and for more than a decade after 1695, was a contrary and recurrent concern among ministers, peers and MPs, the clergy, and vested interests in the book trade, to regulate printing and the press by statute; to restrict their freedom and power; even to return to some form of pre-publication censorship.

After tracing and evaluating the various attempts at statutory regulation and containment of the press in the decades after 1695, this chapter will consider the role and the machinery of the law in matters of press regulation, taking Fox's libel act of 1792 as the *terminus ad quem*. Recourse to the law, it will be argued, had its successes as a means of disciplining the press and, in the case of the Jacobitish press of the early years of George I's reign, was capable even of destroying a segment of it. But though severe, the law was fundamentally powerless to contain the growth of the press and probably less influential in determining the contents of eighteenth-century newspapers than were the economics of contemporary newspaper production or parliamentary privilege, which effectively prevented regular and full-scale reporting of parliamentary debates until the successful challenge to Parliament's privacy of debate by Wilkes in 1771. And recourse to the law on the part of government

was often counter-productive. It will be further argued that though
the law might do something to eliminate or minimize a bad press,
it could do little to ensure a good press. Ensuring a good press became an enduring concern of governments, a concern which required far more than the most efficient official press could have provided. The official press in England, in the shape of the *London Gazette*, was far from efficient or sufficient. In the final section of this
chapter attention will be directed to the consequences of a free press
for the conduct of English government in the eighteenth century,
and to the role of a free press in widening and shaping political
discourse.

≺ I ≻

The argument that the framers of the Revolution believed that liberty of the press was an essential and sacred part of the liberties of
the kingdom provided the opposition to Sir Robert Walpole with a
main theme in the years after 1726. Concern for liberty of the press
as a bulwark of the constitution, together with attacks on standing
armies and official corruption, legitimized the opposition by representing Walpole and the ministerial Whigs as betrayers of the Revolution. In particular, it legitimized an opposition of disaffected
Whigs vulnerable to a charge of having reneged upon their Whig
beliefs. Moreover, concern for liberty of the press as the bulwark of
the constitution, even its sole remaining bulwark, came appropriately from an opposition apparently impotent in Parliament, and
came most appropriately from an opposition one of whose principal
leaders was barred from the Lords, and whose newspapers were subjected during the years between 1733 and 1737 to a legal assault
unequalled in its severity until the surge of prosecutions inaugurated by the French Revolution.[2]

The particular argument that liberty of the press was at the heart
of the Revolution was easily refuted. *The Daily Gazeteer*, a newspaper supporting Walpole's ministry, indeed subsidized by it, was
right to say that the men of 1688 did not regard the press as "the
proper instrument to restrain the excesses and correct the misbehavior of men in power," and that there was no reference in the Decla-

ration of Rights to liberty of the press; "that was a thing not so much as dreamt of in those days."[3]

Nor is there any evidence of liberty of the press in any sense having been raised in Parliament in 1689. However, there could be no doubt that the success of the Revolution owed much to the use of the press as an instrument for bringing down James II and for advancing the cause of William III.[4] That was not an argument *the Daily Gazeteer* chose to make. Instead, it pointed out that the press was neither ignored nor favored at the Revolution: the legislation of the later Stuarts in respect of the press and printing was simply maintained. Long concerned with the power and deployment of the press for propaganda purposes, William as king in England urged the pursuit and punishment of Jacobite libellers.[5] When the question of the further renewal of the Licensing Act of 1662 came before Parliament early in 1693, the government pressed strongly and successfully for its renewal, as might have been expected from a recently established revolutionary regime, still at war and under threat internally as well as externally.

A contemporary Jacobite pamphleteer suggested that renewal was secured only after "great struggling."[6] But it does not appear that opponents of renewal were motivated by a realization of the potential significance of the freedom of the press as a guarantor of the constitution. The evidence in Parliament itself points to narrower and non-political concerns. There was opposition from the independent sector of the book trade complaining of the inequitable restriction upon its trade imposed by the Licensing Act as compared with the restrictions imposed on other trades. There was also opposition from a small group in the House of Lords, mostly Whigs and including authors and patrons of literature estranged from the court, on the grounds that the existing licensing system, in addition to being monopolistic, subjected learning to the arbitrary will of a mercenary and ignorant licenser—a reflection on the earl of Nottingham, the secretary of state, and on the licensers he employed. These critics suggested that any book containing the names of its author and printer might be published without a license.[7]

That particular idea was rejected in 1693 and it never commanded much support from authors, patrons, or even from politicians as they became habituated to the constant necessity for press management.⁸ But after 1695, when pre-publication censorship ceased and printing proliferated, it was thought necessary to have some means of identifying those held responsible for offensive literature in order to bring them to account. In a sense this was a logical development of the Licensing Act of 1662. The preamble to that act asserted that the most effectual means of preventing the printing and selling of "heretical, schismatical, blasphemous, seditious and treasonable Books and Papers" was to restrict and limit the number of presses.⁹ In short, to restrict output as well as content. If content was not to be restricted before publication, and if output was to become increasingly difficult to restrict, there appeared to be a need to devise some system or formula for facilitating legal accountability and thereby encouraging the practice of self-censorship among printers, publishers, and authors.

It was certainly a need addressed in February 1695 when the Commons was required to consider renewal of the Licensing Act of 1662. The House decided at first that a renewal should not be included in a bill, then before it, for continuing various acts about to expire; instead it favored a replacement bill for better regulating printing and printing presses. In some respects the bill proved more sweeping and more stringent than the act the Commons had declined to renew. It required the owners of presses to register them with various specified registration authorities, but for the first time they would be able to establish presses in any city or corporate town in the kingdom, ending the monopoly of London and the universities. Those who did not register became liable to a fine and disablement from trade. Printers of all new books, pamphlets, and papers (and also of portraitures, omitted from the 1662 act) that dealt with religion, the laws, or history of England, were to deliver them sheet by sheet as they were printed—another novelty as compared with the 1662 act—to specified authorities. Anyone who printed anything contrary to the laws of the realm, or contrary to the Christian religion as established by law, would be disabled from his trade and have his press and equipment forfeited. Printers were to be answerable as if they were the authors. All publications were to bear the names and addresses of the master printer and publisher upon pain of forfeiture of the copies printed, with their presses and other equipment. All registration authorities were empowered to issue

search warrants to enter any printing house or other place when
informed upon oath that it housed a private printing press; to seize
any copies of treasonable, seditious, heretical, or atheistical publications; and to bring to justice all persons concerned in the printing
or selling of such publications. No distinction was made between
the houses of peers and of commoners. The numbers of presses or
apprentices were not restricted as they had been in the act of 1662.
No restrictions were placed upon the import of books. There was no
clause limiting the period of copyright.[10]

It is difficult to imagine a bill more calculated to offend vested
interests. The London book trade strongly disliked a bill that ended
London's monopoly but said nothing about copyright. By tradition,
copyright was established by entry in the Hall book of the Stationers
Company, and entries were compulsory in law for as long as the
Licensing Act was on the statute book. If the proposed bill went
through, and the Licensing Act was allowed to lapse, then the only
remedy would be a long and costly suit in chancery. John Locke was
concerned with the general rights and needs of scholars and authors
and with copyright, and was concerned also, as the author of *The
Reasonableness of Christianity*, about the implications of the references to heretical literature in the bill. If Locke was of the opinion
that in respect of religion the bill had gone too far, the bishops
thought that it had not gone far enough. For them the prevention of
mischief was preferable to its punishment, especially since punishment could only follow conviction, which might be difficult to secure. Even severe punishment did not necessarily deter, and a public
trial would give publicity to the very views it sought to silence.
They preferred a licenser.[11]

In these circumstances it was not surprising that the replacement bill failed to pass. The Commons presented its reasons for refusing to concur with the Lords in a lengthy document which owed
much to a memorandum from Locke. It listed arguments about the
unnatural and damaging monopolies of the Stationers Company,
membership of which was necessary to open a printing press, to import books, and to set up as a bookseller; the lack of definition in
the Licensing Act of 1662 as to what constituted 'offensive' literature; that act's failure to achieve the purposes for which it had been
enacted; the invasion of privacy involved in authorizing officials to
search "all mens houses, as well Peers as Commoners," upon prob-

able suspicion of the presence of unlicensed books; and the adequacy of prosecutions at common law. It contained no argument in favor of liberty of the press, and there was no specific reference at all to the newspaper press.[12]

Whether the Lords was persuaded to agree to the lapse of the Licensing Act by the pragmatic arguments it had heard from the Commons is uncertain. There seems to have been concern to avoid conflict with the Commons by initiating a new bill which because of its pecuniary penalties might be regarded as a money bill and might excite a constitutional dispute between the two Houses at a time when the government desperately needed cash.[13] It is also uncertain whether the reasons given by the Commons for refusing to concur with the Lords were its only reasons. The efficacy of the licensing system depended in large part upon the licensers appointed by the secretaries of state. Those appointed after the Revolution had been men of strong and markedly different views on the character of the Revolution, who had performed their difficult duties in a manner which antagonized a wide spectrum of political opinion. Their difficulties arose from a sharply divided and keenly contentious political society and must have seemed certain to persist; even in 1693 doubts had been expressed as to whether the system was not too onerous for any licenser, however talented.[14] In the circumstances, it is not surprising that the Licensing Act was allowed to lapse.

The lapse left the press in a situation like that of the Dissenters under the so-called Toleration Act, which had secured no rights, only removed restrictions, and perhaps had removed them only temporarily. Thus, liberty of the press was not established in Britain in 1695, or indeed at any time subsequently, in any strict, separate, or formal sense as came to be the case in the United States in the late eighteenth century. Nor can it even be said to have been allowed, much less encouraged, to grow. Rather, it was suffered to grow, as had largely been the case in that other palladium of press liberty in the seventeenth century, the Dutch Republic. There liberty of the press found its best support in the diffused sovereignties of the Republic, and fundamentally in the autonomy of its towns, whose decision or non-decision or procrastination in executing resolutions and placards against the press, the States General and the provincial States had to accept.[15]

In England the occasional voices that spoke out in favor of liberty of the press in the 1690s came from those on or beyond the bounds of contemporary political and religious orthodoxy. The most eloquent advocate was Matthew Tindal. Like John Milton, Tindal approached the matter largely as an extension of liberty of conscience, essential for the discovery and preservation of religious truth, and as the peculiar gift of Protestantism. For Tindal, liberty of the press and Protestantism went together, as naturally as slavery and popery: they were twinned; and where separated, as Tindal admitted had occurred "in Denmark, Sweden and several other countries," restraint upon the liberty of the press had enabled ignorance, superstition, and bigotry to abound. Liberty of the press, argued Tindal, was the mother and the offspring of Protestantism, its achievement and its guarantor, as well as the guarantor of all other liberties; an educative and liberalizing force, and one which would keep Parliament alert. Restraint of the press was a popish invention, practice, and snare. Licensers were spiritual dragons: licensing was the Romish inquisition transplanted. All that was required was that either printer or bookseller should set his name on what he published.[16]

The cause of liberty of the press in England was weakened by the fact that Tindal was a Socinian. Throughout the 1690s the Church of England was much concerned with the spread of Socinianism into England. To high-church divines like Francis Atterbury and Francis Gregory, its spread was part of a wider contagion, even a conspiracy, of immorality, threatening to undermine and overthrow the Catholic faith and the manners of the country. They saw a free press as a prime communicator of that contagion, as a prime instrument in that conspiracy; and they also saw liberty of the press as an ideological cover for those who were part of that conspiracy.[17]

In their opposition to a free press Atterbury and Gregory appear to have found support, or a ready audience, among a substantial body of moral reformers in the House of Commons. These men pressed for the reformation of contemporary manners, urging the suppression of duelling, lotteries, cursing, profaneness, debauchery, and gaming.[18] They were also active after 1695 in the attempts made in the Commons to regulate the press and the printing trade; to restrain or prevent their licentiousness and to re-introduce licensing.

In the decades after the expiration of the Licensing Act frequent attempts were made to re-introduce a system of licensing and to pass bills regulating the press. All failed, but the establishment of an entirely new form of censorship in 1737—over theaters—shows that the atmosphere was not unfavorable. These attempts provoked opposition from vested interests in the publishing trade and from scholars, but it was mainly practical considerations that contributed to their failure. In a deeply divided political society licensers could not have avoided partisanship and, given the volatility of politics, a party or faction which exploited a licensing system might soon see it turned against itself. Furthermore the growth in the number of publications and places of publication made licensing logistically an increasingly daunting proposition: between 1666 and 1680 an estimated 3,550 "books" were published; this rose to 10,828 in the years 1710–15. Printing and bookbinding were said to employ 5,000 persons in London and Westminster alone in 1710, and an extensive provincial book trade existed by then which had developed entirely after 1695.

Proposals for licensing did provoke objections of principle. In 1738 Milton's *Areopagitica* and another classic argument for liberty of the press, *The Trial of Peter Zenger*, were republished; and in 1747 Horace Walpole wrote as a Whig who could not "sit by (as) an unconcerned Spectator and see this darling privilege (liberty of the press) openly and publicly attacked."[19]

Between 1695 and 1713 eight bills were initiated for the general regulation of the press—five in the Commons, three in the Lords—but none was completed.[20] The motives behind several of them were as much religious and moral as political. The objective was to prevent the publication of blasphemous and heretical as well as seditious and treasonable literature, to put restraints on those who "are endeavoring to destroy the true worship of God and religion, without which no good government can long subsist."[21] However even in the Lords, where such a bill was introduced in 1698 and strongly supported by the bench of bishops, such arguments proved to be insufficient. Faced by the problems of enforcement, the drafters of most of these bills relied on the requirement that printers and publishers should register, with penalties for those who did not comply; but the logical extension of this requirement to authors, which would strip them of anonymity and expose them to the malicious resentment of ministers, provoked considerable opposition.[22]

In 1712 new sanctions were imposed upon printers and publishers of pamphlets by legislation that obliged them to register their publications with the Stamp Office, or its officers. The so-called Stamp Act of 1712 imposed on papers containing public news, intelligence, or occurrences, a stamp duty charge that varied according to the size of the paper; it also imposed a tax on every advertisement, irrespective of length, contained in any printed paper or periodical published weekly or oftener. One copy of every pamphlet published in London or Westminster was to be taken to the Stamp Office within six days of publication, where duty was to be paid and the pamphlet registered. Pamphlets printed elsewhere had to be taken to a head collector of stamp duties. The penalties for printing an unregistered pamphlet, or one which did not bear the names and addresses of printers and publishers, were heavy. A fine of £20 was imposed upon the printers and publishers and extended to all those involved in the sale of such pamphlets, and copyright was lost even if it had been secured as provided for under the Copyright Act of 1710, which had established the first statutory protection of copy ownership. Further, any person could then freely print and publish the pamphlet, free of prosecution or penalty, provided he or she had paid the duty.[23] Since publication of pamphlets constituted an important part of the business of a London printer and publisher and pamphlets often went into more than one edition, such a potential loss of property was to be taken seriously.[24]

By virtue of its provisions for the registration of pamphlets, the 1712 act may be regarded as the culmination of some of the previous proposals for the regulation of the press. Yet in other respects it was undoubtedly innovative, as well as influential.

A controversy continues among historians whether the act was concerned principally to raise money, or to contain and reduce the press, particularly the opposition press.[25] However, to describe it as a stamp act is not only to prejudge the issue of its main thrust, but grossly to misrepresent its scope. For the laying of duties on a wide variety of printed papers made up only about one third of the act's clauses. Further, like the duties imposed by the act on soap, callicoes, and linens, the duties on printed papers were intended to fund prizes for a lottery: hence its contemporary description as the Lottery Act.[26] There can be no doubt that the primary intention of the act, as evidenced at least by its title, its preamble, and its contents, was to raise money; and it realized about £7,000 in the first year of operation.

What seems most to the point in the present context, however, is the act's recognition that newspapers had come to stay and were as much consumables as other commodities on which it imposed duty. Newspapers had come a long way since 1695. Within five months of the Licensing Act lapsing, there had appeared the three great newspapers of William's reign: *The Post Boy, The Flying Post*, and *The Post Man*, all tri-weeklies. They were accompanied by others, some of them short-lived: in the next six years at least fourteen new newspapers began publication.[27] In 1702 the first regular daily newspaper appeared. The *Daily Courant*, a small half-sheet, provided news but seldom expressed opinions. Comment as well as news was provided at first by the tri-weeklies, but late in Anne's reign dailies appeared in London giving both news and comment, as did weeklies. By 1712 London possessed twelve newspapers and fourteen provincial newspapers had been established; after 1719 the number of provincial newspapers never fell below twenty.[28] Taxing newspapers, therefore, proved an enduringly attractive and increasingly lucrative weapon of fiscal policy. By the middle of the century the annual revenue from the whole range of stamp duties was £260,00, just over three per cent of the annual budget.[29] From the modest acorn of 1712 a sturdy oak had grown.

If intended as a weapon for checking the growth of the press, the so-called Stamp Act of 1712 was successful in that some newspapers disappeared (but mostly low circulation weeklies in the provinces) and others amalgamated; and increased prices produced a decline in the circulation for those which survived. However, it was only a short-term success, for the fall in circulation proved only temporary and was soon recovered.[30] The act of 1712 had been initiated by a Tory ministry and passed by a Tory Parliament, but in 1717 the first Whig ministry of George I's reign extended indefinitely the lottery and its supporting duties.[31] In 1725 a new act stopped evasions of duty cause by bad drafting in the act of 1712, compelling weekly newspapers to pass on the tax to their customers.[32] No weekly newspapers have been shown to have ceased publication solely as a result of the act, and in general more newspapers probably died of natural

causes than were killed by stamp duties.[33] Unstamped newspapers
were not greatly affected until a 1743 act made hawkers liable to up
to three months hard labor, but even then unstamped newspapers
appeared occasionally.[34]

Criticized as an injury to trade and to the employment of the
poor, and as a tax on knowledge, cutting off the poor from improving
literature and family instruction,[35] the early stamp acts do not seem
to have excited much contemporary criticism as a restraint upon the
liberty of the press, though *The Craftsman* made the point in its
first issue.[36] But the same was true of the celebrated Stamp Act of
1765. In all the resolves of the colonial assemblies, there was only
one mention of the Stamp Act as a restraint upon the liberty of the
press: it came from the colony of New Jersey, which lacked a newspaper of its own.[37] It may be argued that silence on the liberty of the
press came naturally, or at least appropriately and decently, from
assemblies which in the eighteenth century showed themselves as
averse to press reportage of their proceedings as the Westminster
Parliament, whose privileges and procedures they copied, and to
whose status they aspired.[38]

≺ II ≻

The end of pre-publication censorship and the limited effects of tax
measures left government and society the problem of controlling the
press. Most agreed that liberty of the press was not an unregulated
liberty but something called an ordered, regulated, legal liberty, a
liberty within and under the law, interpreted by an independent judiciary and brought to its conclusion with the aid of a jury.[39] A licentious press was widely deplored across the whole political spectrum.
But what seemed to some licentiousness seemed to others liberty.
And some, particularly those in opposition to government, as long
as they remained in opposition or out of office, argued that a degree
of licentiousness must be suffered as an inevitable evil, compared
with the greater good afforded by a free press as the chief bulwark of
the constitution. This was an argument advocated consistently by
the opposition organized by Bolingbroke against Walpole, and earlier
in the 1720s by independent Whigs, whose minds were concentrated

on the issue by government prosecutions for libel.[40] But those in government, both Whigs and Tories, seldom responded to press attacks in a detached and tolerant fashion. Judging from their pronouncements and actions, what mattered to them was not the glory of a free press, but the need to control it. After 1695 their main weapon in this struggle was the law of the land.

The strict legal position in England found its classic formulation in Sir William Blackstone's *Commentaries* of 1772, one that would have seemed acceptable to many in England earlier. According to Blackstone, liberty of the press consisted "in laying no previous restraint upon publication, and not in freedom from censure for criminal matter when published."[41] Blackstone was glossed by the legal historian A. V. Dicey in the following century. All that had happened, wrote Dicey, glorying in the minimalist nature of the change, was that the press had become subject only to the ordinary law of the land: liberty of the press was no more than the mere application of the general principle that no man was punishable except for a distinct breach of the law, in the ordinary courts of the country.[42]

Minimalist though the change was in legal terms, it was in retrospect, and in comparison with contemporary Europe, a change of profound significance. The failure to act in 1695 proved the greatest and most creative discontinuity of the period of the Revolution, a discontinuity which marked off England sharply from its past and from contemporary Protestant as well as Catholic Europe, even from the Dutch Republic. For in Europe the publication of any form of news, whether political, literary, artistic, or scientific, required the previous permission of authority. In Europe the press enjoyed not liberty, but liberties—especially conferred privileges. In the cases of France and Spain, these were conferred by royal authority; in the case of the Dutch Republic by the provincial States or the municipal authorities; and in all three cases, to a named beneficiary who in consequence possessed a monopoly in the provision of information in a given domain. These rights were usually for a period, sometimes for an indefinite period, and capable of being passed on to heirs and sold by them.[43] Thus in France, Théophraste Renaudot, the creator of the *Gazette*, founded in 1631 and the first of Europe's official gazettes, established a monopoly of publication which lasted until 1749, when the privilege of the *Gazette* was sold by his heirs.[44]

The publication of news in France was formally compartmentalized. Political news could only be diffused legally via the *Gazette*, published in Paris. Numerous provincial republications of the *Gazette* constituted what passed for an indigenous local press in France.[45] Scientific news in France was the monopoly of the *Journal des Savants*; literary news and society gossip, of the *Mercure*, which in 1724 took the name of the *Mercure de France*.[46] All were published in Paris. This was a far cry from the situation of the press in England, whose multiplicity of indigenous public papers, and "extreme liberty" in communicating what they pleased to the public and in censuring king and ministers, became a matter for comment and for wonderment among European visitors and commentators.[47] The contrast was real enough, but the limits imposed upon liberty of the press in England were also real, for in the absence of preventative censorship there was recourse to punishment under the law for offenses against the law.

The law under which the offenders in England were to be punished was the law of criminal libel. Criminal libels came in a number of varieties, according as they treated of personal, sexual, religious, or political matters. In practice, after 1695 the most important and frequent were political: offenses of seditious libel. Cases of treasonable libel were rare. The Treason Trials Act of 1696 allowed all persons accused of treason, whether peers or commoners, to have a copy of the indictment five days before trial, to make their defense by counsel, and to subpoena their witnesses and have them sworn; and the evidence of two witnesses to an overt act of treason was required.[48] The chances of conviction were thereby substantially reduced. In Anne's reign the law of treason was extended to make it high treason for any person maliciously, advisedly, and directly to maintain and affirm in writing or in printing that Anne was not the lawful queen, or that any person had any right to the Crown, other than a statutory right.[49] But only one case of treasonable libel under the act was carried to a conviction, in 1718 when the printer of *Vox Populi, Vox Dei*, John Matthew, aged 18, was convicted and subsequently executed for the offense.[50]

Prosecutions for blasphemous libel were also a rarity, taken reluctantly by the civil power, and only when the scandal had become so notorious, and the scandal-monger so incorrigible, that action was unavoidable. For example, the eccentric Thomas Woolston deliberately provoked prosecution in exasperation at the indifference of others to his opinions, which led him to conduct disputations with himself in the form of anonymous answers to his own publications. In 1729–30 he was tried for writing that an allegorical interpretation of the biblical miracles was the only one that was not anti-Christian, which was construed as tending to alter and ridicule the religion established by law and therefore to undermine the authority of the law, to the detriment of peace and order. The prosecution avoided using the Blasphemy Act of 1698, because doing so would have required providing proof of the denial of the truth of Christianity and of the divine authority of the Bible.

Apart from Woolston, a few blasphemous works are said to have been presented to local grand juries as public nuisances. These prosecutions did little to stanch the flow of anti-Trinitarian literature and sentiments. The bishops were distressed or roused by the publication of "lewd, profane and blasphemous books," and by divergences from strict Anglican orthodoxy. But they came to accept the need to avoid the appearance of persecution for conscience's sake. They were as aware as was the Crown of the difficulties of discovering those responsible for writing and dispersing blasphemous tracts, and of establishing legal proof against their printers and sellers. In the end, as Wake conceded sadly, it came down to "prayers and pens in defence of Christianity."[51]

The coupling of lewd and blasphemous books was often made. The licentiousness of the press usually encompassed the immorality of the press: the one seemed to lead inescapably to the other. It was a small step from promiscuous slander, which destroyed reputations, to pornography, as small as that perceived by contemporaries from liberty to libertinism, from blasphemy to obscenity, which was originally a religious offense.[52] Though England was quick to import and naturalize, via translations and adaptations, erotic writing from the Continent in the mid-seventeenth century, it was not until 1727, with the successful prosecution of Edmund Curll for publishing and translating a French erotic work, that it became an offense at common law to corrupt the morals of the king's subjects, and that an act against morality was judged against public order.[53]

Curll was convicted and sentenced to the pillory. This example did little to discourage others and in 1748, with the first volume of John Cleland's *Memoirs of a Woman of Pleasure*, England became an exporter of erotic literature. Erotic literature multiplied, making a fortune for Cleland's publisher, and went largely unchecked until the vogue for piety and virtue launched, or sealed, with royal approval in the late 1780s. It can be argued that the main consideration was (as with other forms of libel) experience that attempted prosecutions of authors gave them publicity and increased sales of their works.[54]

In practice most press cases involved seditious libel. The law was sweeping in its definitions of seditious libel and publication. Publication was held to involve all those concerned in the writing, printing, distributing, and selling of the offensive matter. Thus a hawker was in law as much the maker of a libel as the author.[55] Every publication was deemed to be seditious if it seemed likely to bring into hatred or contempt the ruler, his heirs and successors, the government, or any of the great national institutions, or to cause disaffection against them. Even a false statement about the ruler's health might be regarded as a punishable offense, because of its tendency to "disquiet the minds of the king's subjects, hurt public credit,"—which was as much a part of the Revolution settlement as the Bill of Rights—"and diminish the regard and duty to the king," if it was repeated often enough.[56] The difficulty was to decide how many repetitions were needed to transform a mistake into a crime.

But the severity of the law of seditious libel was evident not only in its scope but also in its rules of procedure. The law of seditious libel did not regard truth as a defense: it was concerned with injurious facts, true or false, not with the imputation of false facts.[57] Moreover, it was for the judge to decide whether the act was done with criminal intent, and whether the writing was seditious. The role of the jury was to determine the fact of publication, and whether the expressions, or innuendos, or literary and historical allusions, in which contemporary pamphlet literature critical of government abounded, referred to the persons or institutions in question. The theory ran that an independent and impartial judiciary, such as had been established as a consequence of the Revolution, could be trusted to determine all questions of law.[58]

The theory did not go uncontested by juries or by writers. It was argued that it was not applied uniformly or consistently throughout the law; that intent was a fit consideration for juries and was considered in some cases, even to some extent in cases of libel. In felony cases, for example, the bench was prepared to accept jury mitigation. But if seditious libel could be likened to homicide, and there was the authority of Chief Justice Holt in 1707 to support the view that libelling was a form of murder—murdering a man's reputation—then there seemed no logic in limiting the role of juries in cases of seditious libel, only an expedient reason—fear of acquittal by juries.[59] It was further argued that even under prevailing practice a writer's intentions were considered by juries, to the extent that they were required to interpret the meaning of the blanks and initial letters, and other devices used by writers.[60]

Liberty of the press and trial by jury were coupled by the London Revolution Society in 1788. The coupling was completed by Fox's libel act in 1792, which gave juries the right to bring in a general verdict. Juries, like judges, responded to the changed temper of the times as the French Revolution gathered momentum, and they convicted more often than they had done before in cases of seditious libel. In the early years of the reign of George I, when prosecution for seditious libel crippled and virtually destroyed the Jacobite press in the space of a couple of years, no difficulties with juries seem to have occurred.[61] Perhaps the perceived and real threat of Jacobitism (as of Jacobinism later) made jurors more prepared to accept a limited role than appears to have been the case in the reign of George II. It is not clear that the provision in the Juries Act of 1730, by which special juries could be empanelled at the request of either the prosecutor or defendant in a trial for misdemeanor, enabled government to secure the appointment of favorable juries in libel cases. No change in social composition is apparent. Juries seem to have been drawn from the solid, middling groups of society: tradesmen, craftsmen, and small property owners.[62]

The 1730 Act was followed immediately by the successful conviction for seditious libel of the printer of *The Craftsman*. The judge in the case upheld the doctrine that in libels the jury was only to decide upon the fact of publication and the application, leaving the judge to decide the point of law as to whether the offense constituted a libel.[63] But overall the conviction was something of a pyrrhic victory. The trial became a piece of popular political theatre, with spectators thronging the approaches to the court and noblemen and gentlemen crowding the court itself. The sales of the *The Craftsman* are said to have increased as a result of the trial, and of what was described in a more general context as "the good fortune to be persecuted."[64] The government took this cautionary tale, one of several, to heart. This is indicated by the high number of cases for seditious libel which never came to trial.[65] But there were other reasons for not coming to court or trial, especially difficulties in establishing responsibility for authorship and for publication, or in obtaining hard evidence against the accused. The printing trade was distinguished by the mutual support of its members, and by the sloppy, hurried, somewhat anarchic manner in which news was assembled and the various responsibilities of newspaper composition were apportioned or executed. It was plausible upon questioning to pass the buck: authors complained that printers had not followed copy, or had inserted changes or additions without consulting them; printers denied having seen the work until it had been published, or claimed it had come from unknown hands.[66]

Often, it seems, a government decision not to proceed reflected a belief that legal terrorism of the printing and publishing trades was sufficient. Putting a defendant through the legal mangle of examination, commitment, and confinement could wring the spirit out of alleged offenders, or sometimes the life. The process could keep an offender searching for bail or recognizances. These could be very high. Excessive bail and excessive fines had been condemned in the Bill of Rights, but unfortunately no definition had been provided as to what constituted "excessive," and even relatively small sums might be excessive for a printer with modest assets.[67] There was frequent recourse to procedure by *ex officio* information, by which criminal proceedings could be instituted without recourse to a grand jury and individuals were incarcerated or bound over without trial. Governments sometimes played a legal cat-and-mouse game with offenders, who could be roughly treated by a king's messenger armed with warrants from a secretary of state empowering him to seize persons and papers; brought before the secretary and cross-examined; confined to Newgate; released and then subjected to a re-run of the whole performance. In short, there were ways in which governments could achieve their objectives whilst avoiding the costs, risks, and adverse publicity which attended a formal trial for seditious libel.[68]

The initiation of prosecution, therefore, was a powerful weapon in the government's armory of legal weapons used to control the press, particularly provincial newspapers, whose contents are held to have become the subject of special and separately financed government surveillance by the comptroller of the post office from 1726. It did not always directly involve central government. Sometimes the initiative came from local ministerial supporters, or from local clergy; sometimes central government paid local lawyers to take up a case. In the 1720s a special annual sum was assigned to a legal officer, the "Solicitor for Criminal Prosecutions," for "carrying on public prosecutions."[69] Crucially, both Houses of Parliament took initiatives to punish press offenses, and particularly those offenses which breached parliamentary privilege, or injured either Parliament in its corporate capacity or individual members of Parliament.

< III >

To make public, in printed or written form, any reference to what went on in Parliament was to take a risk after 1689. If existing notions of parliamentary privilege had been strictly and systematically enforced, nothing could have been published, save what Parliament itself authorized. In the case of the Commons, a printed account of the proceedings of the House was available continuously from 1690 in the *Votes* with only one interruption in 1702–3. The *Votes* was an abbreviated account of the corporate actions of the House containing no information on its debates. Permission to publish the *Votes*, under the supervision of the Speaker, had to be granted anew by the Commons at the beginning of each parliamentary session. In short, the Commons operated a licensing system with the Speaker as licenser.[70]

Theoretically the House of Lords was enshrouded in even deeper mystery; no printed equivalent of the *Votes* was made available until 1824, when the House authorized the printing of its *Minutes*. To print any of the Lords' proceedings without the leave of the House was a breach of privilege under standing order 92, first enrolled in

1698 and thereafter read out regularly at the beginning of each session.[71]

Apart from these small loopholes through which, it must be stressed, only snatches of Parliament's proceedings reached the public "out-of-doors," and apart from the publication of the sovereign's speeches to Parliament, royal messages, the addresses of both Houses, and the titles of parliamentary acts in the *London Gazette*, the rest should have been silence.[72] In theory, the speeches of MPs were hidden from sight and sound behind an impenetrable curtain of secrecy. The Bill of Rights enacted freedom of speech in Parliament as a right. That right did not extend, nor did any other part of the Bill of Rights convey a right, to freedom of speech outside Parliament. Moreover, the right to freedom of speech within Parliament was not absolute, as the Jacobite MP William Shippen discovered when sent to the Tower in 1717 for overstepping the bounds of parliamentary language in describing the king's speech opening Parliament as "more fitted for the meridian of Germany than that of Great Britain," and the king as "a stranger to our language and constitution."[73]

Yet in practice some information about proceedings and debates reached wide sections of the public. Individual MPs anxious to speak to opinion outside Westminster printed speeches. Public disclosure also continued in a form peculiar to the House of Lords, in the published protests of dissentients that gave a highly condensed but accurate summary of the arguments of the opposition. Protests frequently reached a wide audience, "printed and handed about in coffee houses and sent all over the Kingdom," but a procedural change requiring protests to be entered promptly had the effect of reducing their number after 1723.[74] Unauthorized lists of how peers and MPs had voted in divisions, and estimates of how they were likely to vote, sometimes attracted wide, indeed foreign, interest. In 1688 a Dutch newspaper published a list purporting to show how peers were likely to vote in the next Parliament on the crucial issue of repeal of the Tests. The division list on the 1710 impeachment of Henry Sacheverell appeared in print with explanations in French, Dutch, and Latin as well as English.[75] Some of these lists, particularly those which appeared during periods of heightened political tension, were printed in very large numbers and were clearly intended to influence the future conduct of business.[76]

A distinctive and largely innovative development giving the public knowledge of parliamentary affairs consisted of the regular publication in manuscript newsletters and printed papers of accounts of proceedings, and frequently of debates also. One diplomat fairly described these as "scraps of parliamentary eloquence."[77] Manuscript newsletters, sent regularly to a circle of subscribers, were popular in early eighteenth-century England as well as in censored Europe. Given the growth of a vigorous and independent metropolitan and provincial press in England, the continued and arguably increased popularity and vitality of manuscript newsletters seem at first sight curious; but they provided a variety of information of a scandalous, confidential, and useful nature. They gave news at the earliest possible moment about public appointments, about the rising and falling fortunes of public men—invaluable knowledge in an age when public office conferred upon its holder access to, or possession of, powers of patronage. Crucially important, they provided information on Parliament and its debates which could be read nowhere else with the same degree of immediacy and often fullness.

However, from the beginning of Anne's reign extracts from Parliament's debates were made public in England in printed form. Extracts and summaries of debates appeared in a periodical of information, *The History of the reign of Queen Anne digested into Annals*, published between 1703 and 1713 and compiled by a Huguenot refugee, Abel Boyer. In the *Annals* materials on debates were published, but well after the debates had taken place. According to Boyer, they were obtained from unnamed MPs who communicated speeches to him, or were obtained via members of Parliament who had procured him opportunities of being an "ear-witness" to their debates.[78] What was unprecedented, however, in Boyer's reportage of parliamentary affairs was his inclusion of regular summaries and extracts of debates, more commonly those of the Commons than the Lords, in another publication, *The Political State of Great Britain*, a monthly periodical begun in 1711.[79] It contained regular reports of parliamentary debates and for the most part published them while Parliament was sitting, an important innovation. Also, with one exception, the reports appeared undisguised. The exception occurred in 1716 when a Commons debate was transposed to the Polish Diet, with a cast of Polish speakers, readily identifiable with English MPs.[80] It was the kind of stratagem which Boyer's immediate successors in the field of parliamentary reporting turned into a general strategy.[81] For the most part Boyer's reportage went unchallenged by Parliament, which is difficult to explain but suggests at least that it was not scandalously unfair, even if partisan.[82]

But if Parliament allowed, and individual MPs connived at or contributed directly to, the publication of extracts and summaries of parliamentary debates in periodicals printed in London, it was a very different matter in respect of the London daily and weekly press. Except for occasional references to some proceedings, more in the evening than in the daily press, the silence in regard to debates was virtually complete. It was easier for readers of the London press to get information about the parlement of Paris than it was about the Parliament at Westminster. Readers of provincial newspapers were marginally better informed as some material was supplied to these newspapers by newsletter writers.[83]

However, parliamentary privilege was invoked to punish those provincial printers, publishers, and newsletter writers who, in newspapers and newsletters, offered the provincial public a glimpse of parliamentary debates as well as proceedings during the reigns of Anne and the first two Georges. It is a measure of contemporary public appetite for parliamentary news, and of the importance newspapers attached to it, that notwithstanding imprisonment and financial loss, provincial printers persisted in the provision of parliamentary intelligence. The repeated flouting of parliamentary privilege in the 1720s by one such provincial printer, Robert Raikes of the *Gloucester Journal*, caused the Commons in 1729 to resolve unanimously to proceed against offenders with the utmost severity.[84] This seems to have persuaded Boyer, who was simultaneously under threat of legal action from the printers of the *Votes* for breach of copyright in publishing details of proceedings, and his successor, that it was unsafe henceforth to publish anything while Parliament was still sitting. The practice thus began, and was followed by two other monthly periodicals launched in the 1730's, *The Gentleman's Magazine* and *The London Magazine*, of postponing reports of Parliament's debates until the parliamentary session was over.[85]

In 1738, the question of the publication of the Commons' debates was discussed at length by the House. There was uncertainty about the validity of the notion that the publication of debates after the end of the session did not constitute a breach of parliamentary privilege. All agreed that publication of debates after the dissolution of the Parliament in which they had occurred did not breach privilege, and that the House of Lords, as a court of record whose "rights and privileges never died" was in a different position in regard to the publication of its debates.[86] Perhaps because it was a court with greater (if rarely applied) powers of punishment, and also because access to the debates of the Lords became more difficult when the gallery of the house was taken down at the end of 1711 session, in order to avoid a repetition of the "inconveniences" suffered during the debates of July of that year, the Lords had less trouble with newsletter writers.[87] Even so, there was a thriving trade in the manuscript minutes of the House by "minute mongers."[88]

The discussion in the Commons on 13 April 1738 led to a unanimous resolution which in theory removed the uncertainties. It became a breach of the privilege of the House for news writers or printers or publishers to give any account of the debates or other proceedings of the House, or any committee thereof, "as well during the recess as the sitting of parliament"; so permitting publication only after its dissolution. Offenders would be prosecuted with the utmost severity.[89] But monthly periodicals merely adopted new artifices in their now customary reportage, continuing to publish summaries and extracts of debates, under the cover of "The proceedings of a political club," in which the identities of the members were concealed in classical names. The Gentleman's Magazine disguised them more imaginatively as "Debates in the Senate of Magna Lilliputa," in which the names assigned to speakers were either anagrams of their true names or altered in a way that still left them recognizable.

Not until 1771 did the reporting of debates in newspapers find an enduring solution, and then as a result of a trap contrived by Alderman John Wilkes, who pitted the privileges of the City of London against the privileges of the Commons. In 1768 the London Evening Post began reporting Parliament's debates and by early 1771 was followed by over a dozen daily, tri-weekly, and weekly papers. The attention of the House was drawn to the breach of privilege, and the publishers of two of the papers were summoned to attend the House. One of the printers defied the House and was ordered to be taken into custody for contempt. The messenger sent by the serjeant-at-arms to arrest him was charged with false arrest and brought before Lord Mayor Brass Crosby and Aldermen Wilkes and Oliver, who discharged the printer and would have committed the messenger, had not the serjeant-at-arms appeared to take him out. The Commons resolved that Crosby was guilty of a breach of privilege and committed him and Oliver to the Tower, where they remained until the close of the session, martyrs in the cause of the City's privileges. Fearful of exciting again the corporate hostility of London, and of getting entangled again with "that Devil Wilkes," the Commons had to rest content with the vindication by the Court of Common Pleas of its power to commit, but it failed to stamp out parliamentary reporting. Reporting recommenced before Crosby and Oliver's release and it continued.[90] Parliamentary reporting was not unfettered after 1771 because journalists were not always admitted into the gallery and, until 1783, had to take notes covertly.[91] But after 1771 the House ceased to assert its claim to control the public reporting of its debates in newspapers. It seems appropriate that the advent of full and regular reports of parliamentary debates in the newspapers press should have been as unheroic, as much the product of the pressures and conflicts of vested interests, and as inconclusively conclusive, as the lapsing of the Licensing Act in 1695.

< IV >

Liberty of the press in England after 1695 was thus constrained not only by the law but also, and more effectively for most of the eighteenth century, by parliamentary privilege. Even so, the press still seemed too free to governments. The power to call to account those held responsible for "possessing the people with an ill-opinion of government" provided only a partial solution. As Lord Chief Justice Holt observed in 1704, it was "very necessary for all governments that the people should have a good opinion of it."[92]

All governments agreed with that and, judging from their actions, saw that the press was crucial to the making of that good opinion. They deemed it necessary to have permanently at their disposal means to inform and guide opinion. This took the form initially of an official gazette, the *London Gazette*. In addition to items of parliamentary news, the *Gazette* had other monopolies: royal proclamations and resolutions of the Privy Council; promotions at court, whose notification was defended as a prized privilege;[93] the publication of the winning numbers in government lotteries; notifications of bankruptcies and notice of projected canals.

The *Gazette* suffered in important ways as a result of its privileged status. Responsibility for the *Gazette* rested with the two secretaries of state, but the actual writing often devolved upon one of the less important clerks of the office. Its style and content and its standards of accuracy over small matters reflected the fact that it was put together hastily by people who were mostly not professional journalists. By the middle of the eighteenth century, there was nothing left but the status of an official government organ.

The decline of the *Gazette* was largely the consequence of the rise of independent newspapers. Newspapers in Anne's reign provided information about foreign affairs, but they also became journals of comment, and more obviously propagandist and party organs, better suited than the *Gazette* to the purpose of procuring a good opinion of government. Robert Harley, later earl of Oxford, alarmed at the inadequacies of the *Gazette*, recognized the importance to government of a permanent, full-time propaganda machine and enlisted writers on a semi-permanent footing to disseminate a flow of propaganda through unofficial government press organs. One writer was Daniel Defoe; his organ was *The Review*, founded in 1704. It is a measure of the importance the press had already achieved in the political process, and of the importance attached by government to winning opinion to its side, that Harley's choice as ministerial writer was Defoe, a great writer and pugnacious controversialist. He did occasionally write and publish pamphlets without consulting Harley, but he was much more under ministerial control than Jonathan Swift, who contributed some of the most influential pamphlets of the day.[94]

Whereas Harley founded a new paper to serve his press purposes, Robert Walpole began his management of the newspaper press by buying out the current leading opposition journal, the *London Journal* (in 1722), and transforming it into the principal government propaganda organ, thus killing two birds with one stone.[95] And whereas

Harley employed major writing talents, Walpole's writers were less talented, but more manageable; duller but more reliable. Under Walpole's direction, most notably in the mid- and late 1730s, the production of propaganda in the form of pamphlets and newspapers was combined with unprecedented, elaborate, expensive, and country-wide arrangements for distribution via the posts. The Clerks of the Road acted as licensed hawkers, assisted in the work of distribution by judges, officers of the customs and excise, and others; the other side of the coin was the systematic denial of postal facilities to opposition newspapers.[96]

Walpole systematically preceded or accompanied parliamentary battles by propaganda barrages, sometimes by publishing documents relevant to an issue about to be discussed or in the process of being discussed.[97] More commonly, parliamentary pump-priming took the form of pamphlets, written by ministers or with their assistance, making use of unpublished documents and distributed to MPs at the beginning of a session or during its progress: in 1730 a leading opposition politician described this as an "annual custom."[98] Analysis of the dates of Defoe's pamphlets indicates that over 60 percent of his attributed output was published either during a parliamentary session, or within a month of its commencement.[99] This anticipates the pattern of publication for pamphlets later in the eighteenth century, with December to March as the most popular months, and the months of July and August as the least popular: a publication period more or less coincidental with the parliamentary year.[100] Such a massive and sophisticated marshalling of the resources of the state for propagandist purposes is hard to square with the view that for Walpole the press possessed only a limited priority.

≺ V ≻

After the Revolution the press became a vital link for both government and opposition in what has been described as a circuit of political communication. In the course of the eighteenth century that circuit became larger and more sophisticated, connecting Crown with Parliament; government and opposition with individual MPs; MPs with each other, and with the opinions and pressures of their constituencies; provincial politics with metropolitan politics.[101] The size of the circuit was obviously affected by the nature and extent of contemporary literacy; however not all those who could read may have read newspapers regularly, and many of those who could not read may yet have listened to the contents of newspapers and other printed matter being read out. During roughly the period between 1714 and 1750, male illiteracy is held to have dropped from around 55 percent to around 40 percent, female illiteracy from around 75 percent to around 60 percent.[102]

If estimates for literacy in the population at large are uncertain and not very reliable, estimates for the sales of newspapers are also rough guesses. Sales of the political press in Anne's reign numbered a few thousands at the most. In the Walpole era, sales of the most successful political papers—the *London Journal*, *Freeholders Journal*, *Craftsman*, and *Mist's Weekly Journal*—may have sold between 8,000 and 12,000 copies per issue, figures that were rarely exceeded in the period 1760 to 1790. Sales of provincial newspapers for the most part numbered hundreds of copies rather than thousands.[103] Sales can be a very misleading and inadequate guide to readership, accessibility, and influence. Readership was certainly larger than sales: the crucial question is how much larger.

Many sales of newspapers, perhaps most sales in London, were made to coffee houses. There were several thousand London coffee houses in Anne's reign, and most self-respecting provincial towns had two or more; their survival depended upon their provision of newspapers.[104] As newspapers multiplied, selection and duplication became more of a problem. By 1731, it seems, only the most eminent coffee houses could take in all the daily printed papers: no hardship for readers since the dailies repeated themselves to a considerable extent, but a concern to newspaper proprietors, to those who advertised, and to those who read advertisements.[105] Judging from the contemporary comment of pamphlets, the clientele of coffee houses was not confined to the upper and middling sections of society, or to townsfolk. Eighteenth-century journalists saw coffee houses as "schools of divinity, schools of politicks, of wit, of polite learning," but primarily they existed to satisfy the voracious appetite of Englishmen for news.[106] Inns, taverns, and ale houses also provided facilities for the reading of newspapers and acted as agents for their distribution, especially in the provinces.[107]

The existence of such varied opportunities for reading news-

papers without buying them makes it difficult to assess the readership of newspapers in the eighteenth century. Historians of the
newspaper press are agreed on the need for a multiplication factor,
but there can be no certainty or agreement about its size. Addison
suggested twenty readers per copy of a newspaper as a modest com-
putation and some estimates went as high as forty readers to a paper.[108] Moreover, even if readership could be more precisely determined, it would not solve the problem of audience, for newspapers
were not closed to the illiterate, who, as contemporaries noted, listened to readings in the streets. If illiteracy did not necessarily prevent access to the contents of newspapers, neither did price. Some
hawkers rented out newspapers. The increasing practice of publication on Saturdays indicated a popular readership both in London and
the provinces, which enabled Mist to reach plebian readers.[109]

There was also available, to Londoners principally, another form
of print culture: prints and cartoons. Concern with "portraitures"
had formed part of the abortive licensing bill of February 1695. No
further attempt to regulate them seems to have been made until the
Engravings Act passed (1735). According to the act it was prompted
by the desire of the inventors, designers, and proprietors of engravings to secure copyright protection against the widespread pirating
of their property in part or in whole. Copyright protection was secured for fourteen years from the first publication, but the price was
the identification of the proprietor on each plate, something which
had been sought as a necessary step towards legal accountability in
1695.[110] This seemed a pressing concern to government in 1735, for
the 1730s, and especially the great controversy in 1733–34 over the
excise bill, witnessed the beginnings of an extraordinary efflores-
cence of indigenous political cartoons, the majority exhibiting a
marked anti-ministerial bias.[111] A factor in this was the thought that
the ambiguous imagery of the print made it more difficult to persuade a jury of its seditious meaning than the printed word, which
was under heavy assault in the 1730s.[112]

Initially the print was not intended for a mass audience. The
prices were higher than those of newspapers and as much as many
pamphlets; the impressions rarely exceeded a few hundreds, though
later William Hogarth's image of John Wilkes apparently ran to
about 4,000 copies in a few weeks; and the season of its publication

was usually in the autumn and the early spring when country gentlemen came to London for the parliamentary session. Moreover,
a complete reading of a political print, with its frequent classical
emblems, its Latin or French inscriptions, and commonly its focus
upon a particular political event, would hardly have been completely intelligible to the semi-educated or politically ignorant, and
only completely intelligible to those whose ability to penetrate its
emblematic and inscriptional mysteries was combined with a reasonable knowledge of current affairs acquired through newspaper
and pamphlet reading.

In the second half of the eighteenth century, prints became more
accessible. More print shops were in business, and the business became more professionalized. Production increased, especially production of political prints, whose number exceeded that of the other
types of print in most years after 1788. The prints themselves shed
their mysteries, with the pioneering work of George Townshend in
the 1750s developing a more immediately recognizable visual vocabulary and a style of political comment that was at once simple,
direct, and grotesque. Prints came to play a continuing part in popular political education, at least in London, which effectually mo-
nopolized their production. In the estimation of worried contemporaries in England, they spoke "a universal language, understood
by persons of all nations and degrees." To continental observers,
the English print—indelicate, irreverent, and scurrilous, even in its
treatment of monarchy—was proof positive of the liberty and license enjoyed by Englishmen and a true expression of the English
genius.[113]

The consequences of the increasing accessibility of the various
forms of print culture for eighteenth-century English politics remain to be considered. Their evaluation depends in the first place
on the sort of information that became available on a regular basis
after 1695. Foreign news dominated English newspapers; it was attractive, it has been argued, because it was less likely to provoke
prosecution for seditious libel, and because copying and translating
foreign news out of European newsletters and newspapers was a
relatively cheap way of filling a newspaper.[114] However, there is evidence for the view that foreign news constituted not just the essential ballast of newspapers after 1695, but a precious cargo. The news-

papers themselves constantly referred to the demand for foreign news, often drawing attention to the excellence of the foreign intelligence they provided.

The reasons why foreign news was read were varied. News about the movements of ships and about conditions in the countries with which Britain traded concerned merchants, bankers, investors, and speculators, especially in the wake of the financial revolution which followed upon the Revolution. To a country involved in major European wars, in which English participation was a direct consequence of the Revolution, and which were fought among other reasons to secure its settlement, there was much to command attention. There were numerous descriptions of the war itself, information about treaty negotiations, and the contents of treaties signed by England or of concern to her. For example, the first knowledge available in England of the existence of the Second Partition treaty of 1700 came via the *London Post* under a heading "The Hague," which cited the news as having come from Spain. In fact, the leak can be traced to Louis XIV. The first partial revelation of the existence of peace negotiations with France in the war of the Spanish and Protestant Succession came in the *Daily Courant* of 13 October 1711. It had been leaked to the press by the imperial envoy a few days after the news had been privately communicated to the representatives of the allies in London. These examples illustrate the extent to which the London press had become a European force, whose management had become a matter of vital concern to European rulers and diplomats.[115]

None of this should be taken to imply that there was open diplomacy after the Revolution, or that informed opinion played a decisive role. But the development of a situation in which members of Parliament were capable of making themselves better informed about foreign affairs led to a qualitative change of large and lasting importance for the formulation, conduct, and presentation of British foreign policy. William learned that it was not possible to keep Parliament in ignorance of foreign affairs, nor even wise, for an instructed Parliament was more easily led than an ignorant Parliament. The advent of a parliamentary foreign policy at the end of William's reign, and its continuance thereafter, went hand-in-hand with the emergence and proliferation of an independent press: they were connected and inter-connected phenomena. One consequence of "liberty of the press," therefore, was to restrict the Crown's liberty to conduct foreign policy as an area of government reserved exclusively for the royal prerogative. In submitting to the need to obtain Parliament's backing for its foreign policy, the Crown submitted to the need to do much more than the constitution strictly required—which was simply the communication to Parliament of certain decisions. Constitutionally foreign policy "lay in His Majesty's breast," but it was agreed that no prudent monarch would act in literal accordance with that view. In practice, if foreign policy was to be conducted effectively, the Crown was obliged to engage in a continuous dialogue with Parliament.[116]

With the lapsing of the Licensing Act in 1695, the press became a permanent voice in that dialogue and ensured that the dialogue was heard "out-of-doors." "Out-of-doors" was an electorate which not only rapidly expanded after the Revolution,[117] but became increasingly informed, or was possessed of the capacity to make itself increasingly informed. The existence of a free, vigorous, and increasingly extensive press required and enabled governments, oppositions, and pressure groups to formulate, conduct, and present their policies in ways which took account of the pervasive and multifarious influences of the press, or face the consequences of the failure to do so. Systematic campaigning in the press did not always ensure political success, or accompany it, but it does seem to have been able to tip the balance at some moments of high political crises, for example, the excise bill crisis of 1733. Walpole's withdrawal of the bill derived in part from the success of the opposition in exploiting the long delay between the first leaking of the government's intention to introduce a bill and its actual introduction to Parliament, by mobilizing popular opinion. The use of the press seems to have been crucial. Judging from the dates of publication of some pamphlets, the opposition was much quicker to state its case just before the opening of Parliament than was the government and concentrated its weightiest, best informed, and most effectively argued pamphlets against the excise bill in the decisive period between Parliament's first consideration of the bill and its second reading.[118] Additionally, the opposition mounted a massive propagandist effort in the provinces, which resulted in nearly sixty constituencies sending instructions to their members to oppose the excise scheme.[119] It may be worth noting in this context that fourteen out of the eighteen borough constituencies which boasted newspapers of their own sent instructions. Walpole, it is true, survived both the excise crisis and the general election which followed in 1734, but he had been diminished, and he had felt obliged to spend more on the press in the years 1733–34 than in any other years during the period 1727 to 1741.[120]

The press did more than serve the specific, changing, and continuing needs of governments, oppositions, and pressure groups. It made for a more instructed and politicized mass of opinion. This is the clear inference to be drawn from much of the pamphlet literature. It is a question not so much of the size of the sales of pamphlets, though some major political pamphlets of the early eighteenth century are held to have had sales, or issues, in the region of 7,000 to 8,000, as of their contents, and of the style and structure of the disputation conducted in them.[121] A significant number of pamphlets on foreign policy published in the 1720s, 1730s, and 1740s presupposed not only a readership in close contact with current international affairs as described in the newspapers of the day, but also a considerable knowledge of international history over an extended period. Pamphlets, therefore, though separate publications, frequently performed the function performed in a modern newspaper by leading articles. They were frequently part of a chain of publications, a voice in existing controversies in print, which became more noisy as more joined in, and which was fully intelligible only to those who were familiar with what had gone before. The gladiatorial aspect of much of eighteenth-century pamphlet literature reflected and exacerbated existing political polarities and came before a wider public through the reproduction and serialization in the newspapers of the controversies generated by pamphlets.[122]

The best documented example of the role of the press as an instrument in eighteenth-century political education is to be found in London. The role of the numerous London newspapers in facilitating the participation of Londoners in the electoral policies of the city and in national politics was large, important, varied, and lasting. Independent newspapers grew apace in London after 1695. By 1709 there were eighteen in the capital, and every week 60,000 or more single newspaper copies were issued. It was a density of political printing activity such as had not been experienced since the revolutionary decades of the 1640s and 1650s, with sales of individual newspapers on a par with sales fifty years later, in the early years of George III's reign.[123]

London printers showed resourcefulness in evading and avoiding the press laws in order to guide the London electorate. Selective references to the names of mayoral, aldermanic, and parliamentary candidates were made in order to favor the electoral chances of one party above another. Newspapers regularly advertised the calendar of municipal elections and the names of party leaders and candidates. Advance notice of common hall polls, in which the liverymen of the city companies elected sheriffs or MPs, allowed the faithful to get into battle order, or withdraw in orderly fashion. The London press fuelled party conflict by associating local and national issues and took party conflict into the coffee houses, which became cells of party as well as centers of sociability, sources of political as well as physical refreshment.[124]

London newspapers circulated widely in the provinces, and provincial newspapers reproduced the running controversies of the leading ministerial and opposition journals published in London. The effect was to enlarge the audience of London and Westminster politics and encourage engagement in metropolitan and national politics in a way, and to a degree, not possible previously. By 1726 there were twenty-six provincial newspapers, some of which were distributed by means of a network of agents and receiving points throughout a large area around the place of publication. The capacity was available to politicize at short notice large areas of the country and a body of opinion that reached far beyond the electorate. Nor was politicization confined to national politics and to easier and better informed participation in national politics. Slowly and reluctantly, windows into local politics opened, often making visible the electoral malpractices and maneuvers of local officials, and the political activities at Westminster of the local MP. Occasional publication of MPs' voting behavior could reduce the distance between an MP and his constituents in a way which discomfited MPs by threatening to make them more accountable to their constituency. A striking instance of this occurred in 1722. An opposition newspaper, *The Freeholders Journal*, printed a list of absentees from the division on the Septennial Bill of 1716, suggesting that their conduct should be taken into account at the imminent general election. The MP for Warwickshire, one of those listed, inserted a notice in *The Whitehall Evening Post*, a London evening newspaper which circulated in the provinces, advertising a meeting at Warwick at which he promised to vindicate his behavior.[125]

The press could be both subversive and supportive of accepted political norms. But subversive or supportive, after 1695 it became a consistent and important feature in the political life of the nation and, in the eyes of Europeans, a distinctive, even unique, feature. In the eyes of the *philosophes* of the eighteenth century England's relative freedom of public discussion made her the freest country in Europe, and a model, perhaps the best model, for the Enlightenment.[126] However the government found itself engaged in a series of bruising encounters with Wilkes in the 1760s. Like many Englishmen in the course of the century Wilkes gloried in the liberty of the press, as the birthright of a Briton and the firmest bulwark of the liberties of the country.[127] What he meant by liberty of the press, apart from the liberty to use the press to advance his own personal and political interests, was the liberty to publish without a license. As he conceded, this liberty was one of the important points passed over in silence by the great patriots who brought about the Revolution, and necessarily so, for "whatever is done on the spur of a present necessity, is seldom mature, perfect or finished in all its parts."[128] What was passed over in silence in 1689 slipped in quietly in 1695. Liberty of the press was gained by default in 1695; but once gained it was not lost, though it remained at risk of being lost or diminished for a decade after 1695, and it always remained subject to the law that was particularly severe as regards seditious libel. In spite of the law, however, and in spite of the prosecutions, or the threat of them, the political literature of the age, as published in newspapers, pamphlets, and prints, was remarkable for its boldness, not its reticence. That was certainly the view of contemporaries from across the channel, and their eyes did not deceive them.

Liberty, Law, and Property, 1689-1776

HENRY HORWITZ

As THE REVOLUTION and settlement of 1688–89 underlined the priority in law of subjects' liberty and property, so celebrations of these birthrights of Englishmen were commonplace in succeeding generations, not least at assizes and quarter sessions. When Sir Daniel Dolins opened the Middlesex sessions in October 1726 by addressing the grand jury and the assembled county notables on "the excellence of our constitution and frame of government; of the wisdom, justice and goodness of our laws ... legally settled, secure enjoyment and free use of life, property and estates," he was expatiating on familiar themes in almost ritualistic fashion.[1] In reciting Englishmen's blessings, Dolins—and others on similar occasions—were drawing contrasts, sometimes explicitly, not only with their ancestors' situation under Stuart rule but also with what they took to be the prevailing circumstances in France and other European monarchies. So, too, continental visitors to eighteenth-century England, among them budding *philosophes*, frequently remarked the differences with their native lands. "I am here," Montesquieu exclaimed on his visit of 1729–30, "in a country which hardly resembles the rest of Europe"; "of all peoples of the world" the English have "progressed the farthest ... in piety, in commerce, and in freedom."[2] Travellers' perceptions were shaped not only by what they saw but even more by what they were told, and Englishmen "at all levels" seem to have had "a powerful awareness of the rights and liberties they had inherited from the struggles" of the previous century. Nor were they loath to brag of their inheritance to foreigners though, as in the instance of Voltaire's London waterman who subsequently was taken up by a press gang, they sometimes learned to their cost that there were limits to the liberty of "the freeborn."[3]

The very prevalence in eighteenth-century England of paeans to the blessings of liberty and property secured by law invites its own questions, many of which have attracted renewed scholarly attention and sometimes debate in recent decades.[4] Here we can canvass, with varying degrees of attention, only a few of these questions, three in particular. First, how far was there agreement on the extent of liberty and the substance of property in this era, and why was it that fears for the security of liberty continued to be voiced after the Revolution? Second, how far did the law become a vehicle after 1688 for propertied interests to serve their own concerns at others' expense? And third, how far did Englishmen (or, rather, after the 1707 union with Scotland, Britons) develop by 1776 new perspectives on the nature and interrelations of liberty, law, and property?

< I >

There can be no doubt that the very widespread attraction of the language of liberty, law, and property encouraged competing applications and rival renditions. On occasion political partisanship engendered contradictory appeals to liberty and property—as in the dispute between the two houses of Queen Anne's first Parliament over the Aylesbury election case. The controversy began with the Tory-dominated Commons exercising its traditional privilege of determining the election returns of its own members; its claims were subsequently deferred to by a majority of the judges of the court of Queen's Bench. But Chief Justice Sir John Holt disagreed and declared that the Commons, by denying arbitrarily the vote to the Aylesbury inhabitants in question and then by imprisoning them for breach of privilege after they sued the returning officer of the borough as a way to make good their claims, was acting unilaterally "to dispose of the liberty or property of the people" and thereby undermining "the security of our English constitution, which cannot be altered but by act of parliament." In turn, the Whig-led Lords endorsed Holt's stance when the case reached the Upper House upon appeal, prompting the infuriated majority below to accuse the peers of "contriving by all methods to bring the determination of liberty and property into the bottomless and insatiable gulf of your Lordships' judicature, which would swallow up both the prerogatives of the Crown and the rights and liberties of the people."[5]

On other occasions, alternate renditions of the rhetoric of liberty and property were offered by economic interests in conflict, as in the popular disturbances of the period variously directed against turnpike commissioners, enclosers, or grain dealers in time of anticipated shortage. Commonly, the protesters or rioters claimed to be defending their customary rights (or their virtual equivalent, existing practice) against the innovatory conduct of their targets.[6] So a recurrent call by food rioters was that local authorities enforce the centuries-old statutes (latterly more honored in the breach in normal harvest years) regulating grain dealers' activities and enjoining farmers to sell their output in the public markets of the district. On the protesters' view, then, the law was on their side and the "liberty" or unfettered right claimed by producers to sell their crop en bloc to dealers from outside the district (at the expense of local wage laborers dependent for their daily bread on small-scale purchases) was not, in the words of a sympathetic pamphleteer, "the liberty of a citizen," but "rather the liberty of a savage; therefore he who avails himself thereof, deserves not that protection the power of society affords."[7]

Nevertheless, it was rare that the rhetoric of liberty *and* property allowed of a clearcut opposition between personal liberty and property rights. Thus, in the sporadic litigation involving the situation of black slaves brought into England, the courts provided no clear lead. To be sure, as early as 1701, Lord Chief Justice Holt had stated, though only by way of *dictum*, that "by the common law no man can have a property in another . . . there is no such thing as a slave by the law of England." While this flat assertion was echoed by later lay commentators such as the author of the widely-read *Present State of Great Britain* and by the admiralty board in a 1758 order concerning the status of an escaped slave who had joined the royal navy only to encounter and be arrested by his onetime owner, Lord Chancellor Hardwicke and a number of other leading legal lights were not prepared to endorse Holt's stance.[8] Thus, the law was still uncertain when Chief Justice Mansfield was confronted in 1771–72 with the case of the slave Somerset, who, aided by the abolitionist Granville Sharp, sought to use the writ of Habeas Corpus to prevent his forcible removal from the realm to be sold in the slave markets of Jamaica. Mansfield, aware of the implications of any disallowance of slavery for British trade abroad and perhaps even more mindful of a potential problem of order at home (there were, by then, perhaps 14,000 slaves in Britain), ruled for Somerset but avoided the general question. The decision in *Somerset*, then, was an important yet limited one. It established that a slave could not be forcibly removed from the realm and that he might use Habeas Corpus to secure his discharge from confinement in England by his alleged owner, but emancipation had to wait until Parliament acted over half a century later.[9]

If the rhetoric of liberty and property was only infrequently threatened by direct contradiction, less straightforward but perhaps more central tensions between personal liberty and property rights have been discerned by some interpreters of John Locke, once the dominating figure in accounts of political thought after 1688. In particular, Locke's use of the term "property" in *The Two Treatises* both in a broad sense to encompass life, liberty, and estate and in the narrow sense of material interests (including one's property in one's labor) encouraged C. Brough Macpherson to read Locke as accepting a "possessive individualism" which sanctioned capitalist economic relations.[10] While the controversy Macpherson's analysis provoked still resonates, of greater positive influence on understanding Locke as a political writer has been Peter Laslett's demonstration that *The Two Treatises* were composed, for the most part, late in Charles II's reign—probably, as Richard Ashcraft has more recently argued, in order to justify the forcible overthrow of that king in the wake of the failure of the "first Whigs" to secure a majority in the Lords for legislation to exclude the Catholic James from the royal succession. But even if Locke's immediate concerns were clearly shaped by the religio-political conflicts of Charles II's day, he only published *The Two Treatises* after James II was displaced by William III. And while the work does not appear to have gained a wide audience in the first decades after its anonymous publication, some of its principal arguments were disseminated, in a series of popular pamphlets, as part of the party polemics of the post-Revolution generation in which the issue of the legitimacy of forcible resistance to government was kept alive by Tory preaching of the doctrine of passive obedience.[11]

≺ II ≻

Although older political questions persisted in modified form during the reigns of William and Anne, it is noteworthy that within a few years after the Revolution some Englishmen began to identify a new form of property—investment in the national debt—as an insidious threat to liberty. The national debt itself was a parliamentary innovation of the post-1688 wars against France, which raised England to a new position of preeminence in European affairs and set in motion or accelerated a complex of domestic developments. A brief review of these war-linked changes will help to pinpoint some key features of eighteenth-century governance and to explain how investment in the national debt came to take on such a malign aspect.

In the first place, the protracted and unprecedentedly expensive warfare contributed to the establishment of Parliament as a regular element in the governance of the realm. The framers of the Declaration of Rights had called for "frequent" parliaments, but annual sessions exceeded their expectations (and perhaps even their desires). Initially, it was the exigencies of war finance that led William III to convene the Houses at least once yearly. After the Treaty of Ryswick of 1697 temporarily halted the fighting, the Commons decided that henceforth peacetime military and naval outlays would be separated from the "civil list," with the former voted on a year by year basis and the latter granted for life. In this fashion, a new constitutional norm of yearly meetings of Parliament took shape in William's reign—a norm adhered to without controversy during the renewed warfare of Anne's reign and hardening thereafter into a constitutional "convention" that has persisted to the present.[12]

In the second place, the annual campaigns William III and his ministers had to wage to win the Commons' backing yielded a significant extension of subjects' rights. William—after first resorting to the Crown's power of veto—eventually accepted a decided restriction upon the monarch's prerogative to keep a complacent House of Commons on foot indefinitely (the Triennial Act of 1694) and conceded that at least two witnesses to the same act were required to secure convictions for treason (the Trials for Treason Act of 1696). Then, to expedite passage in 1701 of the act designating the electoral house of Hanover as successors in reversion to the English throne, William acquiesced in the inclusion of clauses barring royal pardons to parliamentary impeachments and enlarging the judiciary's tenure from the royal pleasure to good behavior. Collectively, these concessions by William chiefly enhanced Englishmen's "negative liberty"—their freedom against the threat of arbitrary governance.[13] At the same time, Englishmen's "positive liberty," their freedom to participate in the political process, was potentially enlarged by the ending of official pre-censorship of the press. The Commons' refusal in 1695 to renew the expiring licensing law opened the way for the rapid growth of that brand of noisy political journalism that impressed and sometimes scandalized visitors from across the Channel.

Third, the funding of William's and Anne's wars brought to the fore a "new species of property."[14] Parliament not only raised existing taxes and struggled to devise new ones; it also resorted to borrowing on an enormous scale and in a novel form. The resulting "financial revolution"—the creation of a longterm debt secured by parliamentary guarantees specifically tied to the yield of some of the additional taxation—went well beyond Charles II's borrowings through the exchequer. The burgeoning debt involved thousands of the English (along with some resident aliens and foreigners) lending to the government, either as purchasers of annuities or as shareholders in the newly-chartered "monied companies" (the Bank of England, established in 1694; the new East India Company, in 1698; and the South Sea Company, in 1711). Of the total war expenditure of close to £50,000,000 by 1714, almost one-third was raised by borrowing. And of the 10,000 or so individual lenders and investors who collectively constituted the mushrooming "monied interest," the bulk resided in the metropolis with a highly visible element being nouveaux riches, Protestant dissenters, or immigrants.[15]

Fourth, the war effort and the creation of the national debt made for a permanent swelling of the central government. To be sure, after the Treaty of Ryswick in 1697 and again after the Peace of Utrecht of 1713, the armed forces were reduced to a peacetime footing. Yet commensurate with the kingdom's enhanced European role and the need to garrison acquisitions such as Gibraltar, the armed forces kept up after 1713 were somewhat larger than the total of those Charles II had maintained in his three kingdoms. In addition, the majority of land and sea officers still on active duty at the end of the fighting were kept on the establishment on half-pay. Nor was there any cutback in the civil administration despite the very considerable wartime expansion of the revenue agencies: these personnel were still needed to collect the levies voted during the war years to serve as security for the government's longterm borrowings (some of the new customs duties and excises had been given for terms of up to ninety-nine years). So, even after Utrecht, the customs, excise, salt, and stamp offices had over 5,000 established officers in the provinces, and the size of the civil administration rose from approximately 5,000 under James II to around 9,000 under George I.[16]

≺ III ≻

These war-generated developments of William's and Anne's reigns were to become permanent features of the eighteenth-century scene, and some of their effects on Englishmen's notions of liberty, law, and property were already discernible by the later 1690s. Indeed, John Pocock has contended that "the first widespread ideological perception of a capitalist form of political relations came into being, rapidly and abruptly, in the last years of the seventeenth century and the two decades following." As the financial revolution spawned "a new class of investors . . . who had lent government capital that vastly stabilized and enlarged it," the sudden visibility of the "monied interest" alarmed the self-selected defenders of the traditional ascendancy of the landed classes who "saw in this process a revolutionary expansion . . . of a system of parliamentary patronage."[17]

These conservative ideologues were neither exclusively Tory nor exclusively Whig; what they shared was a set of premises which leads Pocock to style them "neo-Harringtonians" (after the mid seventeenth-century writer James Harrington because of his and their preoccupation with the balance of property and its political consequences) and "civic humanists" (because of their concern to preserve "civic virtue" from the corrupting effects of "luxury"). By "civic virtue," writers such as Walter Moyle, John Trenchard, and Charles Davenant meant the capacity of the citizen (in English terms, the freeholder preeminently) to play a public-spirited part in the process of self-governance; by "luxury," they meant the intensification of men's propensity to consume amidst the enhancement of national prosperity.[18]

For Pocock, then, it is the expansion of government by war and especially the "new species of property" associated with "public credit" that translated the growth of luxury into a political menace. The "mode of property" the neo-Harringtonians began to attack in the later 1690s and to "denounce as a new force in history, transforming and corrupting society," was not the property in exchangeable commodities (including one's own labor) which is the focus of Macpherson's analysis of seventeenth-century political writing. Rather, it was "property in government office, government stock, and government expectations to which the National Debt had mortgaged futurity" so rendering "government dependent on its creditors and creditors dependent on government, in a relationship incompatible with classical or agrarian virtue."[19]

To be sure, the immediate focus of political controversy after the Treaty of Ryswick was the attempt by William and his junto (or "modern") Whig ministers to persuade the Commons to authorize a sizable peacetime army. But in arguing this question, the neo-Harringtonian or "old" Whig Andrew Fletcher, who advocated disbandment and reliance (in both England and his native Scotland) on a reformed militia, and the "modern" Whig Daniel Defoe, who was supporting the king's proposals, were—in Pocock's view—staking out positions in what would take shape as a political version of the battle of the books between ancients and moderns. For Fletcher and the "ancients," steeped in a particular brand of neo-classical humanism that owed much to Machiavelli's *Discorsi* and that had been domesticated in England by Harrington, the prerequisite of civic virtue was the possession of sufficient property to ensure one's independence and to facilitate one's participation in the governmental process both in war and in peace. From this perspective, one of the foundations of liberty (in the positive sense of civic virtue) was the traditional militia force composed of citizen proprietors. But for De-

foe and the moderns, who tended to think of liberty primarily in the
negative sense of freedom from arbitrary rule and who saw the de-
mise of feudalism and the expansion of commerce of recent centuries as socially "liberating" developments, it made no sense to try to
sustain or resuscitate civic virtue by instituting a reformed militia.
A moderately-sized professional military force would be much more
effective than any amateur militia and funding such an army by annual bills of supply passed by Parliament would be a sufficient safeguard of civilian authority.

As Pocock points to the 1690s as a critical moment in the shaping of political perceptions, so on his reading the history of political
ideas from 1689 to 1776 ceases to be the once familiar progress from
"Locke to Bentham" and becomes in large measure the continuation
and elaboration of the debate between the neo-Harringtonians and
their opponents.[20] The polemic reached new heights in the paper
warfare waged by Viscount Bolingbroke and his fellow "patriots"
against Sir Robert Walpole and the Whig ministerialists in the 1720s
and 1730s. Bolingbroke and his cohorts denounced Walpole for operating a corrupt and corrupting system of political management
that threatened liberty at various levels: constitutionally, "the
power of money" as represented by government patronage and finance subverted the independence of the Commons and so endangered the balance between the executive and the House; socially, the
public spiritedness of the freeholder (and his analogue, the urban
freeman) was being undermined by the spread of luxury. In reply,
Walpole's defenders elaborated the argument, sketched in earlier by
Defoe, that the foundations of liberty were not ancient but modern,
and that in fact power now resided not with the Crown but with
"the people" as represented in the Commons. Moreover, some went
on to suggest that the real danger to liberty in their day was posed
by an overmighty Commons which, if uninhibited in its exercise of
the power of the purse, could overturn the balance of the constitution and even lead to oppression of the subject. Was not unchecked
power in any form potentially dangerous? On this analysis, the
Crown's exercise of "influence" in the form of patronage (office,
benefit, and honor) was a legitimate and necessary ingredient of the
"modern" political order: "the Civil List thus becomes historical
successor to the feudal prerogative."[21]

Pocock has extended his revisionist account of eighteenth century political discourse into George III's reign (and also across the Atlantic), but perhaps we have followed him far enough to make clear the nature of the political quarrel between "ancients" and "moderns" and the relevance of that debate to the various and shifting meanings of liberty and property in the half century after 1689. Given the breadth and boldness of his remapping of the contours of political discourse in these decades, it would be surprising had Pocock's views gone unchallenged. Here, it will suffice to take note of two main points raised by his critics.

First, it has been suggested that Pocock overstates the centrality and distinctiveness of the debate between "ancients" and "moderns." After all, the neo-Harringtonians had no role as such in the prolonged contention over the legitimacy of resistance—the principal issue in dispute in the oath of allegiance controversy of the early years of William's reign and in the even more virulent controversies that culminated in 1709–10 in the Whigs' impeachment of the high-flying Tory clergyman Henry Sacheverell. Again, the sharp separation that Pocock makes between the languages of civic humanism (virtue) and natural jurisprudence (right) may obscure their more or less simultaneous deployment either by different writers aligned together in a given controversy or by the same writer in different contexts. Thus, during the disbanding debates of the late 1690s we certainly hear at least as much of the danger of absolutism a standing army posed as of the threat of corruption it represented. For Trenchard, perhaps the leading anti-army writer, the crux of the matter was that "in all ages and all parts of the World a standing army has been the never-failing instrument of enslaving a nation."[22] Yet in the wake of the passage of the Septennial Act in 1716 (amending the Triennial Act to allow up to seven years between general elections) and the South Sea Bubble of 1720 with its stock market manipulation and the bribing of well-placed courtiers, Trenchard, as co-author of *Cato's Letters*, primarily emphasized the insidious advance of corruption. Similarly, while Defoe may be labelled a "modern" Whig on the strength of his views on a standing army and public credit, this should not lead us to overlook his consistent defense of the legitimacy of resistance and of "Revolution Principles."[23] The overlapping of the languages of virtue and right is also apparent in the polemical warfare during Walpole's primacy—especially in the excise controversy of 1733–34. In attacking the proposed revamping of fiscal administration by shifting a series of levies from the customs to the excise, the opposition made at least as much of the threat to individual liberty posed by the excise officers' powers of search and the excise commissioners' powers of summary jurisdiction as they did of the potential enlargement of ministerial patronage the scheme entailed, and perhaps their most "popular" argument was that the new excises were a further step down the road towards a "general excise" on staple commodities that would be highly burdensome to those of limited means.[24]

Second, "mere" political historians find Pocock's aerial map of political discourse in the decades between the 1690s and the 1740s fitting somewhat uneasily at key points with their own knowledge of the terrain at ground level. Perhaps most important, Pocock's dichotomy of "old" and "modern" Whigs (and its analogue, the opposition of "country" and "court") is at odds with the prevailing consensus that the primary division in English politics between 1689 and at least the early 1720s, if not the 1740s, was that between Whig and Tory. Granted, the 1690s did see a partial realignment in Parliament as a small band of "old" Whigs led by Robert Harley gradually moved from Whig to Tory ranks. However, the sizable backbench Whig vote for a drastic reduction of the army after Ryswick was but a temporary regression to the party's anti-Court orientation under Charles II. Meanwhile, the Tories, out of office for much of the 1690s, were more closely identifying themselves with country positions on questions such as the desirability of reducing the number of members of the House of Commons in receipt of the Crown's patronage. As David Hayton has observed: "from the Junto's assumption of power in 1693–94, the bulk of the Country interest was accommodated within the Tory party, and by Anne's reign Country sentiment seems to have been largely absorbed into backbench Toryism." But it does not follow that the Tories in Anne's reign were primarily a country party. Not only did many Tories scrabble furiously for places in 1702 and again in 1710 when they had parliamentary majorities, but the Harley ministry of 1710–14 managed to stave off four successive place bills while finding new sources of profit for friends and allies in its own monied company, the South Sea. It is possible, then, to talk of "*a* country party" composed of both Whigs and Tories which manifested itself "from time to time" during these years, as in the late 1690s, but "*the* country party did not have a continuous existence"; rather, Whig versus Tory was the dominant alignment of politics for most of Anne's reign as well as much of William's.[25]

What, then, of the political alignments of the years of the opposition to Walpole mounted by the Tory Bolingbroke and the Whig Pulteney on a "patriot" platform? As Quentin Skinner has persuasively argued, the "patriots'" espousal of such "country" shibboleths as limitations upon the number of placemen sitting in the Commons, the reinstatement of the Triennial Act, and the reduction of the standing army was the expedient of a clique of ambitious politicians reaching out to backbenchers still divided along Whig-Tory lines yet often at one in their suspicions of the sincerity of their aspiring leaders. Similarly, Bolingbroke's and Pulteney's patriotic rhetoric can be interpreted as a necessary form of camouflage for their unconstitutional conduct in maintaining a "formed opposition" to the king's chosen ministers and as a means of rallying a body of opinion in London and beyond disgruntled at the ministers' seeming neglect of all the kingdom's commercial interests save those of the chartered companies.[26] Then, too, the "patriots'" repeated setbacks in their drawn-out campaign to oust Walpole have led some political historians to proclaim the "utter insignificance" of neo-Harringtonian ideas in terms of "practical politics."[27] This is surely too total a dismissal. Still, it is apparent that the backbenchers' recurring doubts about Bolingbroke's and Pulteney's "honesty" handicapped the opposition and postponed Walpole's departure. And when at last he withdrew from office in early 1742 over his administration's mismanagement of the war against Spain, his political disciples and heirs, the Pelhams, dealt piecemeal with a motley parliamentary opposition without ever having to make any concessions (such as the repeal of the Septennial Act) by way of constitutional reform.

So, the upshot of the fall of Walpole was not the revival of virtue but a relapse into disillusionment evidenced in the conduct not only of former patriots such as Henry Fielding but also in the *Essays, Moral and Political* published in 1741 and 1742 by the young Scotsman David Hume.[28] Yet, the appearance of the *Essays* and thereafter a flood of works from north of the Tweed has led Pocock to suggest that the debate between "ancients" and "moderns"—moribund at least temporarily in an England apparently "without significant ideological dispute . . . in the late 1740s and early 1750s"—may simply have shifted northwards so "that the growth of political economy in the Scottish Enlightenment might be viewed as an effective response to, and outgrowth of, neo-Harringtonian civic humanism and its denunciations of the new order."[29]

≺ IV ≻

We will have occasion later to revert to the writings of the Scots. Here, we may observe that the very placidity of the years following the making of peace in Europe in 1748 allowed ministers and MPs to take up domestic reform measures. Although the third Viscount Townshend opined to Josiah Tucker that were the kingdom so "happy" as to be able in peace time "to break through the Custom" of annual sessions of Parliament "*Electioneering Jobbs* and *Jobbs of all kinds* would be less frequent," the Houses continued to convene annually.[30] And among the measures of general public import passed in these years were the 1751 statutes to lessen the consumption of gin and to modernize the calendar, the 1752 and 1754 statutes to provide a degree of public funding for criminal prosecutions, and the 1753 statutes against "clandestine" marriages and for the naturalization of Jews (although the last had subsequently to be repealed after xenophobic popular demonstrations in the metropolis).

The legislative activity of these peacetime years should serve to remind us that Parliament was more than an engine for approving supply; it was also an increasingly active legislative body. So, as we move from the realm of political discourse to consider how changes in the law affected the scope of liberty and the nature of property in eighteenth-century England, we need to consider the contents of the expanding statute book as well as the activities of the courts. Certainly, annual parliamentary sessions from 1689 onwards of four months or more yielded a swelling corpus of legislation. During the 25 years of Charles II's reign, some 533 bills reached the statute book—a considerable expansion on the legislative totals of his father's and grandfather's reigns. Even so, William III's reign of but 13 years yielded 809 statutes, and this pace was either matched or bettered under each of his successors in the 1700s.[31] Of this legislation, nearly three-quarters was private or local in substance (for example, estate, naturalization, enclosure, local transportation, and improvement acts) and perhaps another one-tenth consisted of governmental measures relating to supply or military matters. So, roughly one-sixth of the total (close to 800 acts between 1689 and 1760) dealt, like the legislation of the early 1750s mentioned earlier, with matters of general public import.[32]

The enlargement of the statute book was coupled with an increasing assurance shown by MPs and lawyers in Parliament's legislative authority. Already in the prolonged Commons' debates over the 1696 bill of attainder against Sir John Fenwick for conspiring to assassinate William III, even those who opposed such retrospective condemnation as subversive of the newly-passed Treason Trials Act and as contrary to natural justice conceded Parliament's "right to do wrong."[33] Occasionally, it is true, voices were still heard to assert that natural law or fundamental law might or ought to limit the power of statute. Fundamental law was unsuccessfully urged in 1716 as a ground for rejection of the Septennial Act. And both natural law and fundamental law were invoked by Lord Camden, future lord chancellor, in the upper House's debates on the declaratory bill of 1766 brought in to vindicate the authority of the Westminister Parliament against American challenges. Yet, it is an indicator of the movement of opinion by the 1760s that Camden could be stigmatized by those supporting the measure for advancing what they characterized as "new-fangled doctrines, contrary to the laws of this kingdom, and subversive of the rights of Parliament."[34] Again, despite some nods in the direction of natural law, Blackstone, writing shortly before the debates on the Declaratory Act, was clear that "if the Parliament will positively enact a thing which is unreasonable, I know of no power that can control it."[35]

However, Blackstone did accompany his oft-quoted assertion of parliamentary sovereignty with some substantial reservations about the wisdom of specific sections of the statute book, particularly legislation in areas in which the Houses "have not [had] the foundation of the common law to build upon."[36] In a similar vein, but directing his criticism more specifically against the Commons, Lord Chancellor Hardwicke in 1756 complained that laws are passed "which are either unnecessary, or ridiculous, and almost every law they pass stands in need of some new law for explaining and amending it."[37] It was probably, then, the expanding but defective statute book that prompted Blackstone, in spelling out the utility of the study of the law for "gentlemen of independent estates and fortune," to stress their future responsibilities as MPs. Certainly, he emphasized the need for pursuit of "the science of legislation," "the noblest and most difficult" of all inquiries, while observing that existing problems in English law were principally owing to "innovations" made in it by acts of Parliament.[38] In turn, Blackstone's comments upon particular categories of the public statutes of the era may serve as useful markers in our survey of the impact of law upon the scope of liberty and the nature of property in eighteenth-century England.

One series of statutes of legal import about which Blackstone voiced serious reservations was that enlarging the number and range of criminal offenses carrying the death penalty. By his reckoning, the number of capital offenses stood at about 160 by the 1760s, as compared to 50 or so in 1688, and he (echoing Hardwicke) condemned the seeming casualness with which Parliament had elaborated this "bloody code." Had public bills, like private ones, been referred as a matter of course to the judges who sat as assistants to the House of Lords, Blackstone believed it would have been "impossible" for Parliament ever to have attached the death penalty to an offense such as the malicious destruction of a fish pond—one of a series of new capital crimes under the notorious Black Act of 1723. Surely, procedures as painstaking as those used for private bills should be required "when laws are to be established, which may affect the property, the liberty, and perhaps even the lives, of thousands."[39]

Since Blackstone's day, the "bloody code" has often figured in portrayals of eighteenth-century England, and perhaps most strikingly in the work of Douglas Hay. Hay contends that the criminal law functioned not as an instrument of indiscriminate coercion but as a "critically important" and finely-tuned means of "maintaining bonds of obedience and deference" in a society marked by a highly unequal division of property, an established church that let too many of its nominal members forget "the smell of brimstone," and a government that lacked the administrative resources to police the land. Criminal justice in this period should be conceived of "as an ideological system" whose three prime features were its "majesty," as exemplified by the solemnity of judicial process; its "justice," as manifested by the *appearance* of equal treatment of the accused, whether the lowly or the great; and its "mercy," as orchestrated chiefly through the judges' discretionary authority to reprieve the convicted and the Crown's prerogative to pardon the reprieved.[40]

Hay's account of the criminal law system is ingenious, yet by no means the whole story.[41] In supplementing it, we may begin by observing that the nearly universal tendency of contemporaries to exalt the law could under some circumstances inhibit the authorities and upon occasion even be turned against them. Thus, despite the passage of the Riot Act in 1715, there was a "widespread conviction" that the use of troops to suppress the not-infrequent popular disturbances of the day was "no part of the English constitution"—a conviction apparent in the military authorities' own nervous efforts to conform to law on those occasions when the government did call out the troops.[42] In turn, the alleged misbehavior of the troops deployed to quell disturbances in Middlesex in 1768 was only one of a number of causes brought before the courts by John Wilkes and his lawyer-associates as part of their oppositional activities during the 1760s and early 1770s. Lord Camden's judgment of 1765 against the secretary of state's use of general warrants was their most important courtroom success; they also scored some significant victories in frustrating Crown prosecutions for seditious libel by appealing to jurors' views that it was rightly their responsibility, not the presiding judge's, to determine whether the material in question actually was "seditious."[43]

Addressing ourselves more specifically to the criminal law system, it would appear that the discretionary dimension rightly stressed by Hay was by no means the exclusive privilege of the magistracy, the judiciary, the Crown, or those with political connections seeking pardons for kin, clients, or dependents. Discretion began well before conviction in the determinations of individual victims whether or not to prosecute suspected offenders. Moreover, it would appear that the bulk of prosecutors of property offenses in the courts—those victims of crime who, largely without official assistance, went to the trouble and expense of identifying suspects and then pursuing them through the legal process—were of middling means (farmers, traders, shopkeepers, craftsmen, and the like). Even more striking, at least one-tenth, and perhaps as many as one-fifth, of the identifiable individual prosecutors of property offenses at quarter sessions were of limited means (laborers, servants, sailors, and so on).[44] Thus, while the administration of the law, and especially the criminal law, was undoubtedly an important element in a structure of authority sustaining the position of a privileged elite whose core consisted of the great landed families, the law as a vehicle for the defense of property can also be characterized as a "limited multiple-use right available to most Englishmen" which was invoked even by some of the laboring poor.[45]

In many instances, too, the trial jurors had the opportunity to exercise their own discretion (normally, but not invariably, with the cooperation of the presiding magistrates or judge). To be sure, the makeup of trial juries was socially skewed because property qualifications laid down by statute excluded a quite sizable segment of the population. The vast majority of trial jurors were men of middling means, and many appear to have served in this capacity time after time. This prior experience may well have lent them confidence in their own opinions; certainly, trial juries frequently exercised discretion by undervaluing the goods involved in property offenses and failing to find the requisite intent in cases of violent death. In these ways, many indicted for capital crimes were found guilty only of lesser ones, with jurors appearing to take into account much the same elements—above all, the accused's character—that seem to have shaped judges' determinations as to which of those found guilty should be reprieved.[46]

If the jury dominated by middling men played the primary role in the disposition of serious criminal cases in its capacity as finder of fact and by its power to mitigate the gravity of some common charges, what significance ought we to attach to a second category of statutes singled out by Blackstone for criticism—those assigning a variety of offenses, some hitherto dealt with by jury trial, to the summary disposition of justices of the peace outside quarter sessions?[47] Such grants of summary jurisdiction were not unknown before 1688, but the statute book indicates that thereafter MPs increasingly vested themselves and their fellow gentlemen with this kind of authority.[48] For Blackstone, to empower JPs, singly or in pairs, to impose even relatively mild penalties (at least by comparison to the "bloody code") as whipping or incarceration in houses of correction ("bridewells") for terms of up to two years for offenses such as poaching, wood or vegetable stealing, or embezzlement of employers' materials was to threaten the very "palladium" of Englishmen's liberties—the right to trial by jury. Summary justice might be more expeditious, but "delays, and little inconveniences in the forms of justice, are the price that all free nations must pay for their liberty in more substantial matters."[49]

Once again, Blackstone's concerns must be set in context. First, he expressed no reservations about the traditional and frequent use of bridewells as places of incarceration for the idle and disorderly poor, often sent there by the decisions of individual JPs. In general, those liable to commitment to these institutions, whether under older or under newer acts, were men and women of the poorer sort. This fact, so often taken for granted by contemporaries, led one anti-regime pamphleteer to observe in 1731 that the poor "have no advantage of the constitution; there is no *Habeas Corpus* to remove out of *Bridewell*; they have no power to defend themselves from an arbitrary Justice of the Peace, if one of that Bench should prove tyrannical."[50] In fact, the pamphleteer somewhat overstated a good case: it was possible for one committed to a bridewell to seek a Habeas Corpus, and a few instances are known of individuals actually availing themselves of this right.[51] To that extent, the person liable to be sent to a house of correction was better protected than those "able-bodied men as do not follow or exercise any lawful calling," for they were subject to being conscripted into the army at the discretion of three JPs and/or commissioners of the land tax under the Press Act of 1709. But as MPs observed in the 1758 debate over broadening the scope of the Habeas Corpus Act of 1679 to make the writ available to those wrongfully taken up under the Press Act, in reality what counted for those committed to bridewells and those conscripted was not their formal entitlement to the writ but their practical ability to make good that right. It was one thing for an individual of limited means to prosecute a thief; it was another for such a person to attempt to use legal process after being committed by the magistracy, whatever the justification. Hence, even were the proposal to extend the scope of the 1679 act adopted, the poor would be unlikely to be able "to bear the expense of suing a habeas corpus," much less would they "find it possible to get security for their not escaping (if remanded) as required" by the 1679 act.[52] Somerset was the beneficiary of the legal aid furnished by anti-slavery campaigners but their benevolence did not extend to the idle and disorderly.

Second, it is apparent that the rapid expansion by statute after 1688 of both summary procedures and capital offenses reflects, in no small part, MPs' recurrent anxiety over a seemingly rising tide of crime, especially offenses against property in the London metropolis. Nor did the Houses simply multiply penal legislation. A series of statutes of the later 1600s and early 1700s sought to encourage the apprehension of criminals by instituting rewards for information or other forms of citizen action leading to the capture and conviction of shoplifters, burglars, housebreakers, and the like. Moreover, in passing the Transportation Act in 1718 (apparently brought in by the Crown's law officers), the Houses authorized the expenditure of public funds to help pay the costs of deporting certain categories of convicted offenders to the colonies; transportation, it was hoped, would help to bridge the sizable gap in the existing array of criminal sanctions between lesser penalties (whipping and incarceration for limited terms) and the gallows while requiring most of those pardoned to be removed from the realm.[53] Again, during the years of the Pelhams' ascendancy, acts of 1752 and 1754 authorized the payment of at least a portion of the costs of individual prosecutors and of "poor persons" bound over to testify as witnesses.

Limited public financing for improvements to the enforcement of the criminal law was accompanied, especially from mid-century onwards, by enactment of a growing number of locally-initiated bills to enable individual parts of the metropolis and also provincial towns to beef up their watch, improve their street lighting, and take other preventative steps at local expense. Even so, most MPs were loath to contemplate the introduction of centralized policing arrangements for the seemingly crime-ridden metropolis. The Pitt ministry's "London and Westminster police" bill of 1785 was hotly opposed both because it overrode existing local governmental boundaries and because, so the City's petition in opposition alleged, it would introduce[54] "a system of police altogether new and arbitrary in the extreme, creating, without necessity, new officers, invested with extraordinary and dangerous powers, enforced by heavy penalties, and expressly exempted from those checks, and that responsibility, which the wisdom of the law has hitherto thought necessary to accompany every extraordinary power." Henry Fielding, godfather of Pitt's scheme, had warned in the early 1750s that the rising tide of crime in London constituted a dire threat to the very health of the body politic, yet a generation later many of his compatriots still had to be convinced that his remedies were tolerable, at least in England.[55]

The readiness with which Englishmen of the era perceived threats to liberty from centralized or unchecked forms of power may be paralleled by the tendency of some historians to detect in the legislation and in other legal changes of the period a pronounced tendency to shape the law to promote economic development. From Blackstone onwards, attention has been drawn to the "multitude" of acts under the "bloody code" extending the law's protection to new forms of property.[56] Indeed, one can instance no fewer than seventeen separate acts passed between the Revolution and George III's accession in 1760 that extended the death penalty (already imposed for forgery by an act of 1563) to the tampering with a range of newer commercial and financial instruments, among them Bank of England notes. Similarly, a series of statutes, particularly a wide-ranging measure of 1749, subjecting acts of "embezzlement" by industrial workers to the summary jurisdiction of JPs has been instanced as evidence of the recourse to statute to define claims to property rights more precisely and then to protect such claims with the sanctions of criminal law. Some of the takings had not hitherto been treated as criminal offenses at all; "chips" kept by dockyard workers or "wastages" retained by framework knitters had been regarded by them as part of their normal compensation—a claim sometimes disputed, sometimes bargained over by their employers. The criminalization of such conduct has been interpreted as a manifestation of employer concern to stiffen industrial discipline and also to define the wage strictly in cash terms, especially in the expanding array of outwork activities.[57]

As the range of criminal conduct appears to have been broadened to protect the needs of the expanding financial and industrial sectors, so a tendency to elaborate property rights has also been discerned in the law generally. The evidence of seventeenth- and early eighteenth-century legal dictionaries suggests to some "the emergence of a definition of absolute individual ownership, resting on the notion of 'the greatest interest' attributed to the person who had the property."[58] And Blackstone is notorious for his grandiloquent peroration to "that sole and despotic dominion which one man claims and exercises over the external things of the World, in total exclusion of any other individual in the Universe."[59] From this perspective, one can see the increasing resort to local enclosure acts (some 850 were passed between 1715 and 1774, with the rate of adoption steadily increasing after mid century) as going far to end overlapping customary rights in agriculture and so epitomizing that process described by Macpherson as the replacement of "limited and not always saleable rights *in* things" by the "virtually unlimited and saleable rights *to* things."[60]

However, the matter is less straightforward than such generalizations suggest. On the one hand, those able to gain parliamentary sanction for their objectives could use statute to override local custom; in the case of the enclosure acts a majority of landowners of a given locality could in effect compel an unwilling minority to accept monetary payment for their rights in common fields and also deprive cottagers and the like of their use-claims without compensation. On the other hand, the courts were more respectful of custom, provided customary claims were supported by the evidence and put forward by men of some property. The case of Cumbria, an area where customary tenures were still quite common in the early 1700s, indicates that tenants sufficiently determined to defend their claims at law generally prevailed; the courts upheld their position on the level of entry fines and, later in the century, on use rights in timber, turves, and the like.[61] However, the well-known Common Pleas' judgment of 1788 against gleaning seems to suggest that, as with enclosure acts, the customary claims of the rural poor were less likely to be upheld, or compensated if abrogated. So Chief Justice Loughborough characterized gleaning as "inconsistent with the nature of property which imports exclusive enjoyment" in the crop to the farmer; even so, in practice gleaning persisted—often without the farmers' consent—well into the next century.[62] Thus, as we must take care to distinguish the interests at stake in parliamentary and judicial action affecting customary claims, we also ought "not to confuse a legal decision of general significance with the general adoption of it in practice."[63]

What seems to have been occurring in law and at the law, then, was a series of overlapping developments. In very broad terms, there is the tendency—already discernible in the seventeenth century—to blur, though not to erase, the traditionally sharp distinction between real and personal property.[64] At the same time, there is the continuation, and probably the acceleration, of a movement apparent in English society well before 1689—a shift away from customary relations as between employer and employee and between landlord and tenant. Concurrently, there is the protection in law that is being acquired by newer forms of property—a phenomenon seemingly unprecedented in scope in part because parliamentary statute was much more accessible in this century than earlier and also in part because the pace of economic change was quickening. Withal, there was a substantial degree of continuity with the past. There is nothing strikingly novel in principle about a statute such as the 1698 act against forging or counterfeiting notes of the Bank of England; an existing legal standard—the death penalty for forgery—was simply being extended to cover a new type of commercial paper. Again, despite the flood of new criminal offenses created by Parliament, most of those executed in the 1700s for crimes against property were in practice tried and punished under the pre-1689 statutes against robbery, burglary, and housebreaking.[65] Nor were the property interests being protected by the expanding list of capital and summary offenses exclusively or even primarily those of the growing financial, commercial, and industrial sectors. One of the leading (as gauged by the number of committals and by the level of public controversy) types of offenses shifted from trial by jury to summary disposition by JPs was poaching, surely a "class concern," but those whose interests the poaching acts protected were the landed gentry at the expense both of the rural poor and of the more substantial tenant farmers prevented from taking game over their own leaseholds.[66]

As trials for offenses against property punishable under pre-1689 legislation were still the staple items of the criminal justice dispensed at quarter sessions and assizes, so the bulk of civil litigation in the central courts consisted of contract actions to collect debts or damages.[67] Yet, while Parliament between 1689 and 1776 passed no less than ten acts to empty debtors' prisons, the actual volume of contract cases carried through to later stages of litigation was falling.[68] The paradoxical conjunction of a rise in the number of debtors being imprisoned in the later 1600s and early 1700s *and* a concurrent falloff in contract cases coming to trial might possibly be ascribed to the relative ease by which a creditor could secure the pretrial committal of a potentially insolvent or recalcitrant debtor. But the decline in the volume of civil suits pursued beyond pre-trial process was not confined to contract cases.[69]

The fall-off in civil litigation is discernible from the 1680s onwards, and a contributing element may have been the substantial rise detectable in lawyers' charges and court officials' fees. The mounting cost of legal proceedings attracted parliamentary attention in the later 1720s in the wake of the impeachment of Lord Chancellor Macclesfield for corruption and amidst MPs' concerns about the seemingly exorbitant fees exacted by the Commons' own staff for the processing of private bills and the like. But public discussion and parliamentary inquiry yielded at best piecemeal reform: legislation was passed in the early years of George II's reign for the regulation of the lower branches of the legal profession (attorneys and solicitors) and for the substitution of English for Latin in common law documents. However, the recommendations of a royal commission appointed in 1732 to investigate the fees collected by court officers were never even published, much less translated into action, save that in 1743 Lord Hardwicke did issue a comprehensive set of orders for the court of Chancery.[70]

However, for those tradesmen and shopkeepers who because of the expense appear to have been increasingly deterred from litigating in the central courts to collect debts, a significant measure of relief came, though somewhat belatedly, in the shape of Parliament's passage of local measures for the creation of small claims courts in individual cities and towns. These "courts of request," in which non-professional commissioners examined the parties and decided smaller claims without benefit of a jury, were not without precedent; one had been operating with parliamentary sanction in the City of London since the early 1600s, and the City's court had served as the model for several erected in provincial towns by statute during William III's reign. But after a bill for a court of requests for Norwich was approved in 1701, a long hiatus followed, with new proposals sometimes being offered but faltering in the face of opposition from vested local interests. Yet, after this logjam was broken in the late 1740s, the pace of enactment was rapid and it is likely that by 1800 the principal form of civil justice Englishmen then encountered was provided by such bodies.[71]

While the courts at Westminster, then, dealt with a diminished caseload dominated by the contract claims of creditors who had the resources to pursue more than small debts, neither the common law courts nor Chancery seems to have been much better-positioned after 1688 than before to handle complex commercial disputes. To be sure, well before Lord Mansfield's much-heralded tenure (1756–88) as chief justice of King's Bench, piecemeal improvement is discernible—as in the law respecting negotiable instruments.[72] Yet, neither clarification of the substance of the law nor expedients to "domesticate" the law of merchants could simplify the evidence or lessen the costs and delays in complicated business litigation; such disputes not only were likely to baffle juries but could also perplex even the Masters of Chancery.[73] To be sure, the passage in 1698 of a government bill to sanction the courts' enforcement of arbitrators' awards duly arrived at held out the promise of greater efficacy in the extra-judicial resolution of disputes of this kind. Blackstone lauded this legislation, which he saw as a ratification of prior judicial practice; even so, examination of the judicial records indicates that it was only well after Mansfield's arrival at King's Bench that the procedure for submitting out-of-court arbitration awards for judicial enforcement began to be frequently employed.[74]

Given the superior courts' limited capacity to satisfy smaller creditors or to adjudicate complicated business disputes, it might seem that the lawyers and their institutions were more an obstacle than a help to economic development. Yet, as it can be misleading to suggest that Parliament and the courts were the handmaidens of emergent capitalism and industrialization, so to concentrate upon litigation (or, even more broadly, upon the various forms of dispute resolution) may result in a neglect of significant aspects of legal professionals' activities—especially the ways in which the growing corps of attorneys, not least in the provinces, facilitated their clients' objectives outside the courtroom.[75] What one economic historian has denominated as "a marvelous proliferation of trusts" in eighteenth-century England is a clear case in point of the lawyers' facilitative role as advisers and drafters.[76]

By the later 1700s, a sizable proportion of the land of England was held under terms whereby the "owner" had much less than an "absolute" or fee interest and whereby a host of other partial interests of family members (living and as yet unborn, female as well as male) were spelled out and protected through trust arrangements. The peer or squire who at any given moment headed such a landed family was in law but a life tenant of an estate so settled; among other limitations, he lacked the right to alienate those lands and had only a restricted capacity even to mortgage them. Such "strict settlements," employing the novel device of trustees charged with preserving the contingent remainders of an as yet unborn generation, were pioneered by professional conveyancers of the mid seventeenth century after earlier devices had been rejected by the courts as coming too close to the creation of perpetuities (abhorrent on the grounds they clogged or hindered a free market in land). The greater, and also middling, landholders who settled their estates, or portions of them, in this fashion had two principal objectives: to safeguard over time these estates from the personal failings and misfortunes of successive family heads, and to provide at any given time for the advancement both of the holder's siblings and of his daughters and younger sons.[77] In turn, the very restrictiveness of the limits on the present holder of settled lands was qualified by Parliament's capacity and readiness to amend or to terminate such arrangements, provided that the interested parties consented to the terms of the private legislation proposed.

For our purposes, the creation, spread, and later judicial validation of this new conveyancing device is of interest for three reasons. First, it serves to remind us that while landowning families gained a greater degree of legal control over their estates in the sixteenth and seventeenth centuries through acquiring the right to devise realty and later through the abolition of feudal tenures, the "absolute" ownership that emerged was not to the land itself but to income streams and capital portions derived from the properties. Historians continue to debate whether the result worked to the advantage or detriment of various classes of family members, particularly daughters, but at a minimum it would appear that daughters enjoyed a greater security in their portions. Even so, it is likely that the fall in the birth rate among landed families in the later 1600s and early 1700s was a more important influence in improving the expectations of female offspring.[78] Second, it is noteworthy that the very rapidity with which landed families adopted the strict settlement worked in the device's favor when individual settlements were subsequently challenged in the courts. Despite the oft-proclaimed hostility of the common law to perpetuities and despite the argument of counsel that the quality of the legal interest of the trustees to preserve contingent remainders (the interests of the yet unborn) was still too "contingent" to merit judicial protection, the judges' affirming opinions acknowledged the disruption that would result in the arrangements of many landed families were this technique to be disallowed.[79] And third, the success of the strict settlement in the courts, coupled with Chancery's new readiness from Charles II's reign to hold trustees to a high standard of accountability to beneficiaries, helps to explain the lawyers' increasing resort to trust arrangements in a variety of nonlanded settings.

The multiplication of trusts in eighteenth-century England owed a good deal to the inherent flexibility of the device but also something to fortuitous circumstances. One such circumstance was the limited freedom of worship accorded trinitarian Protestant Dissenters from 1689 onwards, for it became common for dissenting congregations, themselves merely voluntary associations, to vest title to their chapels (and any other assets) in trustees. Similarly, the proliferation over the course of the century of voluntary organizations, particularly philanthropic bodies possessing sizable tangible assets (such as hospitals), often produced a similar result. Another contributing circumstance was the growth of the "new species of property" generated by the financial revolution. As some successful urban families chose to provide for children and grandchildren by investing considerable proportions of their assets in the monied companies' securities (rather than in land) the trusteeship mechanism was

adapted to their needs with the trustees also taking on the responsibility of managing the invested corpus.[80] Still another stimulus to
the use of trusts was the South Sea Bubble, for the Bubble Act of
1720 erected new obstacles to the legal process of the incorporation
of businesses. To be sure, both before and after 1720 the partnership
was the usual choice of form for enterprises involving several individuals. Yet, trust arrangements did have some of the advantages
that incorporation offered over partnerships—the separation of ownership from control, the protection of investors by limited liability,
and an indefinite life. For instance, when the Sun Fire Office, ances-
tor of one of the great modern British insurers, was established mid-
way through Anne's reign, trustees were named to hold its realty and
investments, and these trustees signed the insurance policies issued
by the Sun and were the parties of record in suits involving its policies and property. Hence, when the Bubble Act threw up additional
barriers to incorporations, new business groupings could and did
avail themselves of trust arrangements, with mutual covenants governing the relations between the investors and the trustees whom
they selected.[81]

In light of the proliferation of trusts (with attorneys often designated as trustees), it is ironic that this phenomenon receives only
passing remark from Blackstone. His virtual silence on this score
contrasts with his usual readiness to stress the adaptiveness of the
law. As he was undoubtedly aware of the spread of the trust, his
"inadequate" account of this development would appear to be "a
fault generated by his scheme of arrangements"—a scheme whereby
he sought to blend the primarily deductive approach of continental
writers on natural jurisprudence with the decidedly inductive approach of the earlier common law literature in which legal change
was commonly seen as a series of piecemeal responses to social
stimuli.[82] If, then, Sir William's topical organization occasionally
failed him, we should not underestimate the scope of his self-
appointed task to make sense to novices of a body of law that had
grown over the centuries by a process of accretion with change disguised and complicated by legal fictions. As he himself observed:
"We inherit an old Gothic castle, erected in the days of chivalry, but
fitted up for a modern inhabitant. The moated ramparts, the em-
battled towers, and the trophied halls, are magnificent and vener-

able, but useless. The interior apartments, now converted into rooms of convenience, are chearful and commodious, though their approaches are winding and difficult."[83]

The history Blackstone presented in the *Commentaries* to explain the changing substance and increasing complexity of English law is, then, an admixture of the episodic and the structural. On the one hand, the periodization of the survey he offered in his final chapter "of the rise, progress, and gradual improvements, of the laws of England" is keyed to governmental changes—the Norman Conquest, the accession of Edward I, Henry VIII and his breach with Rome, the Restoration of 1660, the events of 1688–89. Again, at various points in his four volumes he introduced historical sketches by way of background so that, for instance, his account of real tenures is preceded by a chapter on feudalism. On the other hand, his history is not simply a series of leading events in *England's* past; he was well aware that "the feodal system" was European in scope. Moreover, in his chapter on the origins of private property (a chapter much influenced by continental natural law writers), Blackstone alluded to a general historical schema—the "stadial" or "four-stage" conception of human history. The definition of private property, he explained, advanced as societies moved from the hunting stage, through the pastoral, and into the agricultural.[84] Britain in his own day he saw as a "commercial society," or at least a society in which commerce had a large role. And he characterized such relatively recent legal changes as the improvement of extra-judicial procedures for dealing with the insolvency of "traders," the elaboration of the law of marine insurance, and the acceptance of the assignability of choses in action (for example, bills of exchange) as "calculated for" the "benefit and extension of trade" and as necessary "in a commercial country."[85]

≺ V ≻

Blackstone's use of natural jurisprudence and of a "stadial" historical framework links his writings to those of his Scottish contemporaries; he drew upon the historical researches of Hume, Robertson, and Kames, and the "four-stage" account of human history is central to Adam Smith's reflections on the progress of civil society.[86] In turn, it was the Scots, with Smith in the forefront, who stand out among the British writers of the mid eighteenth century for their innovative perspectives on the interrelationship of liberty, law, and property. By contrast to the lawyer Blackstone, to Smith the study of law was of value in helping "to form some general notion of the great outlines of the plan according to which justice has [been] administered in different ages and nations." Thus, while eschewing "the detail of Particulars," Smith was especially interested in the development of the common law, reckoning it, as he remarked in his lectures on jurisprudence, "more deserving of the attention of a speculative man" because its antiquity meant it was "more formed on the natural sentiments of mankind" than any other extant body of European law.[87] It is indeed, the connections that Smith and other of the Scots drew between economy, social values, law, and governance through history that encourages Pocock to see them as responding in a dialectical way to the civic humanists' analysis proclaimed in England (and also by some Scots) in previous generations. Yet, Scottish thought also drew extensively on the study of natural jurisprudence, and not least in Smith's own case.[88]

Smith is best known still to the general reader as the progenitor of laissez-faire economics and as the scathing critic of that "mercantile system" which he saw as governing Britain's overseas commerce in his day and whose enforcement was a central element in the Anglo-American crisis that took shape between the publication of the first editions of his *The Theory of Moral Sentiments* (1759) and *The Wealth of Nations* (1776). Over the last generation, however, Smith specialists have begun to explicate the full range of his intellectual concerns as evidenced by his early writings in moral philosophy, the surviving notes of his lectures on jurisprudence (part of his course on moral philosophy), and also his various references to a plan to produce "a sort of theory and History of Law and Government."[89] Indeed, it has been suggested that *The Wealth of Nations* was itself a part of this larger project in which a system of political economy would serve as one leg of that "Account of the general principles of law and Government" which Smith promised his readers at the end of *The Theory of Moral Sentiments*.[90]

In this endeavor, Smith developed and deployed the "stadial"

view of history in his lectures, possibly from the early 1750s onwards, in order, as his former student Millar recounted, "to trace the
gradual progress of jurisprudence, both public and private, from the
rudest to the most refined ages, and to point out the effects of those
arts which contribute to subsistence, and to the accumulation of
property, in producing correspondent improvements or alterations
in law and government."[91] Smith spelled out some of the connections he perceived between economy, law, and government in Book 3
of *The Wealth of Nations*—that is, subsequent to the analysis of
economic principles presented in Books 1 and 2 and prior to the de-
lineation and denunciation of the "mercantile system" in Book 4.

Smith's central historical thesis was that "order and good government, and along with them the liberty and securities of individuals"
were first established in medieval Europe "in cities, at a time when
the occupiers of land in the country were exposed to every sort of
violence." Townsmen, benefitting from royal protection, had the security "to better their condition and to secure not only the necessar-
ies, but the conveniences and elegancies of life."[92] Over the centuries, the "increase and riches of commercial and manufacturing
towns . . . gradually introduced order and good government, and
with them, the liberty and security of individuals, among the inhabitants of the country."[93] The towns had these effects, above
all, by promoting luxury among the great landowners; the availability of consumer goods attracted the lords to market the output of
their estates in the towns, eventually generating a transformation in
landlord-man relations. Lordly retainers were dismissed and tenants
no longer treated primarily as a source of military manpower, with
the upshot that "the great proprietors were no longer capable of in-
terrupting the regular execution of justice or of disturbing the peace
of the country. Having sold their birthright . . . in the wantonness of
plenty, for trinkets and baubles, they became as insignificant as any
substantial burgher or tradesman in a city."[94] So, Smith concluded,
with his characteristic invocation of the logic of the unintended
consequence and his usual disdain of mercantile judgment, "a revolution" was thereby "brought about by two different orders of people
who had not the least intention to serve the public"—the great proprietors acting out of "the most childish vanity" and the merchants
and artificers pursuing "their own pedlar principle of turning a
penny whenever a penny was to be got."[95]

By comparison to the neo-Harringtonians, Smith unmistakably stands out as a "modern," and even some of his conclusions, though not usually his route to arriving at them, had been anticipated by Defoe. On the one hand, Smith (as Hume before him) clearly distinguished between personal liberty, essentially security of person and property, and political liberty, freedom to participate in the process of governance. For Smith, personal liberty could even exist in modern monarchies such as France because there, too, judicial power was generally separated from executive power. However, political liberty was possible only under a "free government" such as Britain's where, along with the independence of the judiciary, there was also the constitutional requirement that the people consent to the levy of taxes and to the making of laws.[96] On the other hand, Smith avoided the determinism that permeated the neo-Harringtonians' accounts of the relationship between commerce and virtue, economy and governance. Smith accepted that a commercial society is compatible with absolute monarchy, so long as the subjects' security and property are protected. Further, he saw England's achievement of "free government" as an aberration from the general European pattern and he accounted for it by pointing to a series of fortuitous circumstances—the kingdom's geography which lessened the incentive for its medieval rulers to maintain a standing army, the Crown's limited ordinary revenues after Elizabeth had sold off much of the royal lands, and the Stuarts' increasing fiscal dependence upon Parliament.[97]

Smith's sanguine view of the prospects for the survival of political liberty in Britain is also striking. As he observed: "The system of government now supposes a system of liberty as a foundation. Every one would be shocked at any attempt to alter this system, and such a change would be attended with the greatest difficulties."[98] For Smith, neither the civil list, though very generous by the 1760s, nor the standing army constituted a serious threat. Indeed, the existence of such a force gave the authorities greater security against occasional riotous outbreaks of plebian discontent and thereby obviated the need for the government "to suppress and punish every murmur and complaint against it."[99] The ideal arrangement in his view probably would have been to supplement a small standing army with a well-trained militia; a militia would keep up the "martial spirit of the people," otherwise liable to decay in a commercial society marked by increasing specialization, and would remove any "real or imaginary" danger to liberty posed by regular troops.[100] Keeping down the army's size would also have the advantage of limiting spending on defense, a matter of concern given the continuing increase of the national debt. But if Smith saw public credit as a "ruinous expedient" in fiscal terms, he did not fear imminent disaster.[101] After all, economic growth had been substantial since 1688 in spite of the mounting public debt.

Nor did Smith express in *The Wealth of Nations* great alarm about "the present disturbances"—that is, the Anglo-American crisis. He, much more than many of his contemporaries, believed that Britain could weather the economic consequences of a separation because he was confident that it had been disserved by the "mercantile system" whose enforcement had helped to precipitate the breach. Indeed, the capacity of merchants and manufacturers to band together and "intimidate" Parliament prompted Smith to liken them to "an overgrown standing army."[102]

Given Smith's condemnation of the success of business interests in swaying Parliament, it should not be surprising that he took little interest in the prevailing state of parliamentary representation—an issue which, thanks to the Wilkites and the American dissidents, had been in agitation in England in recent years. To be sure, as an expedient to avert a separation between Britain and America, Smith did suggest the creation of an imperial Parliament in which the colonies would have a share in representation proportional to the burden of taxation they agreed to assume.[103] But though well aware that the formal structure of parliamentary representation in Britain had been outdated by longterm shifts in wealth and population, he was not even prepared to second Blackstone's opinion that it was a "misfortune" that representatives of "deserted boroughs continued to be summoned."[104]

Overall, then, what we have learned to call Smith's "science of politics" focused primarily upon issues of personal liberty rather than upon those of political liberty. From this perspective, the "mercantile system"—that misguided body of legislation shaped by the "mean rapacity and monopolizing spirit" of merchants and manufacturers—was but the most prominent example of existing law which abridged individual liberty.[105] In *The Wealth of Nations*,

Smith's targets mainly lay in the economic realm—that is, with forms of unjustified interference in the individual's right to enjoy and improve his own property. Hence, he condemned governmental meddling in the grain trade as only aggravating the problem of dearth, denounced the apprenticeship laws as "a manifest encroachment upon the just liberty both of the workman and of those who might be disposed to employ him," and excoriated the operation of the settlement provisions of the poor law as a grievous "oppression" deserving of the kind of "general popular clamour" that had recently been raised against the use of general warrants.[106] Elsewhere, Smith suggested the possibility of a more encompassing critique of existing law; his students' surviving notes from his lectures on jurisprudence show that he was dismissive of the game laws, adjudged the use of capital punishment against theft to be unreasonably severe, and would have repealed as superfluous the mass of anti-Catholic legislation on the statute book.[107]

< VI >

With the Scots, then, and with Smith in particular, we have travelled a long way from the fears of Catholicism and royal absolutism that beset Locke when he drafted *The Two Treatises* and we have also travelled some distance from the shock to civic humanist sensibilities inflicted by the financial revolution with its attendant threat of corruption to the body politic. Rather, both Blackstone in his account of English law and Smith in his wider-ranging inquiries into "the general principles of law and government" were denizens of a much more settled, more confident world. Not that all was well-ordered in British society; each, after all, found ample cause to criticize the fruits of Parliament's legislative propensities.

As Blackstone has sometimes been characterized by commentators as an apologist for the established order, so it would also be misleading to take Smith as typical of British thinking on liberty, law, and property as the American crisis escalated. The year 1776, after all, saw the publication not only of *The Wealth of Nations* but also of Richard Price's bestselling *Observations on the Nature of Civil Liberty* (a distinctive admixture of neo-Harringtonian themes with radical Lockean notions), not to mention John Cartwright's strident call for electoral reform in *Take Your Choice!* and Jeremy Bentham's *A Fragment upon Government*. By contrast to those of his contemporaries who agitated for reform of Parliament and to the American colonists who chose to resist the authority of the Westminster Parliament in defense of their liberty and property, Smith accepted the existing structure of representation and took the principle of parliamentary sovereignty for granted. Yet, on the eve of the loss of the American colonies, and over half a century before Britain's system of representation would be reformed, *The Wealth of Nations* offered a penetrating analysis of how best to promote liberty and property within the broad framework of the established governmental order. As Stewart said of Smith, he "aimed at the improvement of society,—not by delineating plans of new constitutions, but by enlightening the policy of actual legislators."[108]

A Dissident Legacy: Eighteenth Century Popular Politics and the Glorious Revolution

KATHLEEN WILSON

THE ATTEMPT TO ASSESS the impact of the Glorious Revolution on politics and ideology in Hanoverian Britain necessarily raises the question, "Whose Revolution?" Most scholars have reached a consensus that the Revolution was largely an episode in patrician politics, unrelentingly "conservationist" in ideological, political, and social effect, which allowed Whig and Tory leaders to rid themselves of an unacceptable monarch without recourse to the extremism of Charles I's reign. On this view, radical Whig ideas received scarcely a hearing in the political turmoil and debates of the moment or the next decade; popular participation in the Revolution was limited to the riotous anticipation of Parliament's actions by anti-Catholic crowds; and the long-standing tensions between the Crown and gentry that had plagued earlier Stuart governments were resolved. The Revolution's most important legacy was to set the stage for the increasingly formalized party conflict and oligarchic "stability" of the next century.[1]

These dominant accounts are, however, inadequate to explain the profound, if unintended, impact of the Revolution on popular political consciousness and political discourse in the eighteenth century. Myriad interpretations and meanings attached to the Revolution and the settlement in the wider political nation, at the time and in succeeding generations, were just as important as the intentions of its elite actors or the continuity of political structures in assessing the Revolution's legacy. Some scholars have been attentive to the radical readings of the Revolution that reverberated throughout the debates and divisions of the 1680s and 1690s.[2] Yet the impact of these ideas on extra-parliamentary political culture in the eighteenth century remains almost totally unexplored, despite ample evidence that they were fundamental to the tenor and content of both loyalist and dissident politics for the next hundred years.[3]

"Revolution principles" were from the start susceptible to widely divergent interpretations; and in the Hanoverian decades, long-standing disagreements over the nature and content of the political precepts sanctioned by the Revolution were exacerbated by vigorous debates over their current significance as prescriptive or legitimating principles of political conduct. Moreover, although readings of 1688 were influenced by elite party divisions and the specific political context in which they were articulated, they were never wholly the product of these forces. The multiple readings of 1688, which became more amplified as popular political culture became a more important force in Hanoverian politics, were expressed through the wide ranging "media" of extra-institutional political culture, from the press and pulpit to the street theatre and tavern life of London and provincial towns. It is in this wider political arena that the propaganda of party elites found their widest audience; it was also here that political ideas were appropriated by those out-of-doors and used in unexpected and innovative ways.[4]

What emerges from the examination of these "unconventional" channels of eighteenth-century political debate is that the Revolution continued to generate arguments bearing not just on the succession, but on the role of "the people" (however variously defined) in the political process and on the basis and nature of English representative institutions and of much-vaunted rights and liberties. The yearly commemoratory observances of 4 and 5 November—the anniversaries of William III's birthday, and of his landing at Torbay and the Gunpowder plot respectively—provide the cultural bases for attempts to criticize the Revolution's legacy or accommodate it to past and present political positions. These anniversaries were frequently used as the occasions for the glorification of the existing establishment in church and state and sought to engrave on public consciousness a view of the Revolution as a great and providential deliverance that rendered Englishmen's liberties, constitution, and religion secure and inviolable. But they could equally be used as springboards for criticism of the status quo, producing a rhetoric

which was rights-based and libertarian (as well as intensely nationalistic), highlighting changing arguments about the nature of representation and the role of consent, accountability, and trusteeship in
the political system. Nourished by Tory populism as well as radical
Whiggism, and borrowing from contractarian and constitutionalist
political theory, this rhetoric was an amalgam, frequently conflating
incompatible elements and used by different groups in different contexts. Nonetheless, it provided a vehicle for the definition of political rights and liberties in terms that were more expansive than Whig
or Tory oligarchs would have sanctioned. In this way, the Revolution
came to be seen in extra-parliamentary political culture not just as
a constitutional landmark, but as an emblem of English liberties and
of the right of a wider public to canvass affairs of state and effect
political reform. It thus served as a crucial building block in the
"invention" of a revolutionary tradition of English radicalism that
could be used by a variety of opposition, reformist, or radical groups
to legitimize demands for greater popular control over Parliament.[5]

In what follows, the articulation and refurbishment of dissident
readings of Revolution principles will be examined in what must
necessarily be an episodic fashion, focusing first on the interpretations of 1688 in the commemorations of that event one century
later, and then looking backward to consider the use of Revolution
principles in two other important political conjunctures: the opposition to Walpole and the radical agitation of the 1760s and 1770s.
This examination will make clear that the alternative interpretations of 1688 that reverberated in popular political discourse in the
Hanoverian decades provided the rationale for a radical opposition
to the form and structure of the post-Revolution state.

≺ I ≻

At first glance, the centenary celebrations of the Revolution seemed
to have had one unifying theme: smug self-congratulation on the
glories of the British constitution. Marked by exuberant junketings
in town and countryside, 4 and 5 November 1788 were nothing if
not occasions for patriotic excess, given form in this instance by the
memory of "that glorious and immortal hero KING WILLIAM THE

THIRD, who rescued this country from tyranny and oppression, and secured to us a free and happy constitution."[6] William and the Revolution were toasted in marketplaces and taverns and on country estates; orange cockades abounded at a glittering series of assemblies and private parties; and replicas of the standard raised at Torbay received pride of place in the processions of magistrates, troops, bands of music, and ebullient citizens that wove their way through the streets of the capital and provincial towns.[7] "The flame of constitutional loyalty seems to have pervaded all ranks of people," noted one observer from Leeds, and indeed the apparent unanimity expressed by the commemorations convinced many that patriotic loyalty and social and political unity had triumphed over the "spirit of party" that had for so long troubled the nation.[8]

A closer examination of the centenary observances would have dashed such sanguine hopes. The patriotic enthusiasm on this occasion seemed to be a self-conscious attempt to compensate for the damage inflicted by a crisis-ridden decade. The American war had disrupted and embittered English politics, intensifying sectarian as well as political divisions and causing citizens outside the radical camp to question the much-vaunted excellence of British institutions that allowed men in power to pursue interests so contrary to those of the public. Loss of the colonies dealt a severe, if temporary, blow to the national psyche, for it shattered the essential unity which empire seemed to have imparted to national experience since the Revolution. In 1786 one writer concluded gloomily that the "new political existence and glory" that Britain had acquired in the last century had been eclipsed: "Nations, like mortal men, advance only to decline; dismembered empire and diminished glory mark a Crisis in the constitution."[9]

Domestic issues had also led to strife. The Gordon riots of 1780, during which mass demonstrations against popery turned into violence against property; divisions in the movement for parliamentary reform; a resurgence in democratic politicking and the organization by radicals of the Society for Constitutional Information; the "constitutional crisis" provoked by the Fox-North coalition's India bill that would have given ministerial nominees control of the operation and patronage of the East India Company; and the recent campaign for the repeal of the Test and Corporation Acts—all had combined to frighten defenders of the status quo with the specter of an insurgent, "levelling," and licentious lower class, led by factious and designing men within and without doors, seeking changes subversive of the established order.[10] At the same time, Pitt's failure to pursue parliamentary reform after 1785 and his about-face on repeal in 1786 had disillusioned and alienated many of his former supporters, reaffirming their belief that the main threat to public liberty came not from the king's prerogative, but from the tyranny of an unreformed Parliament.

The crisis of the 1780s, then, engendered bitter divisions in the nation that the patriotic mottoes of the centenary celebrations glossed over. Of course, the starkness of these divisions should not be overdrawn. Parliamentary politics by the late 1780s seem to have settled down into the familiar eighteenth-century pattern of a stable administration on one hand and an energetic if ineffective minority on the other.[11] Out-of-doors, political allegiances and positions were fluid and mutable. Campaigns for moral and social reform such as anti-slavery, prison reform, and the reformation of manners provided a common ground that drew together individuals of disparate political views, while also demonstrating a shared concern with corruption in high places and a rising faith in the ability of collective action to effect social transformation.[12] But in the late 1780s party rivalries, and even more the rifts between moderate and radical reformers, kept extra-parliamentary politics divisive, unsettled, and dynamic. The centenary of the Revolution accordingly provided the perfect opportunity for different groups to revitalize and refurbish long-standing, as well as more recent, agendas and alliances; and the anniversary was appropriated to legitimate a multiplicity of political positions. In the process, however, the celebrations embodied the wide gulf that existed between those who sought political change and those who stood for political stasis, crystallizing, eight months before the storming of the Bastille, the sharp disjunction of opinion between the advocates of radical constitutional reform and the champions of an establishment already poised for reaction.

"The spirit of the Revolution must be maintained in its purity and vigor ... using every art and means for its support," it was urged in a London newspaper a few days before the anniversary. That spirit was the "right of resistance ... superceding [sic] and abolishing all names and forms that stood in opposition to the liberty and happiness of a nation." Elsewhere in the country, too, the right of resistance was toasted along with William and the Bill of Rights in order to recall that the "original power" of the people had been demonstrated one hundred years earlier. From this perspective the Revolution had been an indisputably popular act. The "whole nation" united to depose the tyrant James II, the Rev. Henry Hunter of Edinburgh asserted, "the South and the North together; men of all parties and denominations; the Parliament, the Church, the Army; conformists and Dissenters; the City, the Country, the Sovereign's own family, and dependents."[13] Citizens in Bristol, Birmingham, Swansea, Yarmouth, Liverpool, and Newcastle equated "revolution principles" with popular sovereignty and the "Cause of Political and Religious Liberty all over the World."[14] At the Norwich Independent Club toasts to the Seven Bishops, the Majesty of the People, the Friends of Civil and Religious Liberty, Freedom to Slaves, "Equal Liberty to all Mankind, and Virtue to Defend it" indicated the unity that its Foxite membership saw between present political concerns and the "Whig" Revolution of the past.[15] In Manchester, one group of enthusiasts counted among the "universal rights of Mankind" embodied in 1688 the accountability of government, the right of resistance, and civil and religious liberty; they ended with the wishes, "May every despotick government experience a Revolution," and "Oppression to those who Attempt to Confine the Blessings of Freedom."[16]

Other commentators were more inclined to criticize than to glorify the Revolution and its legacy. One writer reflected, cynically but with some justice, that British aristocrats were the true beneficiaries of 1688: many of their ancestors (his list included the Whig duke of Portland) had come to England as "needy adventurers," only to be raised to rank and fortune by William III.[17] Others condemned the Revolution for its paltry guarantees of political rights and even more illusory religious liberty. The Unitarian minister William Wood claimed that the promise of 1688 could only be fulfilled by the removal of the remaining obstacles to full citizenship for all. "Precedent is not reason, and prescription is no bar to the sacred claims of universal justice," Wood pronounced. The claims of "antiquity of long prevailing forms" as the rationale for denying the rights of conscience could only be accepted by "plodding slaves." If government would but recognize this, men would not be tempted into more violent acts of change.[18]

William Enfield, also a Unitarian clergyman, took a more optimistic view of the achievements of 1688, although he also offered a prescription for their improvement in the present. He saw the Revolution as having embodied and established three irrevocable principles: that government was a trust, based on the contract between the people and their governors; that the people had the right to resume any delegated trust that was abused; and that "when Political Liberty is infringed by the Ruling Powers, as to create a general conviction of the necessity of recurring to first principles, a revolution may be effected without bloodshed or violence." Given the rapid advances in moral and political knowledge of the previous century, these principles were especially relevant because a corresponding alteration in political institutions had become imperative. Britain cannot allow her progress to be "retarded by a timid policy, which represents all innovations as dangerous," Enfield warned, for inevitably "enlarged views and a liberal spirit will obliterate the false maxims of ignorance and ... every institution, which is ... inconsistent with that share of natural or political liberty to which every member of a free state is entitled, will be abolished."[19] The Revolution, then, set the precedent for, and showed the ability of, the people to effect non-violent political change; the course of history, the "moral progress of mankind," would ensure that they would do so again.

These interpretations of revolution principles would have been incomprehensible to most of those who hastened James II's departure in 1688. The events of 1688 were reconstructed to embody, and were seen as justified by, the principles of popular sovereignty and natural, as well as historical, rights: a crucial moment when "the people" of England, faced with a recalcitrant monarch who had betrayed the terms of his trusteeship, reclaimed their residual power and asserted their natural (that is, extra-constitutional) rights to refashion government to better protect their interests (while also confirming certain ancient or historical liberties). Even those writers who criticized the Revolution for having not gone far enough in protecting the subject's liberties, proceeded from the premise that "the people" had had the *power* so to act, had they but been more vigilant or prescient.

Of course, this theoretical justification of 1688, in its essentials, would have been broadly acceptable among the radical Whig writers of the 1680s; but it was taken much further than Wildman or Locke would have gone by the infusion of ideas of enlightened "moral progress" and the "universal rights of mankind." The belief in the progress of a "liberal spirit," wrought by the growth of enlightened opinion, had been a central tenet of rational dissenting philosophy for the past two decades and had recently been incorporated into Dissenters' arguments for religious liberty.[20] It was an innovation of the utmost significance, for it implied that reform and the enlargement of civil liberties would be inevitable (because divinely sanctioned) outcome of human history. Additionally, many participants chose to emphasize not only that the Revolution was the act of the "whole people," but also that it embodied the "universal rights of mankind" that provided the model for political change elsewhere (America and, it seemed likely, France) and for all time. Hence, 1688 was exalted as a paradigm of popular revolutionary activity, a "bloodless revolution" effected and directed by an enlightened people that provided a laudable example to the world, and as such a source of nationalistic as well as reformist ardor.

The conflation of these arguments in the contemporary interpretation of the Revolution, and their propagation to a wide audience, were demonstrated in the centenary celebrations of the Revolution Society of London on 4 November. Originally a club of Protestant dissenters, the Revolution Society was revitalized specifically for the centenary observances. Among the members were Lord Stanhope, supporter of the repeal campaign; the duke of Portland, chairman of the Foxite Whig Club; the marquis of Carmarthen, friend to political reform; Henry Beaufoy, Westminster MP who had moved for repeal in Parliament in March, 1787; and Sir Watkin Lewes, John Sawbridge, Thomas Brand Hollis, James Martin, William Smith, Joshua Grigby, and Capel Lofft, of whom the first two were Wilkite veterans, the latter four members of the Society for the Abolition of the Slave Trade, and all current leaders of the Society for Constitutional Information. In addition, the eminent Unitarian ministers

Drs. Andrew Kippis and Richard Price; the printer, political pamphleteer, and Presbyterian minister Rev. Joseph Towers; and many members of the London Committee for Repeal and the Society of Constitutional Information had also joined the society, along with 300 others committed to its political agenda.[21]

Given that its personnel included a remarkable cross-section of current radical leadership as well as veterans of previous campaigns, it is not surprising that the society's purpose was aggressively propagandistic. It was to turn the tide against the opponents of reform who had sought, all too successfully, "to infuse in [the people] a dread of innovation . . . to keep the people blind to their future interests for the sake of the present interest of certain individuals."[22] The observances of the day were thus tailored to "preserving and disseminating the principles of Civil and Religious Liberty." The sermons, odes, and orations were all subsequently published in cheap pamphlet form, while accounts of the meeting appeared in many London and provincial newspapers, a strategy reflecting members' experiences in other political campaigns.[23] They also demonstrated a keen appreciation for the theatrical aspects of eighteenth century politics: members paraded to the London Tavern for their dinner behind the original flag that William had flown at Torbay, while the Tavern itself was decorated with illuminated transparencies "emblematic of that glorious event" inscribed "A TYRANT DEPOSED AND LIBERTY RESTORED, 1688."[24] The rest of the day was spent interpreting the blessings of the Revolution in a way that gave primacy to its populist and radical implications.

The toasts established the scale of priorities, deliberately striving to identify current preoccupations with the radical causes of the past. Prominent were salutations to the Whig heroes of the seventeenth century, Hampden, Milton, Russell, Sidney, and Locke; and to more contemporary celebrities of dissident politics, such as the late Timothy Hollis and John Jebb. The English liberties allegedly confirmed or guaranteed by 1688—freedom of election, trial by jury, liberty of the press (twice), Magna Carta, Habeas Corpus, the Bill of Rights, and "The Majesty of the People"—received appropriate homage. Other toasts drew attention to the list of reforms on the radical agenda: the revision of the game laws, the eradication of electoral corruption, abolition of the slave trade, repeal of the Test and Corporation Acts, and a "just and equal representation of the people." The resolution to press for a bill to designate the sixteenth of December, the day the Bill of Rights was enacted, as the appropriate anniversary of the Revolution aimed at dissociating the holiday from the Protestant 5 November and the preservationist, potentially conservative, message of "deliverance," in order to identify it instead with libertarian issues and the reform cause. In this way, it was hoped, the "example of one revolution will prevent the necessity of another."[25]

The oration of Joseph Towers, a seasoned political activist in reform campaigns, was perhaps the most ingenious piece of popular propaganda on the significance of Revolution principles in the present.[26] Towers was a firm Lockeian, committed to the principles of natural rights, popular sovereignty, and the right of the people to alter the form of government as they saw fit. But in his oration, Towers conflated his view of natural rights with the lessons of English history and the belief in enlightened moral progress, in a manner which privileged the right of resistance as the "prime mover" in past English struggles to protect and expand the people's liberties. The English people had always resisted tyranny in any form, Towers declared, by asserting their "rights as men, and as citizens," and on each occasion that resistance was resorted to, the subject's rights and liberties became a little more secure. English history, and especially the Revolution, proved that "opposition to tyranny is not only defensible, but meritorious"; and that "the welfare and dignity of a nation depended upon their firm and intrepid adherence to the *great principles of public freedom, of just and equal liberty.*" Accordingly, a sincere attachment to Revolution principles would compel the present generation "to engage in every measure that may tend still more to enlarge, to establish, and to confirm the freedom and felicity of our country." Towers thus appeared to accommodate the historical bias of anti-reform arguments, while actually giving the people's continual resort to resistance a trans-historical significance that deprived the principles of 1688 of their specific and limited historical meaning which establishment Whigs had attached to them since 1710. As he stressed, "the mere event of the Revolution" was of secondary importance to "those principles by which that event was produced ... and to those principles to which we must still continue to adhere."[27]

A century later, then, some of the more extreme radical Whig ideas articulated in 1688–90 had an enthusiastic audience, though their principles were pushed farther by the infusion of ideas of equality and of inexorable moral progress that were not yet modified by the excesses of the French Revolution. "Equality" had emerged as a central concept in both the repeal and reform campaigns. It referred to Dissenters' demands for equal treatment, *de jure* as well as de facto, in civil society—the equal power of members of the state to arrive at public office, as Priestley argued.[28] It also connoted the current radical demand for a representative system based on personality rather than property. The extreme radicalism of the "rational optimism" that was so marked a feature of dissenting thought in the 1780s was all too obvious to supporters of the establishment. This was the premise of Priestley's famous "gunpowder" sermon, given in Birmingham on 5 November 1785, in which he described the ideas of rational dissenters as gunpowder, laid "grain by grain, under the old building of error and superstition, which a single spark may thereafter inflame, so as to produce a substantial explosion"—a metaphor that laid the foundation for future misconstructions of his intentions.[29]

Of course, the contribution of dissent to the Revolution Society's rhetoric was just one strand in the startlingly hybrid ideological statements produced by the celebrations. Whig and Anglican members tended to champion natural rights in conjunction with more historically grounded English liberties. This is indicated in the tripartite declaration which, the society argued, encapsulated the "true and genuine principle of our free constitution": that the people were the source of all civil and political authority; that the right of resistance was justified by the abuse of power; and that trial by jury, freedom of the press and of election, liberty of conscience, and the right of private judgment ought "ever to be held Sacred and Inviolable."[30] This version of Revolution principles combined natural and historical rights to make the case for reform, a strategy less threatening to the uncommitted or wavering than appeals to the inexorable march of "resistance." But radical critiques clearly adhered to

a populist interpretation of the Revolution that sanctioned the expansion of existing rights and liberties; they agreed that 1688 had
(or should have) embodied principles that could be used to justify
not just the amelioration of present political and religious discontents, but their direct and forceful rectification.

In conjunction with the arguments for a more "just and equal"
representation currently being made by radical reformers, the Revolution principles of the society postulated a specific relationship between individual liberties and the forms of the state. The maintenance of the balanced constitution was no longer deemed sufficient
to ensure the liberties of the people; its structure had to be altered
in order to secure greater extra-parliamentary control over the
House of Commons. The essence of political liberty was now held
to consist in the right to formal political participation through the
vote, without which civil liberties could never be protected.[31] The
meeting did not address the question of who constituted "the
people" as the Society's politically diverse membership differed on
this issue. Those belonging to the Society for Constitutional Information supported universal manhood suffrage as well as annual parliaments, the use of instructions to representatives, and equal electoral districts.[32] Others advocated the gradation of electors according
to wealth and social rank, with the most dependent members of society voting for the lowest offices.[33]

That this view of the significance of 1688 did not enjoy universal
acceptance was made clear by the rival commemorations that occurred in the metropolis and localities. The Foxite Whig Club, a
"party" headquarters for Whig aristocrats and MPs, slanted its celebrations to glorify its members' status as heirs to the principal architects of the "Whig Revolution." Portland (who had also attended
the Revolution Society's fete) chaired the festivities, "supported on
the right and left by the houses of Russell and Cavendish," (Bedford
and Devonshire, whose dukedoms originated with William) and "a
most numerous body of the most distinguished names for hereditary
patriotism . . . and exalted endowments of the mind." Their toasts
ended with a flamboyant reminder to George III of the principles—
and families—which placed the house of Brunswick on the British
throne. The club then voted a subscription of £1500 for the erection
of a commemoratory column at Runnymede, the site where Magna

Carta was signed, in a deliberate attempt to outshine the Revolution Society.[34]

The most striking contrast to the observances of the Revolution Society was provided by the celebrations in Westminster of the Constitution Club, arch-rival of the Whig Club and opponent of reform. Meeting on 5 November, the club of 1200 celebrated those principles of 1688 which had led to the "present happy establishment in Church and State."[35] Under the motto of "the Rights of the People, and the Freedom of Election," the observances sought to place the Revolution in the context of a series of "deliverances" in English history. A song written for the occasion, entitled "The Three Eighty-Eights," apportioned among the Armada's defeat, the Revolution, and Pitt's ministry the responsibility for the nation's present flourishing condition, all three having saved the nation from attacks on its constitution and established religion. Other songs exploited the traditional associations of the "double deliverance" of 5 November, stressing the roles that the discovery of the Gunpowder plot and James II's abdication had had in preserving king, Lords, and Commons. Above all, the festivities were devoted to the celebration of the Revolution's provisions for constitutional permanence: the restoration of true religion and liberty in 1688 had been fixed, immutably, in the Bill of Rights, and it conveyed to posterity the patriotic injunction to "*Revere Laws* and *Commons*, and *honour the King!*"

The commemoratory celebrations clearly demonstrated the facility with which the Revolution could be appropriated by different groups to serve as a source of political legitimation in the present. Under the mask of patriotic unanimity, the centenary celebrations of the Glorious Revolution focused and expressed the political and ideological divisions within the nation. Yet two important features stand out. First, the French Revolution clearly only exacerbated, rather than created, existing polarities in British political opinion on constitutional reform. Second, and more important for our purposes, the 1788 observances strikingly exhibited the widespread endorsement of populist readings of the Revolution. The principles of popular sovereignty, the right of resistance, and accountability of government were toasted as Revolution principles; and the Revolution itself was reconstructed and admired as a great popular event by those sympathetic to political reform, as well as by those who merely took nationalistic solace in Britain's role as a model for revolution elsewhere—the first to recognize "the universal rights of mankind."

≺ II ≻

The political discourse of opposition under Walpole challenged establishment Whig arguments that security of the *form* of British government—a mixed and balanced constitution—ensured the preservation of liberty under it. In the post-Revolution period, the central focus of fears about the influence and power of the state shifted to that reputed bulwark of liberty itself, the House of Commons.[36] The once pervasive fear under the Stuarts that the king would rule without Parliament had thus been transformed into an intense anxiety at the way in which the king and his ministers ruled through it. Government finance, the growth of the civil list, electoral venality and, above all, the Septennial Act of 1716, whereby a sitting Parliament extended its life as well as those of its successors from three to seven years without consulting the electors—all appeared to have subverted the independence and accountability of the Commons, enabling ministers to build up a slavish court party that passed and defended unpopular and anti-libertarian measures in terms of the public interest.

Fears of parliamentary malfeasance of course, antedated Walpole's regime: seventeenth-century Whig MPs had denounced the threats to liberty posed by corrupt and managed Parliaments; and in the 1720s, John Trenchard and Thomas Gordon, authors of the anti-ministerial *Cato's Letters,* railed against the "mock Magistrates and pretended Representatives who, under the Colour and Title of the Protectors of the People, were at the People's Expense the real Helpers and Partakers of the Tyrant's Iniquity."[37] This notion of "legal tyranny"—that is, the introduction of oppression under the mask of legal forms of government—gained greatly increased credibility under Walpole, who, using the doctrine of parliamentary sovereignty to justify unconstitutional measures and unprecedented corruption, seemed to embody Cato's prophetic description of ministerial tyranny. Executive patronage, following expansion of the fiscal bureaucracy, had greatly increased since the Revolution, rotting the social and political fabric to such a degree that "the freedom of the people [was] much subjected, and sometimes explicitly restrained."[38] Although the form of the constitution appeared unchanged, executive corruption had altered its balance, so that Parliament itself had been rendered useless as the guardian of public liberty. As Lord Lyttleton noted, the crucial place of Parliament in the legislature had been guaranteed by the Revolution, but it had not brought government more into line with the people's wishes or rendered their liberties more secure.[39]

It is in this ideological context that the parliamentary opposition began to argue that the locus of British liberty under Walpole's political machine was extra-parliamentary, a claim in which their interests and those of the wider political nation converged. Court Whig measures that aimed at closing the electorate and circumscribing parliamentary accountability; the Riot Act, which sanctioned the use of troops to quell domestic unrest; the Black Act, which extended the number of offenses incurring capital punishment; the suppression of the Tory press and the imposition of censorship on the theater; and such attempted or actual fiscal measures as the salt tax of 1732, excise bill of 1733, and Gin Act of 1736 stimulated apprehensions in the extra-parliamentary nation about Walpole's intentions. The "country programme" of Tories and self-styled "patriot" Whigs accordingly lambasted executive corruption, attacked the administration's anti-libertarian measures, and championed a delegatory view of parliamentary authority in order to argue that Walpole had betrayed the very "revolution principles" which the Whigs had long trumpeted as crucial to the maintenance of the constitution. While playing down the monarch's culpability in executive corruption, the opposition pressed for measures that, they argued, would restore both the constitutional balance confirmed at the Revolution and the accountability of Parliament to its electors. Hence, triennial Parliaments, the eradication of placemen and pensioners, a reduction in the size of the army and in the national debt, and freedom of the press were all stressed as measures and liberties guaranteed by the Revolution settlement (in which they included the Act of Settlement of 1701 but not, significantly, the repeal of some of its "country" provisions in 1705).[40]

By condemning the policies that contradicted the spirit and

terms of the settlement hammered out between 1689 and 1701 the
opposition focused popular fears about the intentions and consequences of Walpolean legislation. At the same time, county and urban electors, whose role in the political process had been sharply
curtailed under court Whig rule, seized upon the latest version of
Revolution principles to justify the right of the broader public to
canvass and criticize political affairs. In this way, the opposition to
Walpole identified the Revolution with the principles of political
accountability and trusteeship.

The opposition's new role as the true heirs of the Revolution included a print campaign to rewrite the Whig version of events of
1688–89 as well as of 1714. In 1733 Viscount Bolingbroke, despite
his checkered past as an aggressive Tory minister and then briefly as
the pretender's secretary of state a brilliant anti-government propagandist, published his *Dissertation on Parties*, the main thrust of
which was to "vindicate" the Revolution as a bipartisan triumph
to which the opposition alone currently remained loyal. In this essay, which was based on a series of articles he had published in the
opposition's main propaganda organ, *The Craftsman*, Bolingbroke
dismissed the court Whig claim that their party alone had been responsible for restoring and confirming England's ancient constitution at the Revolution as simply untrue. "Many of the most distinguished Tories, some of those who carried the highest doctrines of
passive obedience and non-resistance, were engaged in [the Revolu-
tion], and the whole nation was ripe for it." Tories should not be
accused of disloyalty to a settlement that they had done so much to
engineer and secure.[41]

A revivified street theater, designed to demonstrate Tory loyalty
to the succession and to undermine Whig pretensions as heirs to the
Revolution and Protestant succession, bolstered the opposition's
print campaign, and for this the political calendar provided the perfect medium. For example, royal anniversaries were feted by Tories
and patriot Whigs in the localities in the most ostentatious manner
possible.[42] Equally pointed were the attempts of opposition sympathizers to usurp the traditional Whig holiday of 5 November, in
order to herald and appropriate those "Revolution principles" which
the administration continually subverted. In some large constituencies, such as Newcastle, local Tories advocated commemorating

5 November as the day William III "came to redeem us from STANDING ARMIES in times of peace, from SEPTENNIAL PAR-LIAMENTS and other encroachments of the *Prerogative*, and . . . restored that inestimable blessing, TRIENNIAL PARLIAMENTS." Even smaller towns and villages participated in redefining the holiday's significance. In 1733, 5 November was observed in Petersfield, Hampshire, with effigies in blue star and garter (symbolizing Walpole), marking the "double deliverance, viz., that of the King from the Gunpowder Plot and that of the Kingdom in general from the late Excise."[43] And 11 April, the day the excise bill was defeated, was similarly used by the opposition to deflate government Whig pretensions. Pointing out in 1734 that the day was memorable not only as the anniversary of "our National Deliverance from the late execrable Excise Plot," but also because it was the anniversary of William III's coronation, the *Craftsman* suggested that "THIS DAY . . . be distinguished in the next Almanacks, like the FIFTH of NOVEM-BER on Account of the Double Deliverance from SLAVERY."[44]

The appeal to the extra-parliamentary nation necessitated a renewed discussion of the origins and nature of the popular political liberties guaranteed by the Revolution. Most opposition writers followed Bolingbroke in adhering to the notion of the ancient constitution, which guaranteed the "Gothic" liberties of the subject, but in current circumstances its populist implications were emphasized. "*British Liberties* are not the *Grants of Princes*," Bolingbroke reminded his readers in the *Craftsman*, but are "*original Rights*, Conditions of *Original Contracts*, coequal with the Prerogative and coeval with our government."[45] Other radical Whig ideas received a new lease on life. The pre-election propaganda of 1733–34 and 1740–41 rehashed notions of the sovereignty of the popular will and natural rights, sometimes using Lockeian language to stress the degree to which rampant bribery and corruption threatened both. Liberty is the "natural right" of everyone, one writer argued, which is not wholly surrendered when one enters into the "compact" of government, as the Revolution had shown. In such circumstances electors must choose representatives who will not bargain away their liberties for the emoluments of office.[46] Opposition spokesmen insisted on the political judgement and sense of the extra-parliamentary nation. The "People of this Kingdom" are the "Best Judges of their true Interests, (such as national Debts, the *Revenue*, the *Civil List*, Treaties, Trade, Etc.)," one pamphleteer argued before the 1741 election; they must act to make "the *Voice of the People* . . . the *Voice of Parliament.*"[47]

Accordingly, the opposition employed extra-parliamentary tactics that emphasized the canvassing role of the people in day-to-day political processes and the accountability of those in power to them. The use of parliamentary instructions against Walpole is a case in point. Walpole's proposed bill to levy taxes on wine and tobacco had stimulated intense anxiety among mercantile groups concerned about their profits and among Englishmen of all persuasions concerned by the threats that an army of excise officers dependent on the state posed to their liberties.[48] Propaganda against it poured from the press; instructions were sent from fifty-nine constituencies which directed their representatives to vote against the bill, and the demonstrations on its withdrawal were wild and vehement, expressing violent antipathy against the ministry.[49] The instructions, of course, were encouraged and sometimes orchestrated by opposition MPs, but their organization and the widespread publicity they garnered strongly reinforced the notion that those out-of-doors had the right to canvass public affairs—a right located in the "original power" of the people, confirmed in 1688, and implying the reciprocal duty of accountability on the part of their representatives.

Instructions were constitutionally problematic. Certainly they were not new: they were used extensively by Shaftsbury's Whigs in the exclusion crisis, and instructions to representatives on matters of local concern had precedents going back to the fifteenth century.[50] The right of the people to *petition* king and Parliament for redress of grievances was a hallowed constitutional practice, confirmed by the Bill of Rights. But instructions were rather different, for they stressed the MP's accountability to his constituents in a way that seemed to sanction popular direction of his actions in Parliament. The government press argued that instructions had no legal basis, and that they could not be binding.[51] Opposition adherents insisted otherwise. Most claimed that such interventions were not only legal—an "inviolable right" of private citizens, sanctioned by the Revolution—but also imperative, particularly when faced with septennial Parliaments and a minister who claimed, as Walpole did in

1733, that those out-of-doors had no right to meddle in public affairs.[52] A few opposition writers even insisted that instructions were
binding: MPs "must in most Cases consult their Constituents," one
enthusiast argued, and can "never dare to Vote in direct Opposition
to what is apparently the Desire of those they Represent," however
misled the latter may be.[53] Walpole's withdrawal of the excise bill
seemed to vindicate the efficacy of instructions in repelling the further advances of ministerial oppression, while infusing those out-of-
doors with a sense of their own political weight. "The *Spirit of Liberty* is not yet extinct in this Kingdom," exulted the *Craftsman*,
"the original Power of the People, in their collective Body, is still of
some Weight, when vigorously exerted and united."[54]

When in 1739 a fresh barrage of instructions greeted Walpole's
defiance of public opinion by concluding the convention of El Pardo
with Spain instead of declaring war, the instructions incorporated
proposals for parliamentary reform. The convention outraged mercantile and public opinion because it seemed to signify Walpole's
willingness to sacrifice Britain's colonial trade and imperial expansion in order to protect Hanoverian interests on the Continent.[55] In
response, seventy-nine constituencies instructed their MPs against
placemen and electoral and other forms of corruption in 1739–41.
The opposition press stressed the clear connection between present
discontents and past political grievances, from the Septennial Act to
the attempted excise—all evidences of ministerial corruption that
could only be checked by the three-point program for parliamentary
reform.[56] It also stressed the right of the public to direct their representatives at such a critical juncture, strenuously defending the delegatory theory of parliamentary representation that was a central
tenet of radical Whiggism. MPs were but the "attorneys of the
people" and must take instructions on matters of national as well as
local concern: "Nothing can be more ridiculous and absurd than to
argue that the Principal, who elects, hath not a right to instruct his
deputy, so elected." It constituted "the original design of Representatives."[57]

If the case for instructions was made on the abstract grounds of
accountability, the case for reform was sometimes made on the basis
of constitutional rights, fixed firmly by the Revolution settlement.
The Septennial Act, electoral venality, and the increase of placemen

in the Commons clearly abrogated the spirit and substance of the Revolution; they also abridged Englishmen's "right" to an uncorrupted and accountable Commons. The "Equilibrium of Power" within Parliament was something "which the People claim as their *Natural, Hereditary,* and *Lawful* Birthrights," exclaimed one writer in a fit of hyperbolic abandon, and it was imperative that they be restored and maintained by parliamentary reform.[58] A number of instructions argued that a pure House of Commons and incorrupt electoral system were rights clearly recognized and confirmed by the Revolution and by architects of the Act of Settlement.[59]

Most of the discussion above has focused on the purchase of the populist reading of Revolution principles for the enfranchised, but these principles also raised issues of general political significance that were relevant to the concerns of elector and non-elector alike. In this respect, the contributions of Jacobite writers are intriguing. Jacobite journalists had proved themselves adept at turning Whig principles on their head since the early years of the Hanoverian succession, and in George II's reign they continued to resent bitterly the suppression, by the self-proclaimed defenders of liberty, of popular political license and festival. Journals such as *Robin's Last Shift, The Shift Shift'd* and *Mist's Weekly Journal* decried the constant and violent infringements of individual liberties perpetrated by government troops and policies, associating them with the malevolent corruption of the (Whig) state since the Revolution. Jacobite writers were also likely to use Lockeian arguments about contract and resistance in their discussions of 1688, eagerly drawing its populist implications.[60] In 1732, Fog of *Fog's Weekly Journal* bypassed the bipartisan view of 1688 put forth by Bolingbroke in favor of the argument that the Revolution had been the act of the people at large. William III had been just a pawn in the people's own deliverance of the nation, Fog asserted, invited over by "all ranks and degrees of men in the Kingdom" to comply with the majority will. The "bloodless revolution" was due less to his efforts than to "the Merit of a Brave People who only called him their leader to reap the Fruits of the Attempt they had determined to make for preserving their liberties."[61] Significantly, Fog's view of the role of popular action in 1688 was echoed by a number of other non-Jacobite writers, who argued that James II's conduct in public affairs led "the people" to take the necessary steps to secure their rights and avoid being made "slaves." As one pamphleteer asserted, "It is very remarkable that this great Event [the Revolution] was brought about not by the Parliament, by the Freeholders, or by any particular Body of Men, but by the *People of Great Britain*; and what they did is the Foundation of our present Constitution." He went on to argue that the events of 1688–89 had demonstrated clearly that government was a trust, based on popular consent, in which people of all ranks had residual rights separate from those of their representatives. These included the right to a free press and lawful assembly and the right to canvass public affairs and protest bad governments and bad laws.[62]

The campaign against Walpole obviously stimulated a consideration of Revolution principles that privileged accountability and the popular will in the political process. Yet the social perimeters of "the people" in opposition ideology were not clearly defined. Bolingbroke argued that men "of all degrees" should be included in the political nation, for all had a role as "actors, or judges of those that act, or controllers of those that judge"; and such a view had resonances elsewhere in opposition literature.[63] Most Tory-patriot writers tended to agree that all those engaged in "honest labour and industry" were eligible for inclusion in the political nation, although the *Craftsman* remained dubious of the ability of the meaner sort to resist venality and corruption.[64] In general, then, opposition spokesmen employed a *political* definition of "the people," appealing to those men who were able to maintain their independence against both ministerial patronage and wages and who possessed sufficient "public spirit" to resist the former. Significantly, however, the opposition's attentiveness to the socio-economic contours of its support, which included the most populous boroughs, negated the emphasis on a stake in the land as the sole requirement for citizenship.

The opposition's refurbishment of Revolution principles under Walpole provided the instruments with which to attack the supports of Whig hegemony. Against court Whig claims of current constitutional balance and parliamentary sovereignty, the anti-ministerial spokesmen argued for the sovereignty of the people out-of-doors and advocated measures that would eradicate executive patronage and corruption, "long" parliaments, and popular political circumscrip-

tion. They thus portrayed themselves as engaged in the latest in-
stallment of the historic struggle to restore the ancient constitution,
confirmed at the Revolution, to its "first principles."⁶⁵ In the process, however, they dusted off some radical Whig arguments of the
1690s and gave them a new hearing—and a new audience. Their
strategy provoked ministerialist writers to deny the myth of Anglo-
Saxon liberties and to assert that in fact the Revolution had inaugurated a glorious new era of liberty that had reached its apotheosis
under the court Whigs, an interpretation which continued to have
great currency in the later eighteenth century.⁶⁶

The opposition's use of "real" Whig arguments, clearly selective,
stopped short of taking commonwealth ideas to their logical extreme by downplaying the right of resistance. Bolingbroke admitted
that 1688 had involved resistance and used it as a precedent in arguing for the right of the people to resist a corrupt Parliament.⁶⁷ But
in general most writers declined to draw out the implications of
arguments about the dissolution of government or right of resistance for the present, largely because of their treasonable associations. Tories anxious to redeem themselves from charges of disloyalty to the Hanoverian sovereigns were understandably diffident
about avowing the principles that their Jacobite cousins had taken
up in 1715, while the vigilance with which Walpole suppressed the
slightest hint of disaffection in the popular press made it politically
imprudent (though possible) to espouse resistance theory. Indeed,
the whole case for the possibility of a "loyal opposition" militated
against the employment of such arguments.

In this respect it is important to note that Tory patriot ideology
and tactics were geared to undermine court Whig oligarchy, not the
oligarchic structure of the post-Revolution state itself. Significantly,
Tory patriot leaders were never very specific on what the role of
their newly-activist public would be if they returned to administration; the out-of-doors supporters of the dissident Whigs found out,
to their great disillusionment and bitterness, in 1742.⁶⁸ However, it
is important to stress that the parliamentary opposition to Walpole
subtly legitimized existing representative institutions by providing
populist arguments as to how they could be made responsive to
public opinion. It may not be too far-fetched to argue that through
their tactics and ideology the opposition had made a case for popular

political opinion as a "Fourth Estate"—an implication that was quickly pointed out and criticized by government spokesmen.[69]

The view that the extra-parliamentary political nation had undertaken a campaign of "resistance" to ministerial oppression had wide currency out-of-doors: as "Cato" had reminded his readers in 1721, "upon the Principle of People's judging for themselves, and resisting lawless Force, stands our late happy *Revolution*."[70] In this way populist interpretations of Revolution principles in the opposition to Walpole infused those out-of-doors with a sense of their own political weight and provided an ideological justification for their continuing role in the political process.

< III >

Opposition writers and journalists in George III's reign were far less reticent than their "country" predecessors in using contract and resistance in their interpretations of the Glorious Revolution in order to attack and criticize the state. "POLITICAL WHIGS ought not to be blinded by names and persons," charged the Newcastle radical activist James Murray in 1774, "but examine MEASURES strictly, and compare them with those of Charles I and James II, and if they find them tending to the same end . . . act as the whigs did then."[71] Other polemicists also used this version of Revolution principles in their opposition to government policy. A writer in Salisbury in 1764 cited Magna Carta, the Revolution settlement, and Locke to prove the right to the community to take up the "supreme power" when threatened by such legislative tyranny as the recent cider tax.[72] Even the rhetoric of regicide appeared in the late 1760s: *The Fate of Tyrants: or the Road from the Palace to the Scaffold* was advertised in conjunction with *Wilke's Jest Book* as essential reading for the Friends of Liberty.

The reasons for the revivification of contract and resistance in the 1760s and 1770s are complex. The 1740s and 1750s had seen a diminution of overt partisan conflict and a correspondingly altered domestic political climate, which internal rebellion and war with France paradoxically reinforced. The rebellion of 1745 temporarily stimulated the revival of the anti-Catholic, libertarian rhetoric, tra-

ditionally associated with the Whigs, in all quarters. Tories joined
in condemning notions of hereditary and indefeasible right and defending the current happy establishment in church and state. The
apparent unanimity and pervasiveness of the response to the rebellion did much to banish the specter of a Jacobite restoration and
dissociate political dissent from treason.[73] In the next decade, Pitt's
"patriotic" ministry also focused both populist and libertarian sensibilities on the government; it was aided by the consolidation of
the first empire under the clarion call of spreading the "Birthrights
of Englishmen" throughout the globe. Hence, by 1760, a modicum
of consensus had been reached on issues which had once provoked
heated and feverish debate. That the British monarchy was both hereditary and, at least once, "elective"; that 1688 had involved resistance, which was justified, however vaguely, by popular consent;
and that the settlement which followed the Revolution guaranteed
political rights for Englishmen found expression in both loyalist and
radical political argument.[74] As a result, out-of-doors political debate
was freed of some of its former restraints.

But the revival of a radical rhetoric informed by late seventeenth-
century ideas was also stimulated by the new configuration of elite
politics after George III's accession, and its drastically altered relationship with an expanding, and more socio-economically complex,
political nation. With the "Tory restoration" to high political office
after 1760, Whigs and Tories were formally reintegrated into a
united ruling class. The result for high politics was the transmutation of the remnants of old party groupings into aristocratic connections competing for office; the most striking consequence for the
extra-parliamentary world was that dissident politics were denied
substantive elite leadership. Parliamentary elites now had only a
limited interest in appealing to those out-of-doors for political support. Certain opposition parliamentarians, particularly those in the
patrician connection headed by the second marquis of Rockingham,
still attempted to exploit popular radicalism for their own ends
(with only limited success). But, significantly, the vast majority deliberately snubbed the political aspirations of those out-of-doors.
Whereas Tory and Patriot Whig MPs earlier had argued that the independence and integrity of representatives were proved by their attentiveness to the "voice of the people" as expressed, for example, in

instructions, almost all opposition MPs in George III's reign turned this argument on its head: the integrity of the representative was severely compromised by constituency instructions, they argued, and the constitutional balance undermined by popular pressure.[75]

Hence, when radical political activists in the localities revived the use of instructions their MPs responded with assertions of their irrelevance to parliamentary proceedings. On receiving instructions from the Newcastle freemen in 1769 to support parliamentary reform, Sir Walter Blackett and Matthew Ridley declared that such instructions were inconsistent with their "independency": they would pursue instead a line of conduct "as becomes the independent and uninfluenced representatives . . . of Newcastle."[76] The response of the freemen to such apostasy resembled arguments heard three decades earlier. One outraged freeman declared, "Have they any freedom, as our servants, to vote or determine contrary to the interest and instructions of Those who appoint them?"[77] Petitions did not fare any better. On learning of the Newcastle freemen's petition calling for a dissolution of Parliament in late 1769, Blackett declared that he would not present it; indeed, he would "sooner have that right hand cut off, than sign [it]."[78] When it is recognized that Blackett's "independence" in the 1730s and 40s had earned him the title of the "Great Patriot," it becomes clear how far the anti-Walpolean champions of the people had strayed from their former position.

Such an about face shattered the facade of unity and shared concerns about corruption and accountable government that had seemed so marked an aspect of the anti-Walpolean campaign. Its disruptive influence was increased by a salient feature of English political sociology: the expansion in numbers and prosperity of the "middling" classes—that is, of men of moveable property with an income between £50 and £400 per annum.[79] During the Walpolean period, many members of the middling sort had been preoccupied with issues of taxation, indebtedness (both public and private), and the growing power of the state. In the decades thereafter increasing numbers of them became disenchanted with a representative system that obstructed equal access of all social groups to the political process and attracted to proposals that would eradicate the capricious and discretionary aspects of the patrician state and secure the accountability of men in power. Not coincidentally, they also came to display both a greater readiness to emancipate themselves from elite leadership and a propensity to market, and consume, politics in innovative and effective ways.[80] The result was that the initiative for dissident politics increasingly came from the middling and professional classes, who felt acute resentment at their marginalized place in a political system now seen as dominated by antagonistic interests.

It is in the context, then, of a dissident politics that rejected elite leadership and was denied official recognition that the proliferation of radical readings of the Revolution in the 1760s and 1770s must be considered. Catherine Macaulay was not alone in indicting the Revolution as a compromise between warring factions of the ruling power and thus the fount of all subsequent corruption. John Almon also argued in his reform manifesto of 1768 that the Revolution had given "the *grandees* . . . powers inconsistent with the first principles of liberty," which had contributed to the subversion of law and liberty ever since. Arguments that the Revolution settled "freedom" only "by transferring arbitrary power from one part of the constitution to another" steadily gained ground in the 1770s.[81] In addition, some writers gave a new twist to the empirical arguments about an ancient constitution by taking up the thesis of the Norman yoke, which contended that an arbitrary monarchy had been destroying the people's liberties since the conquest of 1066. They accordingly postulated a more distant past when all men had full political rights and sovereignty resided in the people, while denying that the Revolution had any effect in turning the tide of arbitrary power.[82] And others repudiated historical arguments about English liberty altogether by taking up Lockeian contract theory.[83]

The political context of Wilkite radicalism is well known. John Wilkes, a former supporter of Pitt, battled with successive ministries over general warrants, his expulsion from the Commons, and its refusals to accept his re-election for Middlesex; and in the process he ignited and skillfully exploited a national radical campaign. But here it is the rhetorical context of the Wilkite agitation that needs to be examined. Through an imaginative use of contract and resistance theory, Wilkite journalists gave primacy to the role of resistance in 1688 and conflated it with "the people's" actions of 1649. The consequences of this extremely innovative construction for political argument have never been adequately appreciated. Apologists and critics alike of the Revolution had long stressed the dissimilarities between the moderate and defensive actions of 1688 and the extremism and subversion that were seen to have characterized the upheavals of the mid seventeenth century. In contrast, the Wilkite attack on "secret influence" exerted by the king's ministers conscripted both the Civil War and the Revolution into the cause of radical politics; it identified past and present threats to the constitution and subjects' liberties and so constructed a tradition of popular resistance to executive tyranny that legitimized extra-parliamentary action in the present.

The deliberate attempt to exploit historical memories of Stuart political conflict is evident, for example, in the emergence of the radical "cult" of seventeenth-century Whig martyrs, which served to symbolize current divisions in terms of seventeenth-century polarities. Caricaturists made good use of this in graphic satire: along with prints that identified Bute, who as first lord of the treasury suffered from being a Scotsman and a royal favorite, as the embodiment of "Jacobitism," "scotch barbarism," and "secret influence," he was also depicted trampling on the British lion, Magna Carta, and Bill of Rights; driving over trade and law; murdering Britannia, and poisoning the king.[84] Wilkes, on the other hand, appeared in the prints in the company of Hampden, Sidney, and Russell, martyrs all in the cause of resistance to executive tyranny.[85] Indeed, the historical parallels between George III's reign and those of Charles I, Charles II, and James II became a radical obsession. Wilke's expulsion from the Commons in 1769 was declared an illegality "more ruinous in consequences than the levying of ship money by Charles I or the dispensing power exercised by James II," and his imprisonment heralded as an "intrepid stand against the prerogative of the Court" comparable to Hampden's stand against ship money in 1637.[86] This language and world view of radical Whiggism were absorbed into the everyday discourse of even "respectable" dissidents. The gentleman merchant and Wilkite Crisp Molineux of King's Lynn referred in 1772 to the "Motley Crew of passive obedient and non-resistant Toad-eating Tories who now Surround the throne and preach up absolute monarchy and hereditary right" and warned that if the ministry continued to deny the people their liberties and laws, they would be roused to "a civil war ... in support of their rights, and who will blame them?"[87]

The revival of the language of seventeenth-century radical Whiggism, denoting England's historical struggles against despotism, marked a deliberate and sustained effort to reconstruct and identify the events of the Civil War and Revolution as part of a legitimate, indigenous radical tradition that justified the people's right to resist tyranny in the present. Historical associations with the Stuarts were used to demonstrate the government's sympathy for absolutism, the inevitable consequences of Crown influence, and the urgency of the need for reform. This demonstration allowed radicals to indict the king in court corruption. Junius's famous threat to George III to "profit by the fate of the Stuarts" is but one of the more famous examples of the often violent rhetoric directed against the king before the American Revolution.[88] Printed reminders of Charles I's fate appeared in radical journals like the *Whisperer* and *Parliamentary Spy*, while the main articles of the Wilkite *Middlesex Journal*, which displayed a steadily escalating hostility to the king from its inception in 1769, were reprinted in many of the provincial radical papers. George III's choice to associate himself and his court with "foreigners" (a reference to the alleged domination of Scots in his councils) led one writer to wonder who would support him if the people rebelled; he went on to make solicitous suggestions of changes in men and measures required to prevent the "sword of millions" from being drawn against him.[89] Other writers accused the king of violating his coronation oath by his persecution of "a most faithful people" and argued that George III's actions had proven him "an Enemy to your own Family and to the British nation at large." And as the *Whisperer* saw it, the "compact" between the house of Hanover and the people of England was inviolable, founded on Magna Carta, secured through the Bill of Rights, and delineated through the Act of Settlement; George III would do well to remember that the consequences of breaking this compact had been demonstrated in two revolutions already.[90]

Admittedly, these virulent arguments emanated from writers on the extreme left of the radical constituency, who were not infrequently rewarded for their pains by government prosecution. But more moderate writers also drew attention to the resistance involved in 1688 in order to argue for the centrality of popular sovereignty and trusteeship in the British political system. "If revolution principles are justifiable, that is, if the people may take the power out of the hands of a king or government, when they abuse it, it follows that the king and government are in all cases responsible to the people," one writer declared in 1774; and variants of these principles appeared repeatedly in the radical literature of the period.[91] Northern radicals were vehement in their assertions that by the principles of 1688, magistrates, MPs, and judges were "not the servants of the King, but those of the people."[92] The cases in which Wilkes was involved had focused attention on a number of issues—freedom of election, freedom of the press, trial by jury, and the law of libel—which necessitated the defense of the more "traditional" rights and liberties confirmed at the Revolution. The official disregard and contempt heaped on the scores of instructions and petitions over the Middlesex election provoked radicals to resort to arguments, once used against Walpole, that the government was repudiating the basic freedoms guaranteed by the Bill of Rights. "No man who acts upon *true revolution* principles can be an enemy to a *Petition*," one writer exclaimed. "It is the cause of *liberty*, it is the cause of the people . . . the *courtiers* in the time of King James II called the *Bishop's Petition* a Libel, and . . . sent them to the Tower for presenting it, and we all know the consequences." To call petitioners disturbers of the peace is "Tory Cant," another wrote; rather they have the spirit to oppose an "arbitrary administration" which had "invaded all the *dearest rights* of Englishmen, and have broke down the MAIN PILLARS of the *Constitution*."[93] Indeed, the Bill of Rights appeared more frequently than ever before in the graphic satire of the late 1760s and 1770s and was a constant point of reference at radical meetings, demonstrations, and processions.[94] It was also reprinted in opposition journals and newspapers, so that "every man may see what are the principles of English liberty, and judge how far the modern statutes of the legislature are agreeable with those constitutional laws."[95]

Whether individual Wilkite journalists and partisans damned or celebrated 1688 itself, in general it is clear that most of them considered resistance to be an historical as well as a natural right, sanctioned by the Glorious Revolution. Arguments for resistance, and the "tradition" of popular action that they invoked and created, were well suited to challenge elite claims of political exclusivity and to redefine the nature of political liberty. Resistance arguments privileged and gave currency to the doctrines of popular sovereignty and political accountability; as such, they were useful in mobilizing support for radical causes from an expanding and increasingly res- tive political public. Indeed, the parliamentary elites' repudiation of the role of popular politics in the political process, and the growth of middle class confidence and initiative, increased the purchase of these principles for men who sought independence and accountable government—that is, independence from the capriciousness of the client economy and a Parliament that protected the commercial in- terests and political liberties of its middling constituents. Attacks on an "arbitrary" Commons and the insistence on the right of the people to resist tyrannical governors were intended to remind an apostate Parliament—"one of the most venal and profligate . . . that ever disgraced the British Annals"—of the origins of its power.[96] Most importantly, they also justified the radicals' demands for po- litical change that would accommodate the sovereign popular will.

In this respect, the relationship of the Revolution principles of contract and resistance to the case for parliamentary reform is an intriguing one. Radical rhetoric in the period reflected nothing if not the extreme frustration of an activist political nation whose role in *formal* political processes—albeit an extra-parliamentary one—had been sharply curtailed. Wilkite radicals accordingly combined in their reform program the old country panaceas of place and pensions bills and more frequent (triennial or annual) Parliaments with newer demands that sought to give those out-of-doors a structural, perma- nent role in the political process that would ensure parliamentary accountability and the representation of newer socio-economic in- terests. Hence, radical reform proposals of the period included con- stituency pledges, which bound parliamentary candidates to pursue their electors' programs or principles in Parliament; secret electoral ballots; and a "more equal representation," which usually meant the elimination of rotten boroughs, a redistribution of seats to reflect new centers of population and wealth and, less frequently, the en- franchisement of all who paid taxes—that is, all except the pauper- ized poor.[97] These measures reflected more than the repudiation of the central tenets of the doctrine of virtual representation: they also demonstrated the hard-won knowledge that extra-parliamentary agitation without substantial official recognition was ineffective. The "voice of the people" needed institutional form if it was to be heard.

The other great issue in the 1770s that provoked debate on the Revolution was the American war. The American colonists' opposition to the Townshend Acts, Quebec Act, and Boston Massacre had long been defended by English radicals with reference to Britain's own struggles against popery, illegal taxation, and military and civil oppression in the seventeenth century.[98] The conformity of the colonists' position to that of English subjects in James II's reign was stressed by a group of outraged Norwich tradesmen and merchants in objecting to the attempt of local manufacturers to petition against government colonial policy on strict commercial grounds. This, they argued, represented a "partial and contracted" approach to the colonial crisis, which was caused by ministerial measures that were clearly inimical to the constitution.[99]

Once hostilities broke out defenses of the colonists' position became more strident. Petitions against the government's actions in the colonies stressed that radical opposition at home—like that of the Americans—followed the sound "Revolution principles" that had animated English patriots in 1688 (a strategy which dissociated their position from treason).[100] By this accounting, then, the administration and king were responsible for inaugurating civil war. Once again seventeenth-century English history seemed the best guide to current intentions. King and Parliament were accordingly indicted in a "Stuart" conspiracy to overthrow legal authority, crush colonial and domestic liberties through judicial subversion and military coercion, introduce popery and despotism throughout the empire, pillage the nation's trade and industry, and impoverish the lower orders by conscripting family breadwinners into the cause of murdering colonial subjects.[101]

The essential unity that was perceived between the colonial crisis and domestic political discontents had been intensively explored.[102] Here it is important for its consequences for radical arguments about the Revolution. Certainly the war in America increased the stridency of English radicals' denunciation of government ac-

tion. Shrill accusations of the ministry's absolutist intentions reverberated throughout the London and provincial press, and writers reminded the English public of the essential sovereignty that the colonists shared with themselves: "the people of England" had delegated
"supreme executive power" to Charles II at the Restoration, to William III at the Revolution, and to the House of Hanover in 1714; this
sovereignty was not forfeited on emigration.[103] But the execution of
a war against fellow subjects by a government fond of celebrating
the "noble structure of freedom" established in 1688 convinced
many individuals that what the Revolution had in fact confirmed
were obstructive political institutions mired in hypocrisy, greed,
corruption, and self-interest; and a church "fond of blood and deso-
lation." Richard Watson (an ardent advocate of moderate reform as
well as regius professor of divinity) recalled in a Restoration day sermon to Cambridge University in 1776 what had happened the last
time the English people had been forced to resist a king who had
attempted to tax them without their consent: "devastation and car-
nage, oppression of the People, ruin of the King, of the Nobility, and
of the Constitution." A 1776 tract claimed that "Resistance when
in Freedom's Cause is Public VIRTUE"; by 1781 it had become a
widely-accepted belief that the right of resistance, a right to which
Britons had long resorted, had become for the colonists the "duty of
self-preservation."[104] And in some localities, pro-Americans showed
their hostility to the current establishment by refusing to observe
the fast-days set by the government or the king's birthday, a tactic
which led to hysterical charges of "unpatriotic" or even treasonable
conduct, particularly after the European powers had entered the
War.[105] The Baptist minister Rees David forcefully articulated the
pro-American position in attacking the government in a fast-day sermon of 1781: to fast in support of arbitrary and despotic principles,
he concluded, challenged the divine ordination of civil liberty, and
thus constituted "an act of SOLEMN MOCKERY . . . highly offensive in the sight of God."[106]

From the perspective of many colonial sympathizers the Americans were defending the "true and complete" principles of Britain's
own revolution nearly a century earlier, a fact which stimulated
both admiration and regret. For by 1780 it seemed clear that the
"Revolution principles" which were triumphing in the former colo-

nies were blocked at home by unchanging political structures. In this way the American war contributed to an analysis of power in the post-Revolution state that indicted its structure and distribution. It led many citizens to perceive the existence of a "conspiracy of Nobles," steering the state into disastrous policies that were obviously contrary to the public interest. Those who saw formerly "independent" gentry and peers become the "most warm and inveterate Tories and Jacobites . . . desert[ing] both their Partys and Principles" in the present crisis, agreed that it was men in positions of power and privilege, along with their ambitious and sycophantic followers, who sustained government measures in America against the wishes of independent citizens.[107]

Not surprisingly, then, the war and its aftermath stimulated the rise of novel forms of extra-parliamentary organization, such as the Association movement of 1779–81, which strove to effect "country" measures of parliamentary reform through the force of nationally-coordinated, extra-parliamentary pressure; or the Society for Constitutional Information, formed in 1780 for the purpose of politically educating "the people" in their rights.[108] Perhaps most importantly, the American crisis gave greater currency to natural rights doctrines, stimulating the advocacy of startlingly democratic arguments for parliamentary reform, based on ubiquitous political rights, that advocated the introduction of institutionalized mechanisms of popular control over the organs of the state. Accordingly, in the formulations of such radical reformers as John Cartwright and John Jebb, and to a lesser degree Joseph Priestley and Richard Price, the essence of political liberty was redefined as the individual's permanent, constitutional role in the political process, recognized through enfranchisement. Hence, radical reform proposals in 1776 advocated annual parliaments, equal electoral districts, and a franchise based on personality rather than property, measures which acknowledged the dispersal of political rights throughout the population.

Through the exigencies wrought by national crisis and decades of extra-parliamentary agitation, the right of the people to canvass and demand accountability from their governors, emphasized in the 1730s, had been transmuted into their right to formal participation in the political process through the vote. As Cartwright emphasized in 1782, in a handbill that was distributed as part of the Society for Constitutional Information's gratis propaganda, those who have "no Voice nor Vote in the electing of Representatives, *do not enjoy Liberty*; but are absolutely *enslaved* to those who have Votes, and to their Representatives."[109] Clearly the colonists had agreed.

≺ IV ≻

The Revolution entered eighteenth-century popular political consciousness in a number of guises. One of these was as the great and providential deliverance that rescued England from popery and arbitrary power and rendered Englishmen's liberties, constitutions, and religion permanently secure. It was this face of 1688 that supporters of the establishment usually strove to engrave on public consciousness, as it was most compatible with their arguments that the Revolution, in either confirming an ancient constitution or erecting a new one, had rendered the distribution of power in the state permanent and inviolable.

There were, however, alternative and competing interpretations of the Revolution reverberating in popular political discourse that provided the rationale for a radical assault on the form and structure of the post-Revolution state. They owed something to "real Whig" arguments about the significance of 1688, to the changing configurations of elite politics, and to the broadening social parameters of the political nation. Through the systematic use of government patronage and the successful exploitation of Tory misfortunes, the Walpolean regime had fine-tuned the mechanisms of the state to protect and maintain Whig hegemony. In response the Tory-Patriot opposition in Parliament campaigned to reverse these trends, in the guise of the "country programme" to eradicate court corruption and restore the constitutional balance confirmed at the Revolution. In doing so, the opposition articulated a populist and libertarian version of Revolution principles that emphasized consent and popular sovereignty and championed the role of public opinion and extra-parliamentary organization in the political process. To be sure, this program implicitly sanctioned existing representative institutions, directing honest, independent men of all ranks to help restore a pure

House of Commons, which was held up as the true guardian of public liberty. But in stimulating the articulation of alternative readings
of the intentions and principles of the Revolution the opposition
campaign against Walpole provided those out-of-doors with a compelling vindication of extra-parliamentary political culture and a
justification for the continuing role of the people in the political
process.

In the decades after George III's accession elite sponsorship of
popular opposition politics increasingly gave way to more sophisticated and socially complex forms of political organization. There
was a corresponding emergence of more radical views of the Revolution and its legacy. Wilkite radicals began to insist that the
people's right to resist a corrupt and tyrannical government was the
most fundamental principle justified by 1688, a strategy well-suited
to challenge elite claims of political exclusivity, emphasize popular
sovereignty, and redefine the nature of popular political liberty. The
colonial crisis led many English citizens to perceive that American
"resistance" was made in defense of those principles which they had
come to believe had animated political action in their own Revolution nearly a century before. In this context, radical readings of the
Revolution invented and gave credence to a "tradition" of popular
action that justified demands for political change in the present,
and the Revolution principles of accountability and resistance became the clarion call of a movement to alter the structure of post-
Revolution political institutions.

By 1788, political opinion on the significance of the Glorious
Revolution was as divided and diverse as it had been a century before. Nonetheless, two positions stood out. A substantial number of
radical and moderate reformers, in London and the localities, celebrated the Revolution for the potential it offered as a model for, and
justification of, non-violent political change; an equally vociferous
constituency of loyalists celebrated 1688 for the safeguards it had
erected against such an eventuality. Of course, "real Whig" ideas
had been carried much further by their later proponents, who infused them with principles of "universal" natural rights and inexorable moral progress to justify the right of the people to refashion
government as they saw fit. But the most striking feature of the radical commemorations of 1788 was the degree to which the conser-

vative, elite affair of the late seventeenth century had taken on the mythic proportions of a great popular event, marking, if not the first, then the most successful intrusion of the people into British politics.

The continual reassessment of Revolution principles in eighteenth-century popular politics produced a rhetoric which stressed notions of consent, accountability, and trusteeship, and which gave rise to new views about the just relationship between the individual and the state. In this way, the Glorious Revolution became the vehicle for the formulation of definitions of political rights and liberties in terms more expansive than those sanctioned by establishment supporters and symbolized, in the end, the right of the people not merely to canvass affairs of state, but to effect political transformation. It thus took on the mythic, populist stature that the first English Revolution was so long denied, providing a bridge between seventeenth-century struggles against tyranny and the democratic struggles that had just begun.

<>

REFERENCE MATTER

≺ ≻

Abbreviations

AHR	*American Historical Review*
BIHR	*Bulletin of the Institute of Historical Research*
BL	British Library
Bod.L	Bodleian Library, Oxford
CD	Anchitell Grey, ed., *Debates of the House of Commons*, 10 vols. London, 1769.
CHJ	*Cambridge Historical Journal*
CJ	*Commons Journals*
CSPD	*Calendar of State Papers Domestic.*
CUL	Cambridge University Library
DNB	*Dictionary of National Biography*
EHD	Andrew Browning, ed., *English Historical Documents*, vol. 8. New York, 1953.
EHR	*English Historical Review*
FSL	Folger Shakespeare Library
HJ	*Historical Journal*
HMC	Historical Manuscripts Commission
HMSO	His (Her) Majesty's Stationery Office
JBS	*Journal of British Studies*
JMH	*Journal of Modern History*
LJ	*Lords Journals*
PH	William Cobbett, ed., *Parliamentary History.* 36 vols. London, 1806–20.
PRO	Public Record Office
SP	State Papers
SR	*The Statutes of the Realm*

ST	*State Trials*, ed. W. Cobbett, T. B. Howell. London, 1809–28.
TLS	*Times Literary Supplement*
TRHS	*Transactions of the Royal Historical Society*

‹ ›

Notes

INTRODUCTION

1. T. B. Macaulay, *The History of England from the Accession of James II* (London, 1913–15), 1311–12.

2. Winston S. Churchill, *A History of the English-Speaking Peoples* 2 (London, 1956): bk 6, chaps. 6, 7, and 8; G.M. Trevelyan, *England under the Stuarts* (London, 1904) and *The English Revolution 1688–89* (Oxford, 1938).

3. David Fernbach, ed., Karl Marx, *Political Writings* 2 (London, 1973): 251; V. F. Semenov, cited in William L. Sachse, "The Mob and the Revolution of 1688," *JBS* 4 (1964): 23 and n.

4. J. H. Hexter, "The Birth of Modern Freedom," *TLS*, 21 Jan. 1983.

5. J. H. Hexter, ed., *Parliament and Liberty from the Reign of Elizabeth to the English Civil War* (Stanford, 1991), 110.

6. J. P. Kenyon, *The Stuart Constitution* (Cambridge, 1966), 17.

7. S. R. Gardiner, *Constitutional Documents of the Puritan Revolution* (Oxford, 1947), 376.

8. See J. G. A. Pocock, *The Ancient Constitution and the Feudal Law: A Reissue with a Retrospect* (New York, 1987).

9. On the concept of "mixed" government see Corinne C. Weston and Janelle R. Greenberg, *Subjects and Sovereigns* (Cambridge, 1981).

CHAPTER I

1. Peter Laslett, ed., John Locke, *Two Treatises of Government* (Cambridge 1960), 433; Vernon F. Snow, "The Concept of Revolution in Seventeenth-Century England," *HJ* 5 (1962): 167–90.

2. See L. K. J. Glassey, *Politics and the Appointment of Justices of the Peace, 1675–1720* (Oxford, 1979).

3. John Miller, "The Crown and the Borough Charters in the Reign of Charles II," *EHR* 100 (1985); J.R. Jones, *The Revolution of 1688 in England* (London, 1988), 128–75.

4. G. W. Keeton, *Lord Chancellor Jeffreys and the Stuart Cause* (London, 1965), 306–10; Lois G. Schwoerer, *The Declaration of Rights 1689* (Baltimore, 1981), 296, 297.

5. Brian W. Hill, *Robert Harley* (New Haven, 1988), 170–73.

6. *EHD*:208, 687–88; J. P. Kenyon, *The Stuart Constitution* (Cambridge, 1966), 465–66.

7 *CD* 2:51–52; 4:227–28; 9:523–38.

8. Ibid. 3:341–47.

9. John Miller, *James II: A Study in Kingship* (Hove, 1978), 196–98; PRO, SP Domestic, James II, Entry Book 56, fol. 451.

10. Miller, *James II*, 135.

11. *CD* 3:321.

12. Ibid. 2:55; 3:320–23.

13. H. T. Dickinson, *Walpole and the Whig Supremacy* (London, 1973), 140–48.

14. Kenyon, *The Stuart Constitution*, 420–21, 428–30.

15. Ibid., 430–32.

16. W. C. Costin and J. S. Watson, *The Law and Working of the Constitution* (London, 1952), 1:249–51.

17. J. R. Jones, *The First Whigs* (Oxford, 1961), 188–93; Bod.L, Rawlinson MSS D 384, fols. 69, 74; PRO SP 29/417, fols. 112–13; *ST* 8 (1812): 563–717, 808–16.

18. Schwoerer, *The Declaration of Rights*, 297–300; E. N. Williams, ed., *The Eighteenth-Century Constitution, 1688–1815* (Cambridge, 1960), 27–28.

19. John Miller, *Popery and Politics in England, 1660–1688* (Cambridge, 1973), esp. 80, 82–84, 124–25, 250–63.

20. Kenyon, *The Stuart Constitution*, 410; Sir Roger L'Estrange, *An Answer to a Letter to a Dissenter* (London, 1687), 12; *Animadversions on a late Paper, entituled a Letter to a Dissenter* (London, 1687), 14–15.

21. *A Letter from a Gentleman in the City to a Gentleman in the Country about the odiousness of Persecution* (London, 1687), 31–32; *A Third Letter from a Gentleman in the Country* (London, 1687), 5–6.

22. Robin D. Gwynn, "James II in the Light of his Treatment of Huguenot Refugees in England, 1685–86," *EHR* 92 (1977): 820–33; Miller, *James II*, 144–45.

23. *An Answer to a Letter to a Dissenter, detecting the many unjust insinuations which highly reflect on his Majesty* (London, 1687), 4–10.

24. *Animadversions on a late Paper*, 19.

25. Kenyon, *The Stuart Constitution*, 411; *A New Test of the Church of England's Loyalty* (London, 1687), 3.

26. John Sheffield, earl of Mulgrave and duke of Buckingham, *Works* (London, 1753), 2:70; J. S. Clarke, *The Life of James II* (London, 1816), 2:569, 619, 621; Meriol Trevor, *The Shadow of a Crown* (London, 1988), 54–57, 61.

27. J. B. Bossuet, *Oeuvres completes de Bossuet* (Besancon, 1836), 7:261–63; Jacques Truchet, *Politique de Bossuet* (Paris, 1966), 180–81; F.

Puaux and A. Sabatier, *Etudes sur la Révocation de l'Edit de Nantes* (Paris, 1886), 39, 67–69, 79–80, 82–83.

28. *CSPD, Jan. 1686–May 1687*, 56–58; PRO PC 2, 71, fol. 300.

29. *A History of King James's Ecclesiastical Commission* (London, 1711); Edward Stillingfleet, *A Discourse concerning the Legality of the late Ecclesiastical Commission* (London, 1689).

30. Kenyon, *The Stuart Constitution*, 407.

31. Ibid., 411; Henry Care, *The Legality of the Court held by His Majesty's Commissioners defended* (London, 1688), 18, 24, 37.

32. *A Brief Justification of the Prince of Orange's Descent into England* (London, 1688–89), 19; Basil Hemphill, *The Early Vicars-Apostolic of England, 1685–1750* (London, 1954), 7, 16, 22–23, 25.

33. John Gutch, *Collectanea Curiosa* (Oxford, 1781), 2:397–403; "The Archbishop of Canterbury's articles to the clergy, 16 July 1688," *Somers Tracts*, 1st collection, 1 (1748): 287–88.

34. *The Project for Repealing the Penal Laws and Tests*; J. R. Jones, "William Penn: Representative of the Alternative Society of Restoration England?", in R. S. Dunn and M. M. Dunn, *The World of William Penn* (Philadelphia, 1986), 63–66.

35. *Three Letters tending to demonstrate how the Security of this Nation against all future Persecution for Religion lies in the abolishment of the Present Penal Laws and Tests* (London, 1688), ii, iii.

36. *A Third Letter from a Gentleman in the Country*, 19.

37. See "A Third Letter to Monsieur Van B—de M—at Amsterdam written Anno 1676," *Somers Tracts*, 1st collection, 4 (1748), esp. 120–23; *A Letter from a Person of Quality to his Friend in the Country* (London, 1676), probably by the earl of Shaftesbury.

38. *EHD*:216–17; *The Representation of London and Westminster in Parliament examined and considered* (London, 1702).

39. *Important Questions of State, Law, Justice and Prudence, both Civil and Religious upon the Late Revolutions* (London, 1689), 3.

40. HMC, *12th report*, app., pt. 6:422.

41. *A Brief Justification of the Prince of Orange's Descent*, 10, 19–20; *Important Questions of State, Law, Justice and Prudence*, 3; *A Letter from a Freeholder to the rest of the Freeholders of England, and all others who have votes in the choice of Parliament-Men* (London, 1688), 7, 11.

42. Williams, *Eighteenth-Century Constitution*, 15.

43. Ibid., 28.

44. *CD* 9:262–71, 271–72, 272–76.

45. *The Times Law Reports* 58 (1941–1942): 35–53.

46. J. H. Plumb, "The Elections to the Convention Parliament of 1688–1689," *CHJ* 5 (1937): 235–54.

47. Williams, *Eighteenth-Century Constitution*, 10–16.

48. Proclamation of 28 September (*London Gazette*, 2386).

49. J. R. Jones, "William and the English," in David Proctor, ed., *The Seaborne Alliance and Diplomatic Revolution* (London, 1989).

50. "The Declaration of the Nobility, Gentry and Commonalty at the Rendez-vous at Nottingham," in *A Second Collection of Papers* (London, 1689), 29–31; "An Engagement of the Noble-men, Knights and Gentlemen at Exeter," ibid., 27–28; Andrew Browning, *Thomas Osborne, Earl of Danby* (Glasgow, 1951), 1:391–406. In general see David H. Hosford, *Nottingham, Nobles and the North* (Hamden 1976).

51. "Lord D . . . r's Speech," in *A Collection of Papers relating to the Present Juncture of Affairs in England* (London, 1689), 23–24; *ST* 12:83.

52. "A Letter to a Friend advising in this extraordinary juncture," in *A Sixth Collection of Papers* (London, 1689), 15–16.

53. Henry Maddock, *An Account of the Life and Writings of Lord Chancellor Somers* (London, 1812), app., 3 (the speaker was Sir Robert Sawyer); *A Second Collection of Papers*, 30; "The Speech of Sir George Treby . . . to his Highness the Prince of Orange," in *A Fourth Collection of Papers* (London, 1689), 33.

54. "The Speech of the Rt. Hon. Henry Powle, Speaker of the House of Commons, Delivered to the King's and Queen's Majesties," *Somers Tracts*, 2d collection, 3:440.

55. "A Letter to a Friend advising in this extraordinary Juncture," in *A Sixth Collection of Papers*, 14; "A Modest Proposal to the Present Convention," in ibid., 24–25.

56. Jones, *The Revolution of 1688 in England*, 315–16.

57. "Proposals Humbly Offered . . . for settling of the Government," in *The Eighth Collection of Papers* (London, 1689), 1.

58. Maddock, *Account of the Life and Writings of Lord Chancellor Somers*, appendix, 13; *CD* 9:34.

59. *CD* 9:51.

60. Schwoerer, *The Declaration of Rights*, 281–85, 286–91.

61. Ibid., 299–300.

62. Ibid., 295–98.

63. *CD* 9:28–29.

64. Williams, *Eighteenth-Century Constitution*, 32.

65. Herbert H. Rowen, *The King's State* (New Brunswick, 1980). See also Carl J. Ekberg, *The Failure of Louis XIV's Dutch War* (Chapel Hill, NC, 1979), 174, 179.

66. Clarke, *The Life of James II* 2:479–88, 502–5, 535–36, 566–72, 572–74.

67. Ibid., 2:483–84.

68. Williams, *Eighteenth-Century Constitution*, 36–39.

69. J. S. Watson, *The Reign of George III* (Oxford, 1960), 395, 401–2.

70. Henry Horwitz, *Revolution Politicks* (Cambridge, 1968), 81–85; Browning, *Danby* 1:426–27, 429–33.

71. "Proposals Humbly Offered," in *Eighth Collection of Papers*, 5–6.

72. Schwoerer, *Declaration of Rights*, 299–300.

73. Williams, *Eighteenth-Century Constitution*, 42–46.

74. Kenyon, *The Stuart Constitution*, 442.

75. *CD* 9:252, 260.

76. J. H. Overton, *The Nonjurors: Their Lives, Principles and Writings* (London, 1902).

77. J. P. Kenyon, *Revolution Principles* (Cambridge, 1977), 88–89; John Sharp, *Sermons Preached on Several Occasions* (London, 1729), 2:45–46, 48–49.

78. Costin and Watson, *Law and Working of the Constitution* 1:87–89, 97–98.

79. Williams, *Eighteenth-Century Constitution*, 53–56; Henry Horwitz, *The Parliamentary Diary of Narcissus Luttrell* (Oxford, 1972), 236–38; Samuel Rezneck, "The Statute of 1696," *JMH* 2 (1930).

80. Clayton Roberts, "The Constitutional Significance of the Financial Settlement of 1690," *HJ* 20:59–76.

81. Lois G. Schwoerer, *No Standing Armies* (Baltimore, 1974), 155–87; HMC, *14th report*, app., pt. 2:601.

82. Ibid., 463.

83. Clarke, *Life of James II* 2:478–88, 502–5, 535–36, 566–74. See also "A Short and True Relation of Intrigues to restore the late King James," *Somers Tracts*, 3d collection, 3:263–68; "A Second Letter to a Friend, concerning the French Invasion," ibid., 93–109; *The Late King James's Manifesto Answered* (London, 1697), esp. 33–37.

84. Clarke, *Life of James II* 2:619–42.

85. Ibid., 2:638.

86. Ibid., 2:621.

87. Daniel Szechi, *Jacobitism and Tory Politics, 1710–1714* (Edinburgh, 1984), esp. chap. 2.

88. John Somers, "A Vindication of the Proceedings of the late Parliament of England AD 1689," *Somers Tracts*, 1st collection, 2:348.

89. Isaac Kramnick, *Bolingbroke and his Circle* (Cambridge, MA, 1968), 73–76, 153–57.

90. Ibid., 154–55.

91. Cited by Caroline Robbins, "'Discordant Parties': A Study of the Acceptance of Party by Englishmen," *Political Science Quarterly* 73 (1958): 509.

92. John Brewer, *The Sinews of Power: War, Money and the English State, 1688–1783* (London, 1989).

93. *CD* 9:388–89, 390–91.

94. John Brewer, "The Sinews of War: The State, War and Public Finance in the Aftermath of the Glorious Revolution," (paper given to the Regensburg conference, Die Glorreiche Revolution und die formation der englischen politischen Kultur, December 1988), 1–8.

95. *CJ* 9:6–7, 9–11 (navy for 1694), 18–20 (army), 24–25 (confederates), 26–27 (secret service), 173–75 Public Accounts report.

96. J. A. Downie, "The Commission of Public Accounts and the formation of the Country Party," *EHR* 91 (1976): 33–51.

97. Brewer, "Sinews of War," 10.

98. Colin Brooks, "Public Finance and Political Stability: The Administration of the Land Tax, 1688–1720," *HJ* 17 (1974): 282, 297, 300.

99. Brewer, "The Sinews of War," 4–5, 12–15. See P. G. M. Dickson, *The Financial Revolution in England* (London, 1967).

100. "A Modest Apology for the loyal Protestant Subjects of King James," *Somers Tracts*, 1st collection, 3:20, 51; "Reflections upon our Late and Present Proceedings in England," *A Tenth Collection of Papers* (London, 1689), 4, 12.

101. Lord Acton, *The History of Freedom* (London, 1922), xxx, 44, 50.

102. Pieter Geyl, *The Revolt of the Netherlands* (London, 1966), 183–84.

103. I. Leonard Leeb, *The Ideological Origins of the Batavian Revolution* (The Hague, 1973), 17, 22, 26–27.

104. Sir William Temple, *Works* (London, 1740), 1:89, 136.

105. Hiram Caton, *The Politics of Progress* (Gainesville, FL, 1988), 228–31, 241.

106. S. B. Baxter, *William III* (London, 1966), 79; D. J. Roorda, *Partij en Factie* (Groningen, 1961), chap. 5 and English summary, 259–60; Andrew Lossky, "Political Ideas of William III," H. H. Rowen & Andrew Lossky, *Political Ideas and Institutions in the Dutch Republic* (Los Angeles, 1985), 49–51. See also Simon Schama, *Patriots and Liberators* (London, 1977).

107. Browning, *Danby* 1:151–52, 159–60, 167–75, 191–95; 3:44–120 (Commons), 122–51 (Lords).

108. Williams, *Eighteenth-Century Constitution*, 192–93.

109. Geoffrey Holmes, *British Politics in the Age of Anne* (London, 1967), 151–163.

110. W. A. Speck, *Stability and Strife* (London, 1977), 196–202.

111. Kramnick, *Bolingbroke and his Circle*, 28, 47, 49–54, 73–76, 165–69; J. G. A. Pocock, *The Machiavellian Moment* (Princeton, 1975), esp. 466–86.

112. Gordon Donaldson, *Scotland James V to James VII* (Edinburgh, 1965), 310–33.

113. Ibid., 313–16; S. R. Gardiner, *Constitutional Documents of the Puritan Revolution* (Oxford, 1906), 124–34.

114. Ian B. Cowan, *The Scottish Covenanters, 1660–1688* (London, 1976), 82–133.

115. *EHD*:631.

116. Donaldson, *Scotland James V to James VII*, 381.

117. Cowan, *The Scottish Covenanters*, 135; Walter Harris, *The History of the Life and Reign of William-Henry* (Dublin, 1749), 179.

118. *EHD*:635–39.

119. Cowan, *The Scottish Covenanters*, 91.

120. D. J. Macdonald, *Slaughter under Trust* (London, 1965); John Prebble, *Glencoe: The Story of the Massacre* (London, 1966).

121. J. G. Simms, *Jacobite Ireland 1685–91* (London, 1969), 1–18.

122. John Miller, "The Earl of Tyrconnel and James II's Irish Policy, 1685–1688," *HJ* 20 (1977): 803–23.

123. Simms, *Jacobite Ireland*, 19–57; Karl H. Metz, "Counter-Revolution: a Pattern of Interpretation," (Paper delivered to the Regensburg conference, Die Glorreiche Revolution, December 1988), 1–3, 7–14.

124. *EHD*:747–49.

125. Miller, *James II*, 224; Simms, *Jacobite Ireland*, 86–89; Harris, *The History of the Life and Reign of William-Henry*, 227–28, 237.

126. *EHD*:749–52, 765–69, 769–71; J. G. Simms, *The Williamite Confiscations in Ireland, 1690–1703* (London, 1956), 27–29, 45–72; Harris, *The History of the Life and Reign of William-Henry*, 231, 337–38, 351.

127. *EHD*:772–76, 781–83; J. G. Simms, *War and Politics in Ireland, 1649–1730* (Dublin, 1986), 235–49, 263–76.

128. Patrick Macrory, *The Siege of Derry* (London, 1980).

129. Peter Laslett, *Locke's Two Treatises of Government* (Cambridge, 1960), x-xi, 45–66; Richard Ashcraft, *Revolutionary Politics and Locke's Two Treatises of Government*, (Princeton, 1986), 544–51, 575–89; Martyn P. Thompson, "The Reception of Locke's *Two Treatises of Government*, 1690–1705," *Political Studies* 24 (1976): 184–85, 188–99, 190.

130. Laslett, *Locke's Two Treatises*, 392, par. 158; 426–27, par. 213–16.

131. Ibid., 426–28, par. 213–17; 431, par. 222.

132. Ashcraft, *Revolutionary Politics and Locke's Two Treatises*, 596–601.

133. Williams, *Eighteenth-Century Constitution*, 56–60.

134. Laslett, *Locke's Two Treatises*, 446, par. 243.

135. Vernon F. Snow, "The Concept of Revolution in Seventeenth-Century England," *HJ* 5 (1962): 167–90.

136. Simon Schama, *Citizens* (New York, 1989), xv, 445–49, 786–92, 859–61; Delacroix's painting is reproduced at page 16.

CHAPTER 2

1. See, for example, the speech of Sir Francis Winnington in Bod.L, Carte MS. 72, fol. 508. For a slightly different version, see *A Collection of Speeches and Other Debates of the Late Honourable and Worthy Parliament* (London, 1681?), 3–4.

2. J. G. A. Pocock, *The Ancient Constitution and the Feudal Law* (Cambridge, 1957).

3. J. P. Kenyon, *The Stuart Constitution*, 2d ed., (Cambridge, 1986), 15; L. F. Mengel, Jr., ed., *Poems on Affairs of State* 2 (New Haven, 1965): 485.

4. M. A. Judson, *The Crisis of the Constitution, 1603–1649* (New

Brunswick, 1949), esp. chaps. 9–10; A. Sharp *Political Ideas of the English Civil Wars 1641–1649* (London, 1983); R. Ashton, "From Cavalier to Roundhead Tyranny," in J. S. Morrill, ed., *Reactions to the English Civil War, 1642–1649* (London, 1982), chap. 8.

5. J. R. Western, *The English Militia in the Eighteenth Century* (London, 1965), chap. 1; *EHD*:795; Leicestershire RO, Finch MS. P. P. 57 (ii), 49.

6. J. Miller, "The Crown and The Borough Charters in the Reign of Charles II," *EHR* 100 (1985): 59–62.

7. Western, *Militia*, 12–16.

8. I. M. Green, *The Re-establishment of the Church of England 1660–1663* (Oxford, 1978).

9. J. Miller, "Charles II and His Parliaments," *TRHS*, 5th ser., 32 (1982): 1–7.

10. C. D. Chandaman, *The English Public Revenue, 1660–1688* (Oxford, 1975); *CJ* 8:498–99.

11. E. Berwick, ed., *Rawdon Papers* (London, 1819), 137–38; Durham University Library, Cosin Letter, bk. 2, no. 70. See also Miller, "Charles II and his Parliaments," 15–17.

12. G. Burnet, *History of my own Time*, 6 vols. (Oxford, 1833), 2:1–2; E. Dering, *Diaries and Papers*, ed. M. Bond (London, 1976), 125–26.

13. J. Miller, *Popery and Politics in England, 1660–88* (Cambridge, 1973), esp. chap. 4.

14. HMC, *Finch* 2:30–31; *CD* 8:158.

15. Miller, *Popery*, 9–12.

16. J. R. Jones, *The First Whigs* (Oxford, 1961).

17. *State Tracts*, 2 vols. (1689–1692), 1:402.

18. Miller, *Popery*, 182–88; T. Harris, *London Crowds in the Reign of Charles II* (Cambridge, 1987), chap. 7.

19. T. Bruce, earl of Ailesbury, *Memoirs*, ed. W. E. Buckley, 2 vols. (Roxburgh Club, 1890), 1:22. See also PRO, Baschet transcripts of French ambassadors' dispatches, ref. PRO 31/3 bundle 139, Barrillon to Louis XIV, 18 April 1678 new style.

20. Leics. RO, Finch MS. P. P. 57(ii), 68–71.

21. BL, Add. MS. 29558, fol. 357; R. North, *Lives of the Norths*, ed. A. Jessopp, 3 vols. (London, 1890), 1:316–17; *EHD* (1953), 188. See also North, *Lives* 2:321; T. Carte, *Life of James, Duke of Ormond*, 6 vols. (Oxford, 1851), 5:161–62; Bod.L, Tanner MS. 37, fol. 262; BL, Add. MS. 36988, fol. 180; Southampton RO, SC 2/1/9, fol. 29; Mengel, ed., *Poems* 2:484–85; Warwickshire RO, CR 136/B413.

22. HMC *Ormond*, n.s., 7:95.

23. Pocock, *Ancient Constitution*, chap. 10.

24. *CSPD 1680–1681*, 660; N. Luttrell, *A Brief Historical Relation of State Affairs, 1678–1714*, 6 vols. (Oxford, 1857), 1:199.

25. A. F. Havighurst, "The Judiciary and Politics in the Reign of Charles II," *Law Quarterly Review* 66 (1950): 235–37; P. Hamburger, "The devel-

opment of the Law of Seditious Libel and the Control of the Press," *Stanford Law Review* 37 (Feb. 1985): 682–87.

26. HMC *Ormond*, ns, 6:143–44; L. K. J. Glassey, *Politics and the Appointment of Justices of the Peace* (Oxford, 1979), 49–62.

27. Havighurst, "Judiciary and Politics," 250–51.

28. *CSPD July-Sept. 1683*, 431–32.

29. E. Newton, *The House of Lyme* (London, 1917), 303; BL, Add. MS. 29577, fol. 401; Dr. Williams's Library, Morrice MS. (hereafter Morrice), P, 318.

30. J. Levin, *The Charter Controversy in the City of London* (London, 1969); A. G. Smith, "London and the Crown;" (Ph.D. diss., Wisconsin, 1967), 284–320.

31. J. Sydenham, *History of the Town and County of Poole* (Poole, 1839), 206; Southampton RO, SC 2/1/9, fols. 47–48; *CSPD 1682*, 423–24.

32. J. S. Clarke, *Life of James II*, 2 vols. (London, 1816), 2:620–21.

33. PRO, PC 2/71, p. 1.

34. J. Miller, *James II: A Study in Kingship* (London, 1989), 124–25, 173–75, and chaps. 9–13; J. P. Kenyon, *Robert Spencer, Earl of Sunderland* (London, 1958), chaps. 4–6.

35. Clarke, *James II* 1:659–60; PRO, Baschet, bundle 155, Barrillon to Louis, 15 July 1683 new style.

36. J. Childs, *The Army, James II and the Glorious Revolution* (Manchester, 1980), chap. 4; J. Miller, "The Militia and the Army in the Reign of James II," *HJ* 16 (1973): 661–63.

37. Miller, *James II*, 126–27, and sources there cited.

38. J. Miller, "Catholic Officers in the Later Stuart Army," *EHR* 88 (1973): 45–49.

39. PRO, PC 2/71, p.1.

40. BL, Egerton MS. 2543, fol. 270.

41. J. Gutch, ed., *Collectanea Curiosa*, 2 vols. (London, 1781), 1:436; A. F. Havighurst, "James II and the Twelve Men in Scarlet," *Law Quarterly Review* 69 (1953): 530–31.

42. Louis XIV, *Mémoires for the Instruction of the Dauphin*, ed. P. Sonnino (New York, 1970), 149.

43. Ailesbury, *Memoirs* 1:151.

44. Miller, *James II*, 178–79.

45. J. R. Jones, *The Revolution of 1688 in England* (London, 1972), chap. 6, and "James II's Whig Collaborators," *HJ* 3 (1960): 65–73.

46. C. H. Cooper, *Annals of Cambridge*, 4 vols. (Cambridge, 1842–52), 3:636–38; HMC, *3rd report*, 319; M. Mullett, "Deprived of our Former Place: The Internal Politics of Bedford, 1660–1668," *Bedford Historical Record Society* 59 (1980): 35; *CSPD 1685*, 123–24.

47. Bod.L, Tanner MS. 28, fol. 183; *CSPD 1687–1689*, 304–5.

48. J. R. Bloxam, *Magdalen College and James II* (Oxford, 1886).

49. Kenyon, *Stuart Constitution*, 406–7; G. V. Bennett, "The Seven Bish-

ops: A Reconsideration," in D. Baker, ed., *Religious Motivation: Biographical and Sociological Problems for the Church Historian*, vol. 15 of *Studies in Church History* (Oxford, 1978), 267–82; R. Thomas, "The Seven Bishops and their Petition," *Journal of Ecclesiastical History* 12 (1961): 56–70.

50. Kenyon, *Stuart Constitution*, 410; Hamburger, "Seditious Libel," 709–13. See also Powell's earlier opinion, Buckinghamshire RO, D 135/B2/1/4–5.

51. Sir J. Bramston, *Autobiography*, ed. Lord Braybrooke (Camden Society, 1845), 325–26; Miller, "Militia and Army," 667–73; J. Miller, "Proto-Jacobitism? The Tories and the Revolution of 1688–1689," in J. Black and E. Cruickshanks, eds., *The Jacobite Challenge* (Edinburgh, 1988), 7–23.

52. See G. Savile, marquis of Halifax, *Letter to a Dissenter* (reprinted in his *Complete Works*, ed. J. P. Kenyon [Harmondsworth, 1969]) and *A Letter Written by Mijn Heer Fagel ... to Mr. James Stewart* (reprinted in *State Tracts* 2:334–37). .

53. BL, Add. MS. 34487, fol. 46; Bod.L, Ballard MS. 45, fol. 20; HMC, *le Fleming*, 227.

54. D. H. Hosford, *Nottingham, Nobles and the North* (Hamden, 1976), 88–90, 109–12; P. C. Vellacott, "The Diary of a Country Gentleman in 1688," *CHJ* 2 (1926): 59; *English Currant*, no. 2 (12–14 Dec.).

55. *London Courant*, nos. 4 and 7 (18–22 Dec. and 28 Dec.-2 Jan.); *London Mercury*, nos. 4, 5, and 7 (22–24 Dec., 24–27 Dec., and 31 Dec.-3 Jan); P. E. Murrell, "Bury St. Edmunds and the Campaign to Pack Parliament, 1687–1688," *BIHR* 54 (1981): 188–206.

56. Ailesbury, *Memoirs* 1:202–7; *London Mercury*, no. 1 (15 Dec).

57. HMC, *Dartmouth* 1:232; E. M. Thompson, ed., *Hatton Correspondence*, 2 vols. (Camden Society, 1878), 2:125.

58. J. Sheffield, duke of Buckingham, *Works*, 2 vols. (London, 1753), 2:74; BL, Add. MS. 32095, fol. 305; HMC, *Beaufort*, 92; A. Simpson, "Notes of a Noble Lord," *EHR* 52 (1937): 95.

59. *CD* 9:13, 21–23; L. G. Schwoerer, "A Jornall of the Convention at Westminster," *BIHR* 69 (1976): 252–55. On the radical Whigs, see M. Goldie, "The Roots of True Whiggism, 1688–1694," *History of Political Thought* 1 (1980): 195–235, especially 213–25.

60. *CD* 9:64; Schwoerer, "Jornall," 251.

61. Schwoerer, "Jornall," 251; P. Yorke, earl of Hardwicke, *Miscellaneous State Papers, 1501–1726*, 2 vols. (London, 1778), 2:408–10, 413.

62. *CD* 9:29; Hardwicke, *State Papers* 2:415; J. Miller, "The Glorious Revolution: Contract and Abdication Reconsidered," *HJ* 25 (1982): 541–55.

63. H. Horwitz, "1689 (and all that)," *Parliamentary History* 6 (1987): 25–29.

64. Horwitz, "1689," 29–30; L. G. Schwoerer, *The Declaration of Rights, 1689* (Baltimore, 1981), 270–73.

65. J. Locke, *Two Treatises of Government*, ed. P. Laslett (Mentor ed., New York, 1965), 447–48; Hardwicke, *State Papers* 2: 409.

66. Schwoerer, *Declaration*; R. J. Frankle, "The Formulation of the Declaration of Rights," *HJ* 17 (1974): 265–79; H. Horwitz, *Parliament, Policy and Politics in the Reign of William III* (Manchester, 1977), chap. 1.

67. Schwoerer, *Declaration*, 90–98.

68. Ibid., 78–81, 98–100, 81–86.

69. Ibid., 65–69; D. Ogg, *England in the Reigns of James II and William III* (Oxford, 1955), 175–78.

70. PRO, Baschet, bundle 173, Barrillon to Louis, 16 Oct. 1687 new style.

71. Schwoerer, *Declaration*, 59, 62–66; Havighurst, "Twelve Men in Scarlet," 530–32.

72. Schwoerer, *Declaration*, 71–74.

73. For heads see Schwoerer, *Declaration*, 299–300; for Act of Settlement, see *EHD*:129–34.

74. *CD* 9:30, 33, 36; C. Roberts, "The Constitutional Significance of the Financial Settlement of 1690," *HJ* 20 (1977): 59–76.

75. E. A. Reitan, "From Revenue to Civil List, 1689–1702," *HJ* 13 (1970): 571–88.

76. H. G. Roseveare, *The Treasury: The Evolution of a British Institution* (London, 1969), 88–91; J. A. Downie, "The Commission of Public Accounts and the Formation of the Country Party," *EHR* 91 (1976): 33–51.

77. G. Gibbs, "The Revolution of Foreign Policy," in G. Holmes, ed., *Britain after the Glorious Revolution: 1689–1714* (London, 1969), 66–76; G. C. Gibbs, "Laying Treaties before Parliament in the Eighteenth Century," in R. M. Hatton and M. S. Anderson, eds., *Essays in Diplomatic History in Memory of D. B. Horn* (London, 1970), chap. 7.

78. P. Langford, *The Excise Crisis* (Oxford, 1975); T. W. Perry, *Public Opinion, Propaganda and the Press: A Study of the Jew Bill of 1753* (Cambridge, MA, 1962); Kathleen Wilson, "Empire, Trade and Popular Politics in Mid-Hanoverian Britain: The Case of Admiral Vernon," *Past and Present* 121 (1988).

79. G. Holmes, *The Electorate and the National Will in the First Age of Party* (Lancaster, 1975); H. T. Dickinson, "Popular Politics," in Jeremy Black, ed., *Britain in the Age of Walpole* (London, 1984).

80. *CD* 10:75–76; H. T. Dickinson, "The Eighteenth-Century Debate on the Glorious Revolution," *History* 61 (1976): 28–45. See below.

81. See the alarmist comments in C. H. Hull, ed., *The Economic Writings of Sir William Petty*, 2 vols. (Cambridge, 1899), 2:630–32.

CHAPTER 3

1. [John Nalson], *England Bought and Sold* (1681), 8.

2. *The Thoughts of a Private Person: About the Justice of the Gentlemen's Undertaking at York, Nov. 1688* (London, 1689).

3. BL, Hargrave MSS 96, fol. 24.

4. Sir William Petty, "Concerning Papists & Protestants" (1685), BL, Sloane MSS 2903/2, fols. 22–22v.

5. *An Essay Upon the Original and Designe of Magistracie. Or a Modest Vindication of the Late Proceedings in England* (London, 1689), 4.

6. Sir Robert Atkyns, *An Enquiry Into the Power of Dispensing with Penal Statutes* (1689), 9. See also J. P. Sommerville, *Politics and Ideology in England, 1603–1640* (London, 1986), 98.

7. *An Essay Upon the Original and Designe of Magistracie*, 4.

8. Robert Sheringham, *The King's Supremacy Asserted*, 3d ed. (London, 1682), introduction, 7–8.

9. Ibid., 4.

10. *Some Remarks upon Government, And particularly upon the Establishment of the English Monarchy Relating to this present Juncture* (London, 1689).

11. *The Debate At Large Between the House of Lords and House of Commons, At the Free Conference . . . 1688* (London, 1695), 145–46.

12. Roger Lockyer, ed., *The Trial of Charles I* (London, 1974), 135.

13. See Charles II's speeches to Parliament, 5 Feb. 1672/73: PRO 30/24/4/238 and 27 Oct. 1673: PRO 30/24/5/265; James II's remarks on his first meeting with his council: BL, Add. MSS 5540, fol.45; and James's speech to Parliament 22 May 1685: BL, Sloane MSS 2281, fol.71.

14. *A Dialogue between two Friends, wherein the Church of England is Vindicated in joining with the Prince of Orange in his Descent into England* (London, 1689), 3.

15. *A Second Defence of the Present Government Under K. William, and Q. Mary, Delivered in a Sermon Preached October the 6th 1689* (London, 1689), 9.

16. *The Declaration of the Lords Spiritual and Temporal, in and about the Cities of London and Westminster, Assembled at Guildhal, Dec. 1688* (London, 1688).

17. *Reasons for Crowning the Prince and Princess of Orange King and Queen jointly; and for placing the Executive Power in the Prince alone* (London, 1689), 18.

18. Daniel Defoe, *The Advantages of the Present Settlement, And the Great Danger of A Relapse* (London, 1689), 6, 11, 25.

19. [Richard Claridge], *A Defence of the Present Government Under King William & Queen Mary* (London, 1689), 8.

20. Atkyns, *Enquiry*, 4.

21. Ibid., 12.

22. PRO, PRO 30/24/5/292; John Nalson, *The Complaint of Liberty & Property Against Arbitrary Government* (London, 1681), 1.

23. *CD* 2:21.

24. "A letter containing some reflections on his majestyes declaration for liberty of conscience," BL, Stowe MSS 305, fol. 44v.

25. *An Essay Upon the Original and Designe of Magistracie*, 8.

26. BL, Stowe MSS 305, fol. 44v.

27. "Treatise of the Nature of Lawes in Generall . . . ," BL, Hargrave MSS 485, fols. 36–36v.

28. [Gilbert Burnet], *An Enquiry into the Present State of Affairs* (London, 1689), 10; Lois G. Schwoerer, "Women and the Glorious Revolution," *Albion* 18 (1986): 212, citing National Library of Wales, Ottley Papers, 1469 (11).

29. "Some Reflections upon his Highness the Prince of Orange's Declaration," *Somers Tracts*, 2d ed., 9 (1813): 293.

30. *A Plea to the Duke's Answers* (London, 1679), 3.

31. For the importance of the idea of the ancient constitution in seventeenth-century thought see J. G. A. Pocock, *The Ancient Constitution and the Feudal Law, A Reissue with a Retrospect* (New York, 1987).

32. William Petyt, manuscript of "Jus Parliamentarium," posthumously published in 1739, Inner Temple, Petyt MSS 512/K, fols. 4v-5; BL, Harley MSS 7165, fol. 5; Petyt's draft of "the rights of the Commons of England asserted against Dr. Brady," Inner Temple, Petyt MSS 512/M, fols. 160–160v.

33. Petyt commenting on Edward Coke, Inner Temple, Petyt MSS 512/K, fol. 7v.

34. Ibid., fol. 7.

35. *The Speech of Sir George Treby, Kt., Recorder of the Honourable City of London, To His Highness the Prince of Orange, December the 20th. 1688* (London, 1688).

36. *Vindiciae Juris Regii: Or, Remarques upon a Paper, Entituled An Enquiry Into the Measures of Submission To The Supream Authority* (1689), 19.

37. *An Essay Upon the Original and Designe of Magistracie*, 2.

38. H. C. Foxcroft, ed., *The Life and Letters of Sir George Savile, Bart.* 2 (London, 1898): 282, 301.

39. Ibid., 285.

40. *An Essay Upon the Original and Designe of Magistracie*, 1.

41. Matthew Hale, *The History and Analysis of the Common Law of England* (London, 1713), 46; [Charles Leslie], *The Finishing Stroke* (London, 1711), 2.

42. Howard Nenner, *By Colour of Law* (Chicago, 1977), chaps. 3 and 4.

43. J. W. Gough, *Fundamental Law in English Constitutional History* (Oxford, 1955), 30.

44. Sir Edward Coke, *Eighth Reports*, 118.

45. Gough, *Fundamental Law*, chap. 3 : 30–47.

46. Petyt concluded that there was absolutely no power of judicial review: Inner Temple, Petyt MSS 512/K, chap. 2; and Nottingham, in his "Treatise on Parliament," denounced any judge-made law as intolerable: BL, Add. MSS 36,087, fols. 125–36.

47. "The Earle of Shaftesburye's Speech in the Court of Kings Bench June the 29th 1677," BL, Stowe MSS 182/13, fol. 46v. See also "The Earl of Shaftsbury's Case, Trinity 29th Caroli Secundi in Banco Regis 27th & 29th Junii 1677," PRO, PRO 30/24/6A/306; *London's Liberties* (London, 1682), 8.

48. Remarks of Sir Leoline Jenkins, *PH* 3 : 1191.

49. *An Essay Upon the Original and Designe of Magistracie*, 3.

50. Robert Ferguson, *A Brief Justification of the Prince of Orange's Descent into England*, (London, 1689), 6–8.

51. Lois G. Schwoerer, *The Declaration of Rights, 1689* (Baltimore, 1981), chap. 4.

52. *The Fourth Part of the Institutes of the Laws of England; Concerning the Jurisdiction of Courts* (London, 1671), 25.

53. Sir Joseph Williamson's notebook, PRO, SP 9/22; Matthew Hale, "Of the Alteration Amendment or Reformation of the Lawes of England" (London, 1665), BL, Harley MSS 711, fol. 392; "A common place book of 'remarkable sentences' compiled by an unknown editor during the reign of Charles II," BL, Harley MSS 4636, fol. 6v; *The Protestant Admirer or, An Answer to the Vindication of a Popish Successor* (London, 1681), 2; "Reasons why protestant dissenters aught to concurre for the legal establishment of the late liberty" (London, 1687), PRO, SP 8/1, pt.2, fols. 138–40.

54. "Of the Alteration . . . of the Lawes of England," fols. 393v, 395v.

55. Debate on the coronation oath, 25 March 1689, *CD* 9:196.

56. Robert Filmer, *Patriarcha* (London, 1679), 101.

57. BL, Hargrave MSS 96, fol. 19v; "Preparatory notes touching the Rights of the Crown," Lincoln's Inn, Hargrave MSS 9, chap. 9:6; and "Discourse or History Concerning the Power of Judicature in the King's Council and in Parliament," BL, Hargrave MSS 492, fol. 12.

58. "Preparatory notes," Hargrave MSS 9, chap. 7:2. In similar language, Nottingham in his "Treatise" spoke of "K. Lords & Commons who are the supreme power by the fundamentall constitution," BL, Add. MSS 36,087, fol. 128.

59. "A Letter to a Friend, advising in this Extraordinary Juncture, how to free the Nation from Slavery for ever" (5 Jan. 1688), in *A Sixth collection of Papers Relating to the Present Juncture of Affairs in England* (London, 1689), 15.

60. [Gilbert Burnet], "A letter containing some reflections on his majestyes declaration for liberty of conscience" (4 Apr. 1687), BL, Stowe MSS 305, fol. 46.

61. *CJ* 9:256, 24 Feb. 1673.

62. Ibid. 9:257, 26 Feb. 1673.

63. Corinne Comstock Weston and Janelle Renfrow Greenberg, *Subjects and Sovereigns* (Cambridge, 1981), especially chap. 8.

64. [Thomas Comber], *A Letter to a Bishop Concerning the Present Settlement, And the New Oaths* (London, 1689), 7.

65. "The Earl of Shaftesbury's Speech in the House of Lords the 20th of October, 1675," PRO, PRO 30/24/5/292, p. 11.

66. *The Advantages of the Present Settlement*, 13.

67. *A Discourse Concerning . . . the Present Conventions*, 11.

68. *The Declaration of His Highness William . . . Prince of Orange* (The Hague, 1688), 1.

69. *CJ* 9:758; [Edward Stephens], *Important Questions of State, Law,*

Justice and Prudence, Both Civil and Religious (London, 1689), 2; "A Letter to a Bishop concerning the present Settlement, and the New Oaths," *Somers Tracts* 9:375.

70. PRO, SP 9/6.

71. [Samuel Johnson], *A Letter from a Freeholder, to the rest of the Freeholders of England, and all others, who have Votes in the Choice of Parliament-Men* (London, 1689).

72. *An Essay upon the Original and Designe of Magistracie*, 10.

73. Atkyns, *Enquiry*, 50.

74. HMC, *12th report*, app., pt. 6:29; *7th report*, 759.

75. "An Argument for the Kings Dispensing power in K. James the 2ds time," BL, Stowe MSS 304, fols. 171–171v; Harley MSS 1200, fols. 193–94; Harley MSS 4139, fol. 98.

76. BL, Hargrave MSS 339/3, fols. 31v-32; "A short discourse in defence of the King's power of Dispensation," BL, Sloane MSS 2753/5, fols. 53, 60–61; Sir William Petty, "The Powers of the K[ing] of England," BL, Add. MSS 27,989/3, fol. 18.

77. E. F. Churchill, "The Dispensing Power of the Crown in Ecclesiastical Affairs," *Law Quarterly Review* 38 (1922): 316, 434.

78. BL, Hargrave MSS 339/3, fols. 33–37v.

79. *Animadversions upon the Declaration of His Highness the Prince of Orange*, BL, Add MSS 10,118, 22; [George Hickes], *A Word to the Wavering* (London, 1689), 4.

80. BL, Harley MSS 4139, fol. 106v; Add MSS 5540, fol. 45.

81. BL, Harley MSS 6810/6, fol. 104.

82. E. N. Williams, ed., *The Eighteenth-Century Constitution* (Cambridge, 1960), 11. See also *Discourse Concerning . . . the Present Conventions*, 8.

83. Foxcroft, ed., *Savile*, 289.

84. *PH* 3:1087.

85. *Somers Tracts* 7:451.

86. For an exception see Sir Peter Leicester, *Charges to the Grand Jury at Quarter Sessions, 1660–1677*, Elizabeth M. Halcrow, ed., Chetham Society, 3d ser., 5 (1953): 81.

87. BL, Harley MSS 6495/15, fol. 234.

88. "A letter to Monsieur Van B. de M at Amsterdam written anno 1676 by Denzell Lord Holles concerning the government of England," BL, Sloane MSS 3828/22, fol. 218; PRO, PRO 30/24/6A/304.

89. "Reflections by the Lord Cheife Justice Hale on Mr. Hobbs his dialogue of the Law," BL, Hargrave MSS 96, fol. 18; "Preparatory Notes touching the Rights of the Crown," Lincoln's Inn, Hargrave MSS 9, chap. 2:15. Also see William Petyt, "Jus Parliamentarium," Inner Temple, Petyt MSS 512/K, fol. 220; BL, Harley MSS 6810/6, fol. 102; and Burnet, *An Enquiry*, 11.

90. *An Answer to Two Papers Called a Lords Speech Without-Doors, And a Commoners Speech* (1689), 20.

91. BL, Stowe MSS 371, fols. 53–53v.

92. "A draft work by William Petyt correcting what he considered to be errors of recent English historians and writers on Parliament," Inner Temple, Petyt MSS 512/N, fol. 43.

93. BL, Hargrave MSS 96, fols. 25v-26.

94. "Reasons against the Bill for the Test by the Earl of Shaftesbury: 1675," PRO, SP 9/24/5/294; *A Letter from a Person of Quality to his Friend in the Country* (London, 1675), 18.

95. Claridge, *Second Defence*, 26.

96. "A Vindication of the Revolution . . . ," BL, Stowe MSS 291, fol. 3v.

97. *Vindiciae Juris Regii*, 17, 24.

98. *A Letter Writ by a Clergy-Man to His Neighbour* (1689), 4.

99. Defoe, *Advantages of the Present Settlement*, 11.

100. Ferguson, *Brief Justification*, 20.

101. "The answer of . . . St. Mary Magdalen College . . . Why they did not obey His Majesty's Letters . . . and admit Mr. Anthony Farmer," in J. R. Bloxam, ed., *Magdalen College and King James II, 1686–1688* (Oxford, 1886), 56.

102. Decree of the Commissioner for Ecclesiastical Causes 16 Nov. 1687, in ibid., 205.

103. Ibid., 121, 127.

104. *Bishop Burnet's History of the Reign of King James the Second* (Oxford, 1852), 177–79.

105. Declaration of the Prince of Orange (30 September 1688), in Williams, *Eighteenth-Century Constitution*, 12.

106. Bloxam, ed., *Magdalen College*, 219, 223.

107. Edward Herbert, *A Short Account of the Authorities in Law, upon which Judgement was given in Sir Edw. Hales His Case* (London, 1688), 29.

108. BL, Egerton MSS 2543, fol. 264; BL, Stowe MSS 293, pp. 8–9; *The Declaration of the Estates of the Kingdom of Scotland, containing the Claim of Right* (London, 1689), 1.

109. "Preparatory notes touching the Rights of the Crown," Lincoln's Inn, Hargrave MSS 9, chap 13 : 1; chap. 7 : 1–2.

110. Ibid., chap. 2 : 14.

111. [Stephens], *Important Questions*, 8.

112. Act of Appeals, 24 Henry 8, c. 12 (1533).

113. George Lawson, *Politica Sacra & Civilis: Or, A Model of Civil and Ecclesiastical Government*, 2d ed. (London, 1689), 133.

114. "Jus Parliamentarium," Inner Temple, Petyt MSS 512/K, fols. 209–209v.

115. Atykyns, *Enquiry*, 57; "Memoranda . . . of Danby," BL, Add. MSS 28,043, fol. 102; "Report of the Oxford Parliament, 1680/81," BL, Hargrave MSS 149, fol. 72v; *The Third Part of No Protestant Plot* (1682); Sir William Petty, "The Powers of the K[ing] of England, 10 Decr. 1685," BL, Add. MSS 27,989/3, fol. 17; *A Dialogue Between Dick and Tom; Concerning the Pres-*

ent Posture of Affairs in England (London, 1689), 6; [Samuel Masters], *The Case of Allegiance in our Present Circumstances Consider'd* (London, 1689), 11.

116. "The Lord Chancellor's Speech in the Exchequer, to Baron Thurland at the Taking of his Oath, 24 Jan. 1672/3," PRO, PRO 30/24/5/242.

117. *Thoughts of A Private Person,* 17.

118. Ibid.; also see BL, Harley MSS 6810/6.

119. Roger Thomas, "The Seven Bishops and their Petition, 18 May 1688," *Journal of Ecclesiastical History* (1961), 62, quoting Morrice's *Entry Book* 2:258.

120. Thomas, "Seven Bishops," 64–65.

121. W.C. Costin and J. S. Watson, eds., *The Law and Working of the Constitution: Documents 1660–1914* I (London, 1961): 262.

122. Ibid., 1:267.

123. Ibid., 1:268.

124. Ibid., 1:269; S. R. Gardiner, *Constitutional Documents of the Puritan Revolution,* 3d ed. (Oxford, 1947), 375.

125. Lockyer, ed., *Trial,* 83.

126. *Thoughts of A Private Person,* 14.

127. *A Friendly Debate Between Dr. Kingsman, a Dissatisfied Clergyman, And Gratianus Trimmer, a Neighbour Minister, Concerning The Late Thanksgiving-Day* (London, 1689), 49.

128. Ferguson, *Brief Justification,* 9.

129. *Some Considerations Touching Succession and Allegiance* (London, 1689), 20.

130. "Opinion concerning the King's power to pardon," PRO, PRO 30/24/6B/425.

131. "Answer to a Letter," BL, Add. MSS 22,589.

132. Henry Horwitz, "Parliament and the Glorious Revolution," *BIHR* 47 (1974): 44 n. 3.

133. Comber, *Letter,* 24.

134. J. D., *A Word Without doors Concerning the Bill for Exclusion,* 11.

135. *Reflections upon a Late Book, entituled, The Case of Allegiance considered* (London, 1689), 12.

136. But in Scotland the thrust of the *Claim* was to suggest that the Convention "had the right to dispose of the crown and reshape the constitution." J. R. Western, *Monarchy and Revolution: The English State in the 1680s* (London, 1972), 377.

137. HMC, *12th report,* app., pt. 6:18; BL, Stowe MSS 371, fol. 27v.

138. *Several Queries Relating to the present Proceedings in Parliament* (London, 1689), 1.

139. "Speech of Heneage Finch to the Convention against the Prince of Orange's assumption of the crown, 1688," BL, Stowe MSS 364, fols. 67v-68v; *Somers Tracts* 9:305.

140. "Good Advice before it be too Late: Being a Breviate for the Conven-

tion," in *The Eighth Collection of Papers Relating to the Present Juncture of Affairs in England* (London, 1689), 23.

141. *The History of England from the Revolution to the Death of George the Second*, 1 (1793): 3.

142. *The Letter Which was sent to the Author of The Doctrine of Passive Obedience and Jure Divino Disproved, &c.* (London, 1689), 24; *The Debate At Large*, 41.

143. "Diary of Thomas Smith, DD, a senior fellow of Magdalen College, Oxford" (entry for 21 Jan. 1688/9), BL, Hargrave MSS 401, fol. 37; Defoe, *Advantages of the Present Settlement*, 22; "A Letter to a Bishop concerning the Present Settlement," *Somers Tracts* 9:377.

144. *A Letter From a Loyal Member Of The Church of England To A Relenting Abdicator* (London, 1689), 18.

145. *Some Remarks upon Government, And particularly upon the Establishment of the English Monarchy Relating to this present Juncture* (1689), 17.

146. Some would go further and assert that property and trust were altogether different things, but that was only when property was taken to mean "absolute dominion": *Salus Populi Suprema Lex: Or, The Free Thoughts of a Well-Wisher for a good Settlement in Scotland* (London, 1689), 3.

147. Stephens, *Important Questions*, 6.

148. "Answer to a Letter," BL, Add. MSS 22, 589, p.31.

149. "Free Conference," BL, Stowe MSS 371, fols. 25, 42; the same arguments could be, and were, applied to contract. "A Vindication of the Revolution . . . ," BL, Stowe MSS 291, fol. 12v; Stowe MSS 293, p.19; "Free Conference," BL, Stowe MSS 371, fol. 34v.

150. *An Essay Upon the Original and Designe of Magistracie*, 5.

151. [Henry Maurice], *The Lawfulness of Taking the New Oaths Asserted* (London, 1689), 5.

152. *An Answer to the Desertion Discuss'd*, in *The Eleventh Collection of Papers Relating to the Present Juncture of Affairs in England* (London, 1689), 4.

153. *Some Considerations Touching Succession And Allegiance.*

154. "The Thoughts of A Private Person," 17.

CHAPTER 4

1. Edward Stillingfleet, *The Mischief of Separation: A Sermon Preached at the Guild-Hall Chappel . . . before the Lord Mayor, &c.* (London, 1680), 58.

2. See J. C. D. Clark, *English Society, 1688–1832: Ideology, Social Structure, and Political Practice during the Ancien Regime* (Cambridge, 1985), 389–401.

3. J[ohn] C[orbet], *The Interest of England in the Matter of Religion* (London, 1660), 73–74.

4. Henry Stubbe, *An Essay in Defence of the Good Old Cause* (London, 1659), 132.

5. These figures are derived from Anne Whiteman, ed., *The Compton Census of 1676: A Critical Edition*, Records of Social and Economic History, n.s., 10 (London, 1986): app. F, 223–24.

6. See Gordon J. Schochet, "John Locke and Religious Liberty," in *The Revolutions of 1688–89*, ed. Lois G. Schwoerer (Cambridge, 1992).

7. For the earliest writings, composed in 1660–61, see Philip Abrams, ed., John Locke, *Two Tracts on Government* (Cambridge, 1967), and Gordon J. Schochet, "Toleration, Revolution, and Judgment in the Development of Locke's Political Thought," *Political Science* 40, pt. 1 (1988): 84–96.

8. See Richard Ashcraft, *Revolutionary Politics and Locke's Two Treatises of Government* (Princeton, 1986); cf. Gordon J. Schochet, "Radical Politics and Ashcraft's Treatise on Locke," *Journal of the History of Ideas* 50, pt. 3 (1989): 491–510.

9. For an excellent account of the variety and vagaries of meanings of the term "toleration" as well as an altogether salutory differentiation of the modern meaning of the term from its usage in the late 1650s, see Blair Worden, "Toleration and the Cromwellian Protectorate," in W. J. Sheils, ed., *Persecution and Toleration*, vol. 21 in *Studies in Church History* (London, 1984).

10. John Locke, *Epistola de Tolerantia* [1689]: *A Letter on Toleration*, Latin and English texts, ed. Raymond Klibansky, trans. J. W. Gough (Oxford, 1968), 103; see also 65, 67, 71, 81, 85, 89, 111, 115.

11. Locke, *Epistola*, 133–35.

12. For the history of English non-conformity, see Michael R. Watts, *The Dissenters* 1, "From the Reformation to the French Revolution" (Oxford, 1978), chaps. 1 and 2.

13. Roger L'Estrange, *Toleration Disscuss'd* (London, 1663), 101.

14. See Thomas Hobbes, *Leviathan: or, The Matter, Forme, & Power of a Common-Wealth Ecclesiastical and Civill* [1651], ed. C. B. Macpherson (Harmondsworth, 1968), 365 and chap. 29, passim. See also 477–78, 550–51, and Gordon J. Schochet, "Intending (Political) Obligation: Hobbes and the Voluntary Basis of Society," in *Thomas Hobbes and Political Theory*, ed. Mary G. Dietz (Lawrence, KS, 1990), chap. 4.

15. [William Warburton], *The Alliance between Church and State: or, The Necessity and Equity of an Established Religion and a Test-Law Demonstrated* (London, 1736), 42, 121–24.

16. See I. M. Green, *The Re-Establishment of the Church of England, 1660–1663* (Oxford, 1978), chaps. 1 and 2.

17. Watts, *The Dissenters* 1:222–23.

18. See for the standard accounts of Latitudinarianism, G. R. Cragg, *From Puritanism to the Age of Reason: A Study of Changes in Religious Thought with the Church of England, 1660 to 1700*, (reprinted Cambridge, 1966),

chap. 4 and pp. 190–92; George Every, *The High Church Party, 1688–1718* (London, 1956), chap. 1; and Margaret C. Jacob, *The Newtonians and the English Revolution, 1689–1720* (Ithaca, 1976), chap. 1. These interpretations have been questioned in recent scholarship by John Marshall, "The Ecclesiology of the Latitude-men, 1660–1689: Stillingfleet, Tillotson and 'Hobbism,'" *Journal of Ecclesiastical History* 36 (1985): 407–27, and by John Spurr, "Latitudinarianism and the Restoration Church," *HJ* 31 (1988): 61–82.

19. See Abrams's introduction to Locke's *Two Tracts on Government* for historical details and analysis.

20. John Locke, "An Essay concerning Toleracon 1667," Bod.L, MS. Locke c. 28, fols. 21–32; quotation from fol. 22r. A modernized and slightly incorrect version of the text was published by Carlo A. Viano in John Locke, *Scritti Editi e Inediti Sulla Tolleranza*, edited and translated with an introduction by Viano (Turino, 1961), 81–105; this quotation can be found on 86. In this respect, Locke had moved a considerable distance from his 1660/61 assertion that the magistrate was empowered to regulate matters of religious indifferency.

21. For the most recent scholarship, See Edmund Leites, ed., *Conscience and Casuistry in Early Modern Europe* (Cambridge, 1988), especially the contributions by James Tully ("Governing Conduct," which deals largely with Locke) and Margaret Sampson ("Laxity and Liberty in Seventeenth-Century English Political Thought"). See also Kevin T. Kelly, *Conscience: Dictator or Guide; A Study in Seventeenth-Century English Moral Theology* (London, 1967).

22. Thomas Hobbes, *Leviathan*, in the Macpherson edition 365, 397; and Locke, *Two Tracts*, 137–38.

23. Locke, *Two Tracts*, 238–39.

24. *EHD*:57–58.

25. See Watts, *The Dissenters* 1:221. Also relevant are J. Miller, *Popery and Politics in England, 1660–1668* (Cambridge, 1973), 96; and J. R. Jones, *Charles II: Royal Politician* (London, 1987), 44.

26. *EHD*:365–70.

27. George R. Abernathy, Jr., "The English Presbyterians and the Stuart Restoration, 1648–1663," *Transactions of the American Philosophical Society*, n.s., vol. 55, pt. 2 (1965): 77.

28. E. C. Ratcliff, "The Savoy Conference and the Revision of the Book of Common Prayer," in Geoffrey F. Nuttell and Owen Chadwick, eds., *From Uniformity to Unity* (London, 1962), chap. 2.

29. For varying interpretations, see Robert S. Bosher, *The Making of the Restoration Settlement: The Influence of the Laudians, 1649–1662* (Oxford, 1951), chap. 4; Anne Whiteman, "The Restoration of the Church of England," in *From Uniformity to Unity*, 61–63, 71–72, and "The Re-Establishment of the Church of England, 1660–1663," *TRHS*, 5th ser., 5 (1955):

111−31. The most recent scholarship on Restoration ecclesiology is to be found in Tim Harris, Paul Seaward, and Mark Goldie, eds., *The Politics of Religion in Restoration England* (Oxford, 1990).

30. *EHD*:375−86, 389−94.

31. Mark A. Kishlansky, *Parliamentary Selection: Social and Political Choice in Early Modern England* (Cambridge, 1986), 155 n. 83. Kishlansky does not comment on this.

32. Thomas Lechford, *Plan Dealing: or, News from New-England . . . A short View of New-Englands Present Government, both Ecclesiasticall and Civill* (London, 1642), 23.

33. There are hints to that effect in Kishlansky, *Parliamentary Selection*, 134, 200, 228.

34. Samuel Parker, *Bishop Parker's History of His Own Time in Four Books*, trans. Thomas Newlin (London, 1727), 32, 33. See also Jones, *Charles II*, 59.

35. George R. Abernathy, Jr., "Clarendon and the Declaration of Indulgence," *Journal of Ecclesiastical History* 12 (1961): 55−73, esp. 72; Whiteman, "Reestablishment of the Church," in *From Uniformity to Unity*, 80−83. But see also Green, *Re-Establishment of the Church*, 212−18; Watts, *The Dissenters* 1:219; and Abernathy, "English Presbyterians," 86, 87.

36. *EHD*:372, 373.

37. *PH* 4:261−62, 263; see also J. R. Jones, *Charles II: Royal Politician* (London, 1987), 56.

38. *PH* 4:294.

39. Ibid. 4:314.

40. Jones, *Charles II*, 75 ff.

41. Clayton Roberts, *The Growth of Responsible Government in Stuart England* (Cambridge, 1966), 159−77.

42. *CSPD 1667*, 437 (dated September 2/12); see also 550 (28 October) and 555 (31 October) for other references to the proposed bill.

43. *A Proposition for the Safety & Happiness of the King and Kingdom both in Church and State* (London, 1667), 8.

44. [Thomas Tomkins], *The Inconvenience of Toleration* (London, 1667), 35, 36.

45. See *Reliquiae Baxterianae: or Mr. Richard Baxters Narrative of the Most Memorable Passages of His Life and Times*, ed. Matthew Sylvester (1696), bk. 3:9−17, 23−25, and 32−49. The Barlow manuscript notes, which I am editing for publication, are in Bod.L, Printed Book B.14.15.Linc. Excerpts were printed as an editorial preface to Herbert Thorndike, *The True Principle of Comprehension* (written in 1667, but not published), in Thorndike, *Theological Works* (Oxford, 1854), 5:301−308. It is a pleasure to acknowledge the assistance and cooperation of Dr. John Spurr in working with the Barlow volume. See also Norman Sykes, *From Sheldon to Secker:*

Aspects of English Church History, 1660–1767 (Cambridge, 1959), 72–74; Roger Thomas, "Comprehension and Indulgence," in *From Uniformity to Unity*, 200–203; and Walter G. Simon, "Comprehension in the Age of Charles II," *Church History* 31 (1962): 440–48, and the same author's *The Restoration Episcopate* (New York, 1965), chap. 11.

46. The quotation is from Bod.L, Printed Book B.14.15.Linc., manuscript preface, fol 6.

47. Copies of both proposals are in the Barlow ms. and a slightly different version of the second one is also to be found in Bod.L, Tanner MS. 290, fols. 242–43.

48. Bod.L, Tanner MS. 290, fols. 242–43.

49. *PH* 4:404, 414; Caroline Robbins, ed., *The Parliamentary Diary of John Milward* (Cambridge, 1938), 179, 206, 214–22, 248–50, 325–26.

50. K. H. D. Haley, *The First Earl of Shaftesbury* (Oxford, 1968), 196–97; cf. Parker, *History*, 129.

51. Schochet, "Toleration, Revolution, and Judgment."

52. W. D. Christie, *A Life of Anthony Ashley Cooper, First Earl of Shaftesbury, 1667–1683*, 2 vols. (London, 1871), 2, app. 1 (pp. v–ix).

53. See Howard Nenner, *By Colour of Law: Legal and Constitutional Politics in England, 1660–1689* (Chicago, 1975), index: "disposing and suspending powers" and "prerogative"; Corinne C. Weston and Janelle R. Greenberg, *Subjects and Sovereign: The Grand Controversy over Legal Sovereignty in Stuart England* (Cambridge, 1981), chap. 8; and Carolyn E. Edie, "Tactics and Strategies: Parliament's Attack on the Royal Dispensing Power 1597–1689," *American Journal of Legal History* 29 (1985): 197–234.

54. PRO, Shaftesbury MS. PRO 30/24/6D, Item 427. The paper was apparently drawn up for Shaftesbury rather than for the king; see Haley, *Shaftesbury*, 297, 304–5.

55. My emphasis. *EHD*: 387–88.

56. *PH* 4:503. In his famous *"delenda est Carthago"* speech, urging vigorous prosecution of the Dutch war also at the opening of session, Shaftesbury too defended the declaration, but not with the force of the king. See ibid. 4:506–7.

57. Ibid. 4:527.

58. Ibid. 4:545.

59. Ibid. 4:551; see also R. A. Beddard, "The Restoration Church," in *The Restored Monarchy, 1660–1668*, ed. J. R. Jones (London, 1979), 169.

60. Watts, *The Dissenters* 1:248; see also Frank Bate, *The Declaration of Indulgence, 1672: A Study in the Rise of Organized Dissent* (London, 1908), a detailed study that needs to be updated.

61. *PH* 4:535–45, 551–54.

62. *LJ* 12:584–85; Andrew Marvell, *An Account of the Growth of Popery and Arbitrary Government in England* ("Printed at Amsterdam" [London, 1678]), 15.

63. William Starkey, *An Apology for the Laws Ecclesiastical Established,*

that Command Our Publick Exercise in Religion (London, 1675), A2, 172–73, 181, 185.

64. *A Letter from a Person of Quality, to His Friend in the Country* (1675), 10, 16, 18, 34. The defense of the 1672 declaration occurs on 4. The *Letter*, once attributed to Locke and included in most editions of his *Works*, is now generally ascribed to Shaftesbury. There are "Lockean" qualities to its arguments and much of its prose, and I suspect that both men had a hand in its composition. The *Letter* freely quoted Shaftesbury and was certainly written by someone with access to him.

65. Ibid., 1.

66. Ibid., 10, 18.

67. *PH* 4:798.

68. PRO, Shaftesbury MS. PRO 30/24/6A, Item 334, fol. 115v. The manuscript is entitled "The Present State of the Kingdom at the Opening of the Parliam^t March 6.th 1678/9" and is on fols. 114–115. There is another, slightly but not materially different, copy in PRO 30/24/7, pt. I, Item 498, fols. 124–24. An incorrect and modernized version of the text of the former was published by Christie, *Life of Shaftesbury* 2:281–83, 309–14. See also Haley, *Shaftesbury*, 502–3, and J. R. Jones, *The First Whigs: The Politics of the Exclusion Crisis* (Oxford, 1961), 55.

69. Haley, *Shaftesbury*, 503.

70. See Tim Harris, *London Crowds in the Reign of Charles II: Propaganda and Politics from the Restoration to the Exclusion Crisis* (Cambridge, 1987), chaps. 5 and 6, for a discussion of religious tensions as part of the exclusion campaign.

71. Stillingfleet, *Mischief of Separation*, 58–59.

72. Henry Horwitz, "Protestant Reconciliation in the Exclusion Crisis," *Journal of Ecclesiastical History* 15 (1964): 201–17. See also Horwitz, *Revolution Politicks: The Career of Daniel Finch, Second Earl of Nottingham, 1647–1730* (Cambridge, 1968), 29; *PH* 4:1308, 1311–13; Thomas, "Comprehension and Indulgence," in *From Uniformity to Unity*, 224; and Haley, *Shaftesbury*, 612, 633.

73. Edward Stillingfleet, *The Unreasonableness of Separation: or, An Impartial Account of the History, Nature, and Pleas of Present Separation from the Communion of the Church of England* (London, 1681), preface, lxxix; see also xxiv and xxxii.

74. Horwitz, *Revolution Politicks*, 86–94, and *Parliament, Policy and Politics in the Reign of William III* (Manchester, 1977), 21–29.

75. R. A. Beddard, "Vincent Alsop and the Emancipation of Restoration Dissent," *Journal of Ecclesiastical History* 24 (1973): 172; G. R. Cragg, *Puritanism in the Period of the Great Persecution* (Cambridge, 1957), chap. 2.

76. Watts, *The Dissenters* 1:254–55.

77. *EHD*: 395–96.

78. Beddard, "Vincent Alsop," 176–77; Thomas, "Comprehension and Indulgence," 234–35. The "Address of Thanks from the Presbyterians of

London" appeared in the *London Gazette* for 28 Apr.–2 May 1687 and is reprinted in *EHD*: 397–98.

79. [George Savile, Marquess of Halifax], *A Letter to a Dissenter* (1687) reprinted in his *Complete Works*, ed. J. P. Kenyon (Harmondsworth, 1969), 106.

80. H[enry] C[lare], *Animadversions on a Late Paper, Entituled, A Letter to a Dissenter* (London, 1687), 14, 105.

81. *EHD*: 400.

82. Sancroft was responsible for the publication in 1685 of the second, "corrected" edition of Sir Robert Filmer's *Patriarcha* and in 1690 of Bishop John Overall's *Convocation Book* of 1606. See for the former, Gordon J. Schochet, "Sir Robert Filmer: Some New Bibliographic Discoveries," *The Library* 26 (1971): 135–60, and for the latter the Library of Anglo-Catholic Theology edition of *The Convocation Book of MDCVI, Commonly Called Bishop Overall's Convocation Book* (Oxford, 1844), introduction. Apart from a very old and not particularly useful biography (George D'Oyly, *The Life of William Sancroft, Archbishop of Canterbury*, 2 vols. [Oxford, 1821]), there is virtually no other secondary literature on Sancroft.

83. Roger Thomas, "The Seven Bishops and Their Petition, 18 May 1688," *Journal of Ecclesiastical History* 11 (1966): 56–70; and G. V. Bennett, "The Seven Bishops: A Reconsideration," in Derek Baker, ed., *Religious Motivation: Biographical and Sociological Problems for the Church Historian*, vol. 15 in *Studies in Church History* (London, 1978), 267–87.

84. Text in *EHD*: 400–403.

85. *PH* 5:265.

86. Dr. Williams's Library, Roger Morrice MSS, *The Entering Book: Being an Historical Register of Occurrences from April An: 1677 to April 1691*, vol. 2:493 (entry dated 9 Mar. 1688 [/9]). For further details and a discussion of the political machinations surrounding comprehension, see Gordon J. Schochet, "The Act of Toleration and the Failure of Comprehension: Persecution, Non-Conformity, and Religious Indifference," in *The World of William and Mary*, ed. Dale Hoak and M. Feingold (Berkeley, 1992).

87. *PH* 5:184.

88. Morrice, *Entering Book*, vol. 2:504–5 (entry dated 16 Mar. 1688 [/9]).

89. P. J. A. N. Rietbergen, "William III of Orange (1650) between European Politics and European Protestantism: The Case of the Huguenots," in *The Revocation of the Edict of Nantes and the Dutch Republic*, ed. J. A. H. Bots and G. M. H. Posthumus Meyjes (Amsterdam, 1986), 36, 39–41, 43–49.

90. *A Letter Writ by Mijn Heer Fagel, Pensioner of Holland . . . Giving an Account of the Prince and Princess of Orange's Thoughts Concerning the Repeal of the Test, and the Penal Laws* (Amsterdam, 1688), 1.

91. Ibid., 2.

CHAPTER 5

1. Thomas Burnet, *The Sacred Theory of the Earth* (Carbondale, Ill., 1965), 5, 68; Willey's characterization is in his introduction to that edition.

See also Stephen Jay Gould, *Time's Arrow, Time's Cycle: Myth and Metaphor in the Discovery of Geological Time* (Cambridge, MA, 1987).

2. *CD* 9: 252–54.

3. Caroline Robbins, *The Eighteenth-Century Commonwealthman* (Cambridge, MA, 1959). See also T. W. Mason on "Nineteenth-Century Cromwell," *Past and Present* 40 (July 1968).

4. *Bishop Burnet's History of His Own Time* (Oxford, 1823), 4:410–11.

5. H. John McLachlan, *Socinianism in Seventeenth-Century England* (Oxford, 1951); Earl Morse Wilbur, *A History of Unitarianism*, 2 vols. (Boston, 1945, 1952); G. H. Williams, *The Polish Brethren . . . 1601–1685* (Cambridge, MA, 1978).

6. Sir James Fitzjames Stephen, *A History of the Criminal Law in England* (London, 1883), 2:446–97; Sir William Holdsworth, *A History of English Law* 8 (London, 1925): 403–18.

7. Norman Sykes, *Church and State in England in the Eighteenth Century* (London, 1934), 310. See also chap. 2 of his *From Sheldon to Secker: Aspects of English Church History, 1660–1768* (Cambridge, 1959); G. V. Bennett, *The Tory Crisis in Church and State, 1688–1730* (Oxford, 1975); Eamon Duffy, "'Whiston's Affair': The Trials of the Primitive Christian, 1709–1714," *Journal of Ecclesiastical History* 27 (April, 1976): 129–50.

8. Charles Leslie, *The Nature and Mischief of Prejudice and Partiality* (London, 1704), 54; Henry Sacheverell, *The Perils of False Brethren both in Church and State* (London, 1709), 25.

9. Geoffrey Holmes, *The Trial of Dr. Sacheverell* (London, 1973); D. Szechi, "The Politics of 'Persecution': Scots Episcopalian Toleration and the Harley Ministry, 1710–1712," in W. J. Sheils, ed., *Persecution and Toleration*, vol. 21 of *Studies in Church History* (London, 1984), 275–87.

10. Norman Sykes, "Queen Anne and the Episcopate," *EHR* 50 (July 1935): 433–64.

11. J. C. D. Clark, *English Society, 1688–1832: Ideology, Social Structure and Political Practice during the Ancien Regime* (London, 1985), 55 and passim.

12. Norman Sykes, *William Wake, Archbishop of Canterbury*, 2 vols. (London, 1957), 2:106–49; and his *Edmund Gibson, Bishop of London, 1669–1748* (Oxford, 1926), 160–82, 259–92.

13. John Potter, *A Discourse of Church Government, wherein the Rights of the Church and the Supremacy of Christian Princes are vindicated and adjusted* (London, 1707). The encomium is in the preface to the seventh edition (London 1845), vii-viii.

14. [Francis Hare], *Scripture Vindicated from the Misrepresentations of the Bishop of Bangor* (London, 1721); I am grateful to Dr. J. C. D. Clark for identifying the author whom Warburton notes only as a "late excellent Prelate."

15. Wake to A. J. Turretini, quoted in Sykes, *Wake* 2:170–71.

16. Sykes, *Church and State*, 316–26; R. W. Greaves, "The Working of the Alliance: A Comment on Warburton," in G. V. Bennett and J. D. Walsh,

eds., *Essays in Modern English Church History in Memory of Norman Sykes* (New York, 1966), 163–80.

17. Michael R. Watts, *The Dissenters, from the Reformation to the French Revolution* (Oxford, 1978), 267–89.

18. Alexander Gordon, *Freedom after Ejection, 1690–1692* (London, 1917); H. G. Horwitz, "Comprehension in the Later Seventeenth Century: A Postscript," *Church History* 34 (1965): 342–48.

19. Roger Thomas, "The Non-Subscription Controversy amongst Dissenters in 1719: The Salters' Hall Debate," *Journal of Ecclesiastical History* 4 (1953): 162–86; Alan Brockett, *Nonconformity in Exeter, 1650–1875* (Manchester, 1962), 74–95.

20. Daniel Defoe, *A Tour thro' the Whole Island of Great Britain* (1724–26, Penguin ed., 1971), 71.

21. F. J. Powicke, "An Apology for the Arians of the Eighteenth Century," *Transactions of the Unitarian Historical Society* 1 (1917): 110–24. The situation was, however, complex.

22. K. R. M. Short, "The English Indemnity Acts, 1726–1867," *Church History* 42 (1973): 367–76.

23. R. W. Davis, *Dissent in Politics, 1780–1830: The Political Life of William Smith, M.P.* (London, 1971), 29.

24. N. C. Hunt, *Two Early Political Associations: The Quakers and the Dissenting Deputies in the Age of Sir Robert Walpole* (Oxford, 1961).

25. BL, Add. MSS 35,598, fol. 342, quoted in Sykes, *Church and State*, 284.

26. Thomas Belsham to his mother, 18 July 1774, Dr. Williams's Library, MS. 24.81. See also Basil Short, *A Respectable Society: Bridport, 1593–1835* (Bradford-on-Avon, 1976).

27. Horton Davies, *The Worship of the English Puritans* (Princeton, 1948); Watts, *Dissenters*, 263–67; Christopher Stell, *Architects of Dissent: Some Nonconformist Patrons and their Architects* (Friends of Dr. Williams's Library, Thirtieth Lecture, 1976); Graham Hague and others, *The Unitarian Heritage: An Architectural Survey of Chapels and Churches in the Unitarian Tradition in the British Isles* (Sheffield, 1986).

28. J. J. Wright, *The Story of Chowbent Chapel, 1645–1721–1921* (Manchester, 1921).

29. Edmund Calamy, "A Brief but True Account of the Protestant Dissenters in England," appended to *The Principles and Practice of Moderate Nonconformists with Respect to Ordination, Exemplify'd* (London, 1717). See also Isaac Watts, *A New Essay on Civil Power in Things Sacred* (1739), *Works* (London, 1753), vol. 6; Richard Burgess Barlow, *Citizenship and Conscience: A Study in the Theory and Practice of Religious Toleration in England during the Eighteenth Century* (Philadelphia, 1962), 102–12.

30. A. J. Carlyle, *The Christian Church and Liberty* (London, 1924), 116–18; Anthony Lincoln, *Some Political and Social Ideas of English Dissent, 1763–1800* (Cambridge, 1938), chap. 6.

31. Dudley W. R. Bahlman, *The Moral Revolution of 1688* (New Haven, 1957).

32. J. D. Walsh, "Origins of the Evangelical Revival," in Bennett and Walsh, eds., *Essays . . . in Memory of Norman Sykes*, 132–62. See also Sykes, *Gibson*, 301–20; Maldwyn Edwards, "John Wesley," in Rupert Davies and Gordon Rupp, eds., *A History of the Methodist Church in Great Britain* 1 (London, 1965): 54–55; Robert F. Wearmouth, *Methodism and the Common People of the Eighteenth Century* (London, 1945), 138–64.

33. The 41 volumes of the Ryder diary are in the Unitarian College collection in the John Rylands University of Manchester Library; the extracts used here are in Herbert McLachlan, *Essays and Addresses* (Manchester, 1950), 20–39. On the Leeds situation, W. L. Schroeder, *Mill Hill Chapel, Leeds, 1724–1924* (Leeds, 1924), 31, and a letter from E. Basil Lupton, 13 Mar. 1922, Nottingham University Library, HI W 46.

34. Herbert McLachlan, *English Education under the Test Acts* (Manchester, 1931); Alexander Gordon, "Early Nonconformity and Education," and "Philip Doddridge and the Catholicity of the Old Dissent," in his *Addresses Biographical and Historical* (London, 1902). On Doddridge, Geoffrey Nuttall, *Richard Baxter and Philip Doddridge: A Study in a Tradition* (Friends of Dr. Williams's Library, Fifth Lecture, 1951), and his edition of Doddridge's correspondence, in progress.

35. Alexander Gordon, *Addresses*, 221–24. The peculiar use of the word "experimental" does not carry a scientific connotation but refers to experience.

36. Barlow, *Citizenship*, 114, 117, touches briefly on Anglican embarrassment about the Athanasian creed.

37. The Rev. Anthony Temple, *A Sermon Preached at the Visitation . . . at Richmond . . .* (London, 1786), 17–24, quoted in Barlow, *Citizenship*, 142–43.

38. J. G. A. Pocock, "Clergy and Commerce: The Conservative Enlightenment in England" in *L'Età dei lumi: studi storici sul Settecento europeo in onore di Franco Venturi* (Naples, 1985), 1:524–62 and works there cited; Lincoln, *Political and Social Ideas*, 54 and works there cited. For interesting illustrations of the new usage, see Philip Furneaux, *Letters to the Honourable Mr. Justice Blackstone, concerning His Exposition of the Act of Toleration and Some Positions relative to Religious Liberty* (London, 1770), 1, 16; and Robert Robinson, "On Candour in Controversy," letter 1 in *Arcana . . .* (1774), *Miscellaneous Works* (Harlow, 1807), 4:21–28. See also Martin Fitzpatrick, "Varieties of Candour: English and Scottish Style," *Enlightenment and Dissent* 7 (1988): 35–56.

39. Barlow, *Citizenship*, 112–14; for other contemporary expressions see John Taylor, *The Glory of any House erected for Public Worship and the True Principles, Religious, Civil, and Social of Protestant Dissenters . . .* (London, 1756), and Lucy Aikin, *Memoir of John Aikin, M.D.* (London, 1823), 1:45–46.

40. Mansfield's speech and other papers relating to this dispute were printed in *The Palladium of Conscience* (Philadelphia, 1773); see also Blackstone *Commentaries* 4: chap. 4, III, 2; Priestley, *The Theological and Miscellaneous Works*, ed. J. T. Rutt, 25 vols. (London, 1817–32), 22:302–34.

41. Priestley, *The Importance and Extent of Free Inquiry in Matters of Religion* (1785), *Works* 15:70–82.

42. R. K. Webb, "And the Greatest of These is Liberty: The Manchester College Motto in its Setting," *Faith and Freedom* 40 (Spring 1987): 4–20. See also George Walker, *On the Right of Individual Judgment in Religion* (Manchester, 1800); Philip Furneaux, *Letters to Blackstone*.

43. William Paley, *The Principles of Moral and Political Philosophy* (London, 1785), chaps. 5 and 7.

44. Herbert Butterfield, *Historical Development of the Principle of Toleration in British Life* (London, 1956), 5–6.

45. Cecil Roth, *A History of the Jews in England* (Oxford, 1949), chaps. 7–11; Ursula Henriques, *Religious Toleration in England, 1787–1833* (London, 1961), chap. 6; Thomas W. Perry, *Public Opinion, Propaganda, and Politics in the Eighteenth Century: A Study of the Jew Bill of 1753* (Cambridge, MA, 1962). Francis Place made the point about Mendoza, BL, Add. MSS 27,289: 145–46.

46. John Bossy, *The English Catholic Community, 1570–1850* (New York, 1976); Sykes, *Gibson*, 292–301; G. F. A. Best, "The Protestant Constitution and its Supporters, 1800–1829," *TRHS*, 5th ser., vol. 8 (1958): 105–27, and "Popular Protestantism in Victorian Britain," in Robert Robson, ed., *Ideas and Institutions of Victorian Britain* (New York, 1967), 115–42; Josiah Tucker, *Religious Intolerance No Part of the Divine Plan* (Gloucester, 1774); Priestley, *A Free Address to Those Who Have Petitioned for the Repeal of the Late Act of Parliament in Favour of the Roman Catholics* (1790), in *Works* 22:499–516.

47. Thomas Sherlock, *The History of the Test Act* (1732), 22–23, 28, quoted in Barlow, *Citizenship*, 83; Kathleen Wilson, "The Rejection of Deference: Urban Political Culture in England, 1715–1785" (Ph.D. diss., Yale, 1985), 152–59; Albert Goodwin, *The Friends of Liberty: The English Democratic Movement in the Age of the French Revolution* (Cambridge, MA, 1979), chap. 3, pp. 65–98. The long-standing analysis by Richard Rose, "The Priestley Riots of 1791," *Past and Present* 18 (1960): 66–88, must now be read against the important reinterpretations by G. M. Ditchfield, "The Priestley Riots in Historical Perspective," *Transactions of the Unitarian Historical Society* 20 (Apr. 1991): 3–16, and David L. Wykes, "'The Spirit of Persecution Exemplified': The Priestley Riots and the Victims of the Church and King Mobs," ibid., 17–39.

48. R. K. Webb, "Views of Unitarianism from Halley's Comet," *Transactions of the Unitarian Historical Society* 18 (April 1987): 180–94.

49. Iain McCalman, "Unrespectable Radicalism: Infidels and Pornography in Early Nineteenth-Century London," *Past and Present* 104 (August

1984): 92, and "Ultra-Radicalism and Convivial Debating Clubs in London, 1795–1838," *EHR* 102 (April 1987): 314–17.

50. G. F. A. Best, "The Constitutional Revolution, 1828–1832, and its Consequences for the Established Church," *Theology* 62 (1959): 226–34.

51. W. J. Fox, *The Providence of God in the Progress of Religious Liberty* (London, 1829).

CHAPTER 6

1. J. Walker, "The Censorship of the Press during the Reign of Charles II," n.s., *History* 34–35 (1949–50): 222; Frederick S. Siebert, *Freedom of the Press in England 1476–1776: The Rise and Decline of Government Controls* (Urbana, IL, 1952), 238 and no. 3; P. W. Thomas, *Sir John Berkenhead, 1617–1679* (Oxford, 1969).

2. Siebert, *Freedom of the Press*, passim; see Elizabeth L. Eisenstein, *The Printing Press as an Agent of Change. Communications and Cultural Transformations in Early Modern Europe* (Cambridge, 1979).

3. Cyprian Blagden, *The Stationers' Company* (London, 1960), 21–27, 75–77, 92–94 for points that follow.

4. *CSPD, 1661–62*, 57.

5. Ibid., 283; see Sir George Kitchin, *Sir Roger L'Estrange: A Contribution to the History of the Press in the Seventeenth Century* (London, 1913).

6. *CJ* 8:417.

7. Ibid. 8:425 (the king's speech) and 435; *LJ* 11:471–72.

8. Siebert, *Freedom of the Press*, 203 n. 1.

9. David Cressy, *Literacy & the Social Order Reading & Writing in Tudor & Stuart England* (Cambridge, 1980), 47; Siebert, *Freedom of the Press*, 191 n. 71.

10. Christopher Hill, *The World Turned Upside Down* (New York, 1972), 14, 301–2.

11. *SR* 5:428–33, 556, 577; 6:20.

12. David Ogg, *England in the Reigns of James II and William III* (Oxford, 1955), 510.

13. James Sutherland, *The Restoration Newspaper and its Development* (Cambridge, 1986), 3.

14. *CJ* 8:439, 636.   15. *SR* 5:428–33, 556, 577; 6:20.

16. Maurice Cranston, *John Locke A Biography* (London, 1957), 112.

17. Leonard W. Levy, *Emergence of a Free Press* (New York, 1985), 91–92.

18. John Milton, *Areopagitica. A Speech For The Liberty Of Unlicensed Printing*, in John Milton, *Paradise Lost and Selected Poetry and Prose*, ed. Northrop Frye (New York, 1962), 500, 501, 504.

19. Sir Roger L'Estrange, *Considerations and Proposals In Order to the Regulation of the Press* (London, 1663), A4, A4v, A5, 24–25, 31.

20. Walker, "Censorship of the Press during the Reign of Charles II," 229; R. R. Steele, ed., *A Bibliography of Royal Proclamations of Tudor and Stuart sovereigns and others*, 2 vols. (Oxford, 1910), 1:no. 3239; 2:no. 2198.

21. L'Estrange, *Considerations and Proposals*, 10; 11–24 for list of books to be banned.

22. *CSPD, 1663–64,* 240.

23. Collection of long-run newsletters includes FSL, "The Newdigate Newsletters, Addressed to Sir Richard Newdigate, 1st Bart., and to 2nd Bart., 1673/74–1715"; The Carl H. Pforzheimer Library, Bulstrodiana: Newsletters, Oct. 1667–June 1689 (a collection preserved by Sir Richard Bulstrode).

24. Siebert, *Freedom of the Press,* 250–52.

25. Phillip Hamburger, "The Development of the Law of Seditious Libel and the Control of the Press," *Stanford Law Review* 37 (Feb. 1985): 666–68 and passim; T. J. Crist, "Francis Smith and the Opposition Press in England, 1660–1688" (Ph.D. diss., Cambridge, 1977), 107.

26. Walker, "Censorship of the Press during the Reign of Charles II," 233–35. For Twyn's trial, *ST* 6:513–39. The other men were William Disney and William Anderton: ibid. 11:466–68 and 12:1246–67.

27. Hamburger, "The Development of the Law of Seditious Libel," 664–66, 690, 763 for list of trials.

28. *CSPD, 1660–70,* addenda, 175.

29. Ibid., 436–37; Siebert, *Freedom of the Press,* 247, 258–59.

30. Blagden, *The Stationers' Company,* 163–64.

31. Walker, "Censorship of the Press During the Reign of Charles II," 225, 227; *CSPD, 1660–1670,* addenda, 227, 502.

32. Leona Rostenberg, "Subversion and Repression: Robert Stephens, Messenger of the Press," in *Literary, Political . . . & Legal Publishing, Printing & Bookselling in England,* 2 vols. (New York, 1965), 2:359; Siebert, *Freedom of the Press,* 253.

33. Blagden, *The Stationers' Company,* 173.

34. PRO, PC 2/68, 229, 292.

35. L'Estrange, *Considerations and Proposals,* 10.

36. Richard Ashcraft, *Revolutionary Politics and Locke's Two Treatises of Government* (Princeton, 1986), 394–98 and chap. 8 passim.

37. Michel Foucault, *The Archeology of Knowledge,* trans. A. M. Sheridan Smith (New York, 1976); Annabel Patterson, *Censorship and Interpretation* (Madison, WI, 1984), esp. chap. 2.

38. Cressy, *Literacy and the Social Order,* 47 and n. 19.

39. Walker, "Censorship of the Press During the Reign of Charles II," 225.

40. Cressy, *Literacy & the Social Order,* 48, 72–75, 176, 189.

41. Roger Latham and Wm. Matthew, eds., *The Diary of Samuel Pepys,* 11 vols. (Berkeley, 1970–83), intro., 1:cxxvii; Tim Harris, *London Crowds in the Reign of Charles II* (Cambridge, 1987), 28–29, 99.

42. Aytoun Ellis, *The Penny Universities: A History of the Coffee-Houses* (London, 1956), 29, 45–47, 69.

43. David Ogg, *England in the Reign of Charles II,* 3d ed., 2 vols. (London, 1961), 1:101; Ellis, *The Penny Universities,* 91.

44. Steele, *Proclamations* 1:3622.

45. Harris, *London Crowds in the Reign of Charles II*, 28–29.

46. Sir Roger L'Estrange, *A Word concerning Libels and Libellers* (London, 1681), 12.

47. *London Gazette*, no. 2394.

48. Walker, "Censorship of the Press During the Reign of Charles II," 225.

49. Ibid., 235; *ST* 12:1247; L'Estrange, *Considerations and Proposals*, 6; Crist, "Francis Smith and the Opposition Press," 68, 102.

50. Leona Rostenberg, "The Catholic Reaction: Nathaniel Thompson, Protector of the Faith," in *Literary, Political . . . & Legal Publishing*, 2:328; John Dunton, *The Life and Errors of John Dunton*, ed. J. B. Nichols, 2 vols. (London, 1818), 1:244.

51. Rostenberg, "The Catholic Reaction," 341; and "English 'Rights & Liberties': Richard & Anne Baldwin, Whig Patriot Publishers," in *Literary, Political . . . & Legal Publishing* 2:415.

52. Blagden, *The Stationers' Company*, 173.

53. Harris, *London Crowds in the Reign of Charles II*, chaps. 5, 6.

54. *CJ* 9:577, 582, 600.

55. *CD* 8:292–95.

56. *CJ* 11:643, 708; Betty Kemp, *Votes and standing orders of the House of Commons* (House of Commons Library document 8, HMSO, London, 1971), 16–23, 28; Peter Fraser, *The Intelligence of the Secretaries of State and their Monopoly of Licensed News, 1660–1688* (Cambridge, 1956).

57. Crist, "Francis Smith and the Opposition Press," 96; Walker, "Censorship of the Press during the Reign of Charles II," 223.

58. Charles Blount, *A Just Vindication of Learning and the Liberty of the Press* (London, 1679), Proem, and 2, 3, 10, 14, 16.

59. William Lawrence, *Marriage by the Morall Law of God Vindicated* (London, 1680), 164–67.

60. PRO, PC 2/68, 60.

61. Ibid., PC 2/67, PC 2/68, 154; 179, 207, 212, 229, 231, 243, 289, 292, 311, 478, 528.

62. Ibid., PC 2/68, 236, 256; Crist, "Francis Smith and the Opposition Press," 111; Blagden, *The Stationers' Company*, 165.

63. PRO, PC 2/68, p. 314.

64. Anon, *A Dialogue Between Dick and Tom* (Licensed 18 Jan. 1689), 4; Blagden, *The Stationers' Company*, 170.

65. PRO, PC 2/68, p. 94; Blagden, *The Stationers' Company*, 163–64 n. 1.

66. Blagden, *The Stationers' Company*, 166–69, 174, 278.

67. PRO, PC 2/68, pp. 76, 94; Longleat, Coventry MSS, fols. 64–71.

68. PRO, PC 2/68, p. 257; Crist, "Francis Smith and the Opposition Press," 114, 116.

69. Sutherland, *The Restoration Newspapers*, 12–15, 49–55, 125, 156–57, 159–74; Crist, "Francis Smith and the Opposition Press," 106–7.

70. PRO, PC 2/68, p. 477.

71. Ibid., 496.

72. Ibid., 512–13.

73. Hamburger, "The Development of the Law of Seditious Libel and the Control of the Press," 688.

74. *CD* 8:60, 206–9.

75. Violet Jordain, ed., *Sir Roger L'Estrange Selections From The Observator (1681–1687)* publication no. 141, The Augustan Reprint Society (Los Angeles, 1970), i, ii, 1, 9.

76. For trial, see Lois G. Schwoerer, *Lady Rachel Russell "One of the Best of Women"* (Baltimore, 1988), chap. 6. For speech, see Lois G. Schwoerer, "William Lord Russell, the Making of a Martyr, 1683–1688," *JBS* 24 (1985): 41–47.

77. Narcissus Luttrell, *A Brief Historical Relation of State Affairs from September 1678 to April 1714*, 6 vols. (Oxford, 1867), 1:271; E. S. deBeer, ed. *The Diary of John Evelyn*, 6 vols. (London, 1955), 4:332; Bod.L, MSS 216, fol. 315.

78. Bedford RO London, HMC 41, 41A.

79. *CSPD, 1683* (J-S), 187, 190, 432; Luttrell, *Brief Relation* 1:271; Gilbert Burnet, *History of My Own Time* (Oxford, 1833), 2:391, 394; *DNB*.

80. *His Majesties Declaration to All His Loving Subjects, Concerning the Treasonable Conspiracy Against His Sacred Person and Government* (London, 1683); *CSPD, 1683* (J-S), 216.

81. *CSPD, James II* 1:no. 605, 1374, 1994; 2:no. 568.

82. *SR* 6:20; Lord Macaulay, *History of England From the Accession of James the Second*, ed. C. H. Firth, 6 vols. (London, 1913–15), 1:516.

83. John Miller, *Popery and Politics in England 1660–1688* (Cambridge, 1973), 255–57.

84. Sutherland, *The Restoration Newspaper*, 22.

85. Sir George Duckett, ed., *Penal Laws and Test Act: Questions Touching Their Repeal Propounded in 1687–88 by James II* (London, 1882), 195, 196, 222–23; Nottingham University Library, Portland MSS, PwA 2141, 2143, 2145, 2147, 2159, 2161, 2167; FSL, "Letter of James Frazer to Sir Robert Southwell," V6, 287, pp. 57–60.

86. See Lois G Schwoerer, "Propaganda in the Revolution of 1688–89," *AHR* 82 (1977): 843–74.

87. Portland MSS, PwA 2124e.

88. For a corrected draft, Koninklijk Huisarchief, Manifest van den Koning Willem III aan de Engelsche Natie, 1688, Oct. 10 (N.S.), Minuut van Gilbert Burnet, IX, a. 15 (old number 2638); see also Burnet, *History* 3:210, 300, 308; H. C. Foxcroft, *A Supplement to Burnet's History of My Own Time* (Oxford, 1902), 495, 522.

89. BL, Add. MSS 41,816, fol. 249.

90. Burnet, *History* 3:301, 302; Foxcroft, *A Supplement to Burnet's History*, 285; N. Japikse, ed., *Correspondentie van Willem III en van Hans Willelm Bentinck, Eersten Graaf van Portland* ('s-Gravenhage, 1928), RGP, Kleine Series, 24:618–19.

91. Burnet, *History* 3:301; John Banks, *History of the Life and Reign of William III* (London, 1744), 207.

92. FSL, "Newdigate Newsletters," L.C. 1938; Sir Henry Ellis, ed., *Original Letters, Illustrative of English History*, 3d ser., 4 vols. (London, 1827), 2:313.

93. *An Enquiry into the Present State of Affairs; Reflections on a Paper intituled His Majesty's Reasons for withdrawing himself from Rochester; A Review of the Reflections on the Prince of Orange's Declaration.*

94. J. S. Clarke, *The Life of James the Second, King of England, etc.*, 2 vols. (London, 1816), 2:274; *His Majesties Most Gratious Declaration to all His Loving Subjects* (St. Germain, 1693); *A Speech of a Commoner to a Fellow Commoner*, in *Somers Tracts* 9:305.

95. Harris, *London Crowds in the Reign of Charles II*, 106–7, 116, 124–25.

96. David Kunzel, *The Early Comic Strip: Narrative Strips and Picture Stories in the European Broadsheet from c. 1450 to 1825* (Berkeley, 1973), 137, 144, 145; Dorothy George, *English Political Caricature to 1792: A Study of Opinion and Propaganda* (Oxford, 1959), 1:3; 1:52, 60, 62, 64; Harris, *London Crowds*, 102.

97. George W. Agar-Ellis, first baron Dover, ed., *The Ellis Correspondence*, 2 vols. (London, 1831), 2:243; HMC, *Le Fleming MSS*, 215; *London Gazette*, no. 2394; *A Dialogue between Dick and Tom*, 4.

98. *London Gazette*, no. 2396; Dover, ed., *Ellis Correspondence* 2:272–73.

99. The Carl H. Pforzheimer Library, Bulstrodiana: Newsletters, vol. 12, 5 Nov. 1688, 2d letter; Dover, ed., *Ellis Correspondence* 2:227–73, 279.

100. *Some Reflections Upon his Highness the Prince of Oranges Declaration*, 1–2. In print by 13 Nov., BL, Add. MSS 34,510, 4:246; *Animadversions*, 61.

101. *London Intelligence*, nos. 7 and 8, 2–5 and 5–9 Feb. 1689; *A Dialogue between Dick and Tom*, 10.

102. Dr. Williams's Library, Roger Morrice, "Entr'ing Book, Being an Historical Register of Occurrences from April 1677, to April 1691" 2:449. I used a photocopy.

103. *A Short History of the Convention; or, New Christ'ned Parliament* (London, by 29 Apr. 1689).

104. Jeremy Collier, *Vindiciae Juris Regii* (London, 1689), 29.

105. Morrice, "Entr'ing Book" 2:437. See Lois G. Schwoerer, "Press and Parliament in the Revolution of 1689," *HJ* 20 (1977): 545–67.

106. *CD* 9:142–47 for the debate.

107. *CJ* 10:45; *CD* 9:273.

108. *CJ* 10:14, 15, 18, 19, 20; Bod.L, MSS Rawlinson D 1079, fol. 12v.

109. Schwoerer, "Press and Parliament in the Revolution of 1689," 549–56.

110. *CD* 9:38, cf. 51, 63, 90.

111. *LJ* 13:42, 49, 54, 55, 60, 61, 64, 65, 122; Schwoerer, "Press and Parliament in the Revolution of 1689," 564–65.

112. Schwoerer, "Press and Parliament in the Revolution of 1689," 565–66.

113. Milton's *Areopagitica* appeared in the Stationer's Register under date of 30 Jan. 1689 but there is not evidence that it was printed. See H. R. Plomer, ed., *Transcript of the Registers of the Worshipful Company of Stationers: from 1640–1708*, 3 vols. (London, 1913–14), 3:345.

114. Edmond Hickeringill, *A Speech Without-Doors: Or Some Modest Inquiries* (London, 1689), 32, 34; James Turner, *The Dolphin's Skin. Six Studies in Eccentricity* (London, 1956); Mark Goldie, "The Revolution of 1689 and the Structure of Political Argument," *Bulletin of Research in the Humanities* 83 (New York, 1980): 478.

115. Hamburger, "The Development of the law of Seditious Libel and the Control of the Press," 714 n. 161.

116. Agnes Strickland, *Lives of the Queens of England*, 8 vols. (London, 1860), 7:369–70; Macaulay, *History of England* 7:472–75.

117. *Some Considerations . . . relating to the bill now before that House for preventing licentiousness of the Press* (London, 1693), a broadside; *Reasons humbly offered to be considered before the Act for Printing be renewed* (n.d., Dec. 1692[?]), 1–4.

118. Raymond Astbury, "The Renewal of the Licensing Act in 1693 and its Lapse in 1695," *The Library* 33, 4 (Dec. 1978): 306.

119. E. S. de Beer, ed., *The Correspondence of John Locke*, 8 vols. (Oxford, 1976–89), 4:614–15; 5:786, 788–91.

120. Charles Blount, *Reasons Humbly offered for the Liberty of Unlicens'd Printing* (London, 17 Jan. 1693), 8.

CHAPTER 7

1. Albert Goodwin, *The Friends of Liberty. The English democratic movement in the age of the French revolution* (London, 1979), 85–87; *An abstract of the history and proceedings of the Revolution Society in London* (1789), 7–15; Joseph Towers, *An oration delivered at the London Tavern on the fourth of November 1788* (1788), the advertisement.

2. Quentin Skinner, "The Principles and Practice of Opposition: The Case of Bolingbroke versus Walpole," in Neil McKendrick, ed., *Historical Perspectives. Studies in English Thought and Society in Honour of J. H. Plumb* (London, 1974), 98–127; Donald Thomas, "Press Prosecutions of the Eighteenth and Nineteenth Centuries: The Evidence of King's Bench Indictments," *The Library*, 5th ser., 32 (1977): 315–32.

3. Jeremy Black, *The English Press in the Eighteenth Century* (London & Sydney, 1987), 1–2.

4. Lois G. Schwoerer, "Press and Parliament in the Revolution of 1689," *HJ* 20(1977): 545–67.

5. Lois G. Schwoerer, "Propaganda in the revolution of 1688–1689," *AHR* 82 (Oct. 1977): 859; Raymond Astbury, "The Renewal of the Licensing Act in 1693 and its Lapse in 1695," *The Library*, 5th ser., 33 (1978): 298–99, 306–7.

6. Astbury, "Renewal of the Licensing Act," 300.

7. Ibid., 300–304; *LJ* 15:280.

8. *LJ* 15:280.

9. W. C. Costin and J. S. Watson, *The Law and the Working of the Constitution*, 2 vols. (London, 1952), 1:29.

10. Astbury, "Renewal of the Licensing Act," 309–11.

11. Ibid., 312–13.

12. Ibid., 314–15; Mark A. Thomson, *A Constitutional History of England, 1642 to 1801* (London, 1938), 298.

13. Astbury, "Renewal of the Licensing Act," 316.

14. T. B. Macaulay, *History of England from the Accession of James II*, 4 vols. (Everyman Library, London, 1966), 3:533–35; Thomson, *Constitutional History*, 299; [Charles Blount], *Reasons humbly offered for the liberty of unlicensed printing* (London, 1693), 5–6.

15. H. A. Enno van Gelder, *Getemperde vrijheid (Historische studies uitgegeven vanwege het Instituut voor Geschiedenis der Rijksuniversiteit te Utrecht)* 26 (Groningen, 1972): 151–94.

16. M. Tindal, *A discourse for the liberty of the press* (London, 1698).

17. "A letter to a Convocation man, concerning the rights, powers and privileges of that body," *Somers Tracts*, 2d ed., 9 (London, 1813): 411–16; Francis Gregory, *A modest plea for the due regulation of the press* (London, 1698), passim; Robert E. Sullivan, *John Toland and the Deist Controversy: A study in adaptations* (Cambridge, MA, and London, 1982), 210.

18. David Hayton, "Moral Reform and Country Politics in the Late Seventeenth-Century," *Past and Present* 128 (August 1990): 48–91.

19. H. Walpole, *A letter to the Whigs. Occasioned by The letter to the Tories* (London, 1747), 6–7; *Areopagitica. With a preface by another hand* (London, 1738): the preface argued that "a free Protestant country without the liberty of the press" was "a contradiction in terms, it is free slavery, or inchained liberty"; *The Gentleman's Magazine* 38 (London, 1738): 35–36; Leonard W. Levy, *Freedom of Speech and Press in Early American History* (New York, 1963), 133–36.

20. Thomson, *Constitutional History*, 300; Fred S. Siebert, "Taxes on Publication in England in the Eighteenth Century," *Journalism Quarterly* 21 (1944): 12–13; John Feather, "The Book Trade in Politics: The Making of the Copyright Act of 1710," *Publishing History* 8 (1980): 21–22.

21. House of Lords Manuscripts, n.s., 3. *The Manuscripts of the House of Lords, 1697–1699* (London, 1905), 271.

22. A. Boyer, *The history of the life and reign of Queen Anne* (London, 1722), 552; *The Craftsman's doctrine and practice of the liberty of the press* (London, 1732), 8–17.

23. 10 Annae, c. 19, in D. Pickering, ed., *Statutes at Large*, 46 vols. (Cambridge, 1762–1807), 12:369–77. See also the publications of John Feather, "The Book Trade in Politics," 19–44; "The English book trade and the law 1695–1799," *Publishing History* 12 (1982): 56–58; and *The Provincial Book Trade in the Eighteenth Century* (Cambridge, 1983), 1–8.

24. The tables provided by Ian Maxted, *The London Book Trades, 1775–1800. A Preliminary Checklist of Members* (London, 1977), xxxi (Table II—Output of books 1700–1826), tentatively suggest that in the 1740s stamped pamphlets amounted to over three times the numbers of books published.

25. Laurence Hanson, *Government and the Press 1695–1763* (London, 1936), 11; Michael Harris, "The Structure, Ownership and Control of the Press, 1620–1780," in David Boyce, James Curran, and Pauline Wingate, eds., *Newspaper History from the Seventeenth Century to the Present Day* (London/Beverly Hills, 1978), 84; J. A. Downie, *Robert Harley and the Press. Propaganda and Public Opinion in the Age of Swift and Defoe* (Cambridge, 1979), 158, 161; and his "The Development of the Political Press," in Clyve Jones, ed., *Britain in the First Age of Party, 1680–1750: Essays Presented to Geoffrey Holmes* (London, 1987), 117–18; Henry L. Snyder, "The Circulation of Newspapers in the Reign of Queen Anne," *The Library*, 5th ser., 23 (1968): 219; James Sutherland, *The Restoration Newspaper and Its Development* (Cambridge, 1986), 32; Siebert, "Taxes on Publication," 17.

26. A. Boyer, *History of Queen Anne*, 552–53.

27. E. S. De Beer, "The English Newspapers from 1695 to 1702," in Ragnhild Hatton and J. S. Bromley, eds., *William III and Louis XIV* (Liverpool, 1968), 122; R. B. Walker, "The Newspaper Press in the Reign of William III," *HJ* 17 (1974): 697.

28. G. A. Cranfield, *The Development of the Provincial Newspapers, 1700–1760* (Oxford, 1962), 13–22.

29. P. D. G. Thomas, *British Politics and the Stamp Act Crisis* (Oxford, 1975), 35, 69.

30. F. S. Siebert, *Freedom of the Press in England, 1476–1776* (Urbana, IL, 1952), 314; Snyder, "Circulation of Newspapers," 215; Harris, "The Structure, Ownership and Control," 84–85; Downie, *Robert Harley*, 159; Cranfield, *Development of Provincial Newspapers*, 14–16; J. M. Price, "A note on the circulation of the London Press," *BIHR* 31 (1958): 215–23; R. M. Wiles, *Freshest Advices: Early Provincial Newspapers in England* (Columbus, 1965), 17–18.

31. 3 Geo. 1, c. 9, *Statutes at Large* 13 (1724): 380–87.

32. 2 Geo. 1, c. 8, *Statutes at Large* 15 (1765): 200–201; *Government and the press*, 135–38; Siebert, "Taxes on publications," 19; M. Harris, *The London Newspaper Press, 1725–1746* (Ph.D. diss., London, 1973), 10.

33. Cranfield, *Development of Provincial Newspapers*, 20, 225–26; Wiles, *Freshest Advices*, 20–22.

34. 16 Geo. 2, c. 26, *Statutes at Large* 18: 132–36; Harris, *London Newspaper Press*, 34; T. N. Brushfield, *The Life and Bibliography of Andrew Brice, Author and Journalist* (n.p., 1888), 39–40.

35. *Reasons humbly offer'd to the parliament in behalf of several persons concern'd in paper-making, printing and publishing the half penny newspapers, against the Bill now depending, for laying a penny stamp upon every whole sheet, and a half penny stamp upon every half sheet of all newspapers* (London, n.d.); Defoe, *The Review* 8:671, no. 2, 29 Mar. 1711.

36. *The Craftsman* (London, 1731), 1:11, 9 Dec. 1726; Wiles, *Freshest Advices*, 21.

37. Edmund S. Morgan, ed., *Prologue to Revolution: Sources and Documents on the Stamp Act Crisis, 1764–1766* (New York, 1959), 60.

38. Levy, *Freedom of Speech*, 20, 46–48; Clyde Augustus Duniway, *The Development of Freedom of the Press in Massachusetts* (New York, 1906), 101–2, 115.

39. Gregory, *A modest plea for regulations*, 19; Defoe, *The Review* 2:423–24, no. 106; ibid. 6:363, no. 91, and 403, no. 101; *Cato's Letters: or Essays on Liberty, Civil and Religious*, 4 vols. (London, 1733), 3:299, no. 100, and 304, no. 101; *The Craftsman* (1731) 1:7–8, 10; *ST* 17 (Trial of Richard Francklin, 1731): 665, 670–71, 675; Black, *The English Press*, 166; Anna Janney de Armond, *Andrew Bradford: Colonial Journalist* (Newark, DE, 1949), 95.

40. *Cato's Letters* 1:100, no. 15; ibid. 1:252–53, no. 32; ibid. 3:293–99, and 302–5, no. 101; *Common Sense*, 338–40, 351–52; *The independent Briton* (London, 1742), 13–14, 16; [H. Walpole], *A letter to the Whigs*, 25; Black, *The English press*, 127.

41. Sir William Blackstone, *Commentaries on the Laws of England*, 5th ed., 4 vols. (Oxford, 1773), 4:151–52.

42. A. V. Dicey, *Introduction to the Study of the Law of the Constitution* (London, 1902), 234–65.

43. Henri-Jean Martin, *Livre, pouvoir et société à Paris au XVIIe siècle 1598–1701*, 2 vols. (Paris, 1969), 2:762–69; van Gelder, *Getemperde Vrijheid*, 186–88; S. Groenveld, "The Mecca of Authors? States Assemblies and Censorship in the seventeenth-century Dutch Republic," in A. C. Duke and C. A. Tamse, eds., *Too mighty to be free. Censorship and the press in Britain and The Netherlands* (Zutphen, 1987), 72; Maria Dolores Saiz, *Historia del periodismo en Espana. I. El siglo 18* (Madrid, 1983): 94–103.

44. Gilles Feyel, *La "Gazette" en province à travers ses réimpressions 1631–1752* (Amsterdam & Maarssen, 1982), 9–13.

45. Ibid., passim.

46. Jacques Wagner, *Marmontel journaliste et le Mercure de France (1725–1761)* (Grenoble, 1975), 15.

47. D. Hume, *Essays, moral and political* (Edinburgh, 1741), 9; J. L. de Lolme, *The constitution of England, or an account of the English government* (London, 1775), 277–92; G. C. Gibbs, "Newspapers, Parliament, and Foreign Policy in the Age of Stanhope and Walpole," in *Mélanges offerts à G. Jacquemyns* (Bruxelles, 1968), 296 and n. 11.

48. 7 & 8 Will. 3, c. 3; Costin & Watson, *Law and Working of the Constitution* 1:80–83.

49. 4 & 5 Annae., c. 20; Costin and Watson, *Law and Working of the Constitution* 1:111–12.

50. R. J. Goulden, "Vox Populi, Vox Dei; Charles Delafaye's Paperchase," *The Book Collector* 28 (Autumn 1979): 368–90.

51. W. H. Trapnell, "Who Thomas Woolston was," *British Journal for Eighteenth-Century Studies* 11 (1988): 143–58; Thomson, *Constitutional History*, 278; Norman Sykes, *Edmund Gibson Bishop of London. A Study in Politics and Religion in the Eighteenth Century* (London, 1926), 256–61; and his *William Wake, Archbishop of Canterbury, 1657–1737*, 2 vols. (Cambridge, 1957), 2:170–71, 264–65; Philip C. Yorke, *The Life and Correspondence of Philip Yorke, Earl of Hardwicke*, 3 vols. (Cambridge, 1913), 1: 80–81; J. C. D. Clarke, *English Society 1688–1832* (Cambridge, 1985), 284–88.

52. *A report of all the cases determined by Sir John Holt, Knt., from 1688–1710* (London, 1738), 425–26; David Foxon, *Libertine Literature in England, 1660–1745* (London, 1964), 49–50; Feather, "The English Book Trade," 60–61.

53. Yorke, *Life of Philip Yorke* 1:81–82; Peter Gay, *The enlightenment: an Interpretation* (London, 1969), 202–3.

54. Foxon, *Libertine Literature*, 54; Thomas, *British Politics and the Stamp Act Crisis*, 320–22.

55. J. Towers, *An enquiry into the extent of the power of juries on trials . . . for publishing seditious . . . libels* (London, 1785), 6–7.

56. Black, *The English Press*, 171.

57. Thomas Andrew Green, *Verdict according to Conscience: Perspectives on the English Criminal Trial Jury, 1200–1800* (Chicago, 1988), 318, 337; *ST* 17:668–70.

58. Green, *Verdict according to Conscience*, 236, 254, 272, 320–21; *A faithful report of a genuine debate concerning the liberty of the press* (London, 1740), 17.

59. Green, *Verdict according to Conscience*, 282, 322, 342–44; Robert C. Palmer, "Conscience and the Law: The English Criminal Jury," *Michigan Law Review* 84:788–99; J. M. Beattie, *Crime and the Courts in England, 1660–1800* (Oxford, 1986), 415, 420, 424, 427; *ST* 17:671, 674; Levy, *Freedom of Speech*, 119; Thomson, *Constitutional History*, 429.

60. Towers, *An enquiry into the extent of the power of juries*, 17–21.

61. Green, *Verdict according to Conscience*, 353–54; P. J. Hyland, "Liberty and Libel: Government and the Press during the Succession Crisis in

Britain, 1712–1716," *EHR* 101 (1986): 863–88; G. C. Gibbs, "Government and the English press, 1695 to the Middle of the Eighteenth Century," in Duke and Tamse, eds., *Too Mighty to be free*, 95.

62. Thomson, *Constitutional History*, 412–13; Green, *Verdict according to Conscience*, 271, 322; Beattie, *Crime and the Courts*, 379, 386–89.

63. *ST* 17:671; *The Gentleman's Magazine* (1731), 534.

64. *An historical view of the principles, character, persons etc., of political writers in Great Britain* (London, 1740), 13; *The Danverian history of the affairs of Europe for the memorable year 1731* (London, 1732), 77–79, 80.

65. Gibbs, "Government and the English press," 95.

66. *A collection of miscellany letters selected out of Mist's Weekly Journal*, 4 vols. (London, 1722–27), 1:14, 2:9; Charles Ribley Gillett, *Burned books: Neglected Chapters in British History and Literature*, 2 vols. (New York, 1932), 1:588–89; Goulden, *Vox Populi, Vox Dei*, 372, 383–88; G. C. Gibbs, "The Contribution of Abel Boyer to Contemporary History in England in the Early Eighteenth Century," in A. C. Duke and C. A. Tamse, eds., *Clio's Mirror: Historiography in Britain and the Netherlands* (Zutphen, 1985), 97; *The Craftsman's doctrine*, 25–26.

67. John Brewer, "Commercialization and Politics," in *The Birth of a Consumer Society. The Commercialization of Eighteenth-Century England* (Bloomington, IN, 1982), 209, 216, 259; Norma Landau, *The Justices of the Peace, 1679–1760* (Berkeley and London, 1984) 23–24.

68. Black, *The English Press*, 160–162.

69. Ibid., 136; Beattie, *Crime and the Courts*, 353–54; Cranfield, *Development of Provincial Newspapers*, 143, 145.

70. H. Hale Bellott, "Parliamentary Printing, 1660–1837," *BIHR* 11 (1933–34): 86–88.

71. M. F. Bond, ed., *The Manuscripts of the House of Lords*, n.s., vol. 10, 1712–14 (London, 1953): xliv, 21.

72. De Beer, "The English Newspapers, 1695 to 1702," 118–19.

73. *CJ* 18:653–54; A. Boyer, *The Political State of Great Britain*, 60 vols. (London, 1711–40), 14:587, 589–90.

74. James E. Thorold Rogers, *A Complete Collection of the Protests of the Lords*, 3 vols. (Oxford, 1875), 1:xxi, xxvii, xxviii, xliii–li; Boyer, *Political State of Great Britain* 23:262–63; Charles Bechdolt Realey, *The Early Opposition to Sir Robert Walpole, 1720–1727* (Lawrence, KS, 1931), 84–85.

75. David Hayton and Clyve Jones, eds., *A Register of Parliamentary Lists 1660–1761* (Leicester, 1979), 16, 36.

76. Frances Harris, "Paper-round: The Distribution of Whig Propaganda in 1710," *Factotum* 9 (1980): 12–13.

77. BL, Add. MS. 37382, fol. 291v (Whitworth Papers), Whitworth to Delafaye 20–31 Dec. 1720.

78. Gibbs, "The Contribution of Abel Boyer," 87–108 and especially 96–97.

79. Ibid., 98–102.

80. Gibbs, "Government and the English Press," 100.

81. Benjamin Beard Hoover, *Samuel Johnson's Parliamentary Reporting: Debates in the Senate of Lilliput* (Berkeley 1953), 16–19.

82. Mary Ransome, "The Reliability of Contemporary Reporting of the Debates of the House of Commons, 1727–1741," *BIHR* 19 (1942): 68.

83. Cranfield, *Development of Provincial Newspapers*, 31, 122, 156–59; *CJ* 19:43, 45; 21:85, 99, 104, 108, 115, 117, 127, 227, 238, 249, 263.

84. *CJ* 14:207–8, 270; 19:43, 45; 20:99, 143; 21:85, 99, 104, 227, 238, 249, 263; Boyer, *Political State of Great Britain* 39:151–52.

85. Boyer, *Political State of Great Britain* 37:iii–vii; Hoover, *Samuel Johnson's Parliamentary Reporting*, 9–11.

86. *PH* 10, cols. 800–811; Siebert, *Freedom of the Press*, 279–88, 346–49.

87. Clyve Jones and Geoffrey Holmes, eds., *The London Diaries of William Nicolson Bishop of Carlisle 1702–1718*, (Oxford, 1985) 86.

88. BL, Burney Collection; *The weekly Journal or Saturday's Post*, 7 Dec. 1717.

89. Hoover, *Samuel Johnson's Parliamentary Reporting*, 14.

90. P. D. G. Thomas, "John Wilkes and the Freedom of the Press (1771)," *BIHR* 33 (1960): 86–98; and his "The Beginning of Parliamentary Reporting in Newspapers, 1768–1774," *EHR* 74 (1959): 623–36.

91. P. D. G. Thomas, *The House of Commons in the Eighteenth Century* (Oxford, 1971), 141–48; A. Aspinall, "The Reporting and Publishing of the House of Commons' Debates, 1771–1834," in R. Pares and A. J. P. Taylor, eds., *Essays Presented to Sir Lewis Namier* (London, 1956), 227–57.

92. Costin and Watson, *Law and Working of the Constitution* 1:285.

93. PRO, State Papers Domestic, SP 44/79a, 312–13.

94. Downie, *Robert Harley and the Press*, 131, 137–38, 142, 193; and his "The Conduct of the Allies—the Question of Influence," in C. T. Brobyn, ed., *The Art of Jonathan Swift* (London, 1978), 118–20.

95. Downie, *Robert Harley and the Press*, 161; C. B. Realey, *The London Journal and Its Authors, 1720–1723* (Lawrence, KS, 1935), passim.

96. Michael Harris, "Print and Politics in the Age of Walpole," in Jeremy Black, ed., *Britain in the Age of Walpole* (London, 1984), 192, 197–202; and his "The Structure, Ownership and Control of the Press, 1620–1780," 89, 95.

97. G. C. Gibbs, "Parliament and Foreign Policy in the Age of Stanhope and Walpole," in *Essays in Eighteenth-Century History from the English Historical Review Arranged by Rosalind Mitchinson* (London, 1966), 342; Boyer, *Political State of Great Britain* 30 (1717): 111.

98. Gibbs, "Parliament and Foreign Policy," 343–45.

99. Robert Moore, *A Checklist of the Writings of Daniel Defoe* (Hamden, 1971); John Harris, "Manuscript Dates on Pamphlets Collected by Thomas Bowdler II: With examples from Defoe," *The Book Collector*, Summer 1981:225–31.

100. John Brewer, *Party Ideology and Popular Politics at the Accession of George III* (Cambridge, 1976), 143.

101. Harris, "Print and Politics," 203–10.

102. David Cressy, "Illiteracy in England, 1530–1730," *HJ* 20 (1977): 1–23.

103. Gibbs, "Newspapers, Parliament and Foreign Policy in the Age of Stanhope and Walpole," 298; Black, *The English Press in the Eighteenth Century*, 106.

104. *A collection of miscellany letters* 2:256; *Arguments relating to a restraint upon the press*, 24–25.

105. BL, Burney Collection; *The Daily Advertiser*, 3 Feb. 1731; *The case between the proprietors of newspapers and the subscribing coffee-men fairly stated, being remarks on their case lately published* (London, 1729); *The case of the coffee-men of London and Westminster* (London, 1729).

106. *A collection of miscellany letters* 1:157; 2:255.

107. Alan Everitt, "The English Urban Inn, 1560–1760," in Everitt, ed., *Perspectives in English Urban History* (London, 1973), 94, 101–2, 111; Angus McInnes, *The English Town, 1660–1760* (London, 1980), 14–15; J. A. Chartres, "The Capital's Provincial Eyes: London's Inns in the Early Eighteenth Century," *The London Journal* 3 (1977): 32.

108. Black, *The English Press in the Eighteenth Century*, 105; *The Danverian history of the affairs of Europe for the memorable year 1731* (London, 1732), 80–81; J. R. Sutherland, "The Circulation of Newspapers and Literary Periodicals, 1700–1730," *Library*, 4th ser., 15 (1935): 110–24; J. M. Price, "A Note on the Circulation of the London Press."

109. BL, Burney Collection, *St. James's Journal*, 1 Dec. 1722; *A collection of miscellany letters* 2:257.

110. 8 Geo. 2, c. 13, *Statutes at Large* 16 (1765): 507–9.

111. Paul Langford, *Walpole and the Robinocracy* (Cambridge, 1986), 23–26.

112. Herbert M. Atherton, *Political Prints in the Age of Hogarth*, (Oxford, 1974) 65, 71.

113. Ibid., 62–65; Langford, *Walpole and the Robinocracy*, 27–30; John Brewer, *The Common People and Politics, 1750–1790* (Cambridge, 1986), 32–33, 41–47; Roy Porter, "Seeing the Past," *Past and Present* 118 (1988): 186–205; Charles Press, "The Georgian Political Print and Democratic Institutions," *Comparative Studies in Society and History* 19 (1977): 216–38.

114. Walker, "The Newspaper Press in the Reign of William III," 703; Gibbs, "Newspapers, Parliament and Foreign Policy," 298–300, 302–4; Sutherland, *The Restoration Newspaper*, 143–45.

115. Gibbs, "Newspapers, Parliament and Foreign Policy," 304–13; G. C. Gibbs, "The Revolution in Foreign Policy," in Geoffrey Holmes, ed., *Britain after the Glorious Revolution 1689–1714* (London, 1969), 74.

116. Ibid., 72–76; G. C. Gibbs, "Laying Treaties before Parliament in the

Eighteenth Century," in Ragnhild Hatton and M. S. Anderson, eds., *Studies in Diplomatic History* (London, 1970), 116–37.

117. Geoffrey Holmes, *The Electorate and the National Will in the First Age of Party* (Lancaster, 1976), 14–23.

118. P. Langford, *The Excise Crisis. Society and Politics in the Age of Walpole* (Oxford, 1975), esp. 44–57, 104–18; E. R. Turner, "The Excise Scheme of 1733," in *Essays in Eighteenth-Century History . . . Arranged by Rosalind Mitchinson*, 42–44; Jacob M. Price, "The Excise Revisited: The Administrative and Colonial Dimensions of a Parliamentary Crisis," in Stephen B. Baxter, ed., *England's Rise to Greatness 1660–1763* (Berkeley, 1983), 303–4.

119. Langford, *The Excise Crisis*, 47 and app. A; Price, "The Excise Revisited," 293, 317.

120. *A report from the Committee of Secrecy Appointed to Enquire into the Conduct of Robert Earl of Oxford* (London, 1742).

121. Gibbs, "Parliament and Foreign Policy," 343; Harris, "Print and Politics in the Age of Walpole," 199–201.

122. Gibbs, "Parliament and Foreign Policy," 344.

123. Gary Stuart de Krey, *A Fractured Society* (Oxford, 1985), 214.

124. Ibid., 213–18, 220–22.

125. Ibid., 150–53; Harris, "Print and politics," 206–7; Linda Colley, *In Defiance of Oligarchy: The Tory Party 1714–1760* (Cambridge, 1982), 78.

126. Gay, *The Enlightenment*, 73–74, 451, 454.

127. *The North Briton*, no. 1, Sat. 5 June 1762.

128. John Wilkes, *The History of England from the Revolution to the Accession of the Brunswick Line* (London, 1768), 19–20.

CHAPTER 8

1. As quoted in William A. Speck, *Stability and Strife* (Cambridge, MA 1977), 20. See also John Beattie, *Crime and the Courts in England, 1660–1800* (Princeton, 1986), 331–32.

2. As quoted in Roy Porter, *English Society in the Eighteenth Century*, 2d ed. (London, 1990), 253–54. And see "Notes sur L'Angleterre," *Oeuvres Completes de Montesquieu*, ed. Andre Masson, 3 (Paris, 1955): 283–93.

3. Beattie, *Crime and the Courts*, 197; J. Churton Collins, *Voltaire, Montesquieu and Rousseau in England* (London, 1908), 88–89.

4. Especially H. T. Dickinson, *Liberty and Property* (London, 1977); J. A. W. Gunn, *Beyond Liberty and Property* (Kingston, ON, 1983). Also Anne Pallister, *Magna Carta* (Oxford, 1971); John Barrell, *The Political Theory of Painting from Reynolds to Hazlitt* (New Haven, 1986); Michael Meehan, *Liberty and Poetics in Eighteenth Century England* (London, 1986).

5. *ST* 14:854; *PH* 5:401. And see E. Cruickshanks, "*Ashby* v. *White*:

the Case of the Men of Aylesbury, 1701–1704," in *Party and Management in Parliament, 1660–1784*, ed. Clyve Jones (New York, 1984), 87–106.

6. E. P. Thompson, "The Moral Economy of the English Crowd in the Eighteenth Century," *Past and Present* 50 (1971): 76–136. Compare D. Williams, "Morals, Markets and the English Crowd in 1766," ibid. 104 (1984): 56–73; J. Stevenson, "The 'Moral Economy' of the English Crowd: Myth and Reality," in *Order and Disorder in Early Modern England*, ed. A. Fletcher and J. Stevenson (Cambridge, 1985), 218–38.

7. Quoted in Thompson, "Moral Economy," 86. Compare I. Hont and M. Ignatieff, "Needs and Justice in the *Wealth of Nations*: An Introductory Survey," in *Wealth and Virtue*, ed. I. Hont and M. Ignatieff (Cambridge, 1983), esp. 14–15.

8. W. M. Wiecek, "*Somerset*: Lord Mansfield and the Legitimacy of Slavery in the Anglo-American World," *University of Chicago Law Review* 42 (1974): 86–146, Holt quotation at 92; *The Present State of Great Britain*, 3d ed. (1718), 186, and 11th ed. (1748), 173; N. A. M. Rodger, *The Wooden World* (London, 1986), 161.

9. J. Oldham, "New Light on Mansfield and Slavery," *JBS* 27 (1988): 45–68.

10. C. Brough Macpherson, *The Political Theory of Possessive Individualism* (Oxford, 1962), 194–262. Compare I. Hont, "Needs and Justice," 35–41; Alan Ryan, *Property and Political Theory* (Oxford, 1984), 14–48; Richard Ashcraft, *Locke's Two Treatises of Government* (London, 1987), esp. 167–73, 301–2.

11. P. Laslett, "The English Revolution and Locke's *Two Treatises of Government*," *CHJ* 12 (1956): 40–55; Richard Ashcraft, *Revolutionary Politics & Locke's "Two Treatises of Government"* (Princeton, 1986); R. Ashcraft and M. M. Goldsmith, "Locke, Revolution Principles and the Formation of Whig Ideology," *HJ* 26 (1983): 773–800.

12. Henry Horwitz, *Parliament, Policy and Politics in the Reign of William III* (Manchester, 1977); H. Horwitz, "1689 (and All That)," *Parliamentary History* 6 (1987): 23–32.

13. Isaiah Berlin, "Two Concepts of Liberty" in his *Four Essays on Liberty* (Oxford, 1969), 118–72.

14. William Blackstone, *Commentaries on the Laws of England* (first ed. in facsimile, Chicago, 1979), 1:316.

15. P. G. M. Dickson, *The Financial Revolution in England* (London, 1967), 10, 262–70; Gary S. De Krey, *A Fractured Society* (Oxford, 1985), 106–11.

16. Geoffrey Holmes, *Augustan England* (London, 1982), 264–65, 280, 254–56. And see John Brewer, *The Sinews of Power* (New York, 1989), esp. 66–67.

17. J. G. A. Pocock, "Authority and Property: The Question of Liberal Origins," in his *Virtue, Commerce and History* (Cambridge, 1985), 69, 68.

See also "The Mobility of Property and the Rise of Eighteenth-Century Sociology," in ibid., 108–09; Pocock, "Early Modern Capitalism, the Augustan Perception," in *Feudalism, Capitalism and Beyond*, ed. E. Kamenka and R. S. Neale (London, 1975), 70–72.

18. In addition to the works cited in note 17, see J. G. A. Pocock, *The Machiavellian Moment* (Princeton, 1975), chaps. 11–13; John Sekora, *Luxury: the Concept in Western Thought, Eden to Smollett* (Baltimore, 1977).

19. Pocock, "Authority and Property," 68–69.

20. For a quite different approach, with a stress on confessional divisions, see Jonathan Clark, *English Society, 1688–1832* (Cambridge, 1986), chaps. 3–5. And see J. Innes, "Jonathan Clark, Social History and England's 'Ancien Regime'," *Past and Present* 114 (1987): 165–200; J. Clark, *ibid.* 114 (1987): 195–207.

21. J. G. A. Pocock, "Machiavelli, Harrington, and English Political Ideologies in the Eighteenth Century," *William & Mary Quarterly* 22 (1965): 578. And see Isaac Kramnick, *Bolingbroke and his Circle: the Politics of Nostalgia in the Age of Walpole* (Cambridge, MA, 1968), esp. 122–24; Gunn, *Beyond Liberty and Property*, 114; T. Horne, "Politics in a Corrupt Society: William Arnall's Defense of Robert Walpole," *Journal of the History of Ideas* 41 (1980): 587; Reed Browning, *Political and Constitutional Ideas of the Court Whigs* (Baton Rouge, LA, 1982), 181–82.

22. John Trenchard, *The Second Part of an Argument* (1697), quoted in L. Schwoerer, "The Literature of the Standing Army Controversy, 1697–1699," *Huntington Library Quarterly* 28 (1965): 199.

23. Martyn Thompson, "Daniel Defoe and the Formation of Early Eighteenth Century Whig Ideology" (paper delivered at the Folger Institute Center for the History of British Political Thought, 9 Oct. 1986).

24. Paul Langford, *The Excise Crisis* (Oxford, 1975), 73–74, 158–62; J. Price, "The Excise Affair Revisited: The Administrative and Colonial Dimensions of a Parliamentary Crisis," in *England's Rise to Greatness, 1660–1783*, ed. Stephen B. Baxter (Berkeley, 1983), esp. 299.

25. D. Hayton, "The 'Country' Interest and the Party System, 1689-c.1720," in *Party and Management*, 65, 38–39.

26. Q. Skinner, "The Principles and Practice of Opposition: The Case of Bolingbroke versus Walpole," in *Historical Perspectives*, ed. Neil McKendrick (London, 1974), 93–128.

27. Langford, *Excise Crisis*, 167.

28. M. M. Goldsmith, "Faction Detected: Ideological Consequences of Robert Walpole's Decline and Fall," *History* n.s. 64 (1979): 1–19.

29. J. G. A. Pocock, "The Varieties of Whiggism from Exclusion to Reform," in *Virtue*, 249; J. G. A. Pocock, "*The Machiavellian Moment* Revisited: A Study in History and Ideology'" *JMH* 53 (1981): 67.

30. HMC, *Eleventh Report*, app. pt. 4, *Townshend Manuscripts*, 371 (I owe this reference to Joanna Innes).

31. Horwitz, *Parliament, Policy and Politics*, 315; Peter Thomas, *The House of Commons in the Eighteenth Century* (Oxford, 1971), 61.

32. Derived from *The House of Commons 1715–1754*, ed. Romney Sedgwick (London, 1970), 1:5; Thomas, *House of Commons*, 61. See also J. Innes, "Parliament and the Shaping of Eighteenth-Century English Social Policy," *TRHS*, 5th ser., 40 (1990): 69–70.

33. R. Frankle, "'Parliament's Right to Do Wrong': The Parliamentary Debate on the Bill of Attainder against Sir John Fenwick 1696," *Parliamentary History* 4 (1985): 71–85. And see H. T. Dickinson, "The Eighteenth Century Debate on the Sovereignty of Parliament," *TRHS*, 5th ser., 26 (1976): 189–210.

34. Pallister, *Magna Carta*, 44–45, 56; *Proceedings and Debates of the British Parliaments Respecting North America 1754–1783*, ed. R. C. Simmons and P. D. G. Thomas, 2 (Millwood, NY, 1983): 321.

35. Blackstone, *Commentaries*, 1:91, and also 157.

36. Ibid., 1:353.

37. *PH* 15:740.

38. Blackstone, *Commentaries*, 1:7, 9, 10. And see David Lieberman, *The Province of Legislation Determined* (Cambridge, 1989), 29–67.

39. Blackstone, *Commentaries* 4:4, 18. See also E. P. Thompson, *Whigs and Hunters* (New York, 1975); J. Broad, "Whigs and Deer-Stealers in Other Guises: a Return to the Origins of the Black Act," *Past and Present* 119 (1988): 56–72.

40. D. Hay, "Property, Authority and the Criminal Law," in *Albion's Fatal Tree*, ed. Douglas Hay et al. (London, 1975), 22, 25, 29, 26.

41. In general, see J. Innes and J. Styles, "The Crime Wave: Recent Writing on Crime and Criminal Justice in Eighteenth-Century England," *JBS* 25 (1986): 380–435.

42. Tony Hayter, *The Army and the Crowd in Mid-Georgian England* (Totowa, NJ, 1978), 11–12, 12–15. See also Thompson, *Whigs and Hunters*, 258–69.

43. J. Brewer, "The Wilkites and the Law, 1763–74: A Study of Radical Notions of Governance," in *An Ungovernable People*, ed. J. Brewer and J. Styles (Rutgers, NJ, 1980), 128–71; Thomas A. Green, *Verdict According to Conscience* (Chicago, 1985), esp. 323–28.

44. P. King, "Decision-Makers and Decision-Making in the English Criminal Law, 1750–1800," *HJ* 27 (1984): 28–32; Beattie, *Crime and the Courts*, 192–98.

45. Innes and Styles, "Crime Wave," 404 and n. 51. Compare D. Hay and F. Snyder, "Prosecution and Power," in *Policing and Prosecution in Britain 1750–1850*, ed. D. Hay and F. Snyder (Oxford, 1989), esp. 389–95; Paul Langford, *A Polite and Commercial People: England, 1727–1783* (Oxford, 1989), esp. 157–58.

46. Beattie, *Crime and the Courts*, 378–99, 419–30. Debate over the out-

look of jurors continues as does the wider controversy over the importance and independence of the "middling sort" in this era: compare P. King's and D. Hay's judgments in *Twelve Good Men and True*, ed. J. S. Cockburn and T. A. Green (Princeton, 1988), esp. 302–4 and 311 (also Green's comments at 386–97). And see E. P. Thompson, "Eighteenth-Century English Society: Class Struggle without Class?," *Social History* 3 (1978): 133–65.

47. Blackstone, *Commentaries* 4:277–80. See also 3:380 and 82 for his critique of the special excise summary jurisdiction and of the spread of small claims courts using summary process.

48. Norma Landau, *The Justices of the Peace, 1679–1760* (Berkeley, 1984), 343–59.

49. Blackstone, *Commentaries* 4:343, 344.

50. Mathias Earbery quoted in Gunn, *Beyond Liberty and Property*, 240.

51. J. Innes, "Prisons for the Poor: English Bridewells, 1555–1800," in *Labour, Law and Crime*, ed. F. Snyder and D. Hay (London, 1987), 85–87.

52. *PH* 15:895 (I owe this reference to Nicholas Rogers).

53. Beattie, *Crime and the Courts*, 50–59, 41–48, 500–506.

54. *PH* 25:900–901.

55. Henry Fielding, *An Enquiry into the Causes of the Late Increase of Robbers* (reprint of the 1751 edition, New York, 1975), xiv-xv. In 1786, centralized policing measures were enacted for Dublin.

56. Blackstone, *Commentaries* 4:246; Leon Radzinowicz, *A History of English Criminal Law* 1 (New York, 1948): 642–50.

57. John Rule, *The Experience of Labour in Eighteenth-Century English Industry* (New York, 1981), 124–46. Compare J. Styles, "Embezzlement, Industry and the Law in England, 1500–1800," in *Manufacture in Town and Country before the Factory*, ed. Maxine Berg et al. (Cambridge, 1983), 173–210.

58. A. Reeve, "The Meaning and Definition of 'Property' in Seventeenth-Century England," *Past and Present* 89 (1980): 139 (summarizing, without accepting, G. Aylmer, "The Meaning and Definition of 'Property' in Seventeenth-Century England," *Past and Present* 86 [1980]: 87–97).

59. Blackstone, *Commentaries* 4:2.

60. *Property*, ed. C. B. Macpherson (Toronto, 1978), 18. Compare E. P. Thompson, "The Grid of Inheritance: A Comment," in *Family and Inheritance*, ed. Jack Goody et al. (Cambridge, 1976), 328–60 at 340–41. For the enclosure acts, see Sheila Lambert, *Bills & Acts* (Cambridge, 1971), 133, 153; and J. A. Yelling, *Common Field and Enclosure in England 1450–1850* (London, 1977), esp. 227–30.

61. C. Searle, "The Cumbrian Customary Economy in the Eighteenth Century," *Past and Present* 110 (1986): 106–33; N. Gregson, "Tawney Revisited: Custom and the Emergence of Capitalist Class Relations in North-East Cumbria, 1600–1830," *Economic History Review*, 2d ser., 42 (1989): 18–42.

62. Quoted in P. King, "Gleaners, Farmers and the Failure of Legal Sanctions in England, 1750–1850," *Past and Present* 125 (1989): 117–50 at 146.

63. Thompson, "Grid," 339–40; King, "Gleaners," 150.

64. Reeve, "The Meaning and Definition of 'Property'," 139–42; D. Sugarman and G. Rubin, "Towards a New History of Law and Material Society in England, 1750–1914," in *Law, Economy and Society, 1750–1914: Essays in the History of English Law*, ed. G. R. Rubin and D. Sugarman (Abingdon, Berks., 1984), 23–42.

65. Beattie, *Crime and the Courts*, 513–19.

66. P. B. Munsche, *Gentlemen and Poachers* (Cambridge, 1981), esp. 106–31, 185–86.

67. C. W. Brooks, "Interpersonal Conflict and Social Tension: Civil Litigation in England, 1640–1830," in *The First Modern Society*, ed. A. L. Beier et al. (Cambridge, 1989), 357–99; C. Francis, "Practice, Strategy, and Institution: Debt Collection in the English Common-Law Courts, 1740–1840," *Northwestern University Law Review* 80 (1986), esp. 807–19, 893–907.

68. P. Haagen, "Eighteenth-Century English Society and the Debt Law," in *Social Control and the State*, ed. S. Cohen and A. Scull (Oxford, 1983), 222–47.

69. Brooks, "Interpersonal Conflict," 360–67.

70. G. Aylmer, "From Office-Holding to Civil Service: The Genesis of Modern Bureaucracy," *TRHS*, 5th ser., 30 (1980): 98–102; Brooks, "Interpersonal Conflict," 377–84.

71. Brooks, "Interpersonal Conflict," 369–74.

72. J. Oldham, "Lord Mansfield's Imprint on Eighteenth-Century Property Concepts" (paper presented to the Center for Seventeenth and Eighteenth Century Studies at the Clark Library, 1989); Oldham, "Reinterpretations of Eighteenth-Century English Contract Theory: The View from Lord Mansfield's Trial Notes," *Georgetown Law Journal* 76 (1988): 1949–83; Lieberman, *The Province of Legislation*, 99–121; J. Baker, "The Law Merchant and the Common Law before 1700," in John H. Baker, *The Legal Profession and the Common Law* (London, 1986), 341–68.

73. For one such litigated case on the equity side of the exchequer, see J. Price, "Sheffield v. Starke: Institutional Experimentation in the London-Maryland Trade, c. 1696–1706," *Business History* 28 (1986): 19–39.

74. Blackstone, *Commentaries* 3:17.

75. Sugarman and Rubin, "Towards a New History," 3–11; M. Miles, "Eminent Practitioners: The New Visage of Country Attorneys, c. 1750–1800," in Rubin and Sugarman, eds., *Law, Economy and Society*, 470–503; P. Aylett, "Attorneys and Their Clients in Eighteenth Century Cheshire," *Bulletin of the John Rylands Library* 69 (1987): 326–58.

76. B. Anderson, "Law, Finance and Economic Growth in England: Some Long-Term Influences," in *Great Britain and Her World 1750–1914*, ed. Barrie M. Ratcliffe (London, 1975), 103. And see F. W. Maitland, "Trust and

Corporation," in *The Collected Papers of Frederic William Maitland*, ed. H. A. L. Fisher, 3 (Cambridge, 1911): 321–404.

77. See, in general, Lloyd Bonfield, *Marriage Settlements, 1601–1740* (Cambridge, 1983) and his "'Affective Families', 'Open Elites', and Strict Family Settlements in Early Modern England," *Economic History Review*, 2d ser., 39 (1986): 341–54.

78. For other perspectives on the position of women whose common law rights were modified by settlements, see Susan Staves, *Married Women's Separate Property in England, 1660–1833* (Cambridge, MA, 1990); E. Spring, "The Heiress-at-Law: English Real Property from a New Point of View," *Law and History Review* 8 (1990): 237–72.

79. M. Chesterman, "Family Settlements on Trust: Landowners and the Rising Bourgeoisie," in Rubin and Sugarman, eds., *Law, Economy and Society*, 135–40.

80. Chesterman, "Family Settlements on Trust," 124–27, 145–67. See also H. Horwitz, "'The Mess of the Middle Class' Revisited: The Case of the 'Big Bourgeoisie' of Augustan London," *Continuity and Change* 2 (1987): 263–96.

81. C. A. Cooke, *Corporation, Trust and Company* (Manchester, 1950), 84–88; Armand B. DuBois, *The English Business Company after the Bubble Act, 1720–1800* (New York, 1938), 217–22; R. Neale, "'The Bourgeoisie, Historically, Has Played a Most Revolutionary Part,'" in *Feudalism, Capitalism, and Beyond*, ed. Kamenka and Neale, 100–101.

82. A. W. B. Simpson, introduction to Blackstone, *Commentaries* 2:viii. And see M. Lobban, "Blackstone and the Science of the Law," *HJ* 30 (1987): 313–17, 321–23.

83. Blackstone, *Commentaries* 3:268.

84. Ronald Meek, *Social Science and the Ignoble Savage* (Cambridge, 1976), 177–79. See also I. Hont, "The Language of Sociability and Commerce: Samuel Pufendorf and the Theoretical Foundations of the 'Four-Stages Theory'," in *The Languages of Political Theory in Early-Modern Europe*, ed. Anthony Pagden (Cambridge, 1987), 253–76.

85. Blackstone, *Commentaries* 2:472, 461, 442.

86. D. Lieberman, "The Legal Needs of a Commercial Society: the Jurisprudence of Lord Kames," in *Wealth and Virtue*, ed. Hont and Ignatieff, 207–9.

87. *The Correspondence of Adam Smith*, ed. E. C. Mossner and I. Simpson (Oxford, 1977), 114; Adam Smith, *Lectures on Jurisprudence*, ed. R. L. Meek et al. (Oxford, 1978), A, 2:74–75, and 5:43 (hereafter cited as *LJ*).

88. Compare N. Phillipson, "Adam Smith as Civic Moralist," with D. Winch, "Adam Smith's 'Enduring Particular Result': A Political and Cosmopolitan Perspective," both in *Wealth and Virtue*, ed. Hont and Ignatieff, 179–202, 253–70. See also Peter Stein, *Legal Evolution* (Cambridge, 1980), 29–46; Richard F. Teichgraeber III, *'Free Trade' and Moral Philosophy* (Dur-

ham, NC, 1986), esp. 144–57; E. Pesciarelli, "On Adam Smith's Lectures on Jurisprudence," *Scottish Journal of Political Economy* 33 (1986): 74–86.

89. Quoted in Winch, "Adam Smith's 'Enduring Particular Result,'" 260.

90. Knud Haakonssen, *The Science of a Legislator* (Cambridge, 1981), 150–51.

91. Adam Smith, *Essays on Philosophical Subjects*, ed. I. S. Ross (Oxford, 1980), 274–75. And see A. Skinner, "Adam Smith, an Economic Interpretation of History," *Essays on Adam Smith*, ed. A. Skinner and T. Wilson (Oxford, 1975), 154–55.

92. Adam Smith, *An Inquiry into the Nature and Causes of the Wealth of Nations*, ed. W. B. Todd (Oxford, 1976), 3:iii, 12 (hereafter cited as *WN*).

93. *WN* 3:iv, 1, 4.

94. *WN* 3:iv, 15.

95. *WN* 3:iv, 17.

96. *WN* 5:i, b, 25; *LJ*, A, 2:135. And see D. Forbes, "Sceptical Whiggism, Commerce, and Liberty," in *Essays on Adam Smith*, ed. Skinner and Wilson, esp. 186–91.

97. *LJ* A, 5:1. And see A. Skinner, "A Scottish Contribution to Marxist Sociology?" in *Classical & Marxian Political Economy*, ed. I. Bradley and M. Howard (London, 1982), 99–104.

98. *LJ* A, 5:5.

99. *WN* 5:i, a, 41.

100. *WN* 5:i, f, 59, 60. And see R. Sher, "Adam Ferguson, Adam Smith, and the Problems of National Defense," *JMH* 61 (1989): 240–68.

101. *WN* 5:iii, 41; and also 2:iii, 36. And see Donald Winch, *Adam Smith's Politics* (Cambridge, 1978), 129–31, 135–36.

102. *WN* 4:ii, 43. And see Winch, *Adam Smith's Politics*, 146–57.

103. *WN* 4:vii, c, 75, 77–79.

104. Blackstone, *Commentaries* 1:168, and also 166. Compare *LJ* A, 5:8–11, 134–35; and B: 64, 94–95, 294. And see P. Langford, "Property and 'Virtual Representation' in Eighteenth-Century England," *HJ* 31 (1988): 83–115.

105. *WN* 5:iii, c, 9.

106. *WN* 4:v, b, 7, and 1:x, c, 12, 61, 59.

107. Haakonssen, *Science of a Legislator*, 139–51.

108. Smith, *Essays on Philosophical Subjects*, 311. And see Keith Tribe, *Genealogies of Capitalism* (Atlantic Highlands, NJ, 1981), 121–26.

CHAPTER 9

1. J. R. Jones, *The Revolution of 1688 in England* (London, 1972); J. R. Western, *Monarchy and Revolution* (London, 1972); J. P. Kenyon, *Revolution Principles: The Politics of Party 1689–1720* (Cambridge, 1977); John Miller, "The Glorious Revolution: 'Contract' and 'Abdication' Reconsid-

ered," *HJ* 25 (1982): 541–55; William L. Sachse, "The Mob and the Revolution of 1688," *JBS* 4 (1964): 23–40; J. H. Plumb, *The Growth of Political Stability in England, 1675–1725* (London, 1967).

2. Richard Ashcraft, *Revolutionary Politics and Locke's Two Treatises of Government* (Princeton, 1986); Gary de Krey, *A Fractured Society: The Politics of London in the First Age of Party, 1688–1715* (Oxford, 1985); Mark Goldie, "The Roots of True Whiggism, 1688–94," *History of Political Thought* 1 (1980): 195–236; Lois Schwoerer, *The Declaration of Rights, 1689* (Baltimore, 1981), and "Propaganda in the Revolution of 1688–1689," *AHR* 82 (1977): 843–74.

3. Some exceptions are Caroline Robbins, *The Eighteenth Century Commonwealthmen* (Cambridge, MA, 1961); John Brewer, *Party Ideology and Popular Politics at the Accession of George III* (Cambridge, 1976); H. T. Dickinson, "The Eighteenth Century Debate on the Glorious Revolution," *History* 61 (1976): 28–45, and *Liberty and Property: Political Ideology in Eighteenth Century Britain* (New York, 1977); J. G. A. Pocock, ed., *Three British Revolutions* (Princeton, 1982); and Pocock, *Virtue, Commerce and History* (Cambridge, 1985).

4. Brewer, *Party Ideology and Popular Politics*, 139–200; Kathleen Wilson, "Empire Trade and Popular Politics in Mid-Hanoverian Britain: The Case of Admiral Vernon," *Past and Present* 121 (Nov. 1988): 74–109; and "The Rejection of Deference: Urban Political Culture in England, 1715–1785" (Ph.D. diss., Yale, 1985).

5. Eric Hobsbawn, "Inventing Traditions," in Hobsbawn and Terence Ranger, eds., *The Invention of Tradition* (Cambridge, 1983), 1–14. Throughout this chapter, the terms "popular" and "populist" are used to describe language or arguments that champion the rights or roles of "the people," however constructed, in political activities; they are *political* and thus socially heterogenous designations.

6. *Bristol Gazette and Public Advertiser*, 6 Nov. 1788.

7. *Leeds Mercury*, 11 Nov. 1788; *Bristol Gazette and Public Advertiser*, 13 Nov. 1788; *Manchester Mercury*, 11 & 18 Nov. 1788; *Cumberland Pacquet*, 10 Nov. 1788; *Norfolk Chronicle*, 8 Nov. 1788; *Morning Chronicle*, 4 Nov. 1788; *An Historical and Descriptive Account of the Town of Lancaster: Collected from the Best Authorities* (Lancaster, 1807), 96 (thanks to Jan Albers for the last reference).

8. *Leeds Mercury*, 11 Nov. 1788.

9. *Newcastle Chronicle*, 19 Aug. 1786.

10. Ian Christie, *Wilkes, Wyvil and Reform* (London, 1962); John Cannon, *The Fox-North Coalition: Crisis of the Constitution* (Cambridge, 1969); *The Times*, 4 Nov. 1788; *Morning Chronicle*, 3 Nov. 1788.

11. Ian Christie, *Wars and Revolutions* (Cambridge, MA, 1983), 204.

12. Seymour Drescher, *Capitalism and Anti-Slavery* (New York, 1986); Joanna Innes, "Politics and Morals: the Reformation of Manners Movement in Later Eighteenth Century England," in Eckhart Hellmuth, ed., *The*

Transformation of Political Culture in Late Eighteenth Century England and Germany (Oxford, 1990), 57–118.

13. *Public Advertiser*, 1 Nov. 1788; *The Universal and Everlasting Dominion of God . . . A Sermon preach'd . . . the fourth of November, 1788* (London, 1789).

14. *Bristol Gazette and Public Advertiser*, 13 Nov. 1788; *Norfolk Chronicle*, 8. Nov. 1788; G. A. Picton, *Memorials of Liverpool* 1:22; *Newcastle Courant*, 8 Nov. 1788.

15. *Norfolk Chronicle*, 8 Nov. 1788.

16. *Manchester Mercury*, 11 Nov. 1788.

17. *Salisbury Journal*, 10 Nov. 1788; *Public Advertiser*, 4 Nov. 1788.

18. *Two Sermons preached at Mill-Hill Chapel . . . in the Celebration of the Hundredth Anniversary of the Happy Revolution* (Leeds, 1788), 16.

19. *A Sermon on the Centennial Commemoration of the Revolution* (Norwich, 1788), 9–10, 16–17.

20. See Joseph Priestley, *Essay on the First Principles of Government* (London, 1768).

21. *Abstract of the History and Proceedings of the Revolution Society in London* (London, 1789), 10–13; *A List of the Society, Instituted in 1787, for the Purpose of effecting the Abolition of the Slave Trade* (London, 1788); E. Black, *The Association* (Cambridge, MA, 1963), 211–15.

22. [Jos. Priestley], *Letter to the Right Honorable William Pitt* (London, 1787), 8–9.

23. *Public Advertiser*, 6 Nov. 1788; *Newcastle Chronicle*, 8 Nov. 1788 and *Leeds Mercury*, 11 Nov. 1788.

24. *Public Advertiser*, 6 Nov. 1788; *Abstract*, 7.

25. *Abstract*, 2–10.

26. See Joseph Towers, *A Vindication of the Political Principles of Mr. Locke in Answer to the Objections of the Rev's Dr. Tucker, Dean of Gloucester* (London, 1782); *An Examination into the Nature and Evidence of the Charges brought against Lord W. Russell, and A. Sydney* (London, 1773); and *A Letter to Dr. Samuel Johnson . . . With an Appendix, containing some Observations on A Pamphlet lately Published by Dr. Shebbeare* (London, 1775).

27. *An Oration Delivered at the London Tavern on the Fourth of November, 1788* (London, 1788), 24–25, 27, 31.

28. R. B. Barlow, *Citizenship and Conscience* (Philadelphia, 1962), 221–29; Priestley, *Essay on First Principles of Government*, 9.

29. Joseph Priestley, *The Importance and Extent of Free Inquiry into Matters of Religion* (London, 1785); John Money, *Experience and Identity: Birmingham and the West Midlands, 1760–1800* (Montreal, 1977), 219.

30. *Abstract*, 14.

31. J. A. W. Gunn, *Beyond Liberty and Property* (Kingston, ON, and Montreal, 1983), 242–51; Priestley, *Essay on the First Principles of Government*; John Cartwright, *Take Your Choice!* (London, 1776) and *Declarations*

of those Rights of the Commonalty of England [1782]; *An Address to the Public from the Society for Constitutional Information* [London, 1782]; Capel Lofft, *A Summary of A Treatise by Major Cartwright* (n.p., 1780).

32. Cartwright, *Declarations of those Rights of the Commonalty*; Lofft, *Summary of a Treatise.*

33. Priestley, *Essay on the First Principles of Government,* 17.

34. Black, *The Association,* 217; *General Evening Post,* 4–6 Nov. 1788.

35. *Public Advertiser,* 6–7 Nov. 1788.

36. John Brewer, *The Sinews of Power: War, Money and the English State, 1688–1783* (London, 1989), pt. 3.

37. John Toland, *The Art of Governing by Partys* (London, 1701), 56; Cato's Letter No. 17, *London Journal,* 8 Feb. 1721.

38. [Hugh Hume, Earl Of Marchmont], *A Serious Exhortation to the Electors of Great Britain* (London, 1740), 22.

39. Persian Letter No. 63, in George Lyttelton, *Works,* 3 vols. (London, 1776), 1:336–37.

40. *An Impartial Enquiry into the Properties of Places and Pensions, as they Affect the Constitution* (London, 1740), 9–10.

41. "Dissertation on Parties" in *The Works of Lord Bolingbroke* (London, 1841), 2:70–75.

42. *Norwich Gazette,* 6 Aug. 1726; *Farley's Bristol Journal,* 24 June 1727; *Whitehall Evening Post,* 14 Oct. 1727.

43. *Newcastle Courant,* 12 Nov. 1737; 1 Dec. 1733.

44. *Craftsman,* 20 Apr. 1734; *Norwich Gazette,* 13 Apr. 1734.

45. *Newcastle Courant,* 8 Aug. 1730.

46. *The Freeholder's Political Catechism* (London, 1733).

47. [Benjamin Robbins], *An Address to the Electors and other Free Subjects, of Great Britain* (London, 1739).

48. *Craftsman,* 21 Apr. 1733.

49. Wilson, "Rejection of Deference," 75–80; Paul Langford, *The Excise Crisis: Society and Politics in the Age of Walpole* (Oxford, 1975); Jacob Price, "The Excise Affair Revisited: The Administrative and Colonial Dimensions of a Parliamentary Crisis," in *England's Rise to Greatness, 1660–1763,* ed. Stephen B. Baxter (Berkeley, 1983), 257–321.

50. J. R. Jones, *The First Whigs* (London, 1961), 20–33, 115–55; Paul Kelly, "Constituents' Instructions to Members of Parliament in the Eighteenth Century," in Clyve Jones, ed., *Party and Management in Parliament, 1660–1784* (Leicester, 1984), 170–71.

51. *Daily Gazetteer,* 6 July 1738; *A Letter to William Pulteney Esq., Concerning the Administration of Affairs in Great Britain for Several Years Passed* (London, 1733); *E[dinburg]h's Instructions to their Member* (London, 1741).

52. *The Right of British Subjects, to Petition and Apply to their Representatives, Asserted and Vindicated* (London, 1733); *Freeholder's Political Catechism,* passim.; *Craftsman,* 17 Aug. 1740, 10 Jan. 1741.

53. *Political State of Great Britain* 45:440–41; *Craftsman*, 17 Mar. 1733; *Champion*, 23 Sept. 1740.

54. *Craftsman*, 21 Apr. 1733.

55. Wilson, "Empire, Trade and Popular Politics in Mid-Hanoverian England."

56. *Great Britain's Memorial* (London, 1740); *Great Britain's Second Memorial* (London, 1742).

57. *Craftsman*, 17 Mar. 1733; 22 Dec. 1739, 16 Aug. 1740; *Political State* 45:331–35; *Champion*, 4 Nov. 1740.

58. *Impartial Enquiry into the Properties of Places and Pensions*, 9–10, 37; *Serious Exhortation to the Electors of Great Britain* and *Freeholder's Political Catechism*.

59. *Salisbury Journal*, 20 Nov. 1739.

60. *Robin's Last Shift*, 10, 31 Mar. 1716; *The Shift Shift'd* 23, 30 June, 7, 14 July 1716; *Mist's Weekly Journal*, 3 Feb. 1722; Paul Monod, "For the King to Enjoy His Own Again: Jacobite Political Culture in England, 1688–1788" (Ph.D. diss., Yale, 1985), 59–65.

61. *Fog's Weekly Journal*, 25 Dec. 1731; 6, 13 May 1732.

62. *The Liveryman: or, Plain Thoughts on Publick Affairs* (London, 1740), 13, 6–32.

63. "Letters on the Study and Use of History (1735/36)," in *The Works of Lord Bolingbroke* 2:237. See also the *Craftsman*, 10 Jan. 1741.

64. *Craftsman*, 23 May, 25 July 1741.

65. Bolingbroke, "Dissertation on Parties," in *Works* 2:8–9.

66. Hervey, *Ancient and Modern Liberty Stated and Compared* (1734), 12–35; Dickinson, *Liberty and Property*, 121–62.

67. Bolingbroke, "Dissertation on Parties," in *Works* 2:8–9; "Letters on the Study and Use of History," in *Works* 2:237.

68. *Norwich Gazette*, 4 Sept., 9 Oct. 1742.

69. *Norwich Mercury*, 31 Mar.-7 Apr. 1733; 20–27 July, 17–24 Aug. 1734; *Daily Gazetteer*, 6 July 1738.

70. Cato's Letter No. 59, *London Journal*, 6 Jan. 1721.

71. *The Contest* (Newcastle, 1774), 12.

72. *Salisbury Journal*, 12 Mar. 1764.

73. Wilson, "Rejection of Deference," chap. 3; Nicholas Rogers, "Popular Disaffection during the '45," *London Journal* 1 (1975): 5–27.

74. Marie Peters, *Pitt and Popularity* (Oxford, 1980), 58–72; *Coronation Anthem* [n.p., 1761].

75. Lucy S. Sutherland, "Edmund Burke and the Relations between Members of Parliament and their Constituents," *Studies in Burke and His Time* 10 (1968): 1005–21; Wilson, "Rejection of Deference," chaps. 4 and 7.

76. *Newcastle Chronicle*, 29 Apr. 1768; *Newcastle Courant*, 20 May 1769.

77. *Freemen's Magazine* 1:4–5.

78. Ibid. 2:41–42; *Newcastle Chronicle*, 14 Oct. 1769; *The Contest* (Newcastle, 1774), 23.

79. D. E. C. Eversley, "The Home Market and Economic Growth in England, 1750–1780," in E. C. Jones and G. E. Mingay, eds., *Land, Labour and Population in the Industrial Revolution* (London, 1967), 206–59.

80. Brewer, "English Radicalism," 334–36, and "Clubs, Commercialization and Politics," in John Brewer, Neil McKendrick, and J. H. Plumb, *The Birth of a Consumer Society* (London, 1982), 197–262; Wilson, "Urban Culture and Political Activism in England: the Example of Voluntary Hospitals," in Hellmuth, ed., *The Transformation of Political Culture*, 165–84.

81. Catherine Macaulay, *Observations on a pamphlet, entitled, Thoughts on the Present Discontents*, 3d ed., (London, 1770); *Political Register* 12: 224–25; *The Whisperer*, 10 Aug. 1771; *London Evening Post*, 5–7 Aug. 1773.

82. Christopher Hill, "The Norman Yoke," in *Puritanism and Revolution* (London, 1955); [Obadiah Hulme], *An Historical Essay on the English Constitution* (London, 1771), 4–7; Dickinson, *Liberty and Property*, 198.

83. Isaac Kramnick, "Republican Revisionism Revisited," *AHR* 87 (1982): 629–64, passim.

84. Dorothy George, ed., *Catalogue of Personal and Political Prints in the British Museum* 4:179, 54–54, 114–15, 298–99, 183.

85. Dorothy George, *English Political Caricature* (Oxford, 1959), 143–45.

86. Ibid., 144; *The Whisperer*, 25 May 1771.

87. Norfolk RO, Bradfer-Lawrence MSS, Molyneux Letter Book, fols. 160, 190, 262–63, 199–200, and Neville Papers, MC 7/349–53.

88. *Public Advertiser*, 19 Dec. 1769.

89. *Middlesex Journal*, 10 Sept. 1772.

90. Mark Goldie, "Roots of True Whiggism 1688–1694," *History of Political Thought* 1 (1980): 221; *Norfolk Chronicle*, 30 Mar. 1771, 29 Jan. 1780; *The Contest*, 7; *Whisperer*, 10 Aug. 1771.

91. *Freemen's Magazine* 2:60; *Norfolk Chronicle*, 29 Oct., 11 Nov. 1769.

92. *Newcastle Journal*, 3 Jan. 1771.

93. *Norfolk Chronicle*, 16 Dec. 1769, 5 Aug. 1769; *Salisbury Journal*, 25 July 1763.

94. *Middlesex Journal*, 11 Apr. 1769.

95. *Middlesex Journal*, 26 Apr. 1770; *Felix Farley's Bristol Journal*, 22 July 1769; *Freemen's Magazine* 1:10; *Society for Constitutional Information, Minutes* (London, 1782).

96. *Newcastle Journal*, 3 Jan. 1771; *Bristol Gazette and Public Advertiser*, 5 Oct. 1774.

97. James Burgh, *Political Disquisitions* (London, 1774), 1:37–88; *Reflexions on the Representation in Parliament* (London, 1766), 15; Brewer, "English Radicalism," 351–55.

98. *Middlesex Journal*, 21 Apr. 1770; *Newcastle Journal*, 9, 30 July, 8 Oct. 1774; *The Contest*, 18; *Innocent Blood Crying in the Streets of Boston* (London, 1770); *Freeholder's Magazine*, Apr. 1770.

99. *Norfolk Chronicle*, 21 Jan. 1775.

100. *Leeds Mercury*, 7 Nov. 1775; Newcastle Burgesses against the American War, PRO HO 55/28/19; *Newcastle Journal*, 18, 23 Nov. 1775; *Norfolk Chronicle*, 21 Jan. 1775; *London Evening Post*, 23–25 Jan. 1776; *Annual Register* 21 (1778): 130–31; *The Bristol Contest* (Bristol, 1780).

101. *London Evening Post*, 16–18 Jan., 30 Jan.-1 Feb., 3–6 Feb. 1776; *The Rise, Progress and Present State of the Dispute between . . . America and the administration* (London, 1776); *A constitutional answer to Mr. Wesley's Calm Address* (London, 1775); George, ed., *Catalogue of Personal and Political Satires* 5 : 198–99, 166–67, 202–3.

102. Bernard Bailyn, *The Ideological Origins of the American Revolution* (Cambridge, MA, 1967); Brewer, *Party Ideology*, esp. 201–18.

103. *The Crisis*, 22 July 1775; *Leeds Mercury*, 26 Sept. 1775; *Liverpool General Advertiser*, 17 Nov. 1775; *Constitutional Address*, 15; *London Evening Post*, 15–17 Feb. 1776.

104. R. Watson, *The Principles of the Revolution Vindicated* (Cambridge, 1776); James Thistlewaite, *The Prediction of Liberty* (London, 1776); William Crowe, *A Sermon Preach'd . . . at Oxford University* (Oxford, 1781); *London Evening Post*, 6–9 Jan., 9–11, 16–18, 1–3, 6–8 Feb. 1776.

105. *Felix Farley's Bristol Journal*, 17 Apr. 1776; *Norfolk Chronicle*, 17 Apr. 1779.

106. *The Hypocritical Fast, with its Design and Consequences* (Norwich, 1781).

107. Thomas Bewick, *A Memoir*, ed. Iain Bain (Oxford, 1979), 94; Norfolk and Norwich RO, Neville MSS, JW to SN, 8 June 1777; *Electioneering Journal*, 28 Feb., 6 Mar. 1777; Society for Constitutional Information, *An Address to the Public*.

108. Black, *The Association*, 31–82, 174–212.

109. *Declaration of those rights of the Commonality of Great-Britain without which they cannot be FREE*; Lofft, *Summary of a Treatise by Major Cartwright*.

Index

Library of Congress Cataloging-in-Publication Data

Liberty secured?: Britain before and after 1688 / edited by
  J. R. Jones.
    p. cm.—(The Making of modern freedom; v.)
    Includes bibliographical references and index.
    ISBN 0-8047-1988-8:
    1. Great Britain—History—Revolution of 1688—Influence.
2. Great Britain—History—1660–1714. 3. Great Britain—
History—18th century. 4. Liberty. 5. Great Britain—
Constitutional history. I. Jones, J. R. (James Rees), 1925–
II. Series.
DA435.L53 1992
941—dc20   91-21532
                                                    CIP